The Illusion of
Progress

This book is dedicated to my mother.

The Illusion of Progress

Unsustainable Development in International Law and Policy

Alexander Gillespie

from Routledge

First published in the UK and USA in 2001
by Earthscan Publications Ltd

For a full list of publications please contact:

Earthscan
2 Park Square, Milton Park, Abingdon, Oxon OX14 4RN
711 Third Avenue, New York, NY 10017

Earthscan is an imprint of the Taylor & Francis Group, an informa business

Notices
Practitioners and researchers must always rely on their own experience
and knowledge in evaluating and using any information, methods, compounds,
or experiments described herein. In using such information or methods they should be
mindful of their own safety and the safety of others, including parties for whom they
have a professional responsibility.

Product or corporate names may be trademarks or registered trademarks, and are
used only for identification and explanation without intent to infringe.

ISBN: 978-1-85383-757-9 paperback
      978-1-85383-756-2 hardback

Typesetting by PCS Mapping & DTP
Cover design by Danny Gillespie

A catalogue record for this book is available from the British Library

Library of Congress Cataloging-in-Publication Data

Gillespie, Alexander, 1966-
    The illusion of progress : unsustainable development in international law and
    policy / Alexander Gillespie.
        p. cm.
    Includes bibliographical references and index.
    ISBN 1-85383-756-3 (hbk.) – ISBN 1-85383-757-1 (pbk.)
    1. Economic development. 2. Law and economic development. 3. International
economic relations. I. Title.

HD82.G523 2001
338.9-dc21

                                                                    00-050404

Contents

Acronyms and Abbreviations

ABM	Anti-ballistic Missile (Treaty)
CFC	chlorofluorocarbon
CFE	Conventional Forces in Europe (Treaty)
CSD	Commission on Sustainable Development
CTBT	Comprehensive Test Ban Treaty
FAO	Food and Agriculture Organization
GATT	General Agreement on Tariffs and Trade
GDP	gross domestic product
GEF	Global Environment Facility
GNP	gross national product
HIPC	Highly Indebted Poor Country
IAEA	International Atomic Energy Agency
ICJ	International Court of Justice
ILO	International Labour Organization
IMF	International Monetary Fund
INF	Intermediate Range Nuclear Forces (Treaty)
ISO	International Standards Organization
MAD	mutually assured destruction
NAFTA	North American Free Trade Agreement
NGO	non-governmental organization
NPT	Non-Proliferation Treaty
ODA	Overseas Development Assistance
OECD	Organisation for Economic Co-operation and Development
SALT	Strategic Arms Limitation Talks
START	Strategic Arms Reduction Talks
TNC	transnational corporation
TNT	trinitrotoluene
UNCED	United Nations Conference on Environment and Development
UNCLOS	United Nations Convention on the Law of the Sea
UNCTAD	United Nations Conference on Trade and Development
UNDP	United Nations Development Programme
UNEP	United Nations Environment Programme
UNGA	United Nations General Assembly
UNICEF	United Nations International Children's Emergency Fund
WCED	World Commission on Environment and Development
WCS	World Conservation Strategy
WHO	World Health Organization

WMO	World Meteorological Organization
WRI	World Resources Institute
WTO	World Trade Organization

Introduction

When I was 19 years of age, in my first year at university, I was a volunteer that offered to help paint the Greenpeace ship *Rainbow Warrior* when it arrived in Auckland harbour en route to monitor French nuclear tests in the South Pacific. Like many young New Zealanders of the age, I had been concerned about environmental issues, with a strong interest in the threat of nuclear war. By the time the *Rainbow Warrior* came to town, I had been involved with such issues for over five years, and going down to help paint a boat which had been a poster on my wall seemed like a good idea.

After a good day's work, when it was freshly painted on the outside, it was sunk and a man was killed by an act of international terrorism by the French government. It was not a surprise (although it did seem a little too obvious) that the French government committed this act. Indeed, New Zealand and Australia had already taken them to the International Court of Justice in the 1970s (and again in the 1990s) in a bid to stop their nuclear testing. At that point, on a very cold Auckland morning, I came to the realization that 'saving the environment' was a much more complicated, deeply political and dangerous task than singing peace songs and making daisy chains.

Soon after, I enrolled in law school at Auckland University, with the intention of becoming an environmental lawyer. At the time, the possibility of becoming an environmental lawyer with an international focus was unlikely, as there were no such courses available. This was not a surprise, as looking back, so many of the global environmental problems we face today were barely recognized in the mid-1980s. However, by the end of the 1980s, phrases like global warming, ozone loss, and species decline were beginning to enter into the mainstream vocabulary. At that point, I decided to stay on at law school, and entered into the Masters programme, with its brand new course on international environmental law. This course, which was run by Dr Klaus Bosselmann, had deep insights that led me to think about new and diverse ideas. Among many of the influential ideas that Klaus passed on was that associated with the word 'paradigm'. Klaus explained that word through a series of diagrams (which I still wonder about) and elaborations. I have come to discover that in essence it means patterns that affect the larger picture. In terms of international environmental law and policy, I took the idea of the larger paradigm to mean that the answers we are looking for are not always in the obvious places, as the overall equation is fundamentally influenced by other, often less than obvious, considerations.

With such considerations in mind, I set off on the next stage of my academic journey to Nottingham Law School, where I did my PhD. In England, courtesy of a number of scholarships, I was given the opportunity to work on a simple question that had been vexing me by that stage for a number of years. That question was: *given 30 years of overt environmentalism and literally hundreds of international agreements, why is the situation worse than when the whole process began?* The traditional answer to this problem has been to focus on which agreements are successful, and try to isolate the key ingredients. And in many ways, this method has much to offer. However, I found it did not answer some of the 'deeper' questions.

It is my contention that there are two reasons why the environmental problem is getting worse. The first concerns *why* we protect the environment and the problem of contradictory and ultimately self-defeating objectives. I have addressed this extensively in my last book, *International Environmental Law, Policy and Ethics* (Oxford University Press, 1997). My thesis in this book is that we often try to protect the environment for the wrong philosophical reasons, and ultimately, these lead to unsatisfactory results.

Hopefully, the second part of the answer is found in this book. In very simplistic terms, it deals with the question of *how* we protect the environment, or to be more specific, the background considerations which go towards the making of a world which has more environmental and social successes than the one we currently occupy. My thesis in this book is that the underlying mechanisms, ideals and paradigms which make up the background of international environmental law and policy need to be addressed before real success can be achieved in this area.

SOCIAL ECOLOGY

To approach this second question, I had to search for a yardstick by which to measure and juxtapose the current legal and policy responses to a multitude of international environmental issues. In my first book the yardstick I used came from a branch of philosophy which focused specifically on environmental questions. In this book, I began with the presumption that if sustainable development is to mean anything, then next to the philosophical reasons of why we protect the environment must be the societies that will implement this ideal. In thinking about the societies, both local and global, I came upon the idea of the social side to the environmental situation, or 'social ecology'.

'Social ecology' is not my label. It is a term which was popularized and critiqued by Murray Bookchin.[1] However, in the context of this book, social ecology is by no means exclusively connected with Bookchin's work. Moreover, it is a mistake to assume that there is one body of work which details the fundamental tenets of social ecology. Indeed, for as many people there are who have written about the social side of environmental problems, there are differing opinions of the 'best' way forward. In many ways, this has greatly complicated matters, for despite optimistic assertions in the mid-1980s that the Green movement was entirely unique with its own distinctive agenda,[2] history has proved otherwise. Indeed, the Green movement and all of its social ecology theorists have fragmented into thousands of pieces with the end of the Cold War and the widespread collapse of traditional ideologies, in addition to the development of multifaceted new international problems with vast environmental and social implications.

There is no one theory, let alone theorist, that can 'solve' all of the socially connected environmental problems at hand. To expect otherwise would be foolish and represent an unrealistic assessment of the radically changing world before us. This aspect of change is fundamental to any thinking about what social ecology should entail. Akin to the continually evolving environmental problems is the continually evolving context that surrounds them. Thirty years ago, only the most coherent in the environmental movement could provide critiques about sovereignty or the limits to growth debate. Ten years later, a few could converse about the inter-linkages between debt, aid and the environment. Others were fully aware of the threat of nuclear war between the superpowers. By the early 1990s, only a few could grasp the intricacies of the free trade debate, and the evolving discussion on development, let alone sustainable development (which only became popularized in 1987) in general. Then, with the collapse of the Soviet Union and the widespread success of neo-liberalism, environmentalists had to quickly establish a grasp of all of the intricacies of market economics, and the changing nature of international security.

This book is about all of these issues. It is about how these issues have developed, and how they are currently recognized in international environmental law and policy. Against the law and policy in each situation, I have attempted to critique the area. To do this, I have typically melded a number of theorists together that originally were under 'Green' or 'social' rubrics. I have often supported the contentions of these people with updated statistics, or sources – if their ideas have become part of the debate in international policy.

Many of the sources I have examined have little to do with each other, and the authors of such works could well be surprised to find themselves mentioned next to areas which they have never directly considered. What they do have in common is that they have all dealt with aspects which are essential to the social component of environmental issues. These social components are concerned, in one way or another, with factors which are instrumental to the creation of societies (both local and global) that may achieve a meaningful form of sustainable development.

I believe the international community needs to seriously rethink some of its assumptions within international environmental law and policy. However, this is not to suggest that the international community does not need some form of development, or trade, or growth etc. Nothing could be more absurd. The international community needs all of these things, but not necessarily in the way they are currently operating. Without this rethinking of direction, I think the global community will continue to head in the wrong direction at an increasingly frightening speed, and the idea of sustainable development will remain little more than Green wool, pulled over the public's eyes.

Chapter 1

Development

THE IDEA OF DEVELOPMENT

In his inauguration speech before Congress in 1949, President Truman defined one of the largest of the world problems as 'underdeveloped areas'. Consequently it was assumed that all the peoples of the Earth were to move along the same track and aspire to only one goal – development. President Truman said the road to development was to be where 'greater production' was the 'the key to prosperity and peace'. Truman then outlined a programme of technical assistance designed to 'relieve the sufferings of these peoples' through 'industrial activities' and a 'higher standard of living'.[1]

Before his speech had finished he had already introduced a whole new paradigm in thinking: that societies of Southern countries are not necessarily as valuable in their choice of social arrangements. Traditions, hierarchies and foreign habits – the whole texture of societies – were to be dissolved, homogenized and improved through the application of Western models and by mimicking the 'American way of life' in an economically liberal international system.[2]

Of course, 'development' is neither a new, nor an American idea. It is part of a process that is as old as history itself. However, since the Enlightenment the pursuit of 'development' and the quest for modernity, imbued with ideals of anthropocentricism,[3] technology and industrialization – all wrapped in distinctive economic and political structures – has been pursued with a global vigour.[4] Moreover, since 1945 the speed of this process by which can societies can emerge purified, both modern and affluent, has accelerated yet again.[5]

THE RIGHT TO DEVELOPMENT

The 'right to development' is widely recognized as part of international law.[6] However, this concept was conceived long before its recognition in international law. For example, in 1944, the International Labour Organization (ILO) stated in its Philadelphia Declaration that 'all human beings ... have the right to pursue their material well being ... in conditions of freedom and dignity, or economic security and equal opportunity'.[7]

Four years later, Article 25 of the 1948 Universal Declaration of Human Rights recognized that:

> *'Everyone has the right to a standard of living adequate for the health and well-being of himself and his family, including food, clothing, housing and medical care and necessary social services, and the right to security in the event of unemployment, sickness, disability, widowhood, old-age, or other lack of livelihood in circumstances beyond his control.'*[8]

Similar objectives were reiterated in 1966[9] and 1974.[10] These aspirations were also evident in the United Nations designations of 'Development Decades'. In 1986, the 'right' to development was expressly recognized in the Declaration on the Right to Development.[11]

It is important to realize that a number of countries (such as the United States) refused to accept *this* right to development. This was because it was seen, essentially, as a socialist objective. This problem reflected the difficulty that raged throughout the Cold War period, where the critiques were not over development per se, but over ideology. That is, while some argued for Keynesian or more free market models, others adopted pro-Marxist critiques. This latter critique did not disagree with the goals of the development process (that the poor countries would come to economically emulate the rich countries). What it did disagree with related to questions of the social and political control of the development process. In this regard, the method (but not the goal) of development was crucial. Accordingly, the debate became entangled in the politics of the time, with ideals like the Right to Development being linked to principles such as a New International Economic Order[12] which was strongly linked to a distinct socialist agenda. Accordingly, more social rights, like the rights to food and housing, could not be acknowledged by all members of the global community until after the fall of Communism. After this event these rights could be interpreted in the light of the market rubric, as opposed to a socialist one.

Once the problem of which interpretation prism to adopt exited from the international arena, the right to development became much easier to embrace than before. Accordingly, the 'right to development [a]s a universal and inalienable right and [as an] integral part of fundamental human rights' could be reiterated by the vast majority of countries in conferences such as the 1993 Vienna Conference on Human Rights,[13] and the Cairo Conference on Population and Development.[14] From this point, specific rights within the general rubric of the right to development, such as the 'right of everyone to have access to safe and nutritional food, consistent with the right to adequate food and the fundamental right of everyone to be free from hunger'[15] have been reaffirmed by most members of the global community. Likewise, the 'goals of ensuring adequate shelter for all and making human settlements safer, healthier and more livable, equitable, sustainable and productive' were endorsed by the international community in 1996.[16]

THE FAILURE OF THE CONVENTIONAL DEVELOPMENT PROCESS

In 1949 the World Bank set off on the first of its missions to Colombia. Upon the return of the 14 experts, the prognosis was given that 'the vicious circle ... can only be broken seriously through a global relaunching of the whole economy'.[17] This view incorporated the generic hope of allowing Southern countries to leap-frog to the economic position of Northern countries by giving them Northern style projects in Southern settings.

However, by 1969 the Pearson Commission on Development noted that 'there was a weariness' with the issue of development and a search for new directions was required.[18] This problem has become greatly inflated since the 1970s as the list of development project failures has generally grown.[19] This overall failure has been recognized in environmental, social and economic terms. As the World Commission on Environment and Development (WCED) stated in 1987:

> *'On the development side, in terms of absolute numbers there are more hungry people in the world than ever before, and their number is increasing. So are the numbers who cannot read or write, the numbers without safe water or safe and sound homes and the numbers short on wood-fuel with which to cook and warm themselves. The gap between rich and poor nations is widening – not shrinking, and there is little prospect, given present trends and institutional arrangements, that this will be reversed.'*[20]

These trends continued throughout the 1990s, during which time the overall quality of human life for many deteriorated to a point of 'crisis' where the 'practical minimum' for 'civilization' in some countries was missing.[21] These claims are supported by the fact that by 1996 around 1.3 billion people in the world were living in absolute poverty, and this number is increasing by 25 million per year. Over 120 million people are officially unemployed.[22] More than 800 million people do not have enough food to meet their basic nutritional needs. Fifty thousand people die daily because of poor shelter, polluted water and bad sanitation. As many as 82 countries are classified as low-income, food deficit, in which up to 12 million children die annually.[23] This figure corresponds with the fact that in 1999 more than 80 developing countries were worse off economically than they were 10 years previously. In 70 developing countries, their level of income is less than was reached in the 1970s. In 19 developing countries, per capita income is less than it was in 1960. Such imbalances are not only restricted to Southern countries. Indeed, deep pockets of extreme poverty (of between 7 and 17 per cent of the population) exist within many Northern countries as well.[24]

Quite simply, as the poor are getting poorer, the rich are getting richer in both national and international settings. For example, the assets of the world's

358 billionaires exceed the combined annual incomes of countries accounting for 45 per cent of the Earth's people. Even more remarkably, it appears that the combined wealth of the 10 richest people on the planet could significantly reduce (if not eliminate) global poverty. Overall, the richest 20 per cent of the world's population were 30 times better off than the poorest 20 per cent in 1960, but by 1997 they were 74 times wealthier.[25]

This is not to suggest that all base indicators of human progress are negative. Distinct progress in terms of overall increasing life expectancy, falling fertility rates and increasing literacy may be noted. The above figures mask the problem that such base threats to human well-being are *not* (directly) universally felt. Rather, they remain concentrated (and often increasing) within specific countries, and often specific areas within countries.[26] Nevertheless, despite these differences, the overall problem remains that although some 'progress' has been made, this inching forward has been, as James Wolfensohn suggested in early 2000: 'painfully slow and uneven. Much remains to be done and future prospects do not look bright.' Accordingly, 'These figures call into question the way we have been doing development and forces us to rethink.'[27] This necessity to 'rethink' development was earlier noted in 1994 by the International Commission on Peace and Food which commented:

> 'Until now development has been largely a haphazard, subconscious or half sub-conscious process of trial and error experimentation, an application of partial strategies, a confusing mixture of productive and counter-productive initiatives, an unscientific and often superstitious clinging to half-truths or old-truths that no longer have any relevance.'[28]

Thus, as Elizabeth Dowdeswell, the former Executive Director of United Nations Environment Programme (UNEP) stated, 'development understood in terms of the values on which the current paradigm is based [environmental destruction, poverty, injustice] is a dead end road ... [thus] ... our fundamental definition of development must change.'[29]

THE ROOTS OF FAILURE

The commonly attributed cause of the current failings of development has been its focus on only singular factors – typically, a myopic obsession with only economic growth, to be achieved by emulating the industrialized paths of the 'developed' world. For example, it was suggested with the First United Nations Development Decade that the object of the Decade was 'to attain in each under-developed country a substantial increase in growth ... taking as the objective a minimum annual rate of growth of aggregate national income of 5% at the end of the decade.' Such calls were added to with pleas for 'the rapid industrialisation [as] an indispensable element and dynamic instrument ... of their development process.'[30] By the end of the Decade, the United

Nations General Assembly was calling for the '*uninterrupted* and diversified growth of the industrial sector' (my italics).[31]

This type of focus – with the overt priority of economic growth, perhaps to the exclusion of other social and environmental factors – was reiterated with the Brandt reports of the early 1980s, which also argued for the continued use of western models of development, industrialization and economic expansion as the substance of development.[32] Despite recognition of the new dimensions of the conventional development debate,[33] the Brandt Commissions still appeared to place environmental and social problems as secondary concerns.[34] Thus, these Commissions tended to attribute the failure of development to the international economy and the macro-economic policies of Northern countries, rather than the idea of development itself.[35]

In a similar sense, the 1980 World Conservation Strategy (WCS) was also limited in its outlook as it seemed to suggest that environmental preservation was somehow independent of the debate encompassing an empowering definition of development. Although recognizing that development was important, it did not begin (at least in any suitable depth) to examine the social and political changes that would be necessary to meet conservation goals.[36]

The WCED was not significantly better at recognizing these issues. Although acknowledging the prima facie need to reorganize the conventional development process, it forthrightly advocated that the solution to the overall problem is economic growth.[37] Moreover, although clearly recognizing the importance of seeking an equilibrium between economic and environmental considerations, the social sides of the equation were not overtly highlighted.

Although the Brandt and Brundtland reports and the World Conservation Strategy were limited, they nevertheless highlighted the same central point – that the contemporary practices of development were not working, and that the development ideal may have to be reorientated. It is in the attempt to correct these omissions that the development debate has proceeded. The first step in this direction was to make sure that development was environmentally sustainable.

SUSTAINABLE DEVELOPMENT

Like the 'right' to development, sustainable development is not a recent arrival in international law and policy. For example, in 1962, the United Nations General Assembly (UNGA) passed a Resolution which recognized that, 'to be effective, measures to preserve natural resources should be taken at the earliest possible moment simultaneously with economic development'.[38] This combination of environmental protection and the continuation of economic development is the essence of the popularized concept of sustainable development. The idea of combining the two concepts reappeared in international documents in 1968[39] and 1970[40] and was also recognized around this period by international institutions such as the World Bank.[41] In 1971, the Founex Report stated that, 'the recognition of environmental issues is an aspect of this widening of the development concept'.[42] The Founex report concluded that the questions of development and the environment must be linked, as they were at the 1972 Stockholm Conference, where it was realized that 'States should adopt an integrated and co-ordinated approach to their development planning so as to ensure that development is compatible with the need to protect and improve the human environment for the benefit of their population.'[43]

This intention was reiterated in international and regional documents in the 1970s.[44] In 1980 the WCS formally introduced the concept of sustainable development which recognized that 'Development and Conservation operate in the same global context.' Consequently, 'The underlying problems that must be overcome if either is to be successful are identical.'[45]

This direct linkage suggested that development must be recognized 'as a major means of achieving conservation, instead of being viewed as an obstruction to it'.[46] In the same year, the Global 2000 Report,[47] the first Brandt report,[48] and the Declaration of the Third United Nations Development Decade[49] came to similar conclusions. The 1982 World Charter for Nature recognized that 'in the planning and implementation of social and economic development activities, due account shall be taken of the fact that the conservation of nature is an integral part of those activities'.[50] Similar ideals were repeated in a number of regional agreements in the early 1980s.[51]

In 1987 the WCED popularized the concept and gave it an original and inspirational emphasis. The Commission concluded that sustainable development was the only way forward for a healthy planet. The primary principle of the report was 'to support development that is economically and ecologically sustainable'.[52]

After it was published, 'more than one hundred heads of State', the United Nations and organizations like the Organisation for Economic Co-operation and Development (OECD) all agreed with its logic.[53] Consequently, the concept was quickly recognized as a 'priority on the international agenda'.[54] This was reflected in a number of international and regional instruments leading up to the United Nations Conference on Environment and Development (UNCED).[55] UNCED was then described, in terms of primary purpose, as attempting to move environmental issues into the centre of the overall development agenda.[56] This was indirectly reflected in all the instruments that were adopted at the Summit. In a direct sense it was recognized in Principle 3 of the 1992 Rio Declaration that, 'The right to development must be fulfilled so as to equitably meet developmental and environmental needs of present and future generations.'[57] Comparable pronouncements were evident in two other major documents from the 1992 Earth Summit.[58] Therefore, as principle 4 of the Rio Declaration declared, 'In order to achieve sustainable development, environmental protection shall constitute an integral part of the development process and cannot be considered in isolation from it.'[59] Since this point, sustainable development has been taken as axiomatic in all following international conferences and settings.

THE IDEA OF SOCIAL DEVELOPMENT

The development of social considerations within the development discourse, whereby 'a new paradigm of development with a human face'[60] would be created, is not a new idea. Rather, 'the interdependence of economic and social development in the wider process of growth and change' was formally recognized by the United Nations in the General Assembly Declaration on Social Progress and Development in 1969. This Declaration suggested as its objective that:

> '*Social progress and development shall aim at the continuous raising of the material and spiritual standards of living of all members of society, with respect for and in compliance with human rights and fundamental freedoms.*'[61]

The importance of this type of approach was largely reiterated in the 1986 United Nations Declaration on Development, which defined development as:

> '*a comprehensive economic, social, cultural and political process, which aims at the constant improvement of the well-being of the entire population and of all individuals on the basis of their active, free and meaningful participation in development and in the fair distribution of benefits resulting therefrom.*'[62]

Such approaches are/were seen as the antithesis of the then operating development process, which as highlighted above was failing (and has largely continued to fail) to meet its own objectives. With such considerations in mind it has been suggested that 'there is a current need for a fundamentally different development model based on an alternative development'.[63] This perspective suggests that if a true alternative and sustainable development is to be attempted,[64] social factors must be at the heart of the equation.[65]

The triage between economy, environment and society was fully recognized at the 1995 World Summit for Social Development,[66] and in the run-up to the Earth Summit II in 1997, where it was recognized that: 'Sustainable development may be regarded as the progressive and balanced achievement of sustained economic development, improved social equity and environmental sustainability.'[67]

COMPONENTS OF SOCIAL DEVELOPMENT

The social component to development is made up of many areas. Some, such as a respect for human rights[68] and a reduction of poverty, have become relatively well accepted. These areas have been joined by a number of other factors which have seen a strong, growing correlation between various strands of Green theory and conventional developmental rhetoric. To demonstrate this, consider the following examples of democracy, gender and the importance of planning communities.

The Democratic Imperative

The right for citizens to exist within democratic regimes is a fundamental principle of human rights, and is well recognized within international law.[69] Nevertheless, the majority of the world's population have little control over the institutions that affect their lives.[70] This is a vast problem as the importance of control over institutions and direct democracy (on the local level) is becoming increasingly recognized as a prerequisite for societies which are both environmentally and socially sustainable. Alternative systems offering non-democratic procedures are often seen as the antithesis to establishing environmental protection.[71]

Direct democracy is very important to the theories of social ecology.[72] The specific importance of democracy for social ecology can be traced in a modern context back to ideas which percolated out of the Enlightenment. For example, pivotal theorists such as Jean Rousseau emphasized self-government in a direct democracy, in which all citizens are actively involved in the process of government, rather than simply voting periodically for a representative to take decisions. Here the idea of self-government is posited as an end in itself and a political order is proposed that will actively involve the affairs of ordinary citizens.[73]

In a contemporary sense, it is suggested that all possible decisions should be taken at the local level, with greater participation of the citizenry in the full decision-making process and greater accountability on the part of the decision-makers.[74] Democracy in this sense means 'equality of power among environmental stakeholders and in people taking control of their own environments, and thus owning both problem and solution'.[75] As such, more democracy, not less, is a vital part of solving the environmental and social condition.[76]

With regard to environmental problems, democracy is important because it is believed it will help lead to decentralization, 'appropriate' scale development and direct control over the processes that affect people's lives. This approach should allow people and communities to resume responsibility for their own development, rather than have it imposed upon them from above. Consequently, they will become the subjects, actors and ultimately the deciders in the process. This is necessary, as it is believed that the best social enhancements and environmental protections will come from those who live and depend upon their surrounding environment and communities.[77] This is in contrast to many conventional developmental and political processes where the question of authentic participation is often outside the ambit of the debate. Consequently, conventional developmental processes have typically been something that has been done for people, to people, sometimes despite them and even against their will, but rarely with them.[78]

This requirement for decentralized democratization has been increasingly recognized by international documents. It was recognized in passing in the first Brandt report as a 'requirement for development'[79] and in the 1980 WCS.[80] In 1987 the WCED was explicit and emphasized the need for 'effective citizen participation in decision making'[81] and 'decentralising the management of resources upon which local communities depend, and giving these communities an effective say over these resources'.[82]

The idea of 'popular participation' as a necessary ingredient of sustainable development was reiterated in a number of important international documents leading up to the 1992 Earth Summit,[83] and at Rio itself, where Principle 10 of the Declaration emphasized that 'Environmental issues are best handled with the participation of all concerned citizens, at the relevant levels.'[84] This type of perspective was again reinforced in 1995 by the Commission on Global Governance[85] and the World Summit for Social Development, where the signatories expressed their conviction that 'democracy and transparent and accountable governance and administration in all sectors of society are indispensable foundations for the realisation of social and people centred sustainable development'.[86] The necessity of this approach was also recognized at the 1996 Habitat Conference,[87] and by the Independent Commission on Population and Quality of Life in the same year. This Commission was forthright in its realization that:

> 'The starting-point of a new social contract will be the legal and pragmatic acknowledgment that sovereignty rests with the people: it is the people who must become the subjects of the enhancement of the quality of life.'[88]

The Design of Communities

Traditionally, the idea of direct democracy has been linked to the design and size of communities, by which numerous theorists have suggested that one could not be achieved without the other. This position has a long history in the basis of Green theory, whereby it has been suggested that all social structures should be small and decentralized.[89] This is deemed beneficial as it should help to lead to an ability to participate and establish grass roots democracy. These mechanisms *should* be beneficial both socially and ecologically.[90] Therefore, large-scale, hierarchical structures are to be avoided.

The optimum size of communities varies with each theorist. While some speak in terms of hundreds, others speak in terms of hundreds of thousands.[91] Accordingly, a critical focus has often fallen on cities and urbanized living generally. This is not surprising given the fact that by the year 2015, nearly 56 per cent of the global population is expected to live in urban areas, compared with fewer than 45 per cent in 1994. The most rapid rates of urbanization will occur in developing countries, with their rates of urbanization increasing from 26 per cent in 1975 to 50 per cent by 2015.[92]

Such huge concentrations of people and all their associated needs can bring intensive social and environmental costs in the forms of air and water pollution, the creation of solid waste and the destruction of surrounding environments.[93] Such degradation may cross the lines of sustainability.[94] Accordingly, the World Health Organization (WHO) has suggested that 'The consequences of urbanisation make a major contribution to the global environmental changes that threaten the very existence of life in the future.'[95] Likewise, the World Resources Institute (WRI), UNEP, United Nations Development Programme (UNDP) and the World Bank suggested in 1996 that:

> *'In the absence of policy reform, stronger institutions, and enlightened political leadership, economic and population growth in developing countries in the near term may lead to a deterioration of the urban environment, both physical and social.'*[96]

These problems have rarely led to romanticized pleas for cities to be dismantled and their inhabitants to be taken 'back to the land'. Rather, the underlying principle has become evident that it is not the size of a structure that is the actual problem, but the failure to deliver face to face democracy and the failure to be able to live in balance with the environment.[97] Both of these conditions are believed to be subsumed beneath larger destructive structures.[98] Indeed, cities, no matter how large they are, can be made politically decentralized and 'environmentally friendly'.[99] Accordingly, although numerous governments are trying to reduce rural to urban migration,[100] it is not assumed that urban living is intrinsically unsustainable. This, as recognized at the 1996 Habitat Conference, is especially so if it is complemented with social development, and careful planning which seeks to incorporate environmental considerations.[101]

Gender Empowerment

As the 20th century drew to an end, the role of women came under increasing scrutiny, yet for the most part they do not have equal access to land, credit, technology, education, employment and/or political power. In every society women play critical roles which have profound and pervasive effects on themselves, their families, communities and the environment. It is in this last respect that a growing body of literature has come to realize that women have a key influence on the quality of the environment in many countries. It has also been widely recognized that women and girls are often, disproportionately, directly and indirectly affected by resource degradation.[102]

The importance of gender equality and empowerment, as an indispensable element of sustainable development, was recognized in the international conferences of 1992,[103] 1994[104] and 1996.[105] The foremost recognition that 'Equitable social development that recognises empowering the poor, particularly women living in poverty, to utilise environmental resources sustainably is a necessary foundation for sustainable development' came with the 1995 Beijing Conference on Women.[106] This Conference emphasized that:

'Through their management and use of natural resources, women provide sustenance to their families and communities. As consumers and producers, caretakers of their families and educators, women play an important role in promoting sustainable development through their concern for the quality and sustainability of life for present and future generations... The strategic actions needed for sound environmental management require a holistic, multidisciplinary and intersectoral approach. Women's participation and leadership are essential to every aspect of that approach.'[107]

Quite simply, it has become apparent that without enhancing the well-being of women, their involvement in their communities and their interactions with the natural environment, then sustainable development will not eventuate.[108]

THE FUTURE OF SUSTAINABLE DEVELOPMENT

Development, as an ideology originally predicated on Northern forms of modernity, has been under active siege since the early 1970s. In mitigation of these challenges, and its unquestionable historical and contemporary failures, the idea of development has been reconstituted over the last 15 years to include environmental and social factors. Consequently, today, key components of the new rubric of development such as human rights, democracy and gender equality have been repeatedly brought to the international forefront.[109] With such changes in the idea of development, it could be suggested that the global community now acknowledges the new paradigms, and is en route to a sustainable future.

The Good Bank

A strong example of the change of direction in the development debate is provided by the World Bank. The World Bank is a prime mover in the development debate. It is the largest non-private provider of loans for 'development'. At the end of the 20th century, it was lending close to US$29 billion per year to over 60 countries.[110] The most visible manifestation of the Bank's involvement in environmental affairs is its implementing role in the Global Environment Facility (GEF).[111] In addition to this direct funding, environmental considerations are also built into every World Bank development. The Bank also has considerable influence as a catalyst and architect for co-financing development packages. It is also a (if not the) leader in development research and idea generation in this area.[112]

The World Bank commitment to ensure that the projects it finances do not have serious ecological consequences goes back to 1970. From this time, the bank has been an advocate of sustainable development.[113] This directive to act in a sustainable manner came to be recognized internationally, *outside* the Bank, in multiple documents including the Stockholm Conference, Agenda 21, and the 1997 review of the Earth Summit's goals.[114] This recognition of environmental factors has been increasingly emphasized, *inside* the Bank, since the late 1980s,[115] leading up to 1993 when the World Bank was reorganized to create a Vice-presidency for Environmentally Sustainable Development. This position is accompanied by about 200 full-time environmental specialists. In 1996, a further step was taken with the initiation of a 'new development compact' in an attempt to introduce greater transparency, accountability and institutional capacity.[116]

Alongside the Bank's environmental pretensions are its social ones, which reach back to the mid-1970s when the then President of the World Bank (McNamara) announced that the development record should not be judged by economic growth, but by the extent that poverty was reduced.[117] McNamara suggested that 'Development is about people. The only criterion for measuring its ultimate success or failure is what it does to enhance the lives of individual human beings.'[118] Therefore, if development does not alter malnutrition, disease, illiteracy, unemployment and early death, it can be said to have failed.[119]

Although this approach became slightly subsumed in the 1980s beneath a neo-liberal agenda, by the late 1990s the fight against poverty ('with passion and professionalism for lasting results')[120] was again at the front of the World Bank's agenda, as was its social (and environmental) focus. Indeed, 'People are the reason and the means of development. Their cultures, societies and organisations provide the foundation on which the development program rests.'[121]

The Bad Bank

Despite such sweeping changes in the development debate, it has been commonly suggested that little, if anything, has changed. Rather, it is suggested that the rhetoric of sustainable and social development will simply put acceptable glosses on an essentially discredited idea. As such, social and sustainable development may not end up as alternatives to the traditional development strategy, but minor modifications of it which are designed to allow larger agendas to continue unabated. An indication of this underlying agenda may be gleaned from the preamble of the Rio Declaration, which actually went so far as to suggest that it is necessary to protect 'the integrity of the global environmental *and developmental system*'[122] (my italics).

There is little question that the World Bank's environmental and social rhetoric and procedures are exemplary. What is controversial is how well it follows them. Indeed, because of this continuing anomaly the Bank has created a distinctly bad image with developmental organizations, environmental and human rights groups.[123] This disillusionment was reflected within the Bank in the 1990s when more than a third of completed World Bank projects were judged complete failures by its own staff.[124] Such perceptions also reflected a general questioning of the environmental implications of a multitude of their projects.[125] For example, according to an independent report from within the World Bank on one of its own projects, there was 'an institutional numbness at the Bank ... to environmental matters ... amounting to gross delinquency ... in so many areas no adequate measures are taken on the ground or even under consideration'.[126]

These problems led to a series of legislative efforts within the United States to increase the transparency of the Bank's operations.[127] Furthermore, in 1993 the Clinton administration began pushing for the creation of an internal watchdog within the Bank.[128] However, this watchdog – the World Bank Inspection Panel[129] – has been plagued with allegations that it only has a limited ambit within which it can act, both in terms of what it can recommend and the fact that it only has jurisdiction over two of the four arms of the World Bank. Additionally, it has been alleged that the Panel's independence has been compromised, that its procedures favour the Bank as against those who challenge it, and that the granting of standing to challenge the Bank in court is unduly restrictive.[130]

Such allegations helped to lead to broad calls by UNEP for the World Bank (and the International Monetary Fund (IMF)) to 'come fully within the UN family, [and] operate according to UN principles of participation and transparency.'[131] Although the UN and the World Bank moved towards 'enhancing their partnership' in 2000, along with increased attempts at becoming a 'more open, transparent organisation',[132] calls continued to resonate from international settings for both the World Bank and the IMF to revise their programmes in terms of the detrimental effects they have had on social development, and the poor in particular.[133]

It is possible that such allegations and the ever growing list of counterpromises made by the Bank cannot solve the overall problem. This is because the real difficulty may not be found with the oversight of a number of social and environmental directives. Rather, the difficulty may be within their forced lending approach, encased in an overall orthodoxy of modernity and neoliberalism.[134] In this regard, it is believed that any attempts to 'green' the bank are destined to ultimate failure due to its over-riding mandate. This is defined in the Bank's Articles of Agreement, to: 'Promote the growth of international trade ... encourage investment ... and rais[e] productivity ... of members.'[135]

Moreover, within this ambit the Bank continually commits vast sums of finance to causes which may not necessarily be environmentally beneficial.[136] This may well be due to the fact that the institution remains primarily motivated by economic, as opposed to social or environmental, concerns. As such, exactly how far the Bank may be truly willing to challenge regimes which may be anything from undemocratic through to unsustainable, is a matter of debate.[137] That is, no matter how hard the Bank may try to alter its behaviour, it may ultimately prove futile due to the over-arching orthodoxy within which it exists.

THE OVERALL PROBLEM

The overall difficulty is that the epicentre of the entire development structure and the vast underpinnings of the debate (that is, questions of political and ecological economy) may be being sidestepped or manipulated. The critically important questions (ones which could call into question the legitimacy of the system itself) have not been asked, or have been answered in a way which suits and does not hinder the status quo. Meanwhile, the conventional paradigm of development remains largely intact. This implies that without serious reconsideration of a number of underlying concerns, all of the rhetoric pertaining to social and environmental sustainability may come to nothing and we may, as Elizabeth Dowdeswell suggested, be doing little more with the label of sustainable development than 'deluding ourselves'.[138]

It is in regard to this debate that the rest of this book is based. That is, it seeks to examine the truly defining issues of economic growth, market structure, free trade, aid, debt, sovereignty, peace and security. Within each of these areas the chasm between the rhetoric and the reality will become apparent.

Chapter 2

Growth

GROWTH, TECHNOLOGY AND PROGRESS

Since the Enlightenment, important commentators such as William Godwin[1] and the Marquis de Condorcet[2] have argued optimistically that there is no limit to human progress. Alternatively, if there are limits to growth, then human ingenuity is such that it will bypass them with technology.[3] This type of argument is common within environmental literature. For example, the WCED suggested that:

> 'The concept of sustainable development does imply limits – not absolute limits but limitations imposed by the present state of technology ... technology and social organisation can be both managed and improved to make way for a new era of economic growth.'[4]

This position is supported by a number of historical examples, which show how the then perceived limits to growth were surpassed by the creation of new technologies. The pro-growth perspective also takes delight in the fact that the resources which the 1972 Limits to Growth Report speculated would be completely, or nearly, physically exhausted have not become so (mercury by 1983; tin by 1985; zinc by 1988 and copper and lead by 1991).[5] Rather, the evidence suggests that the world is not running out of most non-renewable resources. Indeed, by a number of measures, reserves of energy and of subsoil minerals are more abundant, and real world prices for such commodities are generally lower today than they were 20 years ago, despite rising consumption. Moreover, new technology is increasingly making possible substitutes for many traditional resource-based materials.[6] Thus, as the World Bank's Report on the Limits to Growth argued:

> 'The concept of resources itself is a dynamic one: many things become resources over time. Each century has seen new resources emerge. The expansion of the last hundred years could not have been sustained but by the new resources of petroleum, aluminum and energy. What about the possibilities of tomorrow – solar energy, sea-bed resources, and what else?'[7]

Such realizations have led some pro-growth advocates to suggest that the Earth and its resources are infinite, that human mastery over Nature through science is limitless, and that 'there is no persuasive evidence that any meaningful limits to growth are in sight.'[8] Some of these cornucopians are so confident in humanity's abilities and the resulting limitless future that they have even suggested that concepts such as the precautionary principle are an impediment to human ingenuity.[9] Lawrence Summers, the former chief economist for the World Bank, epitomized this overall, no-limits to growth belief when he stated in 1990 that:

> *'There are no limits to the carrying capacity of the earth that are likely to bind any time in the foreseeable future. There isn't a risk of any apocalypse due to global warming or anything else. The idea that the world is hanging over an abyss is profoundly wrong. The idea that we should put limits on growth because of some natural limit is a profound error.'*[10]

THE LEFT, THE RIGHT AND THE SOUTH

It is widely believed within modernity that economic growth is beneficial. This growth is seen as the incantation for national happiness and consequently countries all over the world have tried to make economic growth an overriding priority.[11] This drive for economic growth is intrinsic to both of the major ideologies of economic liberalism and state-fostered socialism. It is also very important for Southern countries.

The Left

Traditional Marxism involved a realization of 'productivism', and how it can be applied to serve the needs of all, and not just the ruling classes.[12] This trend has continued through to modern doctrines of socialism. Therefore, it is still argued that full mobilization of modern productive forces is necessary before socialism can be established. This perception suggests 'that there is too little growth'[13] and any limits that do eventuate represent political and social issues, *not* ecological ones.[14]

   However, the type of growth that Marxists desire is different from capitalist orientated growth. Marxists seek growth to meet needs, as opposed to being motivated by private profit and competition. Despite the difference, this approach does not question the overall problem of unlimited economic growth. Consequently, the ecological problems that result have been very similar to those in capitalist economies, if not worse.[15]

The Right

For economic liberalism, a large part of the economy is material growth. The doctrine that 'more is better' which is intrinsically linked to economic growth can be traced predominantly to Locke's thesis on ontological substitution.[16] This ideal 'legitimated virtually endless accumulation of material goods.'[17] The liberal thesis was also bolstered by the idea that the more money people have, the more pleasure they can indulge in. This idea of insatiability is central to modern economics and modern Western societies and manifests itself in a contemporary setting as consumerism.[18] Furthermore, the possibility that there are ecological boundaries to economic progress was not entertained by traditional liberal theorists.[19]

The contemporary preoccupation with economic growth is also entailed by the logic of capital and the pursuit of profit. The restless nature of these dictate continual new investments, improvements and turnover in the production and consumption of goods and services.[20] The primary objective of such economic systems is the expansion of economic growth, whereas goals of environmental protection (or social equity) are secondary. This becomes particularly evident in times of economic recession.[21] Nevertheless, economic growth is seen as necessary as theoretically it allows the generation of these secondary goals.

In the context of the sustainable development debate, the argument for economic growth is justified for two reasons. The first reason is the eradication of poverty, for when economic poverty exists, environmental problems may persist. The solution to this is believed to lie in increased economic growth, which will theoretically reduce poverty, and consequently protect the environment.[22] The second reason, as the 1980 Brandt Commission recognized, is that 'many forms of environmental protection are assisted by growth and the public resources which growth can provide.'[23] In this sense, it is argued that it is essential to have some form of sustainable growth in order to pay for the necessary environmental protection.[24]

The South

Most of the Southern countries on the planet invoke either a form of market liberalism or state-fostered socialism. Some combine various aspects of both, while others add unique specialities to suit their own situation. However, whichever way it is looked at, economic growth is strongly advocated by most (if not all) Southern countries in an attempt to break the economic stranglehold that they find themselves in. As the Charter of Economic Rights and Duties of States proclaims, it is desirable to attain 'the acceleration of the economic growth of developing countries with a view to bridging the gap between developing and developed countries.'[25] Likewise, the 1998 UNDP advocated that, 'poor countries need to accelerate their consumption growth.'[26] Thus, ideals of zero or limited economic growth are primarily viewed as invitations to 'stay poor' while Northern countries retain their current benefits.[27]

To obtain the alleged benefits of economic growth, many Southern countries are willing to endure environmental exploitation if it will lead to an overall improvement in their situation.[28] This ideal was mirrored in the demands from Southern countries for a New International Economic Order, which called for, 'the recovery, exploitation and development, marketing and distribution of natural resources ... with a view to accelerating the development of poor countries.'[29] This problem has become more pronounced on an environmental front, as problems such as climate change have become more urgent. For example, as the Commonwealth Group of Experts stated with regard to climate change and Southern countries:

> *'Developing countries face particular problems in relation to climate change. They have an immediate, and immense, task in reducing poverty which climate change could make more difficult. To realize this goal they will need to achieve rapid rates of growth albeit in a sustainable manner. They cannot, in these circumstances, be expected to curb that growth in order to alleviate a global problem which they have, in any event, done little to create.'[30]*

Extrapolating from similar objectives from an earlier period, Principle 11 of the 1972 Stockholm Declaration stated, 'The environmental policies of all States should enhance and not adversely affect the present or future development potential of developing countries.'[31] Therefore, as Principle 11 of the 1992 Rio Declaration stated, 'Environmental standards, management objectives and priorities should reflect the environmental and development context to which they apply.'[32]

Economic growth is also seen by Southern countries as a remedy for 'environmental deficiencies'. This was reflected in Principle 9 of the 1972 Stockholm Declaration.[33] The Beijing Declaration of the Group of 77 in 1991 reiterated this point in the following terms: 'Environmental problems cannot be dealt with separately; they must be linked with the development process, by which the environmental interests are in line with the imperatives of economic growth and development.'[34] These last points have led to economic growth being a foremost consideration within conventional definitions of sustainable development. This is evident as the modern sustainable development debate has tended to shift the focus away from growth versus the environment, to one of alleged complementarity of growth and the environment. Here, economic growth is advocated as a method to protect the environment and move the planet onto a path of sustainable economic development.

ECONOMIC GROWTH AND SUSTAINABLE DEVELOPMENT IN INTERNATIONAL ENVIRONMENTAL LAW AND POLICY

All of the above positions have culminated in the recognition of economic growth as necessary, if not central, to international environmental law and policy. This recognition of economic growth as an integral part of sustainable development was noted in 1972 by the Council of Europe, which stated that, 'Sustained economic growth is a necessary pre-condition of the availability of means by which the deterioration of the environment may be combated.'[35] In the same period, Robert McNamara, then the head of the World Bank, argued, that:

> 'The question is not whether there should be continued economic growth. There must be. Nor is the question whether the impact upon the environment must be respected. It has to be ... there is no evidence that the economic growth – which the developing countries so desperately require – will necessarily involve an unacceptable burden on either their own or anyone else's environment.'[36]

Similar positions linking economic growth and environmental protection were reiterated in 1979,[37] 1980,[38] 1982,[39] 1983,[40] 1984[41] and 1985.[42] In 1987 the WCED called for a 'new era of growth' and emphasized accelerated economic growth in order to build the foundations for sustainable development. Thus,

> 'Growth has no set limits in terms of population or resource use beyond which lies ecological disaster ... a sustainable world economy requires ... more rapid economic growth in both industrial and developing countries.'[43]

This vision is predicated upon the need to maintain and revitalize the world economy. They suggested that there are *no* absolute limits to growth per se. However, environmental considerations must be woven into the development paradigm. This emphasis on economic growth as an essential ingredient to environmental sustainability was seized upon by multiple governments between 1988 and 1992 in the run-up to the Earth Summit.[44] At the Summit, the recognition that, as George Bush stated, 'Growth is the engine of change and friend of development',[45] was fully enshrined in Principle 12 of the Rio Declaration on Environment and Development. This stipulated that:

> 'States should co-operate to promote a supportive and open international economic system that would lead to economic growth and sustainable development in all countries, to better address the problems of environmental degradation.'[46]

By the mid-1990s the link between sustainable development and economic growth was taken as axiomatic. For example, the 1995 World Summit for Social Development invoked a call for 'promoting sustained economic growth, in the context of sustainable development'.[47]

THE NO-GROWTH POSITION

The need to realize the limits of growth that Nature may impose is a foundation stone of the Green argument.[48] However the realization that it is necessary to control growth is a debate that predates Green theory by many centuries. For example, in antiquity, Plato,[49] Aristotle,[50] Seneca[51] and Tertullian[52] all came to question the limits of growth that a society could achieve and still remain healthy. In the late part of the Enlightenment, J S Mill asked very similar questions and was very scathing of the effects that uncontrolled economic growth could have upon both society and Nature.[53] Implicit within all of these perspectives was that it may be in the best interests of society to be limited in certain areas. In contemporary Green theory, this is known as the 'steady state'.

THE STEADY ECONOMIC STATE

Many Green theorists suggest that economic growth must be limited and that it cannot exceed the level of renewable resource inputs.[54] The central features of a steady state economy are the rejection of capital in the form of the accumulation of producers' and consumers' goods, and the rejection of ever-increasing human numbers. Overall, there is an emphasis on the balance of human impact upon the biosphere.[55] Additionally, the qualities of self-sufficiency, equity and quality of life, as opposed to quantity of output, are stressed.[56]

This form of sustainable development requires a concerted 'reorientation' of the modern market economy towards environmentally benign and socially conducive activities. Inevitably this approach entails a reduction in what is said to be the *needs* of the current consumer society. The ideal here is to draw a line between 'real' needs and 'false' needs. An indication of what real needs may be was given by Article 25 of the Universal Declaration of Human Rights, as food, clothing, housing and medical care and necessary social services, and/or the International Labour Office, which included the minimum requirements for private existence (food, shelter, clothing); essential collective goals (safe drinking water, sanitation, education) and the protection and enhancement of human rights (with an emphasis upon social, as well as civil rights).[57] 'False' needs are typically seen as 'unnecessary' and consumer driven.[58] The exact line where some of these 'needs' are classified as 'necessary' is a matter of debate among numerous theorists.[59]

Growth would be acceptable in a steady state economy, but only if it was truly required and was not driven solely by profit. Further, the steady economic state needs to be carefully planned. Therefore, the issue is not whether to grow or not, but how to grow. Consequently, it needs to be realized that it is a mistake to equate a no-growth state with a resource-frugal one. If environmentally sensitive activities and results are achieved, it may be quite possible to continue to grow.[60]

The usual objection to limiting growth is that it will hurt the poor.[61] This, however, is not necessarily the case. The no-growth position, as originally recognized in the 1972 report and again in the 1992 report, emphasized that the 'basic material requirements of all people must be met'.[62] However, this is not to be a process to simply accelerate uncontrolled economic growth. Rather, it could require cutting back on the part of those who have already benefited from substantial economic growth and transferring or sharing portions of the unnecessary surplus. This point is imperative. Despite the needs to limit and reorientate the economic growth process, it is essential that the conditions for the poor in both Southern and Northern countries be 'substantially improved'.[63] The imperative is summed up by the saying that 'the rich must live more simply, so that the poor may simply live'.[64]

CROSSING ENVIRONMENTAL THRESHOLDS

The steady economic state is advocated because it is believed that many environmental thresholds are currently being crossed by modern society. This idea is not new. It first appeared with force in the middle of the Enlightenment, when some theoreticians began to become pessimistic about humanity's future. The foremost exponent in the environmental context was Thomas Malthus, who postulated that:

> '*The power of population is infinitely greater than the power of the earth to produce subsistence for man. Population, when unchecked, increases in a geometric ratio. Subsistence only increases in an arithmetic ratio. A slight acquaintance with numbers will show the immensity of the first power in comparison with the second.*'[65]

The basis for his theory was that resources, particularly food, were limited, and food was necessary for survival. At the same time, certain classes would always continue to bear plenty of children because 'passion between the sexes was necessary and constant'. Because these were contradictory facts, a limit to growth would eventually come into existence.

For the next 150 years, Malthus's prognosis was of academic interest only as technological innovations (such as the Green Revolution) pushed any hypothetical nutritional limits to the parameter of academic curiosity. However, since the early 1970s the limits to growth debate moved has back into the centre of environmental and public discourse.[66]

The enhanced position of the debate has been supported by three considerations. The first of these pertains to historical evidence which has shown examples of communities that have reached their physical limits of growth and then collapsed.[67] The second reason has to do with a questioning of how far technology can go, and the third reason has to do with current and projected exponential growth rates and the possible effects that these may have on the environment.

The Technological Question

One of the main reasons why the Green, 'no-growth' position differs radically from the conventional 'pro-growth' position is the divergent views about the capacity of technology to cross environmental boundary limits. This is perhaps the main issue that separates the resource optimists from the resource pessimists. The 'no-growth' position does not believe that technology alone will solve all of humanity's problems. There are five principal reasons for this lack of faith in technology.

The first reason has to do with an argument put forward by some 'deep' green theorists that technology is a principal actor in the destruction of the environment. Some have taken the position against technology to its extreme and have classified 'technical man' as the 'modern Judas'.[68] Additional perspectives claim that technological rationality is dominating and attempting to reform Nature. This argument has recently appeared with force in the debate over genetically modified foods. However, this is not a new altercation, and similar debates about technological progress date back to the 19th century with concerns pertaining to the 'Frankenstein factor'.[69] Likewise, in the 20th century, important theorists such as Martin Heidegger,[70] Lewis Mumford[71] and Rudolf Bahro[72] have attacked the technological basis of modern society for its alienating effects and its manipulative, positivistic paradigm.

However, most Green theorists do not subscribe to this anti-technology perspective. Rather, they suggest an *alternative* approach to technology, that although it may have undesired effects, the answer is not to abandon it, but to re-examine it, re-direct it, and control it with tighter reins to make sure it is *appropriate*. This is broadly in accordance with the traditional Luddite position, where it is not technology itself, but its application and social control that is the central concern.[73]

This perspective is consistent with many of the aspects of social ecology which recognizes some of the benefits that modern technology can offer in solving environmental problems. These can be from improving democratic communication systems and thereby helping to empower people, through to giving insights into the natural world and providing the knowledge of how to repair the environment where it is already damaged. It may lead to new environmentally sustainable exemplars, such as alternative energy.[74]

Technology may also be beneficial in the sense that, as Marx saw, it can be used to do the worst jobs that humanity is currently required to do. Thus, it may also have a beneficial liberatory effect.[75] However, for technology to be truly beneficial it must be 'appropriate' and fit within the requisite economic, social, cultural and environmental factors of the place of its application.[76]

This is a problem that has been appreciated since at least the beginning of the 20th century.[77] An oft-quoted example of this is the debate between Gandhi and Nehru. Nehru sought all forms of Western projects so as to 'develop' India. Gandhi retorted that India did not have enough money to employ everyone with modern technology and that even if the capital could be found, the drain on resources would be unsustainable. Consequently, Gandhi advocated indigenous goals and means for social change, which were rooted in the traditions and technologies of the people. He also sought a revitalization of the village economy, the decentralization of production, and a move towards self-sufficiency.[78] In a more modern context, Fritz Schumacher is the best known exponent of these views, with his thesis 'small is beautiful'.[79]

The second reason why technology as an environmental saviour is often frowned upon is that technology, in attempting to solve one environmental problem, may well generate others.[80] The problem here is not so much one of technology itself, but of the limits to human knowledge and the unknown consequences that may flow from applying the technology. The cases of the development of DDT as an insecticide,[81] CFCs as a method of refrigeration, or nuclear power for increased energy demands are all good examples of this point.

The third justification for being sceptical of the technological argument is that it often does not address root causes of the environmental problematique. Accordingly, as the *UNEP GEO-2000* report suggested: 'Environmental gains from new technology ... are being overtaken by population growth and economic development.'[82] The problem was earlier recognized by the Commission on Sustainable Development:

> 'The positive developments mentioned above [increased efficiency resulting in lesser environmental effects] have been largely offset by larger volumes of production. Consequently, many natural resource and pollution problems persist or continue to worsen. The car industry has, for example, produced cleaner and more efficient cars; however, the growth in the number of vehicles has offset the positive environmental effects of that development. Similarly, results have been achieved in waste reduction ... but total volumes of waste produced have been growing.'[83]

The solutions to such problems require large-scale social and political change, which challenges the overall consumption ethos. This is not to argue that technology will not be important; rather, that it is only part of the equation.[84]

A fourth consideration is that many present forms of technology are inherently limited in terms of their actual and potential capacity to solve the various environmental problems. For example, in 1992 the Presidents of the US National Academy of Sciences and the Royal Society of London warned: 'Science and technology may not be able to prevent either irreversible degradation of the environment or continued poverty for much of the world.'[85] In addition many basic ecological services (such as fresh water) cannot be replaced by human technology. Even if they can be replaced, often the costs are prohibitive.[86]

The final concern about technology relates to the social problems that it may create.[87] A good example of this problem is the technology of the 'green revolution', where there has been a displacement of small farmers and households, and a subsequent widening of the class divide between those who can afford to use the new technology and those who cannot. In turn, this has led to an avoidance of 'deeper' social issues such as land reform.[88]

Exponential Growth and Environmental Limits

Exponential growth of the human world has become so rapid that it is believed that certain types of environmental limits have presented themselves. Two examples illustrate this well. These are the problems of population and consumption.

Population Growth and Unsustainable Practices
The world population is increasing by around 80 million people every year. This is the equivalent of 10 new Swedens every year, or an entire Latin America every 5 years. Estimates of future population size are highly uncertain. The UN projections for 2050 suggest a medium projection of 8.9 billion.[89] Much of this growth will be concentrated in Africa and Asia.

The rapid growth that is occurring in these countries may cause unsustainable practices[90] when it is linked to a number of other aggravating factors such as poverty, social inequity and lack of civil and social rights. That is, population growth by itself is prima facie neither good nor bad, but the underlying social and ecological circumstances that people are born into can make it so.[91] Therefore, to quote the Report from the 1994 Cairo Conference on Population:

> *'Demographic factors, combined with poverty and lack of access to resources in some areas, and excessive consumption and wasteful production patterns in others, cause or exacerbate problems of environmental degradation and resource depletion and thus inhibit sustainable development.... Pressure on the environment may result from rapid population growth.'*[92]

The difference in the over-consumption and environmental degradation of the South as opposed to the North, is that the Southern effects are primarily local (relating to areas such as the over-consumption of freshwater resources, soils, forests, habitats and biodiversity),[93] whereas the Northern over-consumption typically results in global problems such as climate change and ozone depletion. In addition, Northern countries can contribute to 'local' problems such as deforestation in Southern countries caused by a demand for rainforest products.

Northern Consumption
The overt consumption of 'non-essential' goods is an integral part of modern life in Northern countries.[94] Such consumption has grown exponentially in a very short time. For example, since 1900 the world's economy has expanded more than 20 times. The consumption of fossil fuels has gone up by a factor of 30, and industrial production by a factor of 50. Four-fifths of that growth has occurred since 1950. Indeed, between 1950 and 1990, the industrial roundwood harvest doubled, water use has tripled and oil production has risen sixfold. The additional economic output of each of the decades since the 1950s is estimated to match that from the beginning of civilization to 1950. Since

1950, Americans alone have used more minerals and fossil fuels than all other peoples of the world throughout human history.[95]

The last sentence of the above paragraph points to the realization that it is not just a question of growth and consumption, but also one of *who* is consuming and how much. This realization first appeared in 1972 at the Stockholm Conference on the Human Environment, where it was argued that the problem of protecting the environment does *not* lie with the unwilling Southern countries, but rather with the Northern countries and with the demands they place on the rest of the world to support their high-consumption economies.[96] However, this realization remained at the back of the mainstream environment agenda for a number of years, and the distinction between the countries responsible for environmental problems was not made. Rather, the generalized problem of growth, as opposed to the problem of who was growing and what the effects of this were, was seen as the culprit. This did not begin to change until the mid-1980s, when it was reiterated that much of the limits to growth debate related to a disproportionate consumption by a minority of people.[97] As the WCED stated, 'An additional person in an industrial country consumes far more and places far greater pressure on natural resources than an additional person in the Third World.'[98]

For example, according to the 1993 UNDP *Human Development Report*, people in industrialized countries consume ten times more commercial energy than people in Southern countries and create 68 per cent of the world's waste.[99] The industrialized countries (and the countries in transition) account for 70 per cent of the world's fossil fuel consumption, 83 per cent of its aluminium, 82 per cent of its copper, and 78 per cent of its beef and veal. Overall, the Northern countries consume five-sixths of the resources that are used in the world, and the South makes do with the remaining sixth.[100]

The average rich nation citizen used 7.4 kilowatts (kW) of energy in 1990. This represents a continuous flow of energy equivalent to that of powering 74 100 watt light bulbs for a whole year. The average citizen of a poor nation, by contrast, used only 1 kW. In a country-to-country comparison, the United States consumes three times more iron ore than India, 4.6 times more steel and 12 times as much petroleum. On a per capita, as opposed to a country comparison, the average American consumes twice as much energy as a Japanese citizen, three times as much as a Spaniard, 19 times more energy than the average Indian, and 100 times more than the average Bangladeshi.[101] In terms of climate change on a country-to-country basis, the United States had a cumulative emission total of carbon dioxide of 168 billion metric tons, whereas India had around 13 billion metric tons.[102] Likewise, in terms of total percentage share of the greenhouse gases, the United States carries the responsibility for 19.14 per cent, whereas India carries only 3.68 per cent.[103]

Overall, each of the 1 billion people in the North consumes around 20 times as much as those in the South. Therefore, the materialist lifestyles of the additional 1.75 million Americans born every year may well do equivalent damage to the environment as that caused by the 35 million people born in the South.[104] Thus, even if there was a substantial population reduction in the

South, unless this was accompanied by a dramatic reduction in consumerism, net environmental damage would still be likely to increase.[105]

Southern Consumerist Growth in the Future

The rapid trajectory in *global* economic growth and the consumption of natural resources is not expected to decrease. Rather, it is expected to increase fivefold in the next century. Current growth rates for the entire world fluctuate between 3 and 4 per cent per annum. This rate of economic growth is deemed necessary just to keep the increasing population supplied with basic needs. This means that growth rates at the end of the 21st century will have to be three or four hundred times the current level.[106] Much of this growth will have to be in Southern countries. For example, the United States is currently the largest economy in the world and is more than twice as big as either Japan or China. However, by 2020, China's economy will be more than 40 per cent bigger than the United States. With this growth will come millions more consumers, demanding all the things that the Northern countries have. This has already started to happen; consider that in 1978 in China there were only a handful of private washing machines, yet by 1995 there were over 97 million, all placing extra demands on water, waste and energy. This consideration of energy also illustrates the same problem when taken as an aspect of growth of the Asia region. Asia is currently doubling its energy demands every 12 years. Accordingly, by 2005 these countries will be producing more sulphur dioxide than Europe and North America combined.[107] However, as much as sulphur dioxide causes local or regional problems (ie acid rain), it will be their increased production of carbon dioxide which will cause global problems such as climate change. Indeed, if current population and energy consumption trends continue, by 2025 Southern countries could be emitting more than four times as much carbon dioxide as industrialized countries do today.[108]

This desire for growth, and the rates at which it is being achieved, has created cause for concern for many. Indeed, as Elizabeth Dowdeswell stated, 'changes in consumption and production patterns need to start in the North, but, we need to broaden the scope of the debate options to include the perspectives of the South.'[109] Such a focus is necessary because if the Southern countries repeat the pattern of resource utilization, pollution and conspicuous consumption that has happened in Northern countries, then vast environmental problems may be anticipated. Indeed, it is unlikely to be possible to maintain the current levels of consumption by industrial societies alone for any length of time, let alone bring the majority of Southern countries up to the same standard.[110] This conclusion was well summarized by the 1996 Independent Commission on Population and Quality of Life which noted:

> 'The whole world cannot sustain the Western level of consumption. If 7 billion humans were to consume as much energy and other resources as do today's industrialized countries, five planet Earths would be needed to satisfy everyone's needs.'[111]

GROWTH AND THE ENVIRONMENTAL NEXUS

The above combination of growing populations and resource consumption is believed to lead to environmental damage in two ways. Firstly, there is the question of resource supply, and secondly, there is the issue of the ability of the biosphere to absorb increasing amounts of human waste.

Resource Supply

In 1972, the Club of Rome released a report entitled *The Limits to Growth*. The report concluded that:

> '1. *If the present growth trends in world population, industriali-sation, pollution, food production and resource depletion continue unchanged, the limits to growth on this planet will be reached within the next one hundred years. The most probable result will be a rather sudden and uncontrollable decline in both population and industrial capacity.*'[112]

It was suggested that as the world's resources are finite, the trade-offs between human activities – namely, the production and consumption of resources and the control of pollution – were soon to meet *absolute* limits.[113]

However, as seen in the earlier section detailing the support of the growth position, many of the predictions made in the 1972 report have been proved wrong and the scarcity of certain resources has actually decreased. However, the debate has reasserted itself along the traditional Malthusian lines – of population outstripping subsistence.

This argument has resurfaced as a massive loss of the momentum in the growth of global food production has occurred, while being juxtaposed against exponential population growth.[114] This problem has affected a number of countries in different ways. For example, in 90 of the poorest countries of the world (of which 44 are in Sub-Saharan Africa) food production, on a per capita basis, is actually falling. Additionally, if current trends in resource use continue and the world's population continues to grow as predicted, it is projected that by 2010 per capita availability of rangeland will drop by 22 per cent, fish catch by 10 per cent, the per capita area of irrigated land by 12 per cent, cropland by 21 per cent and forestland per person by 30 per cent.[115] Unfortunately, these trends need to be working in the opposite direction, as the demand for food in Southern countries is projected to double by 2025.[116]

This question of whether the world will be able to feed its future population is a matter of debate; the central issues are questions of increasing yields, efficiency, irrigation and croplands. The Food and Agricultural Organization (FAO) believes that by the year 2010 overall (declining) production increases will still be able to accommodate effective demand and rising world population in a global sense. However, they are much less sanguine about reducing malnutrition generally. Indeed, certain areas are expected to get worse in terms of feeding themselves, and in some localized areas, expanding populations, dwindling resources and ecological devastation are expected to create a 'vicious circle' which may actually reflect localized ecological limits in the ability to feed the local population. The solution to such localized deficits is hoped to be offset by global increases in food production which can be transferred between countries (via free trade).[117]

This position was recognized by the World Food Summit in 1996, which stated that despite a rising world population, 'Availability of food for all can be obtained.'[118] This position was qualified by the points that national and international communities must remove a number of multifaceted, political – *not* ecological – causes underlying food insecurity.

Others are much more cautious about the technical and ecological ability to produce more food. For example, Elizabeth Dowdeswell stated:

> *'It was clear ... that ... at some point, the limits of the earth's natural systems, the cumulative effects of environmental degradation and limitations of yield raising technologies would have to manifest themselves, and this is now happening.'*[119]

Such a position argues that future food production will be constrained by the shrinking backlog of unused alternative agricultural technologies (ie organic), by the approaching limits of the biological productivity of fisheries and rangelands, by the increasing scarcity of water, the declining effectiveness of additional fertilizer applications, and generally by social disintegration in a number of Southern countries.[120] These trends may put severe strains on the world's ability to increase global food production in parallel with population growth.[121] The pessimistic nature of this outlook is greatly enhanced when taken from the even longer term (ie beyond the population levels of 2010 focused on by the FAO). With this longer-term view, the already qualified hopes of the FAO become problematic, as what the Commission on Sustainable Development classified as 'serious questions about long-term sustainability' arise.[122]

Environmental Absorption Capacity

In a contemporary context, despite the growing debate about whether humanity can feed itself or not, the central environmental limits to growth are seen in the *renewal and absorption capacity* of the environment, which may indicate the initial limits to growth.[123] Specifically, as the 1980 *Global 2000 Report* concluded, 'the problems of preserving the carrying capacity of the earth and sustaining the possibility of a decent life for the human beings that inhabit it are enormous and close upon us.'[124]

Since the early 1990s, this recognition of a carrying capacity of the Earth, and the possibility that this is being crossed has become increasingly prominent.[125] With regard to both the carrying capacity and the absorption questions, the limits to growth were reasserted in 1992 in the 20-year sequel to the original report. It added to the original report by both confirming the original scenario while, at the same time, widening its aim. Specifically, it recognized that the 1972 prognosis that focused on the physical limits of natural resources, or their increasing scarcity at affordable prices, had *not* eventuated. However, if the parameters to growth are foreseen as deriving from the regenerative capacity of the biosphere, then the limits are being reached. The 20-year sequel concluded that:

> '*Human use of many essential resources and generation of many kinds of pollutants have already surpassed rates that are physically sustainable. Without significant reductions in material and energy flows, there will be in the coming decades an uncontrolled decline in per-capita food output, energy use, and industrial production.*'[126]

Although nowhere near as dire, similar realizations about the unsustainable path of the planet were made in 1997, by the Commission on Sustainable Development[127] and at the Earth Summit Review.[128] These were followed in 1999 by UNEP's *GEO-2000* report which suggested:

> '*The present course is unsustainable and postponing action is no longer an option ... signs of improvement are few and far between... If the new millennium is not to be marred by major environmental disasters, alternative policies will have to be swiftly implemented.*'[129]

Such statements suggesting that a limit to growth may be coming into existence are commonly being supported by multiple examples of hard evidence that environmental sustainability may be being transgressed in certain instances. For example, in 20 of the world's largest cities, air pollution levels already exceed WHO guidelines. One-third of the world's population live in countries experiencing moderate to high water stress.[130] Eleven per cent of the Earth's fertile soil has been either eroded, chemically altered or physically compacted to such a level that it cannot fulfil its original functions.[131] Sixty per cent of the world's important fish stocks are being fished at, or beyond, their limits.[132] Between 1960 and 1990 a full one-fifth of all natural tropical forest cover was lost. Global forest, woodland and scrub cover declined by 2 per cent in the 1980s. This deforestation is expected to increase as both Northern and Southern countries increase their consumption (a total doubling of the 1990 consumption figures by 2010) of forest products.[133] Thirty-four per cent of the world's coasts are at high risk of degradation, and another 17 per cent are at moderate risk.[134] By the year 2000 between 5 and 20 per cent of some groups of animal and plant species could become extinct.[135] All of these problems are expected to get worse as population increases.

As dramatic as these statistics are, it is *not* primarily in these areas that the limits to growth debate approximates the theoretical literature to such a high degree. This is reserved for the debates pertaining to ozone depletion[136] and climate change.[137] Within these areas, one cannot help but be struck by the similarities between the various reports and the simulated limits to growth 'overshoot' projections.

CONSUMPTION IN INTERNATIONAL ENVIRONMENTAL LAW AND POLICY

The problem of disproportionate consumption was recognized in 1974 with the Cocoyoc Declaration, which acknowledged that:

> *'the point in the existing world situation is that the huge contrasts in per-capita consumption between the rich minority and the poor majority have far more effect than their relative numbers on resource use and depletion ... the world today is not only faced with the anomaly of underdevelopment, we may also talk about over consumptive types of development that violate the inner limits of man and the outer limits of nature.'*[138]

Similar concerns to these re-emerged in the Brandt report of 1980, which realized that, 'industrialised countries will have to alter their lifestyles', owing to the fact that they use a disproportionate quantity of resources.[139] In 1982, wasteful consumption patterns as a lead to over-exploitation of the environment were noted in the Nairobi Declaration.[140] In 1987 the WCED suggested that, 'sustainable development requires the promotion of values that encourage consumption standards that are ... ecologically possible'.[141] The argument reappeared in 1990 at the World Summit for Children,[142] and then again, with increased focus, in the Bergen Ministerial Declaration on Sustainable Development which pointed out that:

> *'Unsustainable patterns of production and consumption, particularly in industrialised countries, are at the root of numerous environmental problems, notably foreclosing options for future generations by depletion of the resource base.'*[143]

Various participants at the 1992 Earth Summit recognized this problem,[144] as did Agenda 21[145] and the 1992 Rio Declaration on Environment and Development.[146] The theme of unsustainable consumption was directly revisited at the 1994 Oslo Roundtable on Sustainable Production and Consumption[147] and the Cairo Conference on Population in the same year. The Cairo Conference recognized that 'unsustainable consumption and production patterns are contributing to the unsustainable use of natural resources and environmental degradation.'[148] Interestingly enough, the Report from this Conference did *not* single out the unsustainable patterns of consumption just from the North (although it did suggest they should take the lead in reducing consumption). This was unlike the Report of the World Summit for

Social Development in 1995, which stated that, 'The major cause of the continued deterioration of the global environment is the unsustainable pattern of consumption and production, particularly in industrialised countries, which is a matter of grave concern.'[149]

A similar approach was followed with the 1995 Commission on Global Governance,[150] the Commission on Sustainable Development in 1996[151] and the Conference on Human Settlements.[152] The Report of the Independent Commission on Population and Quality of Life was particularly forceful:

> '[I] t is urgent and even imperative to change production schemes and consumption patterns, a shift amounting to no less than a new economic revolution. Because this will affect the future and perhaps the very survival of the world.'[153]

In 1997, recognition of the problem of consumerist growth of Southern countries was achieved at the Global Partnership Summit on Environment.[154] In the same year, at the Earth Summit II, despite *no* targets being set to reduce consumption or production patterns, it was recommended that '*All* countries should strive to promote sustainable consumption patterns [but] developed countries should take the lead' (my italics).[155] However, the exact question of responsibility was far from settled, and this issue remained a source of heated debate at the Commission on Sustainable Development in 1999.[156] Finally, the UNEP *GEO-2000* report swung back the focus onto industrialized countries (and newly industrialized countries which in some cases had per capita consumption patterns equal to established industrialized countries) with their assertion: 'a tenfold reduction in resource capacity in the industrialised countries is a necessary long-term target if adequate resources are to be released for the needs of developing countries'.[157]

This approach is consistent with the drive in this area whereby direct reductions in consumption are being increasingly linked to ideals of enhanced efficiency in production, recycling and consumer choice. For example, the 1995 Draft International Covenant on Environment and Development suggested that to reduce unsustainable consumption patterns, the Parties shall:

> '(a) collect and disseminate information on consumption patterns and develop or improve methodologies for analysis;
> (b) ensure that all raw materials and energy are used as efficiently as possible in all products and processes.
> (c) Require recycling of used materials to the fullest extent possible.
> (d) promote product designs that increase reuse and recycling and as far as possible eliminate waste; and
> (e) facilitate the role and participation of consumer organisations in promoting more sustainable consumption patterns'.[158]

This approach, whereby unsustainable consumption itself is barely questioned, was supplemented in 1999 when Consumers' Rights were added to the ambit of consideration by the Commission on Sustainable Development. The overall problem is that aside from certain conventions such as those on climate or ozone and various areas with regard to oceanic pollution, specific mandates requiring reduction targets in the output of either products or processes or increases in the efficiency of their manufacture which may have negative environmental effects have *not* yet eventuated in the international sphere. Moreover, even the width of the debate – on whether this is a problem for Northern and Southern countries alike – has become increasingly entrenched.

THE POPULATION QUESTION IN INTERNATIONAL ENVIRONMENTAL LAW AND POLICY

Uncontrolled population growth, when *combined* with a broad set of economic and social pressures, may have a distinctly detrimental effect on the environment and the development process in general. This has been well recognized since the 1960s.[159] For example, in 1969 the Pearson Commission recognized that:

> 'No other phenomenon casts a darker shadow over the prospects for international development than the staggering growth of population... It is clear that there can be no serious social or economic planning unless the ominous implications of uncontrolled population growth are understood and acted upon.'[160]

Despite the strong recognition of the necessity to limit population growth, it took many years for the issue to become fully focused in the international arena. Indeed, despite the suggestion at the 1972 Stockholm conference that 'Demographic policies ... should be applied in those regions where the rate of population growth or excessive population concentrations are likely to have adverse effects upon the environment',[161] these policies have been very slow to appear in international forums. For example, the first official international conference on population at Bucharest in 1974 got no further than entrenched argumentation over whether development policy or population policy came first. Indeed, there were many delegations that maintained that rapid population growth was *not* a problem.[162]

In 1980 the first Brandt report reactivated the debate, by suggesting forcefully that exponential population growth could pose distinct problems for development.[163] In the same year, the Global 2000 report suggested that:

> 'Perhaps the most troubling problems are those in which population growth and poverty lead to serious long-term declines in the productivity of renewable natural resource systems. In some areas the capacity of renewable resource systems to support human

populations is already being seriously damaged by efforts of present generations to meet immediate needs, and the damage threatens to become worse.'[164]

The 1984 International Conference on Population in Mexico City met a similar fate to its predecessor, in that it quickly became embroiled in debate. Nevertheless, it was recognized that 'To be realistic, development policies, plans and programs must reflect the inextricable links between population, resources, environment and development.'[165] Despite this recognition, no firm commitments on reducing the growth rate could be reached.[166]

The impasse of failing to fully confront the population issue was directly crossed by the 1987 Brundtland Commission, which stated clearly that 'present rates of population growth cannot continue'.[167] The Commission was promptly followed in 1989 by the (non-official) International Forum on Population in the Twenty-First Century held in Amsterdam. This Forum emphasized that 'Balancing population and resources as well as protecting the environment are key elements to ... sustainable development.' Accordingly, the Forum went on to issue specific figures by how much the population growth rate *must* be reduced for sustainability to be achieved.[168] This necessity to reduce population growth was also endorsed by the South Commission in 1990, which emphasized that the 'explosive' pace of population growth in many Southern countries was 'unsustainable'.[169]

Unfortunately, the drive from the Brundtland and South Commissions, as well as the International Forum in Amsterdam, did not follow through to the Earth Summit. The population question was only dealt with in Agenda 21, where a new, international consensus on population growth as a foremost environmental concern was *not* defined. Nowhere did Agenda 21 suggest clearly and unambiguously that the world should try to limit its population growth, with a view to ultimately stabilizing it, as was demanded earlier.

Despite the failure of population growth to be confronted at Rio, the Earth Summit did finally witness a breaking down of the traditional lines of North and South antagonism over the 'population question', with the South finally acknowledging that uncontrolled population growth could be a potential problem. Accordingly, from this point, most nations have come to recognize that population dynamics play a distinct role in environmental issues, and a new sense of urgency was established.[170] This urgency, and the environmental nexus, was finally recognized in a formal sense at the 1994 Cairo Conference on Population which stated that, 'To achieve sustainable development... States should promote appropriate policies, including population-related policies.'[171] Accordingly, the Report of the Conference went on to issue calls to 'slow down population growth'.[172] This theme was reiterated at the 1995 World Summit on Social Development which recognized that 'continued growth in the world's population ... challenge[s] ... the natural environment'.[173] This link was also recognized by the 1996 Report of the Independent Commission on Population and Quality of Life.[174]

With such a background, it can now be asserted that the linkage between population growth and sustainable development in both ecological and social terms has become fully recognized.[175] However, specific targets to reduce this problem have *not*.

Limitations have also appeared with regard to the specific methods by which reductions in fertility (contraception) may be achieved. Indeed, although the Programme of Action from the Cairo Conference finally[176] recognized that governments and the international community should use the full means at their disposal to support the principle of voluntary choice in family planning, the reality has proved something different. That is, approximately 200,000 unplanned conceptions happen daily on the planet. This figure reflects the fact that although contraceptive use has increased in Southern countries, it remains available for no more than 50 per cent of all couples. Unavailability may be due to cost, politics or simply not being available in the marketplace.[177] When the Cairo Programme of Action was reviewed in 1999, the target of 100 per cent availability of contraceptives for all couples was set for 2050[178] – by which time the human population should have swelled to 8.9 billion.

CONCLUSION

Growth, as manifested in all of its diverse forms, is an essential part of most conventional ideologies. It is also now considered intrinsic to the quest for sustainable development. The idea of limits to how far humanity can grow, both in terms of numbers and their effect upon the environment, has been traditionally dismissed. This has especially been the case with early predictions, which suggested that limits would become apparent in terms of scarcity of static resources, such as minerals.

However, over the past 20 years the realization has grown that there may indeed be physical limits to growth which humanity may be facing that are not necessarily to do with static resources, but more to do with the absorption capacity of the environment. In this regard, environmental problems such as ozone depletion or climate change are already showing that physical limits may be transgressed. On the traditional Malthusian question of whether humanity will be able to feed the forthcoming doubling of world population, the commentators and international institutions remain divided.

The above realizations have begun to force the international community to consider ways of reducing human impact on the environment; firstly, through reducing consumption, and secondly by reducing population growth. Unfortunately, both directions have, to date, proved largely fruitless.

The difficulty with current attempts to reduce consumption is twofold. Firstly, these attempts focus on ideals of efficiency and getting 'more for less'. The *overall* question, of whether to consume or not (with the limited exception of set areas),[179] is steadfastly avoided. Rather, the misplaced assumption remains that consumption itself is not the problem. However, even this very restricted approach to blunting the edges of consumption is restricted by the continuing failure to set international goals or targets about how to achieve the desired efficiencies. Such considerations go to the heart of the next chapter, dealing with questions of markets and market structure.

This failure even to consider whether consumption itself is the central difficulty feeds into the second issue, which is that at the moment the considerations of reducing the impacts of consumption are only placed upon Northern countries. This myopia will radically adjust itself as Southern countries soon eclipse Northern countries with their overall impact on the environment. Even if Northern countries do make extremely good progress in their quest for efficiency, it is highly unlikely that this will offset the overall impact of the other four-fifths of the world, who seek to replicate the Northern consumption-driven economies.

The second area where the international community has been struggling for 25 years has been in efforts to reduce population growth. Here, despite slow progress towards actually recognizing that population growth can directly contribute towards environmental problems, specific mandates or goals for what are sustainable levels of population remain off the international agenda. Even the lesser goals, such as access to contraception, have target dates that coincide with a time when the problem will have already fully arrived.

Chapter 3

Markets

NEO-ECONOMIC LIBERALISM

Edmund Burke, writing in the 18th century, characterized the time as 'the age of the economist'. If he could see the beginning of the 21st century, then perhaps he would recast his classification. Today, economists are key players in nearly all parts of society. This is not a new phenomenon. What is new, is the emphasis that it has taken. This is largely due to the fact that many administrations around the world are now influenced by 'new right' liberal ideologies. This ideology lends ardent support to the free economic market as the ideal basis for a free (and 'efficient') society.[1]

This reborn neo-liberal ethos grew in a post-war period with the Chicago School of Economics, which preached the virtues of the free market with an intellectual and ideological rigour. By the late 1970s and early 1980s this drive became crystallized in the Conservative government of Margaret Thatcher and the Republican administration of Ronald Reagan. Both of these leaders entered power with the most conservative agendas and *ideological* perspectives for half a century. This agenda represented part of what the 1990 South Commission classified as, 'a rigid ideological position prevalent among decision makers in many developed countries who saw the unfettered operation of market forces as always best, whether at the national or international level'.[2]

For example, Ronald Reagan perceived the growth of federal government, particularly its regulatory functions, as a threat to political liberty, as well as the source of many of his country's economic and social ills. Deregulation was thus seen as a tool for economic revival. This meant that private interests were favoured and the role of the government became downplayed.[3] Accordingly, Reagan rejected traditional Keynesian techniques for managing aggregate demand through fiscal and monetary policies, in favour of a new 'supply-side' doctrine. This entailed reducing public expenditure on non-defence programmes, increasing military spending and deregulating the economy. Additionally, the Reagan administration explicitly rejected the welfare state and the limited collectivism that existed in America. Thus, a number of frontal attacks were made on laws of the 1970s covering occupational safety and health, consumer protection, energy conservation and the environment.[4]

In the UK since Margaret Thatcher took office, successive administrations have all been believers in the principles of the free market. Their main concerns were reducing public spending in the public sector, adopting monetarist economic targets, privatizing state enterprises, and weakening trade unions in the political economy. The central mainstay came from two liberal precepts: reducing the government's role in the economy and giving greater power to market forces.[5] Inevitably, this flowed on to a limiting role of the government in environmental decision making.

The adoption of free market principles has not been such a voluntary process in many Southern countries. There, despite the long-standing endeavour to establish in international law that economic choice was a matter of inviolable sovereignty and that the Bretton Woods institutions were politically 'neutral',[6] the international debt crisis has given the IMF and the World Bank the ability to 'reorientate' many of the economies of the debt-ridden countries.[7] Indeed, over 70 Southern countries were 'structurally adjusted' in the 1980s alone.

The IMF was created at the end of the Second World War, and is controlled by the top ten OECD countries. This control is manifested through the voting rights of the donor governments, which are granted in accordance with the size of their contributions.[8] The IMF Charter states that its purpose is to assist its members which 'encounter balance of payment difficulties' and to promote a 'liberal regime of international payments'.[9] In exchange for assistance with balance of payment problems, recipient governments must agree to accept the IMF's conditions that govern the use of the Fund's resources.[10]

The IMF came into its own with the advent of the debt crisis, which engulfed the developing countries in the early 1980s. With this crisis, the IMF found itself advising dozens of countries and arranging crisis loans in situations that turned out to be long term. Obtaining renewed IMF finance has become conditional on following IMF advice. Few governments were or are in a position to resist the conditions that come with the loans. Consequently, the IMF has been given a unique opportunity to influence and reorientate these countries' economic policies. In accordance with this position, the IMF Group of 24 Communique in 1981 asserted that:

> *'The solutions to the payments problem of developing countries in the present unfavorable world economic environment will require adjustment of a structural nature, and of long duration, involving considerable social cost.'*[11]

The structural adjustment in question focuses on a number of economic prerequisites that are central to IMF assistance. These conditions work on the central precept that debtor countries should grow out of the crisis economically. This objective is to be achieved through a series of market economic initiatives, which aim to reduce expenditure and increase revenue. Specifically, the IMF and the World Bank insisted that to achieve economic recovery for these countries, it was necessary,

> *'to improve the structure of government budgets and reduce deficits, primarily through reduced spending and a determined attack on structural rigidities including protectionist measures, which impede the efficient functioning of markets.'*[12]

The policies pursued to achieve these objectives are known as 'structural reforms'. The IMF explained in 1988 that:

> *'Structural reforms ... being undertaken ... are part of a program of modernisation that would allow market forces to play a larger role in the economy. The reforms emphasise a redefinition of the role of the state, including narrowing the scope of government regulation and the privatisation of state enterprises. In addition, the modernisation program contemplates ... the liberalisation of foreign trade and reforms in the financial system.'*[13]

On the domestic front, this entails reductions in government expenditure, especially on social services and economic infrastructure, removal or reduction of subsidies, an increase in tax revenue, restriction of money supply and bank credit and an increase in real interest rates.[14] This policy of structural adjustment is expected to continue for the foreseeable future.

The countries that fail to meet or agree to these objectives may not be eligible for IMF financial assistance. On top of this, countries 'in need' may not get loans from any other international sources without an IMF seal of approval. This seal helps to provide a guarantee that the country will henceforth behave in accordance with the prerequisite economic doctrine. With such requirements needed, it can be seen that the IMF has a huge influence on debtor countries.[15]

THE FREE MARKET AND ENVIRONMENTAL PROTECTION

Domestic Environmental Approaches

Between 1970 and 1980, a vast amount of environmental legislation and environmental protection was established in the United States. However, Reagan, acting in accordance with his economic doctrine and his drive 'designed largely to reverse the institutionalisation process', made budgetary reductions and weakened public bodies.[16] Furthermore, he indirectly but effectively attacked the Environmental Protection Agency and environmental laws on both a domestic and an international level. Where environmental issues had to be addressed, 'market principles' were to be incorporated in all possible situations.

The few specific principles which the Reagan administration did adopt to guide environmental policy were threefold. Firstly, the use of cost-benefit analysis to determine the value of environmental regulation. Secondly, reliance as far as possible on the free market to allocate resources. Finally, environmental responsibilities were to be decentralized.[17]

Reagan's successor, George Bush, decided to slightly distance himself from the 'Reagan revolution' in regard to its attack on environmental initiatives. However, Bush remained committed to the ideal of the introduction of market principles in the field of the protection of the environment.[18] He also reflected the view that the underlying problem for environmental concerns is market failure, in that markets are operating imperfectly and causing environmental *externalities*. Therefore, the best approach for government action is to 'reconstitute' the market. This objective was reflected in 'Project 88, Harnessing Market Forces to Protect Our Environment: Initiatives for the New President'. This report contended that:

> '*Conventional regulatory policies need to be supplemented by market based strategies which can foster major improvements in environmental quality by enlisting the innovative capacity in our economy in the development of efficient and equitable solutions ... market-based instruments belong in our portfolio of environmental and natural resource policies.*'[19]

With the advent of the Clinton/Gore administration, environmental concerns came much more to the fore than with the previous two administrations.[20] Nevertheless, the market-orientated emphasis within this arena has continued.[21]

In the UK, the former Thatcher administration was unsympathetic to environmental concerns in its first two terms of office. In her third term in office Mrs Thatcher changed direction and apparently accepted the need for government intervention to protect the environment. However, nothing substantially changed within the Thatcherite free market ethos and the ideals of the 'enterprise culture' based on concepts like voluntarism, self-regulation, competition and small government, continued largely unabated.[22] Consequently, as Michael Howard stated, 'Government policy will make market forces work for the environment'.[23]

This approach continued with the Major government. For example, in 1993 and 1994 in the course of a 'war on red tape', a number of 'useless regulations' that protect the environment were abolished in accordance with the government's 'commitment to the principle of deregulation' and 'lifting the burden on industry'.[24]

The International Recognition of Market Mechanisms and Environmental Issues

Ever since the establishment of the OECD Environment Committee in 1970, the OECD has consistently promoted greater use of economic instruments to make sure that the polluter pays their fair share. By the 1980s, market-orientated instruments were being heralded elsewhere as quite compatible with sustainable development. This idea was noted at various international meetings in 1982,[25] 1984,[26] 1987,[27] 1990[28] and 1991.[29] Such views were then (re)endorsed by the Environment Committee for the OECD (unsurprisingly),[30] the Business Council for Sustainable Development,[31] and the World Bank, which forcefully argued that, 'Market-based instruments are best in principle and often in practice.'[32] These views strongly influenced the 1992 Earth Summit. Consequently they became incorporated into most of the major documents. For example, the Rio Declaration on Environment and Development recorded in Principle 12, 'States should co-operate to promote a supportive and open international economic system that would lead to economic and sustainable development in all countries.'[33]

Agenda 21 was more forthright in its advocacy of the market-orientated principles. For example, Chapter 2.38 (e) stated that Southern countries should:

> 'Encourage the private sector and foster entrepreneurship by improving institutional facilities for enterprise creation and market entry. The essential objective would be to simplify or remove the restrictions, regulations and formalities that make it more complicated, costly and time-consuming to set up and operate enterprises in many developing countries.'[34]

The 'trend in thinking away from a command-and-control regulatory approach to achieving environmental goals'[35] that UNCED evinced was followed through in the final years of the 20th century. Accordingly, the Commission on Sustainable Development stressed in 1998 that: 'Governments should review their regulatory policies and systems of economic incentives and disincentives ... and should support the environmental protection efforts of industry ... governments should encourage industry's voluntary initiatives.'[36]

The 'New Model' of the role of market mechanisms, as supplemented by the community and government to achieve environmental objectives, was reiterated in 2000 by the World Bank, with a strong emphasis on developing countries.[37]

MARKET SOLUTIONS TO ENVIRONMENTAL PROBLEMS

The Importance of Private Property

The starting point for the free market approach to environmental protection is that private property is conducive to environmental preservation. This maxim proceeds from the neo-liberal conception of common property, that is to say, property that is open to unrestricted use because it is neither owned by an individual nor controlled by the international community. This idea was *traditionally* well recognized in international law and the idea of complete freedom of fishing on the high seas.[38] In such a setting, no nation or individual had the unilateral authority, let alone the responsibility, to control general activities in the international commons.[39] This failure of ownership was/is seen as one of the fundamental reasons for current environmental problems. This approach gained prominence in 1968 with Garrett Hardin's famous 'tragedy of the commons' thesis.[40]

Hardin's central argument was that 'freedom in the commons brings ruin to all'. This is because all are driven by self-interest to exploit the commons before anyone else does, and since everyone adopts this approach, it leads to the overall physical exhaustion of the common property in question.[41] This, he postulated, resulted from the very nature of a common, in that the common property resource is owned by everyone, and at the same time, owned by no one. Since it is used by everyone, it is therefore rapidly and thoroughly depleted as no one has any incentive to maintain or preserve it. The only way that any of the users can capture any of its value, economic or otherwise, is to use or exploit the resource as rapidly as possible, before someone else does. It is also argued that coordination through agreement is extraordinarily difficult in the absence of property rights. Additionally, often the individual exploiting the common cannot be identified.[42]

This form of unlimited and uncontrolled open access within a limited common is reckoned to lead to environmental disasters in both domestic and international settings. This has been particularly well documented in the past with regard to the high seas.[43] For example, at the 1992 Earth Summit in Section 17.45 of Agenda 21 it was noted that:

> 'Management of high seas fisheries, including the adoption, monitoring and enforcement of effective conservation measures, is inadequate in many areas and some resources are over-utilised. There are problems of unregulated fishing, over-capitalisation, excessive fleet size, vessel reflagging to escape controls ... unreliable databases and lack of sufficient co-operation between States.'[44]

Hardin's initial solution to the tragedy was that the environment must *not* be treated as a commons or it 'will be of no use to anyone'.[45] He refined this conclusion some years later with the argument that:

> 'The fundamental error of the sharing ethic is that it leads to the tragedy of the commons. Under a system of private property, the man (or group of men) who own property recognise their responsibility to care for it, for if they don't, they will eventually suffer. A farmer, for instance, if he is intelligent, will allow no more cattle in a pasture than the carrying capacity justifies ... but if a pasture is run as a commons open to all, the right of each to use it is not matched by an operational responsibility to take care of it.'[46]

This suggestion has been advocated not only for the open commons, but also for environmental resources under *public* control. Conversely, it is believed private owners have a direct and immediate incentive for the wise use and careful management of their resources, as they receive the benefits of their wise management or bear the costs of bad management. Thus self-interest and economic incentive are believed to drive the owner to maintain the long-term environmental capital.[47] Consequently it is argued that *private* property rights work to protect the environment because private owners will choose generally not to despoil it. Conversely, these incentives are not believed to exist within bureaucracies or with unowned property. This problem is believed to be further complicated in regulatory settings owing to vested interests and political manipulation.[48] Therefore, it appears obvious that the recognition of private property over common property is a sound way to secure environmental protection.[49]

Restructuring the Free Market with New Property Rights and the Incorporation of Externalities

Externalities

As new environmental problems have presented themselves in areas that were previously non-property (such as the atmosphere), a number of new, de facto property rights over these areas have been created in places. Additionally, these new property regimes can be structured to attempt to correct economic externalities. Once these externalities and subsidies have been corrected, then the free market working upon the strictures of supply and demand should achieve environmental protection.[50]

Economic externalities are created where the activity of one person or entity affects the welfare of other persons or entities, and the costs of this interference are *not* reflected in the price of the good or process that creates this interference. Thus, as Ernst von Weizsäcker stated, 'prices do not tell the ecological truth'.[51] In essence this means that the effect the product or process had on the third party goes unnoticed in an economic sense for the producer, but not the victim of that externality. The inequitable result is that the person or entity that causes the externality is receiving a public or neighbourhood subsidy for their product as the price of the product or the process does *not* reflect its true cost.[52]

The solution to this problem is believed to lie in internalizing the cost of the externalities. Internalization creates an incentive to reduce the activity that produces the external cost, as the prices paid for the item in question rise to reflect the full value of all the environmental and social costs accrued to produce it.[53] Such a process is believed to be essential to achieve significant shifts in consumption and production patterns, so as to achieve sustainable levels.[54] This argument was recognized in Principle 16 of the 1992 Rio Declaration on the Environment and Development, which states that:

> 'National authorities should endeavor to promote the internalisation of environmental costs and the use of economic instruments, taking into account the approach that the polluter should, in principle, bear the cost of pollution, with due regard to public interest.'[55]

Environmentally Destructive Subsidies

The importance of the polluter paying the full price of the pollution necessitates that the product or process causing the damage is not assisted by subsidies from any national, regional or international body. For as the World Bank recognized in 1992, 'Some government policies are downright harmful to the environment. Notable here are distorted prices in general and subsidised input prices in particular.'[56] This realization gained renewed prominence with the 1997 UNGA Special Session on the Review of the Implementation of Agenda 21, where it was recognized that:

> 'There is a need for making existing subsidies more transparent in order to increase public awareness of their actual economic, social and environmental impact and to reform or, where pertinent, remove them.'[57]

Such actions have been deemed necessary because, as the world currently operates, there is a vast multitude of environmentally destructive activities, covering energy, transport, forestry, agriculture and water wastage that are subsidized by governments.[58] Global energy subsidies currently total US$200,000 million per year. OECD countries spend some US$82,000 million a year subsidizing energy production, mostly through tax breaks, cheap provision of public infrastructure and services, subsidized capital and price support. Eighty per cent of these subsidies concern fossil fuels. Nuclear energy receives a further 8 per cent (which is more than alternative energy sources receive).[59] Some specific examples of such damaging subsides can be seen in China, Mexico and Poland, where users pay less than 40 per cent of the production costs of electric power. The figure for coal in the former USSR is 10 per cent. In India and Bangladesh, irrigation water is practically free.[60] However, high figures are believed to be falling as governments begin to weed out their subsidies. For example, fossil fuel subsidies between 1990 and 1995 in five countries in Eastern Europe have fallen from US$14.4 billion to 6 billion. The result of the reduction of these subsidies has been a slackening in demand, and subsequently less pollution in terms of emissions of sulphur and nitrogen oxides and carbon dioxide.[61]

It should be noted that not all subsidies used by governments for environmental purposes are destructive. For example, subsidies for reforestation or environmentally sound technologies (such as alternative energy), recycling,[62] or environmentally progressive practices such as in farming may be beneficial in the quest to protect the environment.[63] Conversely, in some areas where subsidies have been removed, such as with fuel or food subsidies, which should theoretically reduce environmental tensions, the opposite has occurred. This is because the loss of support has helped to force poor people into vulnerable ecosystems, such as tropical rain forests, in search of cheaper forms of energy or alternative ways to fulfil their subsistence needs.[64] All of these examples reflect that *the link between subsidies and environmental destruction is neither direct nor clear-cut.* Moreover, it should force the recognition that if certain goals (such as specific types of environmental protection) are to be obtained, then certain subsides may need to be maintained. They may, however, be illegal under the new trading regimes. I shall discuss this problem in the next chapter.

Permits

Once the market-distorting subsidies by governments are removed, it then becomes necessary to examine other ways in which the market can be structured to protect the environment. Within this vision, the synthesis of new property and the internalization of externalities have come through two areas. The first involves tradable emissions permits and the second deals with 'green taxes'.

The idea of emissions permits dates back to the early 1960s and the Canadian economist J H Dales, who devised a system which would make environmental destruction economically unattractive to those who *own* the rights to destroy or pollute the environment.[65] Since this time they have grown in political popularity. For example, Section 33.18 of Agenda 21 suggests in the paragraph on 'innovative financing' that 'the feasibility of tradable permits'[66] should be explored.

The idea of transferable quotas is well illustrated by the fishing industries in New Zealand and Australia. Here, an overall level of fish-catch is set (and revised annually) and quotas within the overall limit are allocated to each fishing company or vessel, which are freely tradable among vessel owners who can buy or sell their quotas to others. This programme was meant to stop over-fishing and rein in an overgrown vessel fleet.[67] This idea of permit trading has also been extensively used in the USA with air pollution,[68] ozone depleting substances[69] and land development.[70] It has also been suggested for international environmental problems from climate change[71] through to population control.[72]

Taxes

The alternative way that de facto property rights, externalities and making the polluter pay have come into existence has been with the much more common idea of the taxation of products or processes which are environmentally damaging. This is a popular idea in both Green theory[73] and contemporary political debate where green taxes have been applied nationally.[74] Their feasibility with international problems is also being examined.[75]

This idea of taxes to counter environmental externalities is typically ascribed to Arthur Pigou. He devised a series of taxes to account for the social and environmental costs which were not reflected in private decision making.[76] Crudely, a tax is placed on the polluter to bring the polluter's cost function into line with what it would have been, had they faced the true social and environmental costs of their production. Thus, environmental taxes are a way of incorporating the externalities into the cost factor, which in turn corrects the shortcoming of the market. Moreover, these forced cost internalizations also help to create level economic playing fields, so that the entities that already voluntarily incorporate these costs (such as some of the makers of green consumer products) are not put at an economic disadvantage by those that do not internalize these costs – and thus have cheaper products.[77]

All of these above ideas, of making the polluter pay, of the internalization of externalities, the use of green taxes and of tradable permits, are believed to offer a successful path to environmental protection within the rubric of the free market. Additionally, the level of environmental protection generated is believed to be at least equal to that generated by traditional command and control mechanisms, but at a much lower cost.[78]

The Individual's Choice and the Redundancy of Regulation

The Good, Green Corporation
Closely interlinked with the market-driven approach to environmental protection is what the WCED identified as the 'socially responsible industry with an awareness of environmental considerations'.[79] Here, a form of environmental awareness on the part of commercial bodies has become commonplace as such entities (allegedly) make voluntary efforts to go *beyond* what is required by environmental laws. For example, through a number of schemes, many commercial entities are running their own environmental audits, have their own environmental goals and are striving towards achieving the goals of sustainable development all on their own initiative.[80] The United Nations Centre on Transnational Corporations' Benchmark Corporate Environmental Survey in 1991 found that a number of transnational corporations (TNCs) had developed their own international environmental policies which went *beyond* the laws of the nations they were operating within. Others have (sometimes) taken steps to improve their environmental performance, even at some cost to their business. Some had acted to improve efficiencies and reduce wastage and pollutants and, finally, some have even extended their own environmental standards to their subsidiaries.[81]

There are a number of documents which purport to reflect this responsible attitude. For example, the International Chamber of Commerce initially published the *Environmental Guidelines for World Industry* in 1974 and 1981.[82] In 1993 the International Chamber of Commerce formed a World Industry Council for the Environment. This council was/is to 'promote the concept of sustainable development through self-regulatory guidelines and environmental educational programs'.[83] Earlier, in 1989, the Valdez Principles (later renamed the CERES principles) were created by the Coalition for Environmentally Responsible Economies after the *Exxon Valdez* disaster. These are intended to focus the pressure of socially conscious investors in order to improve the environmental conduct of corporations.[84] In 1990 Japan's major business organization launched its environmental charter, which exhorted companies to care for the ecosystem.[85] In the same year the Canadian, British and American chemical companies formed 'Responsible Care Programs'.[86] In 1991, the Business Charter for Sustainable Development was created[87] and by 1992 this had been endorsed by over 600 companies worldwide.[88] By the mid 1990s the International Standardization Organization had created ISO 14000 (and 14001) which detailed some overall schematic views within which businesses can comply with effective environmental management in tandem with socio-economic needs.[89] Finally, the Banking Industry in 1993, and then the Insurance Industry in 1995, both in collaboration with UNEP, issued statements of Environmental Commitment.[90]

The thrust of many of these initiatives was reflected at the Earth Summit, where Chapter 30 of Agenda 21 dealt with 'Strengthening the Role of Business and Industry' and talked of 'encouraging transnational corporations' and of 'voluntary private initiatives'. It also suggested that these 'entrepreneurs' should be 'encouraged' to be 'self-regulating stewards' of the environment.[91] Not surprisingly, the advocates for corporate-driven sustainable development are also strong advocates of the idea that governmental regulation is inefficient, and self-regulation is a much better approach.[92]

From an economic standpoint, the message of all these pronouncements is that there is no fundamental incompatibility between protecting the environment and the interests of business. As the American Council for Environmental Quality noted in its 1990 report, there are 'broad corporate benefits that attend efforts to reduce pollution'.[93] Quite simply, as Sir Martin Holdgate, the President of the Global 500 Forum, told the Commission on Sustainable Development in 1996, 'It is ... a fallacy that environmental protection adds costs. Often, when a Company applies its ingenuity, high environmental performance and profitability go hand in hand.'[94]

The International Free Market and Transnational Corporations

The interface between corporate environmentalism, the self-regulating commercial entity and the free market has been well demonstrated in the international arena with the deregulated international sphere within which TNCs operate. Whereas previously there were movements to control these hugely powerful entities, there is now a trend to free up their economic playing fields. This has been assisted by two separate factors.

First, the creation of expanded international economic freedom has enabled TNCs to thrive. This goal was radically furthered through the Uruguay General Agreement on Tariffs and Trade (GATT) round and the current global neo-liberal atmosphere. These changes have allowed TNCs to capitalize on the opportunities that have arisen.

Secondly, despite the fact that TNCs constitute a critically important element of the global economy and have an undeniable part to play in sustainable development, their importance and reach is *not* matched by international regulation. This is largely a result of the fact that many TNCs have continually lobbied against excessive controls against their actions on both a domestic and an international level. Self-regulation, as noted above, is their preference.

Green Consumerism

The force which is hoped to keep the market and the entities within it on a 'green track' is believed to be the modern, powerful 'green consumer'. Thus, as the 1997 Tokyo Declaration from the Global Partnership on the Environment Summit noted, 'The achievement of sustainable development depends upon citizen awareness that encourages environmentally responsible consumerism and personal behavior.'[95] Such trends, it is argued, will not allow environmental damage to occur. This should be achieved through the consumers' exercise of their purchasing power, which should direct the market towards environmentally benign activities. As Madsen Pirie explained:

> *'The consumer is able to exercise a degree of control on private firms by deciding whether to shop with them or seek satisfaction elsewhere. The goods and services have to be orientated toward consumer satisfaction in order to attract customers and make profits.'*[96]

Thus, the free market will be directed by an orchestra of environmentally conscious consumers who will force the creation of a 'green tinge' to a progressive market. This argument is supported by the rapid growth of a powerful international consumer movement.[97] This type of approach, with its emphasis on changing the type of consumption through public awareness about the impacts of various types of consumption, as opposed to challenging consumption generally, was largely recognized by the 1994 Oslo Roundtable on Sustainable Production and Consumption. That is, the market and its overall consumption ethos was *not* thought to be the problem of over-consumption. Rather, the type of consumption was at issue. Indeed, it was recognized that 'Political reality in democratic societies is such that it will be much easier to change consumption patterns than consumption volumes.'[98]

THE LIMITS OF THE FREE MARKET

Green theory traditionally does not have any preference for either the free market or the controlled market, as the ideal method for achieving its objectives.[99] However, it has become apparent that there are distinct limitations on the market-orientated ideals and the pursuit of goals consistent with environmental protection. As such, it is being increasingly mooted that many environmental and social goals need to be centrally and democratically planned and enforced, or else devastation may follow.[100] As such, *intervention* in the free market may be necessary.[101] Indeed, as Karl Marx suggested, 'cultivation when it progresses spontaneously and is not consciously controlled ... leaves deserts behind it'.[102]

Ethics

The first problem with the market-orientated approach is that it is often considered *unethical*. For example, for many the idea that society may set a limit of tolerable pollution, and then use the market to enforce this, is repugnant. For not only do they disagree with the method, they also disagree with the basis – that there is an acceptable level of destruction.[103] This position is very disparaging about the whole interface between economics and environmentalism. I have already discussed this argument at length elsewhere.[104]

When the Market Needs to be Controlled

If the free market is to have a dominant role in responding to environmental problems, there is still the necessity of strong, centralized state intervention in a number of areas, in order to help make it function in accordance with the desired goals. Often the most effective ways in which these goals can be achieved are by tempering the free market, and *enhancing* the role of the state.[105] This is not a radical suggestion, as even great ideologues like Adam Smith stipulated that the state has an active role in the market society.[106] This idea that government may have a distinct role to play in civil society (as markets alone cannot do everything) has once more come back into fashion – as it became apparent (to the South Commission[107] and the World Summit for Social Development)[108] in the 1990s that governmental intervention was the most effective mechanism to achieve certain goals such as social equity. The situation, with regard to the choice between markets or governments, was well summed up by the World Bank in 1999:

> 'There have been three phases of development thinking. In the first, market failures were seen as pervasive and complete, and government as the only solution to all ills. In the second there was a brief period when government failure was seen as pervasive and complete, and markets (if not the solution) as the only hope. Today's third view – pragmatic but not ideologically satisfying – is that both markets and governments have pervasive failures but that these usually are not complete ... we need to recognize the limits and strengths of markets, as well as the strengths and limits, of government interventions aimed at correcting market failures.'[109]

Within the environmental context, the necessity for governmental intervention (as opposed to market alone) was recognized earlier in a weak form by the WCED, which spoke of the need for incentives and disincentives for commercial enterprises.[110] Gro Brundtland went on later to stipulate that, 'The environmental problems cannot and will not be solved through market forces or any "invisible hand"'.[111] This recognition was repeated by the Council of Europe, in their Pan-European Conference on the Protection of the East-West Environment, where they declared that it is sometimes necessary for governments to, 'Integrate environmental policy systematically into other sectoral policies, while accepting the subordination of the market economy to ecological requirements.'[112] This point is also recognized in section 20.13 of Agenda 21.[113] The need for market intervention is also particularly acute in Southern countries and certain former eastern European countries, which require all the intricacies of public infrastructure, in both a physical and social sense, to move towards any form of sustainable development.[114] There are a number of areas where this need is obvious.

Enforcement, Information and Creation

Firstly, as an over-riding goal, the state must confront and control the environmental and social externalities. Indeed, in this regard both the market-orientated Greens and the perspectives from social ecology are in congruence. Both agree that externalities *must* be internalized and government subsidies for environmentally destructive processes and products *must* be stopped. Accordingly, the state must command and control the environmentally progressive markets through a framework of incentives, infrastructure, regulation and leadership.

There are numerous examples of these areas. For example, governments must monitor and enforce environmental standards.[115] The role of the state here is essential due to the absolute power of some of the entities that willfully, and often illegally, destroy the environment. These entities often have the ability to defeat any challenges brought against them by all but the state and the resources and power that it can bring to bear.[116]

Another important area for the state is to ensure the availability of unbiased and complete information that will allow individuals, groups or entities to make informed choices. This information needs to span from full and complete corporate reporting (with regard to environmental and social effects of their activities)[117] all the way through to full and clear information on consumer products. However, despite such information being available in some countries, and despite calls for it to be made available through the international or regional community[118] through schemes such as 'eco-labelling', many commercial entities (and countries) continue to manipulate environmental information and deliberately keep it obscure, inaccessible, or plainly secret.[119] The Commission on Sustainable Development saw the overall situation as one whereby,

> *'the majority of consumers still have little knowledge of the environmental impact of their consumption habits and lifestyles ... a large number of consumers ... are unable to tell which producers make environmentally friendly products ... they also have limited knowledge of life-cycle effects.'*[120]

Consequently, green consumerism is substantially hampered by entities that misrepresent or withhold facts in order to get on to the green bandwagon. Strong, independent standards, which are validated by the state, are required to rectify this.[121]

The above points, highlighting the necessity of the state to allow the suitable functioning of the free market, face an even greater difficulty in the international arena. This is because strong forms of international authority would be required to enforce the market rules in question, adjudicate disputes, and provide coercion when agreements are not kept.[122] However, as discussed in the following chapter on free trade and the last chapter on sovereignty, the only international bodies which are gathering power are those within the Bretton Woods rubric. Unfortunately, these bodies may not be overtly receptive to the idea of forcing the issue of externalities.

Equity

The market may also need to be closely controlled so as not to generate inequitable results. This is very important in an environmental context as disempowered poverty is often the antithesis of sustainable development,[123] and market-orientated approaches designed to combat environmental problems can easily become inequitable and exacerbate this problem. Of course, this is not a problem of the market instrument per se, but rather a problem of how it is implemented. Indeed, if green taxes are tempered with an appropriate reworking of the entire tax system, then the effects of such taxes need be neither politically regressive nor economically stifling in an overall sense.[124]

However, as they currently operate, green taxes are often regressive with the poorer economic classes. This is because poorer people often spend a higher proportion of their total expenditure on certain products that may need to be inflated in price for environmental purposes, such as energy. Unfortunately, such people may not have the choice of 'doing without' as the product or process is part of an inelastic demand. If this is the case, then a greater economic burden will fall on specific classes of people.[125] This problem may be expected to become more severe, as green taxes will have to be set at quite high levels to achieve their objectives.[126]

Another problem relating to economic wealth is when the economic 'choice' to protect the environment is moved to optional goods or processes, such as those presented by green consumerism. With such consumerism, the typically higher economic costs of the products or processes tend to exclude all but the more affluent consumers. Indeed, green consumers tend to be high-income, educated and professional. These people represent only between 10 and 20 per cent of all consumers.[127] This niche market has three implications. Firstly, the poor are excluded from the process. Secondly, those who can afford it may come to regard themselves as being financially exploited and may react by becoming increasingly unwilling to pay extra for green products.[128] Finally, there is still a market of at least 80 per cent of all consumers who are willing to purchase environmentally unfriendly goods and processes. This huge percentage necessitates the realization that the protection of the environment through the ambit of the market, via the power of the individual consumer, may *not* be achievable. Indeed, the solution to the problem may require *collective responses* governed by democratic procedures, rather than individual responses governed by exclusionary price mechanisms.

The problem of equity is also omnipresent with the establishment of international market mechanisms designed to confront global environmental problems. For example, suppose the problem of climate change is to be addressed by an international taxation system, which is linked to the causation of the problem. This sounds entirely fair, but the question of how this is calculated is very problematic. This is demonstrated by indexes which argue that current 'greenhouse' emission responsibilities are equal between Northern and Southern countries. This is arrived at by looking at the Southern contributions to climate change caused by carbon dioxide release resulting from deforestation and their methane emissions, as opposed to carbon dioxide emissions from 'luxury' lifestyles from Northern countries.[129] While this analysis may be correct in terms of the amounts of greenhouse gases in the atmosphere, it makes no mention of per capita (as opposed to sovereign) emission rates of the greenhouse gases. It also fails to consider the historical contribution of the countries' emissions to climate change, or the distinction drawn between 'survival' gases, such as those caused by methane from rice fields and livestock, and carbon dioxide generated by modern industrial living.[130]

Accordingly, such indexes, which are based on simple numbers, without the contextual background of these figures could prove to be very detrimental, or very beneficial to certain countries. It all depends on how the index is constructed, that is, in accordance with per capita emissions, per country emissions, singular or comprehensive perspective on the gases involved, and the consideration of historical causation.[131] Each variable could throw the system to favour one group over another. Such problems are *not* just technical. Rather, they are deeply political and philosophical, and to ignore them may be to build castles in the air. To quote the Commission on Sustainable Development:

> *'Advocates of such taxes and charges tend to assume that they would easily become widely accepted by national governments and have thus chosen to focus on technical details. Unfortunately, this may not be a realistic approach because global taxes and charges, even if technically feasible, may not be readily accepted. There is currently little apparent willingness on the part of many governments to cede sovereign taxation power to any international body. In addition, global taxes would probably result in enormous wealth transfers ... this factor alone would make the negotiation of global taxes extremely difficult.'*[132]

Indeed, many market theories typically do not acknowledge these considerations which in reality (as opposed to economic theory) are the epicentre of any international environmental agreements.

When the Market will not Work

Despite the rhetoric that commercial pursuits within a free market and environmental protection are complementary and represent a 'win–win' situation, the reality is often the antithesis of this belief. For example, when considering ideals such as the public guiding the commercial world through their purchasing power, it needs to be realized that such approaches are of little use when the market has already been 'captured'. This is because markets run the risk of being distorted by monopolies, which result in *no* competition with 'essential' products or processes.[133] The same rule also appears to hold for exceptionally large and open markets. Accordingly, only oligopolies seem truly receptive to green consumer behaviour. As such, not only the number of commercial organizations engaging in 'green consumer' response is small, so too is the range of products and processes they provide (such as recycled paper and tissue products, solvent free paints and varnishes, cosmetics and more recyclable packaging).[134]

Just as the commercial entities in monopolistic positions are largely immune from market directions, so too are a number of other commercial entities that are greatly removed from end products or processes, and are therefore – in part – *isolated* from the market reactions to these.[135] A similar difficulty, which is known as the 'landlord–tenant' problem is reflected with attempts to increase costs of environmentally damaging activities. The problem is that the responsibility for protecting the environment is often separated from those who are paying the higher costs of the environmentally destructive processes or products. Accordingly, since the former group (the landlords) are not paying the economic cost imposed by an environmentally sensitive market mechanism, they have no incentive to change. Conversely, those paying the bill (the tenants) may not be able to change.[136] Thus, the 'economic logic' of market protection for the environment is *not* responded to appropriately.

Finally, market mechanisms are also unsuitable when environmental problems need to be solved very quickly or directly. The examples of standard setting for objectives such as energy efficiency, air and water standards or technology-forcing roles such as the banning of CFCs, or forceful restrictions on the international trade of endangered species, are all superb exemplars of how direct, state-focused mandates may be the most efficient way to solve the issue.[137]

Profit

Probably the most important justification for why the state must intervene in the movements of the free market is that free market environmentalism can only go so far. This is because the market, left alone, will ultimately only go to the locations where profit can be made. While it is true that some commercial entities will pursue (forms of) sustainable development, others will not. This is because in a competitive market economy, the competitive direction, if it is *not* structured, will flow to practices which are profitable, even if these have detrimental environmental and social consequences. Additionally, the bottom line necessity of the free market – to generate profit – will always limit how far the actors within the market will be willing to tolerate non-profit generating environmental and social concerns. Thus, as the World Bank explained in 2000: 'Although public spirit moves a notable minority to pollution control, most managers are bound by pressures from markets and shareholders.'[138]

Or as Milton Friedman stated in a more direct fashion: 'There is one and only one social responsibility of business – to increase its profits.'[139] It is this paradigm that has forced many to acknowledge that the free market and the actors within it, at the end of the unregulated day, may not necessarily be in congruence with social and/or environmental objectives. For example, according to a 1993 Report by the Office of Technology Assessment of the US Congress:

> *'The interests of all nations ought to be fairly straight forward – quality jobs, a rising standard of living, technological and industrial development ... a high quality environment at home and globally... As compared to nations, the interests of Multinational Enterprises are far more situation orientated and linked to opportunity.'*[140]

This pursuit of economic gain (or at least, the minimization of economic loss) over environmental considerations has been well documented.[141] This has been especially so with some specific environmental problems, such as the oil and auto industry (with the debate over climate change),[142] the energy industry (with the debate over acid rain),[143] the CFC industry (with the debate over the ozone hole)[144] and the tropical logging industry (with the debate over deforestation).[145] This problem of profit is a realization that is common to the socialist and anarchist tradition. For example, as Karl Marx stated, 'Money is a jealous God ... before whom no other God may exist, and the worship of it has given birth to an actual contempt for and practical degradation of nature.'[146]

Or as Fidel Castro said at the 1992 Earth Summit, 'The main responsibility for the atrocious destruction of the environment lies with the consumer societies ... less profit means less hunger in much of the world.'[147] The overall problem with regard to much of the environmentally conscious free market, and its offshoots such as green consumerism and environmentally friendly companies, is that they are only *voluntarily* pursuing these objectives because it is currently in their financial interest to do so. Their ultimate interest cannot be that of environmental protection; rather, it *must* be commercial success. This is essential, as the commercial enterprise which protects the environment, but not its balance sheet, will cease to exist. Thus, the social and environmental concerns of a number of commercial entities must always be focused by the bottom line of market existence (profit). Accordingly, for many entities, once the financial benefits are gone or the financial costs are too much, so too may their commitment to the environment vanish.[148]

Additionally, as nebulous as the pursuit of environmental objectives are for commercial entities, when done on a voluntary or a self-regulatory basis, only a few 'enlightened' companies can be expected to respond, and even these will only be in set situations.[149] Indeed, as the Commission on Sustainable Development noted in 1997 in their review of overall progress achieved since UNCED:

> *'Although there are numerous examples of good practices by business and industry, the number of companies that are making strides in becoming sustainable development enterprises is small relative to the global total... It appears that relatively few companies have integrated sustainability requirements into their overall corporate strategy with a commitment to follow it even in the absence of stringent regulations... Even in developed countries, the bulk of the investment is compliance investment. Voluntary, non-compliance investment, such as investing in environmental controls over and above required compliance, does not play a major role.'[150]*

This problem is not only limited to TNCs that choose *not* to take voluntary measures to further environmental or social goals. There are also instances where TNCs have engaged in activities that are outright illegal (ie corrupt practices)[151] or very unscrupulous practices, such as actively trying to subvert United Nations goals – such as the WHO's International Code on Breast Milk Substitutes.[152]

Such realizations have helped lead to the proposition that the market and the players within it must be directed, for they will probably *not* set appropriate standards by themselves. As such, commercial entities must be forced to follow directions given by democratic choice – such as environmental and social protection, rather than market profitability. This is essential, because if profitability is the objective, environmental goals may well be omitted.

Green Consumerism

Another good example of where the market and real environmental responsibility may be leading in opposite directions is presented by the oxymoron of green consumerism. The central difficulty with green consumerism is that although it has made many people think about the role that they, as individuals, play in environmental destruction, it has only brought about a superficial change in the way that individuals relate to the environment. This superficiality is reflected in the danger that people may be misled into thinking that if they consume more wisely, then they can continue to consume at the same rate. In doing so, green consumerism is spreading the message that by substituting good materials and designs for bad ones, then it is possible to marry the growth economy and protection of the environment. Many Green theorists are profoundly sceptical as to whether this is in fact the case.[153] As Christopher Plant explained, 'While green goodies are perhaps welcome, they are also mainly a diversion from the urgent deep structural task ahead. We can hardly hope for societal transformation from recycled toilet paper.'[154]

Green consumerism may be sidestepping the central issues and, at best, is only 'heading towards the cliff at a slightly slower speed'.[155] As such, green consumerism may only be buying time. It still uses raw materials, it still contributes stresses, albeit weaker ones, to ecological systems and, fundamentally, it still assumes that growth is perfectly acceptable, so long as some of the rougher edges are taken off it. Green consumerism is still consumerism, which is the fundamental paradox. Indeed, a central answer to the greater environmental problem is not to consume *appropriately*, but rather, to consume *less*.[156]

Additionally, the pursuits of green consumerism do not question or challenge the consumer on key issues.[157] For example, the issue of the whole development process involving indigenous peoples in the Amazon is avoided, whereas the economic benefits of the 'rain forest harvest' (of which these indigenous cultures play a part) are proudly displayed.[158] Likewise, the solution to the air pollution issue is not to be found primarily in lead-free petrol and greater engine efficiency; rather, it is to be found in fewer cars and more public transport.[159] Unfortunately, the individual green consumer is not, prima facie, confronted with such paradigmatic choices when asked to exercise their individual consumer choice at the petrol pump.

The above problem of green consumerism, like that of the profit driven economy, reflects the general concern that economic liberalism may *not* necessarily lead to environmental protection.[160] Accordingly, the entities which operate within such a market place and the overt free market paradigm may need to be controlled. One of the foremost examples of this concerns the possibly most powerful economic forces on the planet – TNCs.

The Control of Transnational Corporations
TNCs are the exemplars of the international free market and the paradigms (from the rejection of limits to growth to the profit-maximizing quest) that they operate within.[161] They are immensely powerful. For example, in 1990 the total number of TNCs exceeded 39,000, with more than 270,000 foreign affiliates. In 1995 alone, these entities were responsible for over US$315 billion in foreign direct investment, although the real figure may be as high as US$1.4 trillion.[162] They employ over 70 million people worldwide, have an estimated turnover of US$3 trillion, or 30 per cent of the gross world product, and control around 70 per cent of world trade.[163] The larger TNCs, such as General Motors, Exxon and Ford, have individual annual incomes that are larger than those earned by many poorer and middle income countries, such as Saudi Arabia, Norway and Indonesia.[164]

Such figures suggest that TNCs represent very powerful forces, with strong economic and political influence.[165] Inevitably, they have a huge influence in the international environmental debate and their cooperation (if not control) is crucial if any progress is to be made towards sustainable development.[166] For example, about half of the Western world's carbon dioxide emissions and half of the Southern world's fossil fuel use is closely connected with TNCs. They are responsible for approximately 10–20 per cent of global methane emissions, and roughly two-thirds of all CFC emissions.[167] Such figures *should* necessitate a control on such entities. However, despite their power and influence, TNCs are only controlled by an ad hoc and fragmented collection of national laws, with little accountability to anyone other than their shareholders.

This freedom and power is juxtaposed against their near absolute freedom to wield this power in the international arena, and the multiple lacunae which permit them to operate in a way which avoids environmental (and/or social) responsibility.[168] This has resulted in numerous calls for a powerful international standards code that could control the conduct of TNCs.[169] To quote from the United Nations 1992 report on World Investment:

> 'international self-regulation by business needs to be embedded in firmer frameworks. In particular, the possibility of pernicious competition in attracting foreign direct investment on the basis of lax environmental regulations (or more likely lax implementation and enforcement) suggests a need for internationally agreed codes and guidelines.'[170]

Similar concerns to this were raised in 1980,[171] 1982,[172] 1987[173] and 1990.[174] The 1995 Commission on Global Governance added that: 'Governance would be strengthened through multilateral agreements that define minimum standards of corporate behavior.'[175] This type of approach was suggested by the IUCN's Draft International Covenant on Environmental Law[176] and reiterated by the UNDP in 1999.[177] Elsewhere, within the Commission on Sustainable Development, it was noted in 1998 that 'voluntary initiatives' may be worthless unless they can prove that they take the industry beyond 'business as usual' and that there is transparency, monitoring and overt public participation in the process. Without these essential ingredients, 'codes of conduct have amounted to nothing more than merely words on paper'.[178]

The approach favouring the international regulation of TNCs has not been the direction of international environmental law. By the early 1990s all draft proposals to control the activities of TNCs, and even simple oversight of them by UN agencies, had been forced back.[179] Additionally, all detrimental references to TNCs were removed from Agenda 21 at the 1992 Earth Summit. Conversely, the positive references of TNCs were emphasized.[180]

This lack of criticism of TNCs has continued with all of the major international conferences of the 1990s. With these conferences, like the Earth Summit, there has been a continual omission of any statements linking TNCs with either social or environmental damage. Rather, the dictates of Conferences such as the World Summit for Social Development speak in terms of 'Encouraging transnational and national corporations to operate in a framework of respect for the environment while complying with national ... and international law.'[181] Likewise, the Habitat II conference only went so far as to endorse calls for 'socially responsible corporate investment'.[182]

THE IMPORTANCE OF PROPERTY FROM THE PERSPECTIVE OF SOCIAL ECOLOGY

The Control of Property

Social ecology is similar to economic liberalism in that it also recognizes the importance of property. However, social ecology may directly challenge the liberal ethos on *private* property. It may do this through the recognition of communally owned and managed common property and also through emphasizing both the importance and limitations of ownership of property.

The Recognition of Common Ownership

Property is a concept that is created by society. It is a creation that can empower, exclude, or control access for many or for a few. As it is an idea created by society, property as a notion is not absolute, but relative. Consequently, there may be many interpretations of what property is, or is not. For example, natural resources may be categorized as exclusive private property, public property, common property, or unowned property.[183]

Despite this number of possibilities, Western definitions of common property generally recognize it as belonging to no one individual. If it is categorized as such, then it is seen as open access and is freely available to any user. This is the interpretation that Garrett Hardin used for his analysis of the 'tragedy of the commons' and the subsequent need for private property. However, social ecology rejects this restricted view of the 'unowned and open to all' interpretation of common property. Rather, it typically views common property as communally owned resources, which are controlled and utilized for the good of the whole community as a worthy objective. This view of common property, as a method to manage natural resources, is found throughout the contemporary and historical world.[184]

In accordance with this community-controlled common property regime, access and restriction to common property are strictly regulated, so that a common benefit for all can be achieved. In each instance, a body of rules sets limitations on use, rights of access and monitoring of use so as to prevent 'free riders'. There are no ultimate private owners. Consequently, the community has to determine the rules for all usage of the commons, with the interests of the whole in mind, rather than those of specific individuals. The interests of the whole are then guaranteed within specific social norms and rules which seek the sustainable, equitable, efficient and interdependent use of collective goods.[185]

The strengths of the communally owned common property view are enhanced by emphasizing a number of considerations that the liberal 'tragedy of the commons' scenario (and consequent advocacy of strict private property) overlooks.

First, the 'tragedy of the commons' approach overlooks the fact that the genesis of overuse may not be because the natural resource is a commons, but because the ideology which is feeding on the commons is privately owned. For example, had the herds within Hardin's paradigm been owned in common there would have been no incentive to overgraze.[186] Additionally, the fallacy in the 'tragedy of the commons' parable lies in the very concept itself. 'Commons' implies a community that holds and controls something in common.[187] However, Hardin's parable assumes that the herders behave according to the principles of the individualistic marketplace, on the basis of economic self-interest and possessive individualism. This is *not* the typical basis for a commons arrangement. Thus, Hardin's case stands only if the desecrated environment is *not* a genuine common and other priorities such as individual economic gain are tolerated.[188]

A second oversight is that to go straight to the market-orientated arguments that flow from the tragedy of the commons thesis is to ignore the possibility that common ownership regimes may have become strained. This may occur through either expropriation, uncontrolled economic growth or technological change, which can outstrip traditional common property regimes. In such situations the ecological resource base may well collapse.[189] The solution to the problem may not lie in rejecting the commons, but in controlling the process which led to the over-exploitation.

Finally, it should be realized that averting the tragedy of the commons by means of exclusive property rights may lead to 'the tragedy of the commoner'. In such situations, not only is the ecological survival of the resources in question, but so too may be the survival of those individuals forced from the common. Such individuals may flee into truly uncontrolled areas, such as some tropical rain forests, where the real tragedy of the commons may occur.[190]

Public and Private Property

In certain societies, communally orientated common property regimes may not be appropriate. As such, the question of continued private ownership needs to be examined. However, as a generalization, Green theory is indeterminate on the question of the use of private property ownership, although there is no question that the use of private property *must* be controlled. For example, some Green theorists suggest that *all* private ownership of land should be abolished,[191] whereas others believe that private ownership is acceptable, although 'current conditions' need further control.[192] However, with regard to considerations such as the privatization of public assets, such as national parks, beaches and wildlife, advanced by free-market environmentalists, then they become increasingly antagonistic. This is typically because such approaches signal a relinquishment of public control over public assets. This is considered bad for democracy because citizens are denied the opportunity to participate in, or otherwise call to account, decisions made by private property managers, other than through common law actions. Accordingly, it is commonly mooted that the environmental commons should not become the possession of private individuals.[193] This approach has its roots in the writings of Gerrard Winstanley,[194] J S Mill[195] and Gifford Pinchot,[196] who stated comprehensively that:

> '*Conservation is the application of common sense to the common problems for the common good. Since its objective is the owner- ship, control, development, processing, distribution and use of the natural resources for the benefit of the people, it is by its very nature, the antithesis of monopoly ... conservation policy has the*

purpose ... to see that the rights of the people to govern themselves shall not be controlled by the great monopolies through their power over natural resources... Monopoly ... its abolition or regulation is an inseparable part of the conservation policy... The earth, I repeat, belongs of right to all its people, and not to a minority, insignificant in numbers but tremendous in wealth and power. The public good must come first.'[197]

The Redistribution of Small-scale Property

Many strands of social ecology recognize the problem that some own too much property and use this power to disenfranchise others. Conversely, others own too little property, and as such have no security or incentive to protect what they have. For example, at the end of the 20th century, nearly three-quarters of all the land in the world that could be owned was controlled by 2.5 per cent of the people. Worldwide, around 138 million rural households are almost landless, two-thirds of them in Asia. In Latin America two-thirds of the land is owned by just 1.5 per cent of landowners. In Guatemala 2 per cent of the landowners own 80 per cent of the land. In Brazil, 20 million rural peasants are landless, while the richest 1 per cent own 15 times as much land as the poorest 56 per cent of the Brazilian farmers put together. In Bolivia, 3 per cent of the largest land-holdings account for over half of the titled land. In Africa, three-quarters of the agricultural population own just 4 per cent of the land. In Egypt the richest 0.4 per cent of farmers control 35 per cent of the land.[198] Inequitable land holdings is not a problem that is unique to Southern countries. For example, in the UK, 6.7 per cent of the population own 81 per cent of the land.[199]

These figures represent a trend that has been continuing for over two centuries. This is the enclosure of the commons or the capture of the private property of the small tenure holder, and the passing over of such property to large estates in private ownership. This problem is now seen by many as one of the central issues in environmental battles worldwide.[200] The pivotal part of this debate suggests that the need is not to *disallow* private property, but rather to *redistribute* ownership, to both small tenure holders or community groups.[201] This drive for land reform, as an explicit and strategic developmental issue, has gained increasing prominence in recent years.[202] This is because types of land tenure, and their reform, have a direct bearing on the question of agrarian reform generally,[203] and sustainable development specifically.[204] For as Elizabeth Dowdeswell, the former Executive Director of UNEP, stated, 'recognising traditional land rights and enforcement of these rights ... and ... encouraging land reforms ... could significantly reduce pressure on marginal and ecologically fragile lands'.[205]

Land reform is important for environmental protection because – as the neo-liberal free market advocates noted at the beginning of this chapter recognized – possession and security of tenure create an incentive to protect it. In many ways, social ecology accepts this precept that secure property rights would often stop those who currently destroy the environment, as they do not 'own it' in either a private or communal sense. Conversely, if the environment, roughly commodified as 'property', is vested with individuals or communities, then not only may equity be served, but so too may sustainability.[206] As Robert Chambers explained:

> *'Poor people with secure ownership of land, trees, livestock and other resources, and where confident that they can retain the benefits of good husbandry and pass them on to their children, can be, and often are, tenacious in their retention of assets and far sighted in their investments ... what appears an inability to invest labor for the longer-term is often a rational recognition of insecurity: who will plant a tree or invest their labor in works of soil conservation who fears that the tree will be stolen, or the land appropriated, or the household itself driven away at will? In contrast long-term tenure and secure rights of usufruct encourage a long-term view and the investment of labor and funds in resource conservation and enhancement.'[207]*

This question of land reform is not purely a modern one. In a historical context it occurred in Europe between the 17th and 19th centuries, and in the USA in the 18th century. It has occurred since the Second World War through democratic procedures in India, military occupation in Japan, peasant revolutions in central and Latin America and communist collectivization in China, Russia and the former Eastern Europe.

In a modern context, despite the precedents for land reform, the issue remains politically unpopular. This is because a restructuring of land tenure may result in changes in the political, social and economic power positions within a society. This is the key obstacle. This change in society is not only resisted by domestic interests, but also by neo-liberal ideologies.[208]

Land Reform in International Environmental Law and Policy

The necessity of land reform was noted repeatedly during the 1960s and 1970s. The high tide mark of this period was probably the 1979 World Conference on Agrarian Reform and Rural Development, which was forthright in its assertions that 'equitable distribution and efficient use of land, water and other productive resources, with due regard to ecological balance and environmental protection, are indispensable for rural development'.[209] Similar ideals were reiterated with the 1980 Brandt report[210] and the 1990 South Commission.[211]

The specific importance of land reform as an integral part of sustainable development was noted in 1987 with the WCED, which recognized that 'In many countries where land is very unequally distributed land reform is a basic requirement.'[212] This point was repeated in the Food 2000 report, which was prepared for the WCED. This report concluded that:

> 'Sustainable livelihood development plans comprise of three elements. First, land reform and redistribution: the extension of principles to include livestock, trees and other assets is essential. Through secure ownership of assets the poor will gain not just livelihoods, but personal stakes in conservation.'[213]

Similar points were repeated in 1989[214] and at the Earth Summit with the Forest Principles.[215] Finally, at the 1996 World Food Summit, the signatories agreed to:

> 'pursue ... land reform policies that will permit farmers, fishers, foresters and other food producers, particularly women, to earn a fair return from their labor, capital and management, and encourage conservation and sustainable management of natural resources.'[216]

These calls for land reform have often been supplemented by a much more refined approach by which to achieve the goals. That is, land reform through compensation packages (as opposed to simplistic, non-compensated compulsion).[217] However, despite this refined approach, the ideal has not been institutionalized in the international community (for example, the FAO has no position paper on land reform) and in general the international community has moved more towards considerations pertaining to security of tenure as opposed to its redistribution. This approach was clearly recognized in Agenda 21[218] and the Habitat II conference.[219]

CONCLUSION

Economic liberalism has returned to the global community with a force that few would have predicted 30 years ago. This ethos has engulfed both Southern and Northern countries alike. Within this ethos, new types of instruments and emphases within the market economy have been brought to bear upon environmental issues. In this area, a focus on governmental subsidies and environmental externalities has been brought to the fore as impediments to a perfectly functioning free market that will secure environmental protection.

Once these impediments have been removed, then the conscience of the consumer and the corporation can be relied on, to direct the market towards environmentally protective choices through consumer directives, and/or through behaviour designed to maximize the economic self-interest of both. To further this goal, regimes such as permit trading or green taxation have been built. Finally, it is believed that wherever feasible, property should be privatized, for only privately owning individuals have the incentive to protect their environment. Most of these arguments have come to be forcefully reflected in both national and international environmental law and policy.

Social ecology agrees with many of the aspects that the neo-liberal analysis has produced. It too advocates that governmental subsidies which destroy the environment should be removed, and environmental externalities should be internalized. Where it differs from the neo-liberal approach has to do with questions of how far the market may be trusted to truly protect the environment. In this regard, it has two central concerns. Firstly, the free market *ultimately* does not promote or even acknowledge social or environmental sustainability. This is not a fault of business. This is a reality of a competitive economy. As such, social and environmental goals are for the public, not the private, sector to establish and enforce.

The second reason why it is possible to be sceptical of market mechanisms is the belief that the profit-driven neo-liberal perspective is of the importance of property as an incentive to conservation. Social ecology differs over the mandate that all property must be private. Rather, it is suggested that common property regimes may be just as effective, if not more effective, as private property. Accordingly, the necessity to redistribute private property to both suitable individuals and communities may need to be recognized. Needless to say, this is the antithesis of the neo-liberal approach. Likewise, despite this recognition within much literature, it is barely recognized in international environmental law and policy.

Chapter 4

Trade

THE FREE TRADE POSITION

The Background

The tendency to see economic affairs as being international was established before the Industrial Revolution. This view evolved when voyages of discovery turned many of the navigable seas into highways for foreign-bound raw materials and goods. However, it was not until the advent of political liberalism and its child, laissez-faire, that the domestic free market and international economic interdependence were fully linked. Adam Smith fully opened the door for this idea with his influential work, *The Wealth of Nations*.[1]

Before Smith, a mercantilist tradition had broadly accepted the necessity for domestic market protection. Smith disagreed with such protectionist ideals, and sought to end mercantile institutions by moving towards the 'free laws of commerce' in an international setting. He theorized that this international community would allow the free market system and the societies within it to find their true balance, and thus create economic efficiency via specialization, which would benefit *all* of those involved.[2] David Ricardo elaborated on this idea with his thesis of comparative advantage. He postulated that:

> '*Under a system of perfectly free commerce, each country naturally devotes its capital and labour to such employments as are most beneficial to each. This pursuit of individual advantage is admirably connected with the universal good of the whole.*'[3]

Over 200 years since the advent of economic liberalism, these philosophies have become commonplace in multiple areas, including the international environmental arena. For example, Section 2.5 of Agenda 21 stated that an 'open trading system which leads to the distribution of global production is in accordance with comparative advantage, and is of benefit to all trading partners'.[4] Today, belief in free trade as a mighty engine of economic growth is a pillar of contemporary economic orthodoxies.[5] These beliefs are reflected in a multitude of free trade agreements which are both regional and global. The most prominent of these is the GATT. The GATT preamble recognized:

> *'that ... trade and economic endeavor should be conducted with*
> *a view to raising standards of living ... developing the full use of*
> *resources of the world and expanding the production and*
> *exchange of goods.'[6]*

To achieve these objectives, the GATT preamble suggested substantial reductions in tariffs and other trade barriers and the elimination of discriminatory treatment in international commerce. Such a trading system is underpinned by rules of conduct, openness, and a mechanism for arbitration.

The Uruguay Round, which was concluded at the end of 1993, was the culmination of an eight-year process of trade negotiations which concluded with the establishment of the World Trade Organization (WTO) on 1 January 1995. The Uruguay addition to GATT was commonly viewed by predominantly Northern countries as the most important issue on the international agenda in the early 1990s.[7] This interest was sparked by the economic benefits that are believed to be generated by free trade. Indeed, by 2005 it is anticipated that the world's GDP will be between US$213–274 billion larger than it was in the mid-1990s, due to enhanced international trade.[8]

International Trade and the Environment

Traditionally, GATT negotiators had viewed the environment as a strictly non-economic factor that had little to do with trade negotiations. However, with the growing awareness of the environmental condition in the 1980s, by the early 1990s the G7 were agreeing to look to GATT 'to define how trade measures can properly be used for environmental purposes'.[9] Accordingly, a working party was created within GATT to examine the inter-relationship between the environment and trade without barriers.[10] Before this point, the idea that trade and environment might be detrimentally linked was discounted, or was seen as a problem that had been adequately addressed within the mechanisms that already exist (and have a long history) within free trade agreements.[11] Accordingly, pivotal occasions such as the 1992 Earth Summit failed to acknowledge that environmental protection, sustainable development and trade issues could be linked in any detrimental manner. Only the alleged benefits of free trade and environmental protection were aired. Consequently, the concept was openly supported. Principle 12 of the 1992 Rio Declaration on Environment and Development declared, 'States should co-operate to promote a supportive and open international economic system that would lead to ... sustainable development.'[12]

Similar objectives were reiterated in a number of the other Earth Summit documents.[13] The positive recognition of free trade and sustainable development was also recognized in the important North American Free Trade Agreement (NAFTA) between Canada, the United States and Mexico,[14] and in the preamble of the WTO Agreement.[15] The situation was summed up by the WTO's Committee on Trade and Environment, which noted in 1996 that:

'There should not be nor need to be any policy contradiction between upholding and safeguarding an open, equitable and non-discriminatory multilateral trading system on the one hand and acting for the protection of the environment on the other.'[16]

It was/is asserted that free trade can affect the environment in a beneficial way though a number of methods.

Escape from the 'Trade Trap'

Free trade is believed to be beneficial for the environment, as it will avoid the quagmire of suppressed prices that commodity exports commonly suffer. This problem is reflected in a number of international environmental documents. For example, in 1972, at the Stockholm Conference on the Human Environment, it was concluded that:

'For the developing countries, stability of prices and adequate earnings for primary commodities and raw materials are essential to environmental management since economic as well as ecological processes must be taken into account.'[17]

The general need for market access for Southern countries had earlier been noted by the 1969 Pearson Commission.[18] This plea was forcefully reiterated in the international commissions of 1980,[19] 1983,[20] 1987,[21] and 1990.[22] The problem was specifically noted in an environmental context in 1980 with the World Conservation Strategy, which suggested that in order to achieve conservation it was necessary to liberalize trade, including the removal of all trade barriers to goods from Southern countries.[23] The incompatibility of protectionism and sustainable development was also reiterated in the Report of the 1987 World Commission on Environment and Development (WCED)[24] and the 1992 Cartagena Commitment.[25]

These calls reflect the commonly perceived notion that many of the economic problems of Southern countries are attributable to low commodity prices in many areas.[26] These problems developed historically through the creation of colonies which were forcibly structured to provide benefits for their colonial masters.[27] By the time these former colonies became politically independent, they had been solidly locked into a pattern of trading dependence which often continues to this day.[28]

Under such structures, certain commodities were given exclusive preference over others, to the extent that vast sectors of entire countries were, and in many instances remain, devoted to working towards their production.[29] Uganda, for example, in the mid-1990s relied on coffee for 95 per cent of its export earnings and Zambia relied on copper for 90 per cent. In Africa, at least ten countries rely on one commodity for more that 50 per cent of their exports. This reliance on primary commodities for export has been assisted in a contemporary sense by the imposition of the IMF policies to pay their debts.[30] Additionally, despite the Uruguay Round, a number of barriers continue to exist to important Southern exports.[31] Consequently, many Southern countries have been unable to diversify their exports.

Despite the fact that Northern countries were often instrumental in the creation of this relationship of dependency, they have also traditionally placed import barriers, such as quotas, subsidies, voluntary export restraints and anti-dumping measures that discriminate against Southern countries' exports. These have tended to encompass most products that are not commodities or raw materials. For example, the average European tariff barrier at the end of the 1980s on Southern iron ore was zero, on unwrought iron it was 2.4 per cent, 9.3 per cent on iron and steel plate, and 20 per cent on knives and forks.[32] In 1991 it was reported by the GATT secretariat that there were 284 discriminatory export-restraint arrangements imposed on the South by industrialized countries.[33] These policies meant that Southern countries are often denied the possibility of extra revenue in terms of billions of dollars annually.[34] Additionally, having to pay high duties on processed goods discourages Southern exporters from developing their own processing industries. Consequently, they remain locked into the role of primary-product exporters. This had been increasing steadily over the past few decades.[35]

The consequences of this overall situation were foreseen in 1969 by the Pearson Commission. The Commission was very concerned with the precarious nature of this situation, which made many nations vulnerable to import duties, price fluctuations and quota systems.[36] The implications of this economic vulnerability were borne out in the mid-1980s when, despite an upturn in the world's economy, commodities were at their lowest price for the entire 20th century, with the exception of the 1930s depression.[37] These low commodity prices continued until the middle of the 1990s, when they began to rise again.[38]

This quagmire of depressed prices evolved as a result of the collapse of a number of international commodity agreements. This was followed by saturation of the relevant commodity markets. Consequently, supply rapidly outstripped demand, leading to further collapses of prices. Such drops in commodity prices have often forced Southern countries to increase production in an attempt to sell more at a lower price, and thereby maintain their level of income. This practice has simply resulted in further gluts of commodities on the world market, which drives prices down even further. Prices have also dropped as a result of the implementation of new technology that has permitted the replacement of traditional raw materials from Southern countries by synthetic ones, which are much more versatile, cheaper and can be produced domestically in Northern countries.[39]

The end result of this problem is twofold. First, economic development (and therefore sustainable development) for Southern countries trapped in closed or restricted trading regimes may not be possible.[40] This was recognized in a number of Earth Summit documents.[41] The second problem with such tariffs is that they allegedly result in environmental destruction. This problem has been aptly demonstrated with the trade in tropical timber, where the exporting countries typically could not export processed wood. Rather, their exports were restricted to only unprocessed logs. Once the timber gets to its destination it is then processed, thus creating jobs and profit elsewhere. Accordingly, nowhere near the maximum value of the product is paid to the original exporting country. Conversely, if the exporting countries could process their timber it would add value to their exports, thereby reducing foreign exchange pressures. However, as it has traditionally stood, the industrialized countries have imposed high tariffs on processed timber products to protect their own processed timber industries. The result of this has been that the exporting countries are forced to rely on increased exports of unprocessed logs to make the same amount of income, thereby adding to the destruction of their environment.[42]

Conversely, if the countries that export the tropical timber were paid more for it, 'they could chop down fewer trees and invest profits in more sustainable forestry'.[43] This same logic has been applied to a number of other examples concerning the production of other natural commodities. Quite simply, increased incomes from exports *should* lead to increased environmental protection, as the environment will not need to be exploited so intensively.[44] Such increased monies generated from trade *should* also help these Southern countries obtain the necessary financial resources to move towards paying some of the financial costs of sustainable development.[45] Indeed, it is worth noting that the increased monies across the board for many Southern countries from trade liberalization could make impressive inroads into their overall financial liquidity.[46] This could be conducive to the funding of sustainable development.

The Efficient Use of Resources and Comparative Advantage

The second way in which free trade is expected to improve the environment is through international competition, which is alleged to be environmentally beneficial because of the efficient use of resources, higher productivity and increasingly efficient technologies. These factors are all deemed necessary for sustainable development.[47] The argument of efficient use involves an important assumption. This is that the environment can be used to achieve comparative advantage, which in turn is in accordance with sustainable development. This was recognized in paragraph 2.5 of Agenda 21, which stated,

> 'An open, equitable, secure, non-discriminatory and predictable multilateral trading system that is consistent with the goals of sustainable development and leads to the optimal distribution of global production in accordance with comparative advantage is of benefit to all trading parties.'[48]

Low environmental standards may be seen as part and parcel of a country's comparative advantage to be exploited through trade.[49] Thus, as the Secretariat of the GATT stated:

> *'in principle there is no difference between the competitiveness implications relating to different environmental standards and the competitiveness consequences of many other policy differences between countries – tax, immigration and education policies for instance.'*[50]

This statement is in accordance with the earlier OECD suggestion that 'Different national environmental policies, for example, with regard to the tolerable amount of pollution, are justified.'[51] Consequently, the international trading system ought *not* to apply to redress or harmonize the different environmental approaches that different countries are willing to tolerate.[52]

Therefore, trade advantages gained by countries willing to accept *lower* environmental standards are treated as part of the 'efficient reallocation of production internationally'.[53] Under this theory Southern countries should take advantage of the fact that their environmental standards are *lower* than in Northern countries, as a possible means to attract more investment. The implicit assumption in this is that eventually, after a country has absorbed a set level of environmental damage, and has enough economic strength to choose otherwise, it will adopt a path that is less environmentally damaging.[54]

'Real Problems' and Pricing

The third argument why free trade should be permitted is that it is not seen as a primary source of environmental problems. The 1992 Cartagena Commitment, which was agreed at the Eighth UNCTAD, explained: 'Environmental policies should deal with the root causes of environmental degradation, thus preventing environmental issues from resulting in unnecessary restrictions to trade.'[55] The root causes of environmental degradation are recognized as being connected to questions concerning development, debt and international financial assistance. Hence, it is suggested that environmental protection should be pursued by focusing on these issues, rather than by distorting international trade.[56]

Specific attention is usually focused on distortions of the free market, which cause environmental damage through environmental externalities, or on subsidies, which are environmentally destructive. Alternatively, free trade should theoretically encourage correct pricing, for it does not allow price distorting and environmentally damaging subsidies. Therefore, as Renato Ruggiero, the former Director-General of the WTO, suggested in 1997:

> *'One of the keys to sustainable development lies in pricing environmental resources to reflect their real scarcity and true social value ... trade liberalisation has an important role to play here by reducing market inefficiencies which distort price signals.'*[57]

The Basis for Free Trade and Environmental Considerations

The Fear

For an effective free trade system, it has been advocated that all debate on international environmental issues that could lead to trade disputes should be resolved by international consensus. Indeed, as the Commission on Global Governance stated in 1995, 'For economic growth to raise the living standards of the poor and be environmentally sustainable, trade has to be open and based on stable, multilaterally agreed rules.'[58] Accordingly, individual *unilateral* actions for environmental purposes affecting trade patterns should be discouraged. This does not mean that all unilateral actions are forbidden. Rather, it suggests that for unilateral actions to be legitimate, they must not be (as Article XX of the GATT prescribes) arbitrary or unjustly discriminate between countries. Accordingly, they must be non-discriminatory, least-cost options and focus only on the product (as opposed to the process that created it). This position was strongly reinforced in the so-called Shrimp–Turtle decision of the WTO, where the efforts of the USA to restrict the importation of shrimp products, which inadvertently caught sea-turtles in the process, were struck down. This was not because it was a unilateral action (which it was) but that the measure was arbitrary (in that different countries were treated differently) and it was unjustified in that they should have adopted 'diplomacy first' rather than proceed straight into sanctions.[59]

The desire to rein in unilateral actions stems from an established fear that individual domestic environmental protection measures which are introduced into free trade arenas could act as potential barriers to products that are produced in a different and, in this instance, environmentally unfriendly way. This fear has been particularly acute in Southern countries. Consequently, they are strong advocates of 'environmentally unhindered' free trade. Differing foreign environmental standards acting as trade impediments are seen to hinder this goal. This concern can be traced back to the 1971 Founex report, which articulated some of the fears of Southern countries regarding international environmental regimes,

> '1. Fear that the developed nations will create rigorous environmental standards for products traded internationally and generate 'neo-protectionism' excluding non-conforming goods from poor lands.
> 2. Fear that emphasis on non-polluting technology and recycling may eliminate or reduce demand for raw materials or agricultural products.
> 4. Fear that the developed lands will unilaterally dictate environmental standards to the developing lands without considering how to relate those standards to the conditions of the developing lands.'[60]

These fears found their way into a recommendation at the 1972 Stockholm Conference which stated:

> *'All countries present at the Conference agree not to invoke environmental concerns as a pretext for discriminatory trade policies or for reducing access to markets, and recognise further that the burdens of the environmental policies of industrialised countries should not be transferred either directly or indirectly to the developing countries.'*[61]

The 1992 Earth Summit also explicitly rejected the use of trade-distorting measures designed to protect the environment.[62]

The question of unilateral measures or 'vigilante action', as Arthur Dunkel, the former Secretary General of GATT, labelled them,[63] has also been increasingly examined since the early 1990s. It has been argued that unilateral actions for environmental protection through trade restrictions are to be avoided because they could be disguised, unjustified restrictions on international trade. Therefore, all trade-related actions that deal with environmental protection should be based on international consensus, as manifested through multilateral environmental agreements.[64] This position was recognized at the eighth UNCTAD prior to the Earth Summit,[65] then repeatedly at the Earth Summit itself.[66] The situation was aptly summarized by the 1996 Caracas Declaration from the ninth UNCTAD which stated:

> *'In connection with sustainable development, the treatment of environmental issues needs to be approached in the framework of multilateral environmental agreements and based on the principles of need, effectiveness, non-discrimination, transparency, the least possible restriction on trade, and shared but differentiated responsibility... Unilateral actions that restrict trade, imposed by the developed countries to address environmental problems outside their borders, should be eliminated ... measures aimed at solving ... environmental problems should be based on multilateral environmental agreements.'*[67]

This outlook reflected the 1991 ruling by a GATT panel on the 'Mexican Tuna' issue, where the USA unilaterally restricted the importation of tuna caught by Mexican fisherman using fishing methods that were detrimental to dolphins. The Panel stated, 'A contracting party may not restrict imports of a product merely because it originates in a country with environmental policies different from its own.'[68] It was suggested that such unilateral actions would only be acceptable if it was an action required by *international* law, such as those applying to the trade in endangered species,[69] the trade in toxic waste[70] or the trade in ozone depleting chemicals,[71] but *not* if it was merely required by domestic law.[72] While a question of precedence exists within certain academic debates between multilateral environmental agreements and free trade agreements, it is generally *assumed* that the specific multilateral environmental agreements over-ride the trade agreements, if the contesting parties are both signatories to the multilateral environmental agreement in question which also has a dispute resolution mechanism.[73] However, should a dispute arise with a *non-party* to a multilateral environmental agreement, the WTO would provide the only possible forum for the settlement of the dispute.[74]

Where there is no multilateral agreement governing the situation, the inference would appear to be that the control of the product in question should be left to individual consumers. In this regard, the importance of transparent, accessible and credible consumer information within international trade has been highlighted.[75] This approach has become pertinent with the trade in tropical timber.[76]

Akin to multilateral solutions to environmental disputes is the desire for a harmonization of environmental standards internationally.[77] The necessity for harmonized international standards in a modern context goes back to the formation of the ISO in 1946,[78] and is already implicit in a number of regional trade agreements. For example, the Central American Economic Association agreement of 1960 stated that:

> '*in order to create a reasonable degree of equality in the trade relations between them, the Contracting parties shall endeavour to achieve uniformity in the legislative or other provisions affecting the production of goods.*'[79]

Likewise, the Latin American Free Trade Area calls on parties to 'promote progressively closer co-ordination of the corresponding industrialisation policies'.[80] This approach was furthered at the 1972 Stockholm Conference on the Human Environment in Recommendations 103 and 104. These suggested with specific regard to products (as opposed to processes, which were deemed to be only the concern of the national state):

> '*in order to avoid an impairment of the access of the developing countries to the markets of industrialised countries because of different product standards, Governments should aim at worldwide harmonisation of such standards ... the United Nations system ... should assist Governments to develop mutually acceptable common international environmental standards on products which are considered by Governments to be of significance in international trade.*'[81]

Since this point, the drive towards harmonizing standards[82] – environmental standards in particular – is an idea which has become popular. For example, in their report for the summit of 1994, APEC's Eminent Persons Group recommended 'the gradual convergence of environmental standards among APEC members.'[83]

For many this drive towards the harmonization of environmental standards is seen as a way by which certain economic bodies in industrialized countries may regain economic competitiveness by competing on 'level playing fields' where all trading competitors must abide by the same standards. This is believed to be helpful for the environment, as it should help to stop the importation of goods from countries with lower standards, and also stops the migration of industries to countries that are willing to tolerate levels of pollution that others would not. Implicit in this drive for international harmonization is the creation, or at least empowerment, of an international standards body. The European Community recognized a similar position in 1973. They stated, 'Major aspects of environmental policy in individual countries must no longer be planned or implemented in isolation ... and national policies should be harmonised within the community.'[84]

The idea of a central body establishing international standards has now been applied to international trade.[85] This objective has been forcefully pursued since 1986 when US negotiators, still smarting from the EC ban on hormone treated beef, put forward proposals to 'increase efforts to harmonise national health and safety standards'.[86] This proposal led to the drafting of agreements requiring national governments to harmonize their environmental and health standards. Where these are not harmonized, if they are used to discriminate in the international trading arena, they must be 'based upon sound, scientific evidence'. The ideals of harmonization and the importance of scientific justification were cemented into place with the success of the Uruguay Round.[87]

THE REJECTION OF FREE TRADE

International trade has the power to create opportunities and support livelihoods. However, it *also* has the distinct ability to destroy both them and the environment. In this regard, the idea that free trade can effectively promote a meaningful form of sustainable development may be an idea that lacks credibility. As it stands, the free trade ethos as a panacea for sustainable development may be closer to allegations of oversight, simplicity and manipulation, than truth. Indeed, contrary to popular belief, there appear to be extensive and significant links between international trade and the environment that can both influence and undermine national and international efforts to address ecological problems. These problems have been increasingly recognized by a number of people, and for many, the rejection of free trade has become increasingly vocal. This was powerfully demonstrated at the 1999 Seattle trade talks.

Despite this growing chorus, the rejection of the free trade position has had *little* recognition in the *official* international environmental arena. While the WCED recognized in passing that the pursuit of sustainable development needed 'an international system that fostered sustainable patterns of trade',[88] their position remained vague. Three years later, a similar position emerged from the Bergen conference, where 34 industrialized nations signed a declaration pledging to undertake a dialogue on the links between trade policy and the environment. In doing so, the Ministerial Declaration on Sustainable Development from the Conference suggested, 'economic instruments, including trade agreements, should so far as practical be structured so as to avoid undesirable environmental effects resulting from international trade.'[89] Finally, in 1999 a major WTO study on the environment, for the first time ever, acknowledged that there may be detrimental linkages between trade and the environment. The linkages that this report made are outlined in the following text. This admission by the WTO was added to by the growing concerns of UNEP that free trade may, in certain circumstances, lead to unsustainable development. As such, 'the need to ensure that trade and environment policies are mutually supporting is more pressing today than ever before'.[90]

From the perspective of social ecology, to avoid the undesirable environmental consequences resulting from free trade, it would require, in effect, the large scale abandonment of free trade as we currently know it. To support this assertion, four issues will be examined. The first concerns some of the outdated basic assumptions of free trade. The second concerns the problems that will be created for environmental protection under the proposed new international regulatory body. The third issue concerns direct links to the problem of environmental destruction. Finally, the way that free trade undermines the social ecology goals of self-sufficiency and poverty alleviating communities will be examined.

Difficulties with Theory

Monopolies, Boundaries, Loyalties and Debt
Free trade theory has been abstracted from many complicated factors. This is because the ideas of free trade have their theoretical roots in the 18th and 19th centuries, and as such, they often fail to meet the political realities of the 21st century. This can be demonstrated in a number of ways. First, capital and labour were assumed to be perfectly mobile only at a national level and international capital flows were *not* accounted for. In today's world, however, national boundaries do *not* inhibit the flow of capital investment. This free flow of capital means that investment is governed by absolute profitability, and not by theoretical dictates of stationary national comparative advantage. Comparative advantage is also undermined by the floating rates of exchange. Violent swings within the monetary system can easily result in varying trade patterns and capital movements. These movements are dominated by monetary fluctuations rather than by comparative economic advantage. This monetary instability can weaken the underlying rationale of comparative advantage in international trade.[91]

The second point is connected to the first, in that the early free trade theorists believed that those with capital to invest would 'prefer the support of domestic, rather than foreign industry'.[92] Indeed, all of the early eminent economists embraced the need for community, citizenship, patriotism, sovereignty and ownership, as being values integral to any investment decision. It was *not* a world of cosmopolitan money managers and TNCs that transcended national preferences. This caveat on free trade is now removed, as profit, and *not* national loyalty, has typically become the primary consideration.

A third difficulty is that technological development was assumed to be transparent and available to all. This is clearly not the case, as certain countries race ahead claiming absolute advantages over others.[93] Additionally, technological advance is undermining much traditional comparative advantage as labour and certain commodities have been replaced by cheaper technological processes.[94] Thus, as the Commission on Global Governance noted:

> *'In an era of rapid technological change, new uses for primary commodities and the development of synthetic substitutes make the roller coaster of international commodity markets an even harder ride for many specialized communities that depend upon them.'*[95]

The fourth concern is that there are a number of assumptions regarding comparative advantage that are no longer appropriate in the modern trade arena. These include the beliefs that there are constant returns to scale (ie no diminishing returns); that there is no trade in common factor inputs, such as raw materials (as otherwise comparative advantage could be manipulated by outside interests); that there is no under-utilization of labour, capital or land, no emigration or capital outflow, no imbalance in international trade and payments (otherwise capital transfers would impair the terms of trade) and no conflict between private sector interests and the objectives of long-term social utility; and finally that inflation, deflation and domestic and foreign debt do not affect comparative costs.[96] This last consideration alone completely obliterates the idea that trading partners may begin on anything even assembling symmetry, or an equal capacity to compete fairly, or indeed, even grasp some of the benefits that free trade purports to offer.[97]

Power Imbalances

An important prerequisite to enter free trade and secure a comparative advantage is that all parties need to be fully aware of all the costs and benefits so they are able to exploit the market. This requires an absence of monopoly[98] so that equal bargaining positions can be achieved, whereby all parties can work to secure a benefit. However, this is not always possible. Consider, for example, the toxic waste trade.[99] Here, the exporting country enjoyed what was clearly an unfair advantage on the transaction.[100] This is because the total costs to the host country over time may not have been properly estimated or shadow-priced. Such information collapse means it is often difficult to determine comparative advantage. This is because the potential short and long-term human and environmental costs may be large enough to completely offset the monetary benefits of the transaction. Thus, because such costs cannot be estimated, let alone realized, it is difficult to establish the benefit that the receiving country obtains.

The consideration described above illustrates that benefiting from free trade depends on two supporting assumptions. First, it is assumed that the exchange is voluntary, and second, that both parties gain from the exchange. However, this is not the usual case for North–South relations.[101] This is because global economic systems are not primarily determined by concepts like 'natural advantage', but by power and resultant strength imbalances between parties. This can be seen on both the macro level, pertaining to the relationship between countries trading on a generic level, and on a micro level, which deals with the actors within markets.

On the macro level, the international political economy necessitates that there are distinct power imbalances between the nations in the free trade debate, with some having unequivocal advantages over others.[102] Accordingly, free trade does not benefit all nations equally. Indeed, as it stands, it is anticipated that 71 per cent of the economic benefits of global free trade will be concentrated in North America and Europe. Southern countries as a whole are expected to reap less than 30 per cent of the overall economic gain, with the majority of this 30 per cent going to the five biggest developing countries.[103] With the economically poorest countries, it is anticipated that they may actually be *net losers from free trade*.[104] In 1996 the Commission on Sustainable Development (CSD) explained the challenges of trade liberalization for small island states:

> *'Globalisation is not likely to be achieved through the integration of all national economies or all regions. Certain categories of countries do not have a resource base or infrastructure to find a sizeable slot in the globalizing economy. Generally speaking, poor countries and small developing countries face the risk of remaining relatively marginalised from global trends... A few Island developing countries may be "net losers" as a result of losses in competitiveness and slow progress in seizing trading opportunities.'*[105]

Very similar conclusions were reached at the 1997 Review of Agenda 21 by the General Assembly. This Special Session reiterated the general concern that Southern countries with highly dependent trade preferences relating to net food importation, and those dependent on only a few commodities for export, are highly vulnerable. Accordingly, such countries may expect to be further marginalized from the benefits of the global economy.[106]

On a micro level, the overt power relationship on the ground is well displayed by the control and oligopoly of some TNCs over complete areas of trade.[107] This power often has much more to do with the overt control of trade than ideals of comparative advantage. For example, with much of the Southern agricultural produce which enters international trade, increases in prices tend to reflect increases in profit for the powerful TNCs who have cornered and exploited markets, rather than a more equitable redistribution and empowerment.[108] Accordingly, for raw cotton, the price the growers receive is less than 8 per cent of the final product price. For coffee, it is around 15 per cent (although often less).[109] In this regard, the gulf between free trade and *fair trade* is vast. Unfortunately, this is not only a theoretical problem, as the quest for equity and empowerment is an intrinsic part of sustainable development. Accordingly, free trade needs to be reconciled with fair trade to move fully towards sustainability, or as Elizabeth Dowdeswell, the former Executive

Director of UNEP, stated in 1995, 'The debate [on free trade] should be between sustainable and fair trade on one hand, and unsustainable and unequitable trade on the other.'[110] In this regard, to quote the 1997 UNEP *Global Environmental Outlook*, 'the reconciliation of environment and trade regimes in a fair and equitable manner still remains a major challenge'.[111]

EXTERNALITIES AND FREE TRADE

Free trade is based on an ideal that the market is pure. However, this is not the case.[112] In economic terms, the environmental effects of free trade are externalized. The Analytical Report from UNCTAD VIII described the situation with international trade and externalities thus:

> 'an important factor behind environmental degradation is that costs and prices of commodities often do not fully reflect their social cost (including that of environmental destruction). In certain cases, natural resources such as water and air are treated as virtually costless. As a result, incorrect price signals are given to producers and consumers. This leads to significant distortions, over-exploitation and mismanagement of resources.'[113]

The countries which typically do *not* internalize the true environmental cost of what they produce and place within the arena of international commerce omit to do so because the current trade system does *not* demand nor encourage that these costs be internalized. Yet for free trade to work well and protect the environment, it *must* internalize such costs.[114] For example, as Elizabeth Dowdeswell stipulated, sustainability requires that 'commodity prices fully internalise the human and environmental costs of their productions'.[115] Without such internalization, the market mechanism is failing, and such failure may be detrimental for the environment. Indeed, as the World Bank has conceded, 'When market failures/or policy distortions exist, an increase in trade may cause environmental harm.'[116] Likewise, as UNEP has noted, 'Trade liberalisation can act as a magnifier of policy and market failures if appropriate environmental policies and sustainable development strategies are not implemented.'[117]

The realization that 'sustainable natural resource use will be more difficult to effect if environmental costs and benefits are not taken into account in the prices of products', was also recognized in 1996 at the Ninth UNCTAD[118] and by the CSD.[119]

However, *free trade is actually based on a converse principle to the internalization of externalities – that of comparative advantage.* Although I have discussed this problem in detail elsewhere,[120] it is still worth revisiting briefly the contradiction between environmental externalities and comparative advantage.

This contradiction is a problem which is largely overlooked. For example, Principle 16 of the Rio Declaration stated that, 'National authorities should endeavour to promote the internationalization of environmental costs ... without distorting international trade.'[121] This is consistent with the 1972 definition by the OECD of the Polluter Pays Principle.[122] This position creates a problem, as the Business Council for Sustainable Development recognized:

> *'The question remains – and to which we have no convincing answer nor indeed know of one – is how can a developing nation charge a price for exports that reflects their environmental costs, and compete against other nations willing to absorb such costs for short term profits?'*[123]

The answer is that it cannot. Environmental externalities, playing on an abuse of the market system, create the comparative advantage that so many nations try to achieve. Indeed, as was noted at the 1994 meeting between UNEP and UNCTAD, 'while internalising environmental externalities [is] ... desirable, it was also recognised that this concept may have several trade implications'.[124] This recognition of the economic cost of internalization has increased in trade circles, and the movement is now away from any direct mechanism which would seek to incorporate these costs, towards more informal 'cooperative' approaches such as international environmental agreements.[125] Unfortunately, such cooperative approaches, or alternative avenues, such as additional financial assistance, do *not* work well within the political economy of international environmental law and policy. It is this fact that has helped engender so many international environmental problems in remaining unresolved. That is why unilateral actions aiming at the internalization of externalities may need to be recognized within legitimate trade restrictive measures.

Environmental externalities are a type of comparative advantage in international trade. However, these are also an oversight in pricing that provide a subsidy by discounting the cost of environmental destruction. This should be a problem which is easily reconcilable as the Subsidies Code of the GATT encourages parties to eliminate (certain) subsidies as a form of domestic trade regulation because they are seen as trade-distorting.[126] Yet, ironically, the definition of subsidy is often stated in very broad terms and incentives for environmental protection (not environmental damage) may be classified as such, and may consequently be challenged as an abuse of free trade.[127]

It is currently an option for states to use trade restrictions for the products of other countries which are believed to be environmentally damaging if the restrictions are applied in a non-discriminatory way (ie similar restrictions also apply on the domestic producers) and are the least-cost option. The most important caveat in this area is that in addition to non-discrimination and least-cost they can only prohibit goods that involve *product* related environmental considerations with trans-border effects. That is, requirements which have some effect on the product itself, and can be detected through inspection. For example, regulations that stipulate that products must reach certain standards, such as set emission levels for vehicles, or products which invoke certain packaging requirements, or measures aimed at recycling, can be upheld.[128] However, GATT (and

NAFTA) through the Tuna–Dolphin decision forbids unilateral actions on *process* standards, because 'the issue of production and process methods lies within the sovereign jurisdiction of each country'.[129] Accordingly, it is illicit to unilaterally restrict foreign goods on the grounds that a country disagrees with the production *processes* of how any such good was produced. Process standards are those which have no effect on the physical characteristics of the product itself and relate only to the production or manufacturing process. In this regard, if goods are produced in a way which other countries find objectionable, say, catching tuna with large incidental catches of dolphins, then, without the backing of an international agreement, the offended country may *not* act unilaterally and via trade actions work against this concern.[130] This principle also means that consumers may be able to purchase products that would otherwise be prohibited in their own countries because the production processes were deemed unacceptable by their own community/government, but not by others.

The effect of this approach on the problem of externalities is that there is even less incentive for commercial entities to internalize their environmental costs when dealing with processes, as opposed to products. Indeed, in this area of environmental processing discrepancies between countries there is *no* possibility for countervailing trade sanctions to protect those who wilfully internalize the true costs of environmental (or social) *process* subsidies.

The paradox of this situation is heightened even further when it is realized that despite the general appearance of GATT and its inherent dislike for subsidies, certain subsidies or outright trade bans continue to be wilfully tolerated within free trade agreements such as those pertaining to national security (ie the American trade embargo on Cuba), public morals, or goods made with prison labour.[131] It could be equally possible to recognize certain subsidies that create environmental or social benefits, which should also be exempt from countervailing duties or other trade penalties in retaliation.

It was this awareness for such democratically desired, minimal standards that led to the establishment of the *social chapter* within the free trade area of the European Community.[132] Such minimal standards are another way of saying that trade which does not comply with them must be retaliated against, for they are in effect receiving an unpaid social subsidy. Likewise, as pointed out above, many (if not most) environmental costs are not internalized. Unfortunately, these types of subsidies, if process orientated, are not actionable under the current international regime of free trade. However, the WTO does not have a social clause within it. Of course, this should not be a surprise, for the objectives of free trade, like that of the free market, are the pursuit of profit and efficiency – not equity and sustainability. This in itself is unfortunate, as most of the governments of the world already talk ad nauseam about environmental sustainability as well as recognizing a number of *social* goals which they have already signed (if not implemented), such as the Conventions of the International Labour Organization, which could collectively form the core of any social clause.[133]

Since many of the costs and environmental subsidies are not being truly recognized, the justification for comparative advantage, premised upon non-internalized externalities, should *not* be upheld. This is because it is being created on a malfunctioning market, which is at the same time being held out as 'pure'. If the trade system cannot be established to internalize these costs and create a level playing field, then the question of restrictions of trade once again becomes of primary importance.[134]

All of these problems with the theory of free trade do not, by nature, suggest that free trade is premised upon mistakes and should be abandoned. Rather, they point out that free trade, as it currently operates, is many miles away from its founding ideas of a mutually beneficial and benign system of exchange. Indeed, a system has developed which protects and enhances power and is based much more on the exploitation of both labour and environment, rather than being based on ideas of level and equal playing fields where the good of all will be achieved.

The Problems with International Regulation under International Trade Regimes

Science
Under the new system for the regulation of environmental concerns within free trade, parties may restrict imports if they feel they violate their domestic product (but not process) standards. They may do this if they believe something is a danger to human health, or they believe the action is necessary to obtain environmental preservation. However, if parties adopt this position they have an obligation to ensure that trade restrictions are only applied to the extent necessary to provide protection. Further, this must be based on internationally accepted scientific evidence.[135] Such a basis leads towards the suggestion that international regulations governing the environment will be 'harmonized' on scientific principles. For example, article XVI of the agreement establishing the WTO stipulates that 'Each member shall ensure the conformity of its laws, regulations and administrative procedures with its obligations as provided in the annexed agreements.'[136]

The consequences of this type of direction may be that a country with higher domestic environmental standards should be able to stop the entry of products that are produced in ways which are inconsistent with those standards, *if* the foreign goods fail to meet internationally accepted scientific norms.[137] However, a country which has standards lower than internationally accepted scientific norms will not be challenged to raise its standards.

The movement to find internationally acceptable standards may lower standards that are currently recognized in many industrialized countries. For example, Codex Alimentarius, a UN food standards body run jointly by the FAO and the WHO,[138] which was classified as 'the only legitimate source of scientific information',[139] has standards which are lower than those currently used in the USA for at least eight major pesticides. Likewise, in Australia, a study revealed that out of 135 cases where Australian standards were at variance with international standards, harmonization would result in the lowering of those standards in 121 cases.[140] This result is unacceptable to many communities, who see such a veto power as contra their democratic decisions.

The scientific regime within the free trade arena also faces the question of whether the precautionary principle will be included in the decision-making process. This question has become pertinent as, traditionally, the lack of scientific certainty has at times been used to prevent progress on important international environmental issues. To overcome this problem of scientific uncertainty, there has been a move towards the 'precautionary principle'. This entails that where there are significant risks to the environment, governments should take precautionary actions to limit the environmental problem, even where scientific evidence is *not* conclusive. This has been introduced into a number of international environmental agreements, statements and declarations.[141]

The choice of using the precautionary principle or preferring to establish scientific causation before making choices has not yet been adequately addressed. Under the Uruguay Round, members can adopt policies where relevant scientific evidence is insufficient, but they must later provide 'objective assessment' of this measure 'within a reasonable time'.[142] The obvious problem is, precautionary acts may be needed in situations where conclusive proof cannot be adduced within 'a reasonable time'. This limiting approach was broadly in accordance with the conclusion in the so-called Beef Hormones case that: 'the precautionary principle, at least outside of the field of international environmental law, still awaits authoritative formulation'.[143]

In many regards, NAFTA is very different to GATT on these points. Firstly, NAFTA explicitly provides that any party challenging another party's environmental, health or safety standards bears the burden of proof in the dispute.[144] Secondly, NAFTA recognizes the precautionary principle where the science is not fully available, and moreover, it allows nations to establish their own 'appropriate levels of protection'.[145] Thus, if a party determines that the risks from a given service or product are too great, the party can choose to ban that product, so long as they do so in a non-discriminatory manner. The pivotal point is that the party must determine that the risk or principle they seek to invoke is 'based upon scientific principles'[146] derived from an acceptable risk assessment process. Once this is done, then their social value judgement about what level of risk is acceptable to them is a legitimate justification to control trade in that product.

Although the steps that NAFTA has taken in this regard are an improvement, an overall difficulty remains where democratic decisions are taken to control trade that reflect ethical or cultural values and not scientific ones. For example, the European Community's decisions to ban the importation of hormone induced beef,[147] genetically modified food[148] (the debate prior to the Biodiversity Convention for Biosafety) or fur that has been trapped with 'inhumane' leg-hold traps[149] reflect distinct cultural and ethical sensitivities. These subjective considerations, like the *subjective* interpretation of *objective* facts purporting to show environmental risk, should be respected on the grounds of democratic choice, rather than invalidated because questions of cultural perception are supposedly outside the ambit of scientific debate.[150]

Control

A second major area of concern within the international harmonization of science is the 'more than probable threat' that any scientific panel in these disputes could end up being entangled with 'predetermined objectives'.[151] This is currently exemplified with Codex, for in this body it has been suggested that there is 'a gross imbalance' between government and industry representatives on the one hand and consumer representatives on the other.[152]

This imbalance mirrors the overall processes of Codex which have historically been closed to public health advocates and environmentalists. Additionally, governmental delegates have traditionally participated in Codex proceedings with the assistance of industry representatives but, until recently, with little assistance from the health or environmental community. Codex meetings, at which standards are debated and adopted, are held in secret and there is no record of the proceedings available to the public. Draft Codex standards are not made available to the public until well into the process, and there is no mechanism for the public to provide input. A further imbalance is reflected in the dominance of representation of Northern countries compared with Southern countries.[153]

Unfortunately, this debate pertaining to accountability, democratic institutions and openness has also been replicated with the disputes panels of the WTO, and the WTO overall. The CSD summarized this situation thus:

> 'The importance of achieving transparency, openness and active involvement of the public and experts, in relation to work on trade and environment... The Commission recognises that there is considerable need for improvement in these areas.'[154]

In 1996 the WTO acted towards remedying this situation by extending observer status on a permanent basis to the inter-governmental organizations which had been granted observer status in the past on an ad hoc basis.[155] Despite the limitations involved in this extension, the process may still be unfavourably compared with NAFTA, where a greater effort has been sought to invoke transparency and the inclusion of democratic, empowering processes.[156]

Unilateral Actions

The resolution of international environmental problems often comes about through the unilateral actions of one country. Or as the World Bank recognized, 'International agreements often follow catalytic unilateral action.'[157] However, since 1994, the idea of one country acting unilaterally to protect the environment has become increasingly difficult.[158] The near prohibition on unilateral actions may well preclude the practice whereby nations occasionally acted to protect the environment unilaterally in the past, in the absence of international agreement to protect the environment.[159] For example, in 1970 the Canadians passed their Arctic Waters Pollution Prevention Act. This Act had the overall purpose of preventing the deliberate or accidental discharge of oil into Arctic waters, which would result in substantial damage to the Arctic ecology. The Canadians believed that they had to act unilaterally to protect their own interests.[160] The process of obtaining universal consent to create a new international environmental rule was believed to be too slow and cumbersome. This remains a common problem with much of international environmental law.[161] In 1990 and 1994 Canada suggested similar measures to protect fish stocks.[162]

Unilateral actions were also important in respect of the protection of the ozone layer. Here, the USA acted unilaterally to control the output of CFC. Subsequently, after the Vienna Convention for the Protection of the Ozone Layer and the subsequent Montreal Protocol, the USA was prepared to legislate unilaterally with trade restrictions against countries not accepting responsibility for their CFC use.[163] The USA has continued to act unilaterally in other fields of environmental concern, such as those pertaining to nations undermining the International Convention on Whaling,[164] or nations which harvest tuna in a way which incidentally kills dolphins in a manner inconsistent with US law.[165] The continuation of unilateral, non-discriminatory actions was approved in principle by the Clinton/Gore administration.[166]

It is important to note that unilateral actions to protect the environment taken by states, if in excess of multilateral agreements, are not illegal per se. However, to remain legitimate, they must be non-discriminatory, take the least-cost approach and deal with product-related (as opposed to process-related) environmental damage.

The importance of non-discrimination has already been highlighted by the Indonesian attempt to place a ban on the export of its felled wood as raw material. Their intention was not only to preserve the forests, but also to stimulate local industries by exporting a small amount of finished products. The European Community referred this to the GATT surveillance body as a forerunner to a formal challenge to attempt to overturn the ban, on the grounds that the Indonesian directive was *not* consistently applied to external and internal restraints.[167]

A very similar problem arose with the US Environmental Protection Agency's attempt to place trade disincentives on foreign gasoline which did *not* meet domestic environmental emission standards. This was struck down by the WTO's Appellate Body on the grounds that their trade discriminating action was taken before alternative, less cost methods were examined. Indeed, the EPA's failure to seek cooperative solutions with the importing nations, and failure to consider the costs that were being cast on the importers, meant that their action was rejected as unjustified by the WTO.[168]

Although the principles of non-discrimination, least cost, and seeking cooperative approaches appear perfectly reasonable, there are distinct situations where they remain problematic. For example, unilateral, trade restricting action may be needed in areas where non-discrimination is not an option, because only one of the aggravated parties produces the good in question; the least-cost options (say, consumer information regimes) are clearly inadequate; or the country producing the environmental concern is highly un-cooperative in seeking any 'solution' to the problem from anything other than their own perspective.

In this regard, nations may need to be 'coerced' to join multilateral environmental regimes that are powerful enough to achieve their goals, and trade controls may be the best method to achieve this coercion. An example of this may be with the trade in tropical timber, where as yet there are no effective international agreements to stop unsustainable practices and deeply uncooperative protagonists.[169] Additionally, coercion may be necessary where international treaties are already established, but the parties differ over how to implement them, such as with the Convention on International Trade in Endangered Species of Wild Fauna and Flora (CITES) and the unilateral bans on the ivory trade.[170] Accordingly, unilateral actions may, once more, become valuable.

It has been suggested traditionally that these unilateral actions may still be justified under Article XX (b) of GATT, if such actions were/are 'necessary'.[171] In this instance, 'necessary' was/is interpreted as pre-empting international environmental agreement. Of course, the axiomatic problem is, if the requisite international agreements need to confront such problems which have not been confronted by the democratic, international community, then such unilateral actions may not be deemed 'necessary'. Working on similar logic, the independent Australian and European initiatives that intended to restrict imported tropical timber from unsustainably logged areas could easily have run foul of GATT.[172]

Likewise, the possibility that nations may try to coerce others into international environmental agreements generally, through trade restrictions, is also something which is viewed within increasing unease from within the WTO. This position manifested itself fully with the second Tuna–Dolphin Panel in 1994,[173] and later in 1998 with the Shrimp–Turtle decision. In the latter judgement, it was stated:

> *'It is not acceptable, in international trade relations, for one WTO Member to use an economic embargo to require other Members to adopt essentially the same comprehensive program, to achieve a certain policy goal, as that in force within that Member's territory, without taking into consideration different conditions which may occur in the territories of those other Members.'*[174]

Finally, it is important to note, as discussed above, that even if unilateral actions are non-discriminatory and the least-cost options, they can only prohibit goods that involve product-related environmental considerations, and not process ones. Aside from the problems that this presents for the vexing issue of externalities, it also presents a difficulty in trying to stop goods which involve production processes with extra-jurisdictional effects, in areas where there are no multilateral environmental agreements. This represents a distinct difficulty from an environmental perspective. This is because all too often the manner in which a product is produced is an essential element of the product, which cannot be parcelled off in determining how a given product is to be treated in the marketplace. This perspective finds support in the fact that the greatest environmental impacts of most products often occur not at the consumer, or post-consumer, level but at the production stage.

Theoretically, this distinct problem within international environmental trade will be resolved, not through the unilateral actions of countries, but by motivated consumers making their own informed choices.[175] However, as examined in the last chapter, the idea of the green consumer within the market driven approach is, in parts, deeply problematic. A specific problem within this area is that of the provision of full and complete information for the consumer to make their decisions. This problem has become magnified within the international trade debate on tropical timber. Within this area, certain countries have gone to elaborate lengths to slow and hinder progress towards any international certification programme.[176] Overall, the situation was aptly summed up by the UNCTAD Report on Trade and Environment, which was released prior to the 1996 meeting. The Report stated:

> *'Timber certification in practice is very complex, and it might be difficult for small holdings and developing countries to fulfil the monitoring and testing requirements. Furthermore, it remains as yet uncertain how the markets would react to certified timber and how efficient a certification system could be ... timber certification can at best only have a marginal effect on the environment.'*[177]

The laboriously difficult nature of international eco-labelling schemes to help consumers to differentiate between products of international trade has also found it increasingly difficult to move forward towards any meaningful standards. Current attempts have often become entrenched, due to the diversity of needs and demands, including a foremost concern of many Southern countries that *process* methods, which are non-product related, should *not* be covered by any eco-labels.[178] There has been 'little progress' on this issue and 'further discussion is needed'.[179] The failure of progress on this issue is because eco-labelling based only on product, not process methods, is clearly in accordance with the current approach in international trade, as exemplified in the Tuna–Dolphin case. Although process costs may have direct environmental and social externalities, they are viewed as domestic considerations and not international concerns. As such, a country may manipulate these as part of its comparative advantage (which, prima facie, cannot be discriminated against by other countries). Therefore, although 'Ecolabelling schemes bring environmental benefits ... these should not be won at the expense of trading opportunities and competitive status.'[180]

Free Trade and Environmental Damage

The Attraction of Environmental Damage
The theory of free trade does *not* take account of the natural limits imposed by finite resources or of the natural sinks set by nature. As such, it is believed that free trade can lead to the exceeding of the carrying capacity of the environ-

ment.[181] However, despite this problem, the willingness to incur environmental damage is *not* seen as an argument against free trade but, rather, as one for it. Such a willingness is seen as a comparative advantage that can theoretically bring benefits to the nation incurring the cost. The logical conclusion of this approach was spelt out in an internal memo by the World Bank's former senior vice-president, Lawrence Summers. He rejected the idea that industries in the North should absorb the costs of toxic waste disposal, if these costs were cheaper in the South.[182] Such shocking scenarios were instrumental in the creation of Article 14 of the Rio Declaration, which declares that 'States should effectively co-operate to discourage or prevent the relocation and transfer to other States of any activities and substances that cause severe environmental degradation.'[183]

Despite this principle, international trade may be working in the opposite direction. The evidence for this assertion can be demonstrated with NAFTA. There, part of the US industrial response to the free trade agreement with Mexico has been an exodus of environmentally damaging firms to Mexico. For example, in 1982 there were about 500 *maquiladoras* (US-owned 'twin plants') in Mexico, whereas in 1992 there were more than 2000. Between 1992 and 1998 the *maquila* workforce grew by more than 60 per cent. It has been estimated that more than 1000 of these factories produce hazardous waste. However, only around one-third of these companies comply with Mexican environmental laws. Although this is deemed illegal under NAFTA,[184] it is believed that this rate is unlikely to decrease, as environmental infringements have become secondary to the importance of economic growth and free trade.

The rapid growth of *maquiladoras* is because Mexican environmental standards are lower than those in the USA. Consequently, commercial entities can produce their goods more cheaply in Mexico than they can in the USA, and they can now sell them on the lucrative US market without any obstructive import barriers. Additionally, it is cheaper for North American firms to go across the border and dump their wastes there.[185]

As a result of these environmental problems, former President Bush was forced in 1992 to allocate US$200 million to help deal with the proliferation of environmental problems on the Mexican border.[186] However, Bush's response to the environmental impacts were not sufficient and the Clinton/Gore administration found it necessary to incorporate supplementary clauses into NAFTA to try to protect the environment and labour.[187] However, these additions have proved to have distinct limitations and have not been able to adequately confront the overall problem.[188]

Unfortunately, such problems have not been restricted to Mexico. Pollution intensive industries have been relocating from a number of industrial countries in a number of areas. This has especially been the case with certain selected industries such as those working with asbestos, heavy metals and leather tanning.[189] However, it should be noted that it is not lower environmental standards *alone* which lead to TNCs migrating.[190] There are also a number of other considerations, such as lower labour costs and multiple other market advantages. Lower environmental standards may often be part and parcel of this overall incentive to relocate.[191] Nevertheless, the argument was conceded by the WTO in 1999 that, 'Numerical models have confirmed the theoretical results that trade liberalisation can harm the local environment in countries with a comparative advantage in polluting industries.' Conversely, within industrialized countries,

> *'While competitiveness concerns seem to have been somewhat overstated in the debate, and while data do not seem to support the hypothesis that investments are fleeing developed countries for developing countries with more lax standards, environmental initiatives are nevertheless defeated from time to time because of competitiveness concerns.'*[192]

Direct Environmental Damage

Around 25 per cent of world trade involves the import and export of primary products such as timber, fish, minerals, tea and coffee.[193] The production of certain (but by no means all) commodities for export can, as the WCED noted, have a marked effect on the environment.[194] This point was conceded by the WTO in 1999 with their specialized report on *Trade and the Environment*. On this issue it noted:

> *'International trade can sometimes exacerbate the effect of poor environmental policies. For example, the additional demand from the world market may induce farmers to increase the usage of agro-chemicals to boost exports. Likewise, the demand from the world market may encourage unsustainable fishing or logging in the absence of a proper management regime.'*[195]

The strongest example of the link between trade and overt environmental devastation involved the mining of phosphate for fertilizer from the island (and community) of Nauru.[196] Less extreme examples which show this linkage involve the international timber trade's role in rain forest destruction.[197] This has remained despite 'soft' attempts to make the world's tropical timber trade 'sustainable'. Indirect environmental damage caused by trade and tropical deforestation can also be seen through the production of non-timber commodities, such as beef or coffee for export, which are often produced on land where rain forests once stood.[198] Likewise, the trade demand for shrimp and shellfish farming, and fish, have all been linked to environmental devastation.[199]

A second means by which direct environmental damage may occur relates to the environmentally damaging processes that produce these export-orientated commodities.[200] For example, in Chile, it is clear that much of their alleged economic success has resulted from an extreme over-use and destruction of the natural resource base. Often this abuse has involved the utilization of techniques and processes which are banned in Northern countries, for example the use of certain toxic and pesticide materials.[201]

Environmental damage may also occur when peasants are forced off their lands or from their commons to make way for trade-orientated objectives, and may be moved into uncontrolled commons, leading to the renowned environmental tragedy.[202] With such considerations in mind, it has been asserted that the ecological roots of certain crises, such as the Sahelian tragedy in the 1980s, can be attributed to the violation of the traditional principles of environmental management in semi-arid conditions. These practices were violated through the drive for export-led economic growth, specifically the establishment of vast cash crop monocultures of groundnuts and cotton for export. This policy marginalized a large number of farming and pastoral households, who were pushed to the more precarious environments on the fringes of the desert, which were, and continue to be, overgrazed. Second, the export crops themselves were environmentally damaging and over a period of years destroyed fragile ecosystems. Third, the collapse of commodity prices in the 1980s forced more people to leave the already degraded land, and seek out subsistence on the fragile desert fringes. Finally, when the rains did not come to sustain the 'unnatural numbers' existing in previously unpopulated areas, the ultimate crisis arrived.[203]

Increased Growth

Increased economic growth is a central tenet of free trade. For example, within the articles of GATT itself there are calls for 'an economic deployment of productive resources'.[204] Within this rubric, it is assumed that free trade will allow nations to grow economically and ultimately create sufficient revenue to protect the environment. It is commonly assumed that if producers get *fairer* prices for their products they will not be driven to destroying their natural environment to the same extent, because smaller amounts of environmentally damaging activities should secure the same revenue. However, there is an implicit and important caveat to this, namely, that both the resource and the trade must be managed with the objective of conservation, and not just profit in mind.

The difficulty is that within the paradigm of the profit-driven market economy is the assumption that producers of environmental damage will voluntarily slow their destruction (as discussed in Chapter 3), or even recognize that there may be limits on economic growth (as discussed in Chapter 2).[205] Increased profit, by whatever means, is not necessarily a panacea for anything but commercial success. If mechanisms which secure this within international trade are created, there is little reason to assume as part of a logical follow-on that this will lead to environmental protection or the recognition that environmental limits may exist. Certain countries already go to extreme lengths to keep trade as free as possible because of the profits that can be achieved by their destructive processes.[206] These people have little intention of limiting the profit margins which free trade provides. For example, as a World Bank study on Malaysian forestry noted, 'The abnormally high, windfall profits ... have created intense pressure to open up the forests for logging ... loggers have sought to harvest as quickly as possible.'[207]

Thus, if import restrictions are removed, the creation of new markets may act as a powerful stimulant for further environmental destruction.[208] This may be reasonably expected, as the countries that want to increase production of their possibly environmentally damaging exports are currently economically deficient. Windfall revenue, via increased trade, is not something that they want to limit. If the level of return is currently sufficient to make them drive hard in the destruction of the environment, then the possibility of even greater returns due to reduced import barriers may only exacerbate this process.[209]

The Undermining of Social Ecology

The Movement to Poverty

It is assumed that all nations can find some form of comparative advantage that is worthwhile to exploit. For Southern countries this has traditionally come from their supply of cheap labour. Yet poverty, while perhaps being beneficial to economic efficiency, should not be exploited (let alone seen as a benefit, as free trade theorists believe) if sustainable development is to be achieved. To move towards any meaningful form of sustainable development, it is necessary to move away from economic poverty.[210] However, free trade works on a theory that the cheaper the production costs, and in this instance, labour costs, or indeed, labour rights, then the better it is for comparative advantage. This presents a problem for both Northern and Southern countries. It has already proved a difficulty for some Southern countries which have already suffered, or are expected to soon suffer from a further de-industrialization under free trade regimes, and have subsequently experienced growing unemployment.[211] In Northern countries, the growth (and fear) of unemployment induced by free trade is even greater.

The theory of the free market is that labour can move to capital, and like the other aspects within the competitive market economy can compete for the high paying jobs, and help keep the overall costs of wage labour down. Alternatively, capital can move to where the cheap labour is and bid up the wage rate. Either way, those who advocate free trade and free capital mobility are simultaneously advocating for the general equalization, if not lowering, of wages. This conclusion is inevitable: the high mobility of modern capital and technology strives to be economically 'competitive' by continually seeking to lower its costs. The result of this on a transnational level was clearly foreseen hundreds of years ago by David Hume:

> '*Manufacturers ... gradually shift their places, leaving those countries and provinces which they have already enriched, and flying to others, whither they are allured by the cheapness of provisions and labour; till they have enriched these also, and are again banished by the same causes. And in general we may observe ... the poorer countries will undersell the richer in all foreign markets.*'[212]

The movement towards unemployed masses which command low wages may be inevitable, as the economic cost of the human labour input is one of the few factors that is generally *not* mobile within a free market, unlike modern capital and technology, which were a traditional monopoly within Northern countries due to the restrictions of trade. However, with free trade, the one factor in production costs which may be lowered – labour – may now be accessible in other countries. Consequently, the market, having searched out the *lowest labour* options, may move accordingly. To stay competitive, the remaining non-employed labour will be implicitly invited to lower their costs or their rights so as to remain 'flexible' enough to respond to international market demand. Essentially this means that the labouring classes in the high wage countries are being expected to compete with the lower labour standards of Southern workers. The over-supply of cheap Southern labour will probably force prices for labour down, not up.[213] The effects of this on Northern countries could be socially disastrous.[214]

Without some form of global minimum wage, international capital will search the globe for the cheapest bargain in the labour department. A world minimum wage is extremely unlikely, as is a globally organized (and powerful) labour movement. A final possibility is an unparalleled growth in the world economy creating a vast number of jobs, thereby increasing demand for labour, and therefore raising wages across the board. However, this is also equally improbable, due to the huge population and unemployment pools in Southern countries.[215]

This situation must be seen as deeply ironic as so many commentators and governments recognize that the poverty of the South is a reason why sustainable development will be very difficult to achieve. However, many of these same people are simultaneously inviting poverty and lower living standards in the North, through downsizing wages because of free trade. Free trade, with movement of capital and labour, only truly benefits the owner of the capital. The replacement labour force of the South is arguably better off, but the former labour force of the countries that the industries migrated from is worse off. In such a situation, the North would be driven to retaliate by attempting to undercut what advantages the Southern countries possess; that is, cheap labour and lax environmental standards.

In an attempt to avert this distinct problem, some free trade agreements, such as NAFTA, determined that the failure to enforce certain domestic laws is an unacceptable means of encouraging investment and development. Specifically, it was stipulated that 'The Parties recognise that it is inappropriate to encourage investment by relaxing domestic health, safety or environmental measures.'[216] The inclusion of such regulations led to President Clinton's suggestion that such side agreements would lead to 'less difference in the cost of production on either side of the border because of different ... regulations'.[217]

This type of approach has already been recognized elsewhere, such as with the European Union, and at the WTO's first Ministerial Conference in 1996. At this conference, a consensus emerged that members were committed to the observance of core labour standards which had been articulated by the ILO and internationally agreed.[218]

Despite progress being made in this area, a number of limitations remain. The first problem is that responses are inherently limited by the starting point of the different nations. For example, NAFTA does not suggest that Mexico must raise its standards, only that it must enforce its existing ones. As such, the underlying problem of different starting points (ie dramatically lower wages), which is the real prompt for relocation, remains unaltered. Secondly, many of the ILO standards are not internationally recognized, and once more, the labyrinth of multilateral and unilateral actions appears. Finally, at the WTO conference, the section on labour standards ended with the caveat that: 'labour standards should in no way be used for protectionist purposes or to put into question the comparative advantage of countries'.

Self-reliance

Free trade is the antithesis of self-reliance. The acolytes of free trade have a horror of self-sufficiency, often equating it with protectionism, inefficiency, economic distortion and a lack of economic growth. However, the alternative to self-reliance is reliance on others. Many social ecologists see such a position as leading to dependency, vulnerability, loss of autonomy and benefits for only a few. Free trade is also believed to contradict the objectives of social ecology because it destroys local control, decentralization and anything small scale in its drive for global economic interdependence. Additionally, economic decentralization based on the utilization of local materials and resources and the economical use and recycling of materials reduces the necessity to import. Because free trade threatens these objectives, it is commonly rejected by Green theorists.[219] Very similar views to this were stated in the 1974 Cocoyoc Declaration which stated:

> 'We believe that one basic strategy for development will have to be increased self-reliance. [This means] self confidence, reliance primarily on one's own resources, human and natural and the capacity for autonomous goal setting and decision making ... it implies decentralization of the world economy and sometimes also of the national economy ... self reliance at national levels may also imply a temporary detachment from the present economic system; it is impossible to develop self-reliance through full participation in a system that perpetuates economic dependence ... the ideal we need is a harmonized co-operative world in which each part is a centre, living at the expense of nobody else, in partnership with nature and in solidarity with future generations.'[220]

The Trade in Agriculture

The best example of the loss of self-reliance is with food production.[221] A typical example of the demand for self-sufficiency in this area can be taken from the UN's Economic Commission for Africa which stated in 1989,

'Africa's vitality, resides, above all other considerations, in its being able to feed its own people from its own internal resources.'[222] This type of call was a basic reiteration of a common theme for the last 50 years.[223] This theme was well stated at the 1981 UN Conference on the Least Developed Countries which recognized that:

> 'Achievement of food security should clearly be one of the prime objectives of the agricultural sector... Every least developed country should take important initiatives to reduce its dependence on food imports.'[224]

These calls for self-reliance in food have often also been associated with demands that food be available on 'equitable' terms within the world market.[225]

The case for increased self-reliance and equity in internationally affected food issues is rooted not only in the inherent dangers for weak trading countries of dependence on volatile world markets, but also in the importance that agriculture maintains as a mainstay of many economies. Despite this desire, the contrary ethos – that free trade in food stuffs is conducive to the food security of net food importing countries – came to dominate the international agenda in the second half of the 1990s.[226]

This belief has coincided with the increasing numbers of countries that are becoming dependent on foreign food imports. For example, by the 1980s, 50 countries that had been self-sufficient in the 1930s had become net importers of food. Overall, it is estimated that Southern countries will be making net imports of food in 2010 of around 160 million tonnes per year. This is double what they currently import. Some countries, such as the 'least developed', may end up in a worse predicament than others in this regard.[227] However, it should be noted that often those countries that are dependent on food imports are still exporters of food produce. In fact, many of these countries actually export more food than they import.

Meaningful forms of sustainable development may be impossible where the two most protein-needy continents, Africa and Latin America, remain the major suppliers of the largest quantities of animal protein feed. Indeed, the Peruvian export of fish catches alone may be sufficient to raise the nutritional standard of protein for the undernourished on the entire South American continent to southern European levels. The corresponding fish meal coming from Africa may be enough to reduce the present protein shortage on that continent by at least 50 per cent. This dilemma is of growing concern as such commodities are now exported to generate lucrative foreign exchange, despite the fact that they are still often the staple diet of many Southern peoples. Thus, because free trade allows foreigners to pay more for the products than locals, self-reliance is diminished. Few Southern countries can compete with Northern countries for the price of these foods. In such circumstances, food can only go in one direction – towards those with the money to buy it.

This problem is exacerbated by the debt crisis, where despite growing food insecurity in many Southern countries, external pressures to repay foreign debt have maintained the institutional bias in favour of export crops at the expense of staple food production. Such policy directions do little to reduce the vulnerability of the poor, and serve only the interests of large-scale commercial enterprises.[228]

This form of economic development through free trade, which forces many people in Southern countries to export their food, may be helping to cause poverty and malnutrition. For example, in Chile nutritional levels have fallen among the poor, while at the same time the economy has grown. Per capita consumption of animal protein has dropped by 15–25 per cent, while calorific intake has also fallen by between 10 and 22 per cent since the early 1970s. This is not surprising, as consumption of local fish and agricultural products has fallen. Likewise, during the 1970s and 1980s when beef production in Costa Rica more than tripled, local consumption levels of beef declined to such a level that the average Costa Rican ate less beef per year than the average North American house cat. Quite simply, vulnerable populations are traded against foreign exchange earnings.[229]

Ironically, it has been found that when a Southern economy is seriously depressed, the poor may actually be eating best. Indeed, this was seen at the height of the 1980s debt crisis. At this point, when market infrastructure and agricultural support services, including market protections, came to a halt, many Southern countries which could not get their food to market were forced to eat it themselves.[230]

Despite all of the above problems, the self-reliance in food of many Southern countries has been undermined by the last round of trade talks. The question of international trade and agriculture had traditionally been outside the scope of liberalization within GATT, due to the perceived importance of attempted self-reliance of domestic agriculture for these countries. However, the Uruguay Round made a successful attempt to bring this within the ambit of GATT.[231] As such, for the first time, agriculture has been incorporated under operationally effective rules, disciplines and commitments regarding market access. Moreover, under Article 20 of the Uruguay Round Agricultural Agreement, countries agreed to work towards substantial progressive reductions in support and protection in agriculture and to continue the process of reform through further negotiations which began in 1999.

The last GATT Round called for limits to be placed on countries' abilities to control agricultural imports. This call was based on the ideological belief that it is better for a nation to buy its food security on the world market than build up the production capacity of its own farmers. This liberalization of trade will probably result in the undercutting of most of the agricultural produce from Southern countries by Northern agricultural products. Indeed, without subsidies, which the South has been losing at a disproportionate rate to those which the North retains, most Southern agriculture will lose any comparative advantage that it may have had.[232]

Cheap agricultural products from primary producing giants like the USA, the EC and the other countries with very strong agricultural sectors, seriously threaten the small farmers of the Southern countries. Small farmers within Southern countries have already been suffering disproportionately under structural adjustment regimes. Their difficulties may be exacerbated by subsidy reducing trading regimes whereby they are forced to compete against Northern agri-business (or at least, that based within the USA or the EC) which remains (after the Uruguay Round) partly subsidized. Small-scale (Southern and Northern) producers are simply unable to produce goods as cheaply as the large competition (for example, the top 10 agro-chemical companies control 85 per cent of the global agro-chemical market) that now accompanies free(r), but by no means fair, trade in agricultural produce.[233]

Other examples of the large and economically efficient opposing the small and vulnerable can be seen with the production of bananas or coffee.[234] With regard to bananas, this commodity is often a mainstay of the exports from Caribbean countries, but they cost up to two-thirds more to produce than those grown in the large plantations in Central and Latin America. The smaller countries of the Caribbean are at a distinct cost disadvantage to the big banana plantations in a free market. If the small markets do not receive specific protection then the tens of thousands of small farmers will probably be driven out of business. It is expected that this could have ecological impacts for the local communities, which may be forced to move from the already precarious ecological nature of their economic existence.[235]

Despite these predicted social and economic outcomes, a GATT dispute panel has ruled that such protection is contra the principles of free trade, as the way that a good is produced (as opposed to the product itself) is not a valid reason to discriminate between producers. Accordingly, the preferential treatment that one group of banana growers gets over another is unfair discrimination.[236] Despite this condemnation by GATT, a similar action concerning the same facts within the European Community before the European Court of Justice held that such importer preference, given the purpose of the discrimination, was not unjustifiable discrimination.[237] However, the ECJ's decision was based on the social objectives of Community policy, not the economic efficiency objectives of GATT – which were reiterated by the WTO in 1998.[238]

A similar problem exists with the loss of agricultural supports in Mexico under NAFTA. It is expected that market prices may drop to such an extent that over 1 million peasant farmers may be forced off the land, as they become increasingly unable to compete with the large-scale factory farms operating in the USA.[239] The attack on the small farmer is not a problem that is restricted to Southern countries. Indeed, millions of small farmers in Northern countries are also expected to become bankrupt once full international competition commences. This is because, as noted above, expanding trade and competition in a world where agriculture is increasingly capital intensive may only speed up the process of concentrating the control of farming resources in fewer hands.

An associated problem here is that trade liberalization in agriculture may also be expected to raise the price of certain agricultural products, once all of their subsidies have been removed and full international competition takes place. This is particularly true for dairy foods, sugar and wheat, and to a lesser extent for coarse grains and meats.[240] This may detrimentally reverberate towards the poor of a number of countries.[241] This presents a distinct problem, for, as seen in Chapter 2, the discussion about whether the world will be able to keep feeding an exponentially expanding population is a matter of intense debate. Importantly, even the optimists within this debate distance themselves from the political obstacles (as opposed to the ecological) that feeding the world may present. In this regard, a system that will drive food towards those that can pay the highest price presents vast difficulties for food hungry people. Accordingly, the poor areas of the planet which already do not have enough food to feed their expanding populations, or enough money to purchase it from elsewhere, may expect distinct problems.[242]

The position of Southern countries is further affected by three additional reasons. First, article 9 of GATT gives all countries the right to impose export restrictions on food and other critical resources in times of shortage. This is designed to prevent the export of food for higher prices in times of shortage. However, the Bush and Clinton Administrations and the European Community have proposed that this provision of GATT be abolished.[243]

Second, following on from the first proposed change concerning agriculture, there is food dumping. This is commonly practised by surplus-producing nations like the USA or the European Community. This has a dramatic effect on the attempts by Southern countries to attain food security, due to the unnatural depression of agricultural prices. This elimination of all trade barriers could make it impossible for Southern countries to protect themselves from food dumping.[244]

The final consideration is that it has been recognized since the first UNCTAD conference in 1964 that 'developed countries should grant concessions to all developing countries ... [and] should not, in granting these concessions, require any concessions in return'.[245] However, the 'special and differential treatment' or the 'development principle' that Southern countries sometimes rely on, is now to be phased out in the *long* term.[246] This means that Southern countries will eventually no longer rely on this exception to avoid taking trade liberalization measures.[247]

The culmination of these changes may not lead to any form of meaningful sustainable development for many Southern countries. For as the WCED recommended, Southern countries' agricultural sector must be supported.[248] The FAO's 1991 Agenda for Action on Sustainable Agriculture and Rural Development summed up the situation well with its statement that:

> *'Unfettered free trade and free market economies pursued with a view to maximising profits for the participants, do not appear to be geared to protecting natural resources and ensuring sustainability, since they are not by their nature concerned with longer-term issues.'*[249]

This vulnerability was recognized within the eventual Uruguay Agreement on Agriculture,[250] the 1996 World Food Summit[251] and the Addis Ababa Declaration from UNCTAD IX in 1996 which noted that 'net food-importing countries' could expect 'significant transitional difficulties and costs'.[252] Similar concerns were reiterated at the 1997 UNGASS Review of Agenda 21.[253]

It was with such considerations in mind that the 1996 World Food Summit continued to recognize limitations of the market as an equitable source of food for countries. Indeed, the Rome Declaration on World Food Security, although recognizing the importance of free trade in foodstuffs, continued to reiterate the language of 'self-reliance' amid concerns that 'trade policies' must also be 'fair' and that the poorest countries continue to receive access to external foodstuffs 'on reasonable terms and conditions'.[254] The problem is that the free market does not recognize bottom lines of 'fair' or 'reasonable'.

CONCLUSION

Environmental concerns have a long history in free trade agreements. This long history, akin to beliefs in the overall benefits of free trade and comparative advantage, is believed to lead to an ultimate economic and ecological utopia for all. Additionally, a general avoidance of any possible negative environmental effects of free trade currently dominates the international arena. If such effects do exist, then it is suggested that these must be dealt with within multilateral settings, away from the possibility of unilateral, trade discriminating measures.

Unfortunately, whether the international free trade system which the world is currently embracing will lead to environmental and social sustainability is far from given, and it appears highly possible that it is actually leading in the opposite direction.

The current regime of free trade is radically distanced from its theoretical roots, and revolves much more around power than equity and fairness. It is predicated on actively excluding large parts of environmental externalities. It actively discourages unilateral acts to protect the international environment (despite the importance of these in the past) and seeks to foster multilateral scientific standards that are based on neither the precautionary principle nor democratic deliberation of these standards.

Moreover, free trade may also exacerbate the prerequisites of social and environmental sustainability in a number of ways. This may be done by encouraging the reckless use of domestic environmental resources, the allowance of environmental dumping in countries with low environmental standards, and the economic exploitation of the overall poverty of Southern countries – at the expense of Northern workers. That is, free trade as it currently works is not based on holding considerations of social and/or environmental objectives. Rather, it is based on commercial viability, in an international marketplace without social markers. All of these last considerations point to the overall lack of control for vast swathes of humanity over the institutions, communities and environment on which they depend. In this regard, free trade is the antithesis of self-reliance – a principle which is very close to the heart of much Green theory.

These points should not be seen as arguments against free trade per se. Rather, it is the recognition that free trade as it currently operates can all too easily be socially and environmentally disastrous. If international trade was based on the basic norms of social justice and environmental sustainability – from the necessity to actively internalize environmental externalities through to disallowing social dumping, and a general movement towards community empowerment leading to fair (as opposed to free) trade – then it might, in certain instances, be quite beneficial to forms of sustainable development.

Chapter 5

Debt

THE DEBT CRISIS AND SUSTAINABLE DEVELOPMENT

The international indebtedness of sovereign countries is not a new phenomenon.[1] However, the debt crisis, which is made up of bilateral debt (country to country), multi-lateral debt (international institution to country) and commercial debt (financial institution to country), of the 1980s and 1990s is much larger, with greater implications, than earlier foreign debts. Modern debt problems developed in the 1970s when there was a vast amount of money in circulation for Western governments and banks to lend.[2] Many Southern countries took advantage of this and borrowed heavily. The money was spent on weapons, large-scale conventional development ideas, increased prices for international commodities (such as oil) or simply squandered by corrupt governments.[3]

The possibility of a major debt crisis at the end of the 20th century was foreseen by the Pearson Commission in 1969[4] and the first Brandt Commission in 1980.[5] Their predictions materialized in 1982 when interest rates rose dramatically, as did the prices of a few important foreign commodities such as oil. Further, the value of the commodities that the Southern countries produced for the industrialized world collapsed.[6] Suddenly, the debts that these countries had incurred earlier could not be repaid.

Since 1982 it has been estimated that over US$50 billion per annum has been leaving debt-ridden Southern countries for Western coffers. In 1999, the total debt was reported as being above US$1.9 trillion.[7] The debtor countries as a group began the 1990s 61 per cent further in debt than they were in 1982.[8] Moreover, the severely indebted low-income countries often pay more to their creditors than they receive (in terms of aid and new loans). Sub-Saharan Africa has a total debt of US$212 billion and paid an annual average of US$10.7 billion on debt service between 1990 and 1994 – substantially more than the US$9 billion which UNICEF estimated was needed for health, nutrition, family planning and education. Accordingly, it is not surprising to find that most of the citizens of sub-Saharan Africa are 20 per cent worse off in real terms than when they obtained independence 30 years ago, and every year they are getting poorer. Additionally, Latin Americans have seen their standard of living fall by at least 10 per cent since the debt crisis began.[9]

In the early 1980s the growing debts forced a number of countries to consider whether it was easier to repudiate their debts.[10] They were persuaded not to by a series of rescue packages set up by Western governments, the World Bank and the IMF as, 'Strong and comprehensive adjustment policies had to be implemented in order to prevent unsustainable current account imbalances.'[11] Accordingly, 'economic adjustment' became the order of the day.[12] Rescheduling debts was conditional on the adoption of new economic policies. They were told to slash their imports, devalue their currencies and cut government budget deficits. Accompanying this, the application of free market principles swept across the indebted countries, resulting in privatization and an increasingly reduced role for governments in the control of their economies.[13] However, this created distinct problems. As Section 2.34 of Agenda 21 noted:

> *'Many indebted developing countries are undergoing structural adjustment programmes ... while such programmes are necessary for improving the balance in fiscal budgets and balance of payments accounts, in some cases they have resulted in adverse social and environmental effects, such as cuts in health care, education and environmental protection.'*[14]

Adverse social and environmental effects may be the direct costs of the debt crisis. For example, the standard of living of many of these countries has been held down (although in some middle income Southern countries it may be beginning to rise again) because of the necessity to repay the debt in accordance with the structural adjustment objectives. As a result, lower real wages, cuts in government spending on health, education and social programmes and cuts in subsidies on basic foodstuffs have become standard under the IMF programmes. Accordingly, in many countries, unemployment and underemployment have skyrocketed, investment has fallen and economies have contracted. Overall, the social costs of many of the structural adjustment programmes have been very high.[15] For example, UNICEF documented in the mid-1990s that:

> *'The current 10 billion dollars that sub-Saharan Africa pays on the interest of its debt is four times as much as [it] spends on its health services and far more than is spent on the health and education of its children.'*[16]

The structural adjustment programmes are, as the former managing director of the IMF, Michael Camdessus, stated, 'very tough and harsh'.[17] This may have been an understatement. Indeed, the death of half a million children each year which is attributed to the debt crisis and the associated poverty in Southern countries reveals a much more human side to the economic conditions that have been forced upon debtor countries.

Conversely, if the programmes are to be assessed by the underlying strategic goals of restructuring Southern economies in accordance with market-orientated ideals, it has undoubtedly been a tremendous success.[18]

However, whether this market-orientated ideal has spurred economic success (irrespective of the social and environmental costs) is in itself highly arguable.[19]

This is especially the case with sub-Saharan Africa, where since the early 1980s there have been over 160 World Bank and IMF loan agreements covering over 30 countries – more than the whole of the rest of the world. Some of these countries have had uninterrupted structural adjustment programmes for over 15 years, which they have largely complied with, while being increasingly supplemented by large amounts of foreign financial assistance. However, as seen above, many of these countries continue to remain in dire straits, and the overall economic benefits of the process remain questionable. To quote one World Bank study of the adjustment lending over this area:

> 'Adjustment lending has not significantly affected economic growth and has contributed to a statistically significant drop in investment ratios... Also, adjustment lending programmes did not significantly affect inflation or saving to GDP ratios.'[20]

Similar problems plague Latin America, where although small amounts of economic growth have started to come from some countries (while others decline), this is often deemed insufficient to combat the economic decline of the last 15 years.[21] Even where economic recovery has placed tenuous roots, this is often highly unstable (as the crisis of the Mexican Peso in late 1994 demonstrated).[22] Thus, as the 1995 Commission on Global Governance came to suggest, many IMF programmes have in recent years failed to achieve their objectives, and the results of their programmes are often disappointing.[23]

Even if it is accepted that a country has greater 'economic health' than before, and that this is beneficial, the question of who has benefited from the success becomes imperative. Indeed, it is quite clear that not all sections of society have suffered equally (if at all) in the debt crisis, as the 'costs' appear to have been borne disproportionately by the poor and vulnerable.[24]

It is on this topic of the 'costs' of the debt crisis that the environmental nexus comes into focus. However, before going on to examine the effects of the debt crisis, it should be noted that rarely can a linear, one-to-one causal link between events be demonstrated. The consequences of the debt crisis are no exception. None of the following examples is solely the fault of the debt crisis. However, the debt crisis is, at the very least, an aggravating factor in the negative trends that make it more a process of feedbacks than linear connections. This, in turn, may make the debt crisis and its consequences mutually reinforcing.[25] If, for example, one concludes that it is the estimated 300 million 'shifted cultivators', rather than the debt crisis itself, that are the principle agents of rain forest destruction, then the investigation must be taken one step further. The landless would not have to resort to slashing and burning the forest had they any reasonable alternative. 'Shifted cultivators', as the term suggests, are almost always displaced against their will – whether by export crops, loss of jobs, poverty, or any other force beyond their control. The debt crisis should be seen here as the push factor.[26]

However, before proceeding, it should be noted that 'solving' the debt problem alone would *not* in itself lead to a suitable form of sustainable environmental (or even economic)[27] development. The environmental problematique is multifaceted and many aspects of this would remain, even if all the debts were forgiven. Moreover, it should be recognized that the situation of many countries before the imposition of structural adjustment policies was clearly untenable, and they *had* to be adjusted as they were already unstable through the lenses of many economic, social and environmental critiques. The question, therefore, is not all or nothing of structural adjustment but, rather, *how* to progress to a sustainable future. In this regard, the debt crisis and the question of how to move on to an alternative (and suitable) path is a major consideration and is still an essential part of any attempt to establish sustainable development.

THE ENVIRONMENTAL COST

In the 1980s, when new lending slowed to a trickle and the debts had to be repaid, many Southern countries were forced to 'mine' their natural resources to pay their debts.[28] This effect is particularly well documented with tropical deforestation where, as Susan George has documented, 'half of the Third World external debt and over two thirds of global deforestation occur in the same fourteen countries'.[29]

The debt and the resultant structural adjustment programmes accelerate the forces driving deforestation and other forms of environmental destruction in several obvious and other more subtle ways. First, there is the pressure to increase exports, which may stimulate unsustainable patterns in the process. The UNEP *GEO-2000* report explained the problem as one whereby:

> *'From the environmental perspective, the need to pay off these debts has driven many developing countries to sell off their natural resources, particularly timber and minerals, for whatever price they could obtain, often in environmentally destructive ways. Export cash crops have often been favored over food production for local consumption. Environmental standards have been kept low or non-existent to help attract foreign investment... The indebted countries have thus been pushed towards further environmental deterioration.'*[30]

The second concern is that debt and structural adjustment have often increased the poverty and marginalization of the most vulnerable in society. In many places this has led to an intensification, diversification or overall exodus of these people into fragile ecosystems in search of means to increase their subsistence levels.

Finally, the detrimental environmental effects of the debt situation often go unheeded, because as the WCED noted, 'Conservation takes a back seat in times of economic stress.'[31] This omission has often been furthered by the lack of environmental protection, enforcement and monitoring capability by many of the respective departments of the countries undergoing structural adjustment. Overall, it has been asserted that structural adjustment, accompanied by the debt crisis, 'without qualification, has failed in putting adjusting countries on a sustainable development path'.[32]

This problem was first acknowledged in an environmental context by the WCED.[33] In 1989 there were a number of regional declarations, such as the Declaration of Brasilia which recognized the strong link between external debt and environmental destruction. The Brasilia Declaration stated:

> *'In Latin America and the Caribbean under-development and the deterioration of the environment ... condemn millions of people to a quality of life beneath the norms of human dignity...*
>
> *This situation has been exacerbated by the severe indebtedness of Latin America and the Caribbean ... the indebtedness crisis and the adjustment policies stemming from the crisis have eroded conditions for economic, social and environmental development. The debt cannot be paid under current conditions, not by increasing hunger and poverty among our peoples, not with further underdevelopment and consequent defacement of our environment.'[34]*

Similar conclusions were noted by the South Commission in 1990,[35] the 1990 World Summit for Children,[36] the 1992 Earth Summit[37] and the 1997 United Nations review of progress since the Earth Summit. At the review conference, it was recognized that:

> *'The debt problems of the 1980s of most middle-income developing countries have been alleviated through a combination of sound economic policies, liberalisation of international trade and capital movements, rescheduling of bilateral external debt and the introduction of new instruments such as Brady-type and debt conversion programmes. However, the debt burden of heavily indebted low-income countries has increased during the past decade, which has hampered their development potential... In many developing countries, the debt situation remains a major constraint to achievement of sustainable development.'[38]*

In 1999, Klaus Toepfer, the executive director of UNEP, reiterated the UNEP position that 'debt relief is a necessary precondition for sustainable development'.[39]

In light of these problems, it has been argued by various people, institutions and countries that the external debt of the Southern countries must be cut by between 50 and 100 per cent, depending on the country in question.[40] As the debt crisis has dragged on, and the focus has shifted increasingly to the least-developed countries, the emphasis is on the latter figure.

ATTEMPTS AT RESOLVING THE DEBT CRISIS

In response to the debt crisis, there have been a number of initiatives for debt reduction and debt rescheduling, designed by the creditors to avoid an all out default. These have traditionally fallen into three distinct areas: commercial, multilateral and bilateral debt. However, post 1996, attempts have been made to bring these under a more coordinated single rubric.

Commercial Debt

The principal way of dealing with commercial debt[41] appeared in 1989 when the USA announced a new initiative aimed at tackling the problem.[42] This was spurred partly by the fear that if there had been a major forgiveness, or large-scale debt default, many banks would have been ruined. However, disastrous economic consequences for most banks are no longer a possibility.[43]

The Brady plan was named after the then US Treasury Secretary, Nicholas Brady, who realized that many of the Southern debts were no longer worth what the commercial creditors pretended, and therefore had to be reduced. This plan was aimed at reducing the commercial debt of middle-income Southern countries. In essence, the plan recognized that commercial debt could be reduced with support by the IMF and World Bank. Creditor banks were invited to accept a range of options for reducing the stock of debt owed to them, in return for assurances by the Bretton Woods institutions and the government involved that the reduced sum would be repaid.

A case-by-case review began that led to a US$15 billion commercial debt reduction for Mexico, a 35 per cent debt reduction for Brazil, and similar deals for Venezuela, Costa Rica and Argentina.[44] However, the plan only dealt with commercial bank debts, and by 1994 the overall debt reduction accounted for by the Brady Plan was around US$24 billion, or 6 per cent of total debt.[45]

The small size of reductions of commercial debt in the face of the overall debt problem is also mirrored by the fact that commercial debt has continually fallen in percentage terms to a point where it now represents only about 15 per cent of the overall debt of the most severely indebted countries (much of it has been converted through the Brady plan, or schemes such as debt buy-back schemes or debt-equity swaps which are discussed below). Nevertheless, the debt remains substantial, although probably not 'intolerable'[46] for highly indebted countries. However, this is not necessarily the case for the countries which are 'middle income' debtors, with whom commercial debt remains a strong concern.

Multilateral Debt

Multilateral debt, as a percentage of total debt share, is rapidly growing. Interest payments on long-term debt to multilateral creditors (the World Bank, the IMF and the Regional Development Banks) increased by 30 per cent during

1987–1993, while combined interest and principal payments increased by 60 per cent. At least seven severely indebted countries now find that over 15 per cent of their total debt is multilateral, whereas for some individual countries, such as Uganda, multilateral debt accounts for over 70 per cent of their total debt overhang.[47]

The possibility of rescheduling or cancelling these debts has continually been steadfastly refused by the institutions that hold them. The standard reason is that to do so would jeopardize the stability of the global financial system. Accordingly, these loans are always preferred creditor status, which gain repayment precedence over all other types of debt, and cannot be forgiven. This defence is highly arguable.[48]

This is not to suggest that these institutions do not recognize the need for debt reduction. Indeed, the World Bank has, after much criticism for its role in structural adjustment,[49] converted parts of its debt holdings into less demanding forms. Even the IMF now accepts that parts of Africa 'need debt relief and concessional assistance'.[50] Moreover, the Bank and IMF have begun to move towards implementing some new proposals (such as the Highly Indebted Poor Country Initiative, HIPC, discussed shortly) and cancellation of parts of multilateral debt may occur. Nevertheless, this movement has only been made with reticence, and the full degree of commitment (especially on behalf of the IMF) towards finding an economically sustainable solution may be a matter of debate.[51]

Bilateral Debt

Bilateral (or official) debt currently accounts for around 61 per cent of total debt stock for the 32 severely indebted, low-income countries. Bilateral debt is on the increase, as is a hardening of its terms. For example, projections for 1992–1997 show that sub-Saharan Africa is scheduled to pay, on average, four times as much as it paid official creditors in 1991.[52] Two-thirds of this type of debt is owed to Western governments (known as the Paris Club),[53] which are at the forefront of debt-reducing considerations. Unfortunately, the US$250–300 billion which is owed to non-OECD countries[54] is not within the ambit of the following proposals.

The necessity for Western governments to reschedule bilateral debt is not a new idea. It is a process that has already been invoked between 1957 and 1969 following problems that a number of countries had repaying their loans.[55] However, since the 1980s, the process has gained a new importance.

The first attempt at rescheduling in the early 1980s was the Montevideo plan, but this was not large enough to confront the crisis.[56] Then, at the annual meeting of the IMF in Seoul in 1985, James Baker, the former Secretary to the US Treasury under Ronald Reagan, proposed what came to be known as the Baker plan. The Baker plan was an attempt to resolve the debt crisis through a policy of economic growth, with each of the middle-income indebted countries adopting appropriate adjustment policies that would permit this goal. This was to be assisted by a minor reduction in the total amount of debt owed, but primarily through new loans by the commercial banks and the IMF and the World Bank (ie more debt) to assist in debt servicing, and the adoption of standard economic monetarist policies.[57]

Not surprisingly, the response to the Baker plan was slow and limited. To substantiate the desired new growth, further investment of foreign capital was required. The multinational lending institutions were not enthusiastic about this. At the same time, the Baker plan was distributing a grand total of US$29 billion in extra loans. If this total sum was split, the debtors would have been trying to secure very small amounts among themselves (approximately a 5 per cent difference in the total owed in 1986, graduating to a 3.4 per cent difference in 1991) while having to submit to even greater structural adjustment conditionality. Due to such limitations, the Baker plan failed to either gain popular acceptance or solve the debt crisis.

Although the Baker plan failed in these regards, it succeeded in the creation of an important precedent – it reinforced and legitimized the policies which were already in place. The Baker plan did *not* address the central issue of the overall debt and interest rates which were causing the problems. It simply intended to make it a little easier for the debtor nations to keep paying. Additionally, the Baker plan was successful in establishing the case-by-case approach to individual debtor nations. This approach subsequently precluded joint actions by debtor nations.[58]

Following the failure of the Baker plan, a number of initiatives from individual industrialized countries developed between 1985 and 1989. In 1988 at the G7 Summit in Toronto, a menu of debt relief for low-income countries was concluded. Under this scheme, creditors could choose from one of the following: they could cancel a third of their debt; they could reschedule all payments over a much longer time period; or they could reduce interest payments.[59] Debt spreading in accordance with the Toronto proposals has been implemented by many low-income African countries, whereas other countries like Poland and Egypt had their entire debts cancelled by the USA, owing to their 'strategic importance'.[60] Likewise, the Philippines' decision to allow a US military base to remain 'opened the way for various US funds to be used for debt relief'.[61] Many of these decisions are political and were/are tied to the overt interests of creditor governments.

In 1990, the UK, in 'an attempt not to transfer the losses of the banks on to the taxpayers, nor to deter the banks from lending again', suggested what were known as the Trinidad proposals.[62] These would have cut across-the-board foreign debts by two-thirds (as opposed to the one-third reduction under the Toronto terms) but this was *not* accepted by the major creditors as a general policy. Instead, cuts of up to 33 per cent for some of the poorer African countries were agreed, whereas others were entitled to the full 66 per cent. This offer was on the proviso that the remaining section of debt was fully serviced.[63]

The UK began to push this policy as the Toronto terms were clearly inadequate, and the poorer nations, such as those in sub-Saharan Africa, were hardly better off.[64] This was due to the restrictive ambit of the Toronto terms, namely that countries are not eligible for debt relief on credit accumulated after the first rescheduling operations in the early 1980s. Thus, for a country like Zambia, less than a quarter of their debt would have been eligible for reduction.

Overall, it has been estimated by the World Bank that taking up any one of the Toronto options could have saved only small amounts. For example, any one option could save Africa only 5 per cent of its overall debt service obligations. Indeed, it was estimated that the increase in the Southern countries' total debt between 1989 and 1990 was 'projected to exceed the debt reductions from the initiative and other programmes of debt reduction'.[65] For a specific example, consider how Mali, which was one of the celebrated cases of bilateral debt forgiveness, was granted 'relief' of US$70 million, while its total debt was US$1790 million.[66]

Progress towards overall and meaningful reductions was slow, although continuing evolvement such as the 1991 Enhanced Toronto Terms introduced the possibility of going beyond the traditional short-term approach, towards direct debt reductions of up to 50 per cent (while the other 50 per cent moved to market rates) or long-term, concessional repayment rates. However, even these 'enhanced' terms only took the problem a few steps further, for against this background a number of countries were 'vehemently against any mass debt cancellation for the poorest Southern countries'.[67]

This lack of progress was also reflected at the 1992 Earth Summit, where despite recognition that the debt problem needed to be solved as one of the prerequisites for sustainable development,[68] only a few individual pledges to reduce the debt crisis by selective countries were given. There was no joint commitment by the economically wealthier nations to reduce debt payments.[69]

The overall drive of the G7 to unsustainable debt began to change in 1993 when the Clinton Administration offered to write off 50 per cent of the debt of Africa's poorest countries in an attempt 'to relieve countries of their crushing debt burdens'.[70] This change of course was hoped to revitalize and expand the Trinidad terms at the 1993 G7 summit in Tokyo. However, this was to no avail,[71] and it was not until the following G7 meeting in Naples that the problem of bilateral debt began to be taken more seriously.

At Naples the British proposed to extend the Toronto terms to cover the entire debt stock and to increase to two-thirds (up to a maximum of 67 per cent) the amount of debt eligible for write-off. They also suggested that countries with 'exceptional' levels of debt may need even higher write-offs. Compliance with IMF programmes for at least three years was a prerequisite.

The Naples terms proved inadequate for a number of reasons. Most obviously, the debt reduction element was not sufficient to restore a number of countries to a position of financial solvency. This is especially so for the countries which cannot currently pay their bilateral debt, because their overall debts to their bilateral creditors are only a small part of their total debts. The terms were also very restrictive in demanding a strict three-year compliance with IMF policies, as few countries have been able to stick absolutely to these dictates. Accordingly, very few debtors were expected to exit the debt treadmill via this avenue.[72] Only Uganda and Bolivia were able to gain any advantage from this scheme, but the overall results were negligible, as only small percentages of their overall debt (11 per cent for Bolivia and 3.2 per cent for Uganda) were eligible for reduction, or else most of their debt was held by multilateral institutions.[73] Thus, as the Commission on Sustainable Development noted in 1996:

> 'Debt problems are far from over for a significant number of countries... Definitive Paris Club action on bilateral official debt ... is unlikely to resolve the debt crisis of countries with high proportions of multilateral debt.'[74]

In 1995 the World Summit for Social Development recognized that debt must be dealt with in a way which was consistent with 'social development'.[75] While the Summit welcomed the Naples terms, and the general search for 'effective, development orientated and durable solutions to external debt problems',[76] it was specific in its call on the international institutions to examine ways of reducing multilateral debt.[77] However, its most forthright calls had to do with demanding, 'Structural adjustment policies, which should include social development goals, in particular eradicating poverty, promoting full and productive employment, and enhancing social integration.'[78]

Accordingly, the necessity of establishing an 'adequate social safety net under structural adjustment programmes' was agreed as a principle.[79] However, looking at the greater picture, the Summit did *not* take bold steps on debt reduction. Indeed, aside from the consensus that structural adjustment should be altered, only Denmark, the Netherlands and Austria announced that they would cancel a portion of their debt to Southern countries.

The HIPC Initiative

In yet another attempt to confront the debt problem, the Heavily Indebted Poor Countries (HIPC) Debt Initiative was unveiled by the World Bank, the IMF and the G7 at their 1996 Summit in Lyon. This initiative seeks to go *beyond* the Naples terms and carries the ultimate objective to take the debt of the over 40 heavily indebted countries to 'sustainable levels'. Importantly, it seeks a cumulative approach by dealing with bilateral, commercial and multilateral debt. In total, debt write-offs may go as high as 80 per cent.

However, before being eligible, the country must complete 'a period of strong policy performance' (originally six years) and their ratios of debt service (above 20 per cent) or exports (over 200 per cent) have to be above the set level. By the middle of 1999, 12 countries had qualified for relief, involving an estimated debt service relief of about US$8.5 billion over time. The initiative also entails (in principle) improvements to basic social structure and poverty reduction (in terms of health care, primary education or immunization objectives) within the goals of the structural adjustment.[80] Although these goals were all highly praised, the three-year review of the HIPC suggested it was not going far enough. Accordingly, the HIPC was reworked in 1999 to make it even more applicable to the poorest countries. This was done by lowering the debt to export ratio (down to 150 per cent), shortening the period of performance (down to three years), and strengthening the components of accountability, scheme ownership and poverty reduction.[81] Finally, as a way to encourage the resolution of the debt issue, in late 1999, first President Clinton, and then the UK pledged to forgive 100 per cent of their bilateral loans to the poorest countries if they meet the goals of the HIPC.[82]

Despite the reworked approach of the HIPC, the mechanism has still been criticized for a number of reasons. These reasons include encompassing a time frame which is too long and too hard in deciding when a debt is or is not sustainable. Indeed, on the prerequisite of (even the reduced) three-year compliance with IMF programmes, this criterion alone may still be sufficient to exclude some countries. Moreover, concern has been raised that the debt to export or servicing ratios are still too high and need to be lowered, or even abolished and the focus placed on humanitarian benchmarks, as opposed to economic ones. Finally, the amount of relief may still not be sufficient. Indeed, with the higher limits of up to a 40 per cent write-off of debt for Mauritania (in 2000), the remaining 60 per cent may still be too large.[83] Also, despite the fact that the UK and Clinton promised to write-off 100 per cent of bilateral debt to HIPC qualifying states, the other members of the Paris club have not.

Small-scale Plans: Debt Swaps for Equity and Nature

The other notable method devised to reduce the size of the problem has been through a series of debt exchanges. The first has been through 'debt for equity' swaps.[84] This involves the creditors selling off the debt on a secondary market, in which foreign parties can trade the debt owed to private banks at a discount. These markets exist today primarily to sell debt to international organizations for use in debt exchange programmes. A debtor nation is not allowed to directly buy back its own debt at a discounted rate. Only outsiders or third parties can purchase the discounted debt. The buyer will then sell it back to the original debtor state for its partial or full dollar value in local currency. The proceeds are then invested locally or in some other venture.[85]

Although this procedure does reduce some of the foreign debt that is outstanding, the debtor country loses control of some domestic equity to foreign interests. This same problem also applies to what is known as 'debt for nature' swaps.[86] At the same time, due to the generally small nature of the swap, the improvement in the net international investment position is rather modest.[87]

These ventures have proved to be highly inflationary. They also require the debtor country to have the money to make the final transaction. Even if they can collect the funds for the transaction, then those funds become diverted from other uses. Also, some multilateral development banks, and governments that took on the loans, do not sell their debt obligations to private investors for political reasons. Finally, only certain countries actually support their banks in debt for equity swaps, for example through incentives like exemption from capital gains taxes.[88]

The second way in which debt exchanges have occurred is through 'debt for nature' swaps.[89] Classified as the 'dignified alternative' to the other approaches of dealing with the debt problem, these swaps have so far received general support from both creditor and debtor countries.[90] By the end of 1996, at least 16 countries had undertaken debt for nature swaps since they first appeared in 1987. The total size of the funds utilized in these bilateral or trilateral (ie a specific NGO is involved) dealings is believed to be around US$1 billion.[91]

Despite the attraction of these swaps, there have been problems with sovereignty and allegedly 'inappropriate Western methods of conservation' which have accompanied debt for nature requirements, such as wilderness parks from which human inhabitants have been excluded. Other problems with this approach are that it legitimizes the debt and that recipient countries often do not, or cannot, implement the conservation directives. Finally, there are also risks of economic underpricing and of being outbid by someone who would rather exploit the environment in question and that only a few international relief organizations have budgets sufficient to purchase debts from commercial banks, even at greatly discounted rates.

Also, it needs to be remembered that those who own the debt will only be prepared to sell it for a very cheap price when it is considered to be without value. This only occurs when a debtor country has a very large external debt, a weak economy, a negative trade balance, and bleak prospects for the future. For this reason, although a multitude of countries in Latin America, sub-Saharan Africa and former Eastern Bloc countries can entertain such swaps, the more wealthy debtors cannot, as they are still considered trustworthy debtors and their debts will not be sold off.

Finally, the overall size of the swaps is minimal. The Southern world now owes the industrialized countries over US$1.9 trillion. Debt for nature swaps over the last five years have accounted for only US$100 million – less than one ten thousandth of the total debt, or about 1 per cent of Brazil's annual interest payments. However, to be fair, proponents of debt for nature, or debt for equity, swaps never claimed that they would solve the debt crisis. Nevertheless, it is doubtful if anyone realized they would have such a small impact, and no matter how successful, are not an answer to international debt.[92]

Default

Default from international debt obligations has a number of historical precedents,[93] and legal arguments in support of it.[94] Perhaps the most famous of these was when the USA took over Cuba shortly before the turn of the 20th century, and cancelled all of Cuba's debts to Spain on the grounds that the burden was: 'imposed upon the people of Cuba without their consent and by force of arms'. Such debts were later called 'odious' by legal scholarship, by which the later government was not bound to repay.[95]

However in a modern context, the possibility of default has been averted by four facts. Firstly, the debts are owed through a combination of commercial, bilateral and multilateral arrangements that have presented a unified front. Secondly, the debtors, despite some distinct solidarity in the mid-1980s,[96] have displayed a lack of unity and have only presented haphazard challenges to their common problem.[97] Thirdly, the fact that the entire international credit system would 'close up' to the debtor country has made few countries openly consider this option.[98] Finally, there has often been little support for the idea by the ruling Southern elites and their governments, as they themselves may have little to gain from debt repudiation but, rather, more to gain from debt repayments and the opportunities gained from them.[99]

CONCLUSION

In total, the debt situation of the Southern countries as a whole appears to be improving. However, this progress has been largely confined to middle-income Southern countries, while the more severely indebted countries continue to struggle with debts that are economically, socially and environmentally unsustainable.[100]

The above paragraph makes two important points. Firstly, the debt 'crisis' is currently over only for the countries that exist above the poverty line, and not the 41 that are classified as extremely indebted. Indeed, in sub-Saharan Africa alone, it would be possible to make social investments which would save the lives of around 21 million African children and provide 90 million girls with access to primary education for *less* than is currently being spent on debt repayments.[101] Despite this alternative scenario, it currently appears politically unlikely that further debt reductions will be made in this area due to the increasingly intransigent polemics of some of the principal debtors.[102] Secondly, although commercial debt has been largely brought under control, and bilateral debt is being confronted, the problem of multilateral debt continues, largely unabated. However, the new HIPC initiative has begun to overcome this problem. Moreover, given the review of the programme in 1999, it is possible that some real progress may be made in this area.

Although progress in this area may be slow, the larger question remains that seeks to examine the new body of thought building on older orthodoxies. This is, whether it is possible to continue to reconcile the traditional structural adjustment goals while retaining the new social and environmental objectives.[103] This type of approach has come to be reflected in a number of international forums. For example, the 1995 World Summit on Social Development, while not rejecting structural adjustment per se, did call on these programmes to encourage 'people-centred development'. Likewise, the 1996 Habitat Conference called on structural adjustment to be made consistent with social objectives.[104]

This need to 'soften' the effects of structural adjustment has been evident within the Bretton Woods institutions since the latter part of the 1980s, when first the World Bank[105] and later the IMF moved to achieve greater external evaluation[106] and refocus their structural adjustment programmes so that they incorporate social welfare safety nets. According to Michael Camdessus in 1995, these nets create an emphasis on 'social objectives', which have been emphasized in an attempt to mitigate the 'short-term adverse effects' on the most 'poor and vulnerable'. The protection of the environment was also supposedly a new goal to be factored into their reworked equations.[107]

Unfortunately, these agreements have proved difficult to enforce, and non-compliance appears to have been tolerated. This in part may reflect the fact that the IMF's structural adjustment programmes do not have explicit environmental assessments attached to them, unlike World Bank loans. As such, this whole effort has been criticized by some as 'tokenism'.[108] Moreover, these new socially focused programmes may have barely dampened the overall thrust of the adjustment process, which continues to have both direct and indirect social effects on the poor.[109] Indeed, no set quantitative targets, minimum spending thresholds on set social/environmental issues or strict budget monitoring on these issues have been set by the IMF. Moreover, of late, they have been emphasizing that: 'In the family of international organisations, the social components of country programmes are primarily the responsibility of the World Bank and other organisations, not the IMF.'[110]

Aside from the short-term ambit of the above considerations is the difficult question: what has the debt crisis and its resolution through structural adjustment set in motion for the long term? Indeed, in the long-term view, even if an economy has been 'redirected' towards high levels of economic growth closely entwined with market principles in the international economy, the question of whether this leads to environmental sustainability and the incumbent question of social equity remain problematic.[111]

Chapter 6

Aid

INTERNATIONAL FINANCIAL ASSISTANCE

Overseas Development Assistance (ODA), or 'aid' as it is commonly known, is the transfer of resources on terms which are more generous or 'softer' than loans obtainable on the world's capital markets. This usually involves loans with at least a 25 per cent grant component. ODA may be bilateral (country to country) or multilateral (where one country gives money to an international institution to distribute).

ODA is typically given from one government (usually a 'developed' country) to another (usually a 'developing' country). In principle, social ecology disagrees with providing an endless supply of international financial assistance to Southern countries. Many social ecologists are also deeply sceptical of aid because of its long history of ecologically and socially disruptive results.[1] Additionally, the kinds of environmental and social sustainability emphasized by social ecology, such as upholding civil and social rights, decentralized democracy and overall empowerment, typically do not require large infusions of external finance.[2]

Nevertheless, this is *not* to argue against all financial transfers. The social ecology perspective generally recognizes that international financial assistance may be *currently* necessary to alleviate the socially and environmentally destructive poverty and disenfranchisement that currently engulfs millions of people in Southern (and pockets within Northern) countries. Moreover, it can be accepted as a principle that aid, when properly conceived, controlled and encased within suitable and supportive foundations (from population control to market structure), can be effective in achieving its goals.[3] The task therefore is to apply the correct types of aid and foundations to help alleviate the crushing burdens and disenfranchisement of millions of people. Such an objective provides a strong argument in favour of financial assistance.[4] Indeed, for dependent low-income countries that are already struggling with the debt crisis, stagnant economic growth, increasing poverty, declining private investment, and are *already* heavily dependent on foreign financial assistance, 'ODA is a main source of external funding'.[5] Without this funding, many countries would lack the resources necessary for the protection of the environment and the reconstruction and improvement of human welfare. Accordingly, the case for such transfers on this ground alone remains 'compelling'.[6]

AID AND INTERNATIONAL ENVIRONMENTAL LAW AND POLICY

The decision to give, or refuse, international financial assistance predominantly reflects political, rather than economic, choices.[7] Contemporary history demonstrates that vast amounts of financial assistance can be transferred between countries without affecting the domestic situation, *if* the objective is perceived to be important enough, for example, war or security.[8] Since the Second World War, the objective of the development of the poor countries of the world has been mooted as such a worthy goal.

The debate about financial assistance has been a permanent feature of international relations since aid donors began to coordinate their efforts in 1960. With regard to the actual level of how much each country should give in aid, the debate fluctuated with various proposals throughout the 1960s.[9] Finally, in 1970 the UN General Assembly set out the International Development Strategy for the Second United Nations Development Decade. For agreed targets for financial resource transfers and ODA flows, they suggested:

> *'Each economically advanced country will progressively increase its official development assistance to the developing countries and will exert its best efforts to reach a minimum net amount of 0.7 per cent of its gross national product ... by the middle of the next decade.'*[10]

Similar calls, reaffirming this goal and requesting donor countries to reach this target, have been reiterated over the following decades.[11]

The specific importance of international financial assistance to help solve environmental problems first appeared in international forums in 1970.[12] Ten years later, the first Brandt Commission suggested that *additional* financial assistance should be made available to Southern countries, to help contend with 'the critical areas of ecology'.[13] Throughout the 1980s, similar ideas proliferated. For example, the WCED recommended that attention be given to setting up 'a special international banking program or facility ... to finance investments in conservation projects'.[14] Towards the later half of the 1980s calls proliferated for the establishment of specific 'Planetary Protection Funds'.[15] These ideas were broadly recognized in 1991 when the pilot phase (1991–1994) of the Global Environment Facility (GEF) was established with the objective of funding (by both grants and concessional loans) initiatives to help avert the international environmental problems of climate change, ozone loss, biodiversity decline and ocean management.[16] The GEF was/is predicated upon funds which are *additional* to existing aid flows.[17] The pilot phase commanded a fund of approximately US$1.2 billion, and the second phase (1994–1997) of the GEF has expanded the core fund to US$2 billion. In the fiscal year 1998, the GEF was replenished with US$1.99 billion in new financing from 23 donor nations. With carryover, the total GEF funding for 1998–2002 was estimated at US$2.75 billion.

The question of exactly 'who pays' for international environmental protection was first brought to the forefront at the 1972 Stockholm Conference on the Human Environment.[18] The Conference concluded that Southern countries should be 'assisted' in their attempts to confront the conditions of underdevelopment causing environmental disruption and redress for the costs of environmental protection.[19] These two principles meant that 'additional international financial assistance'[20] was required. The linking of the need to meet financial assistance for development *and* additional environmental assistance was recognized in the World Conservation Strategy, which suggested that:

> *'assistance should be made available to enable requesting nations to carry out national conservation strategies ... [and] ... the flow of finance and development assistance should be increased, to a minimum of 0.7 per cent.'*[21]

Similar calls appeared in 1980,[22] 1983,[23] 1987,[24] 1989,[25] 1990[26] and 1991.[27] The importance of additional international financial assistance generally, and in the environmental context, was repeatedly recognized at the 1992 Earth Summit,[28] and has been subsequently reiterated.[29]

THE ARGUMENTS FOR AID IN INTERNATIONAL ENVIRONMENTAL LAW AND POLICY

There are two motives for the giving of international financial assistance. The first of these is primarily ethical, revolving around ideas of the 'awareness that we live in a village world, that we belong to a world community'[30] and pleas of 'humanitarianism'.[31] Such arguments are typically supported from many perspectives.[32] However, directly ethical arguments receive little attention in the raw politics of the international arena, which tends to be dominated by justifications that could be classified as more practically based.

Southern countries often feel they should be assisted with international environmental initiatives because they are to blame for only a small amount of the causation of a number of international environmental problems. This causation imbalance has led to the acceptance of the idea that if Southern countries are to participate in helping to avert international environmental problems, such as climate change, then it is necessary to assist them financially. This was recognized in a number of international documents both prior to the Earth Summit[33] and at Rio itself.[34]

Akin to the idea of causation is the view that as industrialized countries have economically developed they have created the international 'ecological debts' through *indirect* routes. For example, the impact of the climate change that Northern countries have caused has often been offset by the 'carbon absorption services'[35] (ie tropical rain forests) of Southern countries. However, this 'service' has not been paid. In doing so, the Northern countries have created an unfair advantage over Southern countries. Accordingly, it is suggested that in the interests of fairness, payments are made to Southern countries.[36] This argument has appeared in many settings.[37]

A further reason why Southern countries believe they should be financially assisted is based on the fact that many of them were once colonies and were environmentally exploited domestically. This may have been through *direct* acts such as nuclear testing, excessive mining[38] or the creation of dependent economies, which were/are tied into ecologically destructive patterns of trade. Such direct damage often continues, partly as a legacy of their colonial status, in the form of the debt crisis which, as the previous chapter demonstrated, may have severe ecological and social consequences.[39] These arguments are supposed to create 'a moral duty of reparation to make up for past exploitation'.[40]

The fourth justification for the transfer of international environmental financial assistance is that many Southern countries are reluctant to participate in international environmental solutions, since there will be associated costs which they may not be able to meet. A number of Southern countries are already highly dependent on external aid. To ask them to give up what little they have (for example, destroying their last forests), for an international problem they did not create (such as the global loss of forestry), may be asking too much. Consequently, it has been suggested that if environmental protection is desirable, the financial burden (or payment for the opportunity cost of non-destruction) should fall on countries that are economically developed.[41]

The final reason in favour of the international transfer of financial assistance is related to self-interest. This was argued forcefully by the 1969 Pearson Commission[42] and by the first Brandt Commission.[43] Over the decades the pure self-interest recognition has come to encompass the dawning reality that the solutions to the major international environmental problems require the participation of *all* countries. Accordingly, for one country to protect their own interests they may have to offer financial inducement to the unwilling countries simply to participate.[44] Tariq Hyder, a negotiator and spokesperson for the G77, has summarized the issue well:

> *'The industrialised countries must realise that the rules of the game in the North/South dialogue have changed. In the past ... the Southern world was seen in terms of "lifeboat" and "triage" theories where the weak might have to be left behind. It is now clear that in terms of the global atmosphere and environment, we are all in the same lifeboat. If the developing countries are not given the trade opportunities, debt relief, credit facilities, financial assistance and the technology flows that they require for their development, we will all eventually pay the price.'[45]*

This self-interest argument pertaining to the necessity to fix international environmental problems that affect Northern countries is also reflected in the self-interest of Southern countries, which have often come to view international environmental negotiations as a very good opportunity to advance a broader agenda of change in the structure of North–South relationships. Consequently, certain Southern countries have not hesitated to start using this leverage.[46] The Indian and Chinese demand for US$2 billion to sign the Montreal Protocol exemplifies the point on linkages between environmental concerns and broader demands on development per se.[47]

FINANCIAL ASSISTANCE AS A CATALYST FOR SUCCESS

Nowadays, international financial assistance is often recognized as holding the key to the success of many international environmental agreements. This is a realization that has long historical precedents. For example, the 1911 Treaty between the four sealing nations of Canada, Japan, the USA and Russia was predicated upon compensation to restrain two parties from 'over-harvesting'. This in turn allowed the other two nations to achieve 'sustainable catches' and the conservation of the seals was assured.[48]

In a modern context, a notable achievement of international financial assistance has been to increase the effectiveness of the international environmental agreement for the protection of the ozone layer. The vague promises of technical assistance under the Montreal Protocol as it was originally drafted,[49] were not sufficient inducement for the pivotal countries of India and China to sign and ratify the agreement. They wanted definite commitments in terms of compensation for loss of economic development that they may have suffered in forgoing the use of ozone depleting substances.[50]

The solution was found in the creation of an international ozone layer protection fund in 1989.[51] This promised Southern countries help with the financial, technical and human implications of complying with any ozone-protecting regime. This promise was clarified and specified in 1990[52] when it was acknowledged that:

> 'special provision is required to meet the needs of developing countries, including the provision of additional financial resources ... the funds can be expected to make a substantial difference in the world's ability to address the ... problem of ozone depletion.'[53]

As soon as the requisite levels of financial resources were reached (US$ 2 billion) India and China indicated that they would accept the agreement.[54]

With the deadlock being resolved relatively quickly, the Montreal Protocol and its subsequent amendments has gone on to be regarded as the modern prototype for international environmental agreements. However, it must be emphasized that the agreement was substantially assisted by the financial incentives behind it. Consequently, the precedent may be taken that the financial linkage acted as a powerful inducement to the participation of particular states.[55]

THE PROBLEMS ASSOCIATED WITH AID

International support for international financial assistance has begun to falter, and has been struggling since the late 1960s to keep up with its hopes.[56] This is not surprising, for as the 1995 Commission on Global Governance noted,

> 'aid has had a very bad press, with programs being attacked from all sides by people worried about waste, corruption, human rights abuses and neglect of the environment in recipient countries.'

Such backgrounds, when mixed with a distinct ideological dislike of foreign aid,[57] have often (but not always) caused some commentators to argue that 'Aid is a waste of time and money. Its results are fundamentally bad. Far from being increased, it should be stopped forthwith before more damage is done.'[58] There are a number of reasons why this call has been instigated.

The Misuse of Aid

One of the most common reasons why aid fails in its objectives, and subsequently receives much antagonism, has to do with the excessive intrusion of either the donor or recipient government in terms of its political (from manipulative patronage to outright corruption) or commercial usage.[59] This has become a specific concern with international environmental issues[60] and was forcefully debated at the Earth Summit, where a number of industrialized countries refused to offer international financial assistance unless there were guarantees that it would be used for specific purposes.[61]

The flip side of recipient governments using foreign financial assistance for misguided purposes is the giving of foreign financial assistance to stipulated (but not necessarily needy) donors, or giving assistance which is closely entwined with conditional purposes that are misguided.[62] This problem may come in two forms. First, the choice of countries that receive the assistance and, second, how this is utilized within the receiving countries.

On the question of allocation of monies, it has been long recognized, as the 1990 South Commission pointed out, that international financial assistance is 'not allocated among recipient countries according to objective economic criteria but ... [is] ... governed by political and security objectives'.[63] Such objectives typically further the donors' wishes, rather than the recipients' needs.[64] For example, as the UNICEF 1994 *State of the World's Children* Report stated:

> 'to a large extent, the size and shape of today's aid programs remain frozen in the pattern of the cold war era. About 25 per cent of US foreign assistance is military aid and for the fiscal year

of 1994 more than 25 per cent of non-military aid is earmarked
for Egypt, Israel and the nations of the former USSR, leaving
only about $6.5 billion for the rest of the developing world.'[65]

The least developed countries of the world, which make up 10.3 per cent of
the developing world's population (but over 75 per cent of the world's chron-
ically poor), receive just over 30 per cent of all international financial
assistance. The low-income developing countries (including China and India),
which account for 78 per cent of the developing world's population, take the
total to 69 per cent of all aid. As it currently stands, the least developed and
other low-income countries have seen their share of aid fall since 1990.
Bilateral aid to sub-Saharan Africa has fallen consistently in real terms for five
years. Nevertheless, upper middle income countries such as Israel, Jordan,
Syria and Egypt still receive a fifth of all aid. Israel and Egypt absorb over half
of the US Aid budget with over US$ 5 billion annually. This is three times the
US Aid budget for the whole of sub-Saharan Africa. High income countries
also take 3 per cent (US$ 1.8 billion) from the international aid pie each year.[66]
Such a situation is, as the Independent Commission on Population and Quality
of Life suggested, 'absurd'[67] because international financial assistance should
go to those who need it.

Even where aid is spent in the poorest countries there is little guarantee that
it will be effective, or even beneficial. Indeed, the recent history of ODA is
littered with examples where it has not achieved its objectives. The World Bank
stated in 1999: 'Foreign aid has at times been a spectacular success – and an
unmitigated failure... And everything in between.'[68] The World Bank suggested
that aid projects may fail for a number of reasons, which often have little to do
with the magnitude of financial resources transferred. These include the lack of
a suitable policy environment (ie sound economic management, commitment to
achieve the set goals) and failures to participate with democratic society and its
civil members (from NGOs to local business interests). Failure is also invited if
projects are not well thought through conceptually; if they are not tailored to
the needs of each individual country; or if they fail to have either a long-term
view or an ability to be involved in capacity building.[69]

Project failure for ODA is often because of the misplaced focus of the
recipient or the conditions attached to the ODA by the donor, or both.
Conditional, or tied, aid involves the situation whereby aid is only given in
exchange for certain acts, which are typically beneficial to the giver of the aid.
This type of conditional financial assistance is still common and amounted to
approximately a quarter of all ODA from OECD countries.[70]

Within this rubric comes the area of conditionality, which seeks to further
sustainable development objectives. On a multilateral level, the contribution
of aid to sustainable development objectives was identified as a central task
for development cooperation in the 1990s. By 1992, the OECD had prepared
Guidelines on Aid and the Environment which were designed to 'promote
international collaboration on environmental problems which transcend
boundaries to become regional or global in nature'. This goal was reaffirmed

in preparation for the 1997 Earth Summit Review, where the Development Assistance Committee (DAC) of the OECD stated they would:

> *'support efforts ... to ensure that current trends in the loss of environmental resources – forests, fisheries, fresh water, climate, soils, biodiversity, stratospheric ozone and the accumulation of hazardous substances – are effectively reversed by 2015'.*[71]

Despite the good intention of such objectives, if these are not augmented with the considerations noted above (on why ODA may fail), the results may also prove unrewarding. In this regard, attempts to stop tropical deforestation through conditionality requirements (alone) on ODA have proved largely unsuccessful.[72]

Other types of conditionality (ie the forced purchase of the donors' exports) have often been seen as a diversion of public funds from the commonly touted axiomatic goals of ODA – poverty reduction and sustainable development. Owing to such concerns, since the early 1960s it has been argued that all conditionality should be removed, *other than* conditionality that requires that assistance should be targeted towards primary considerations such as basic education, health and local environmental protection.[73] Prior to the 1995 Social Development Summit, this idea became encapsulated in what has become known as the 20/20 compact (which became solidified at the Summit) under the terms of which donors would agree to give at least 20 per cent (the NGO target was 50 per cent) of their foreign aid for priority goals (basic education, primary health care, clean water supply and family planning). Simultaneously, the developing countries would earmark 20 per cent of their budgets for the same areas of activity.[74] Such a proposal was considered necessary at the time because in the early 1990s the corresponding shares spent on basic needs were only 7 per cent of foreign assistance and 13 per cent of developing countries' budgets.[75]

At the 1995 Social Development Summit and the following Conference on Human Settlements[76] this proposal was *not* accepted by all countries as a firm plan of action. Rather, it was posed as a recommendation, much in line with the objectives of the Development Assistance Committee of the OECD,[77] that interested participants may wish to take up. This objective has not been taken up despite continuing recommendations from international commissions to do so.[78] Moreover, despite much rhetoric to the contrary, there has been no increase in spending on the key areas of basic health and basic education. Overall, less than 0.1 per cent of total aid is allocated to basic education (such as primary schools and adult literacy) and 0.3 per cent for basic health.[79]

The problem of the direction of international finance in these areas has also been played out specifically in the international environmental field with the GEF. The problem is that the GEF focuses predominantly on environmental problems from a Northern perspective. That is, it seeks to fund projects that address climate change, biological diversity, international waters and depletion of the ozone layer. Although this ambit was expanded when the GEF was reconstituted to include land degradation, primary desertification and deforestation, these additional areas must relate to the four focal areas.[80] Thus, the GEF has been explicitly excluded from financing or even examining the broader critiques pertaining to the overall debate about development per se or the specific issues of free markets, poverty, trade, structural adjustment, debt or aid.[81] It also implicitly excludes a host of new claims in respect of environmental 'services' provided by Southern countries which have been laid before Northern countries. For example, certain countries have demanded payment for not exploiting their rain forests, and allowing the continuance of international 'carbon absorption services'.[82] Such claims have typically been seen to go beyond what could be considered 'legitimate' and, accordingly, many Northern countries are unwilling to pay for what they consider to be illegitimate 'extras'.[83] The structuring of the GEF goes to the heart of this issue and the recognition of what is, or is not legitimate.

The problem of the control of international financial assistance (as opposed to the focus) has also been forcefully played out within the GEF, where questions of who controls the decision-making process have been asked since its creation.[84] Initially, the World Bank was the chosen vehicle for implementing the GEF.[85] This was despite opposition from both environmentalists and Southern governments, due to the undemocratic nature of the Bank and its previous social and environmental track record.[86]

To help begin to address the concerns of democracy it was suggested prior to, and at, the Earth Summit that greater democratization of the decision-making process of the GEF should be achieved by giving Southern countries 'an appropriate influence in allocating these [GEF] funds'.[87] Accordingly, after the pilot phase of the GEF was reviewed in 1994 and the second stage implemented, the actual structure of the GEF was changed so that a basic parity now exists between donors and recipients.[88] The World Bank now retains a more neutral position, acting as a trustee for the GEF.[89]

Despite this greater equity between Northern and Southern countries, the power continues to be predominantly exercised by governments. That is, the bodies that are neither international agencies nor independent states have remained largely excluded from the decision-making process.[90] This exclusion, as one of the foremost downfalls of the GEF, was highlighted by the Independent Evaluation of the Pilot Phase of the GEF, where it was recognized that 'the shaping of projects, where local participation and co-operation are essential to outcomes, has been particularly problematic during the pilot phase'.[91] By 1999, indications suggested that this problem was being corrected, although residual problems such as coordinating interested agencies (both multilateral and private) remained.[92]

Numbers and Willingness

The demands for international financial assistance are increasing. Simultaneously, the willingness to provide such assistance is declining. The demands for increased international financial assistance can be ascertained by examining the size of the international funds over the previous decades and how they have grown exponentially. For example, the World Heritage Fund is US$ 2.2 million annually, and the fund for the Montreal Protocol is around US$2 billion.[93] It is estimated that it could cost US$4.5 billion annually to stop desertification,[94] a total of US$250 billion to conserve biodiversity[95] and anything up to US$100 billion per annum to slow global warming.[96]

Total costs for annual sustainable development range from Maurice Strong's suggestion of US$ 8.8 billion,[97] to the (accepted) UN suggestion of US$625 billion per year, of which 125 billion of this is expected to come from external sources. This 125 billion figure is US$70 billion more than *all* current aid flows.[98] Needless to say, the OECD countries refused to accept the figure at the 1992 Earth Summit and suggested a target figure between US$2 and 10 billion on top of the existing aid budgets.[99] Accordingly, most OECD countries[100] (including the USA, despite pronouncements that 'the days of the open cheque book are over')[101] promised to increase their international financial assistance for environmental purposes.

Multilateral efforts (and promises) to 'secure an expansion of the aggregate volume of resources made available to the less developed countries' date back to 1961.[102] However, these early promises never got any further than the ones made at the Earth Summit, where despite the overall intentions of reaching the 0.7 per cent target for overseas aid, the pivotal G7 countries all declined to give a timetable as to when their countries would reach this limit.[103] No timetable was placed in Agenda 21 in 1992, and when the issue was revisited in 1997, it was again avoided, despite the promises made at the Earth Summit for additional assistance, which had not materialized.[104] As such, the Programme for the Further Implementation of Agenda 21 noted that:

> '*Most developed countries have still not reached the United Nations target, reaffirmed by most countries at UNCED, of committing 0.7 per cent of the GNP to official development assistance... Regrettably, on average, ODA as a percentage of the GNP of developed countries has drastically declined in the post-UNCED era... Developed countries should therefore fulfil the commitments undertaken.*'[105]

Overall, environmental aid has often struggled to make the levels that were promised.[106] With certain international environmental funds, they have struggled to meet minimum requirements. For example, the Earth Increment, a US$5 billion fund which was established at the Earth Summit and was designed to help Southern nations implement Agenda 21, has, since its inception, been in perpetual danger of total collapse.[107] Disappointment has also come to pass on the promises of extra money for the GEF's second phase, with only 78 per cent of its target being reached. Accordingly, as the 1997 Special Session of the General Assembly noted, 'its levels of funding and replenishment have not been sufficient to meet its objectives'.[108]

Despite the above shortfall within the GEF, it must be recognized that this achievement is favourable when compared with the failure in the international arena to meet the 0.7 per cent target of external assistance. Indeed, by the mid-1990s only a handful of the developed countries (Denmark, Netherlands, Norway and Sweden) who give foreign aid surpassed the 0.7 per cent of gross domestic product (GDP). Overall, after peaking in 1991, the real value of aid began to fall to just 0.3 per cent in the middle of the decade.[109] This percentage term, in the mid-1990s, represented the *lowest level for 30 years* despite the so-called 'peace dividend'.[110] It was only in 1999 that development assistance from the OECD countries began to rise again, thus ending a five-year decline. Nevertheless, the combined gross national product (GNP) average was only 0.25 (which was well below the 0.33 per cent average of the 1970s and 1980s).[111]

The problem of declining aid flows and a refusal to set concrete commitments to meet the 0.7 per cent target have plagued the international community to such a degree that by the mid-1990s the Commission on Sustainable Development began suggesting that *additional* mechanisms (such as global taxes) may need to be seriously considered if sustainable development is to occur.[112] Very similar conclusions were reached by the 1995 Commission on Global Governance[113] and the 1996 Independent Commission on Population and Quality of Life.[114] Unfortunately, such proposals face distinct difficulties, and as the Commission on Sustainable Development noted in its 1997 five-year review of progress since UNCED, 'there is currently insufficient political will to go much beyond the discussion of technical details'.[115] This conclusion was reflected at the Earth Summit II conference.[116]

CONCLUSION

International financial assistance has a distinct role to play in moving towards a society which is both socially and environmentally sustainable. Moreover, it has a pivotal role in enticing a number of countries into international environmental agreements. Without such assistance, it is arguable that the crucial steps towards acceptance of certain international environmental agreements would not be reached.

However, as it currently operates, international financial assistance is commonly abused and misused by both donors and recipients alike. In this regard, movements towards the 20/20 compact represented a good starting point for assistance which actually helps environmental sustainability and social equity. However, as noted, this option has not been accepted by the majority of donors.

This refusal to delink financial assistance has also been mirrored by a refusal to raise international aid flows to the requisite level of 0.7 per cent of GNP. This type of general assistance is very important to a number of least developed countries and their attempts to move towards the social issues of sustainability that deal with distinct problems such as poverty and empowerment. Even where assistance has broadly kept up with its demands and promises, such as with GEF, its ambit has been tightly curtailed to also exclude these issues.

In a nutshell, aid has a very important role to play in the movement towards a socially and environmentally sustainable society. However, when viewed from its current position of abuse, self-interest, manipulation and limited ambit, it has few redeeming features. Accordingly, the traditional mechanisms and motivations for aid need to be carefully rethought and care needs to be taken not to throw out the baby with the bathwater.

Chapter 7

Peace

SECURITY

Social ecology has always possessed a strong link with the pursuit of peace and disarmament.[1] This has been reinforced by the idea that a strong military as the basis of security for the nation state is outdated, diversionary and dangerous. Accordingly, *the concept of security has radically changed.*

This change has become evident because what nations may now need to protect themselves from in an age of overt interdependence (from the ecological to the economic) is rapidly making traditional ideas of defence outmoded. In particular, the environment – which was once seen as barely important to debates about security – is now often damaged (both directly and indirectly) in conflicts, as well as being a catalyst (both directly and indirectly) for conflicts because of resource shortages.[2] As such, environmental stress can play a contributing role to both the causation of conflicts, and the developments within them. Therefore, as the WCED suggested: 'a comprehensive approach to international and national security must transcend the traditional emphasis on military power and armed competition'.[3]

Accordingly, as the 1994 Commission on Peace and Food stated, 'what is needed is a quantum shift from the competitive security paradigm' because 'as the face of global society has changed, so too has the nature of global security'.[4]

Despite these changing world views, the traditional military paradigms remain largely intact. Such military build-ups, maintenance and balance are a threat to any meaningful type of sustainable development in two ways. Firstly, the economic costs of military security divert scarce funds from elsewhere. Secondly, war, from local internal conflicts to the possibility of a full-blown nuclear exchange, represents the antithesis of sustainability.

The Economic Costs of Military Security

The financial costs of overt military structures are detrimental because they divert scarce resources into military budgets which are often critically needed elsewhere. This is a problem that has been long-recognized,[5] and has been reiterated by a number of international conferences and commissions.[6] It was hoped that with the end of the Cold War this problem could actually be reversed with the so-called 'peace dividend', which was supposed to amount to a cumulative saving of the reduced spending on weapons from its peak in 1987 (of an estimated US$995 billion annually) to an estimated US$745 billion in 1998. Such reductions could have had a huge impact on the funding of sustainable development. However, virtually all of these savings went into budget deficit reductions and non-development expenditures.[7] The lion's share of the reductions was made by the industrialized countries, who reduced their arms budgets by around 20 per cent. The USA spent approximately 30 per cent less in this area at the end of the 1990s than it did at the end of the 1980s, and Russia's arms budget is currently less than a tenth of what it was for the same period. The overall reduction for developing countries has been around 10 per cent.[8] However, it must be realized that although Southern countries only account for about 15 per cent of the world's military spending, their expenditure on the military has risen twice as fast as national incomes. For some regions, such as South-east Asia and sub-Saharan Africa, military spending has been increasing, not decreasing.[9]

The industrialized countries spend, on average, 3 per cent of their GDP on defence. Conversely, with developing countries, 24 already spend over 5 per cent of their GDP on defence, and a further 12 spend more than 10 per cent. The average industrialized country now spends twice as much on health as it does on the military. Conversely, among the 94 developing countries for whom data are available, no less than 52 spent more on the military than on health. The average developing country spent 2.5 times more on arms and defence than on health.[10] In some of the most needy countries, this has reached extreme lengths. For example, in Sudan, the government allocated a direct figure of 5.6 per cent of its budget (although the indirect costs probably take it to around 13 per cent) to the military (in 1997), and 0.3 per cent to its health budget.[11]

Overall, although global military spending has fallen, military budgets are still very high and represent great sums of money. For example, in the decade 1990–2000, it is estimated that the world spent US$9 trillion on military equipment It has been suggested by various international commissions that such sums should be reduced in the order of 50–75 per cent.[13] Such reductions could easily outstrip current levels of overseas development assistance. The USA had a budget of US$270.6 billion for 1999. Conversely, the UN budget for peace-keeping in 1998 was US$1.3 billion. This comparison suggests the obvious point that the finance from military budgets could be used for other objectives which may accord more directly with the needs of sustainable development. For example, the costs of meeting the health and education targets agreed at the 1990 World Summit for Children represent *only* 16 per cent of developing countries' current spending on weapons.[14]

War as the Antithesis of any Meaningful Form of Sustainable Development

War and violence are the antithesis of development. From local wars to global Armageddon, war kills people, destroys lives, communities and society. War continues to claim hundreds of thousands of lives (an average of 450,000) per year.[15] When coupled with the damage that war does to society and environment, it becomes axiomatic, as the UNGA declared in 1984: 'that life without war serves as the primary international prerequisite for the material well-being, development and progress of countries and for the full implementation of the rights and fundamental freedoms proclaimed by the United Nations'. Accordingly, 'the peoples of our planet have a sacred right to peace'.[16] The 1992 Rio Declaration added to this by recognizing this concern in the context of sustainable development:

> *'Warfare is inherently destructive of sustainable development. [Accordingly] States shall therefore respect international law providing protection for the environment in times of armed conflict and co-operate in its further development, as necessary.'*[17]

The Effects of Nuclear Weaponry

Before 1945 the greatest explosive effect of bombs was produced by TNT (trinitrotoluene) devices of about 20 tons. The nuclear weapons which exploded in Hiroshima and Nagasaki had the explosive power of 15 and 12 kilotons respectively, that is, 15,000 and 12,000 tons of TNT. Many of the weapons existing today represent several multiples of these first atomic bombs. Today, bombs range from the megaton (equivalent to a million tons of TNT) through to the multiple 20 megaton (the equivalent of 20 million tons of TNT). A single 5 megaton bomb represents more explosive power than all the explosive force of all the bombs used in the Second World War.[18] Between them, Russia and the USA (alone) have upwards of 30,000 nuclear weapons in various states of readiness. Collectively, they have some 7000 warheads ready to be fired with less than 15 minutes notice.[19]

Technologically advanced weapons have already caused vast environmental damage. This has become manifest from the direct effects of warfare (from the use of Agent Orange in Vietnam, to the effects of the nuclear weapons used in the Second World War, or the approximately 2050 nuclear tests since then)[20] and the indirect effects generated by the disposal of such weaponry.[21] However, the costs already associated with nuclear weaponry are minuscule compared with the near incomprehensible apocalypse that they could create if a full-blown exchange were ever to take place. In the words of the UNGA, such an exchange would be capable of destroying civilization on Earth.[22] Likewise, the 1982 Independent Commission on Disarmament and Security Issues warned, a full-scale nuclear exchange could bring about the extinction of humanity.[23]

The possibilities of nuclear war represent the worst possible environmental threat imaginable.[24] The extent of damage was summarized by the 1987 WCED in the following terms:

> 'The likely consequences of nuclear war make other threats to the environment pale into significance. Nuclear weapons represent a qualitatively new step in the development of warfare. One thermonuclear bomb can have an explosive power greater than all the explosive used in war since the invention of gunpowder. In addition to the destructive effects of blast and heat, immensely magnified by these weapons, they introduce a new lethal agent – ionizing radiation – that extends lethal effects over both space and time.'[25]

Nuclear weapons have the potential to destroy the functioning of most of the important ecosystems on the planet.[26] This could follow from the possible after-effect of a nuclear exchange – the nuclear winter.[27] A full-blown nuclear exchange could lead to the direct death of up to 1 billion people. It could also destroy civilization, in terms of social institutions, economic structures and cultural treasures[28] and cause untold damage to future generations.[29] Despite the possibility that such weapons could bring the end of the human race, in terms of international law the question of whether they are either illegal to possess, or use in self defence *if necessary*, has been avoided.[30] That is, despite the cataclysmic risk that they represent, they are not prohibited per se. Accordingly, any decisions to reduce weapons have to be made by negotiation.

LAYING DOWN ARMS

Humankind's efforts to control the consequences of the possession of weapons followed quickly on the heels of weapons development. History records negotiations between the Greek city-states of Sparta and Athens concerning limitations to fortifications in the 5th century BC.[31] Similar attempts to control the worst weapons of the following ages, such as cross-bows and cannons, received periodic interest.[32] However, it was only with the onset of industrialization and a new genre of weapons that international arms control came into its own. The Hague Conventions of 1899 and 1907 outlawed such weapons as dumdum bullets and asphyxiating gases.[33] These were the first in a long line of such conventions designed to limit the impact of future wars. Such objectives were soon eclipsed with the 'war to end all wars' and the advent of a new generation of terror weapons. The League of Nations which followed this debacle was predicated on disarmament, and further international conventions designed to remove the inhumanity from international conflict were attempted.[34] Once again, these were belittled by another World War, which was only brought to an end by the terrifying precedents of Hiroshima and Nagasaki. Atop this precipice came forth the Cold, and occasionally hot, War.

The axiomatic necessity to control and disarm the nuclear build-up between the two superpowers was a continual topic in international relations throughout the period of the Cold War. Realizations that reducing the nuclear build-up actually enhanced defence and promoted national security (from reduced risks to reduced economic costs) provided a strong background to international negotiations of this and subsequent periods.[35] That is, the desire to reduce arms was not necessarily to promote peace, and reductions were *not* conducted out of altruism. Rather, self-interest and security were the foremost motivations.

The Control of Nuclear Weapons

One year after atomic bombs were used on Japan, the USA put forward the first attempt to control the future use of such weapons. This (the 'Baruch Plan') was at the first session of the UN Atomic Energy Commission. The plan consisted of the complete transfer of all US atomic weapons, atomic power facilities, and atomic know-how to international control. The plan called for the creation of an international organization under the auspices of the UN Atomic Energy Commission to be responsible for all aspects of the development and use of atomic energy. However, the Soviets rejected the US proposal, calling it a transparent attempt to monopolize nuclear weaponry to the disadvantage of all other states.[36] Three years of sterile negotiations in the UN Atomic Energy Commission followed, until the work of the Commission came to an end in 1949 with the detonation of the first Soviet atomic bomb.

The beginnings of the 1950s saw the continuation of the Korean war and the beginning of the competition for influence between the USSR and the USA in the Middle East. These events, and the mind-set of the time, meant there was little chance for the control of armaments between the superpowers. However, the realization that nuclear technology could possibly spread around the globe and be used for either peaceful or military purposes resulted in an attempt to control its distribution. This was done so as to achieve a strict control of its use for peaceful purposes ('atoms for peace')[37] under the auspices of the International Atomic Energy Agency (IAEA).[38] Although this avenue was controlled (and later strengthened),[39] this source of nuclear technology would eventually help to lead to the testing of the nuclear bomb by India in 1974,[40] as well as moving towards the possible nuclear arming of Iraq, North Korea, Libya and Iran in the 1980s and 1990s.[41]

The technological achievement of the launching of the Soviet Sputnik in 1957 stripped the US psyche of the idea that it was 'safe' from the reach of the USSR. This shattering of illusions was quickly followed by the Berlin crisis of 1959–61, the U-2 incident of 1960 and finally the Cuban missile crisis of 1962.[42] The nuclear background of this period was the deadliest that humanity ever experienced in terms of the vast amount of megatons of nuclear weaponry available.[43] This background helped propel the superpowers towards the necessity for arms control. However, despite much rhetoric and the mutual recognition that this was necessary, there were very few concrete limitations or controls.[44] The first tentative steps in this area were the 1963 Partial (Atmospheric) Test Ban Treaty[45] (which only the USSR and the USA abided by) and the 1968 Non-Proliferation Treaty (NPT).[46] The NPT (which was reviewed in 1995 and 2000) tried to stop the proliferation of nuclear weapons to states other than the five superpowers; the nuclear powers affirmed security assurances to non-nuclear states that they would not use their weapons against parties to the NPT unless they or an ally were attacked;[47] the NPT tied non-nuclear states to the IAEA; and stipulated that the overall goal for the signatories was to: 'pursue negotiations in good faith on effective measures relating to cessation of the nuclear arms race at an early date and to ... complete nuclear disarmament under strict and effective international control.'

In 1972, towards the end of the Vietnam war, the first Strategic Arms Limitations Talks (SALT)[48] agreement was signed, which was a temporary accord restraining the growth of US and Soviet strategic forces while a more elaborate treaty was negotiated. The cornerpiece of SALT I was the Anti-Ballistic Missile Treaty (ABM)[49] which banned nationwide anti-ballistic missile systems. The basis of this Treaty was that neither nation would be allowed to develop defensive systems (anti-ballistic missiles). This was necessary because if such systems were developed (such as the 'Star Wars' system)[50] then the vulnerability of each superpower and the associated balance of terror represented by mutually assured destruction (MAD) could not be maintained.[51]

The following agreement, SALT II,[52] which set limits on the number of deployed strategic systems the sides could possess, was not ratified by the US Senate. This was due to the 1979 USSR invasion of Afghanistan. Any hope of SALT II reappearing before the Senate for ratification was distanced on Ronald Reagan's entry to office. Reagan set up an entirely new approach to arms control (and proliferation) which was eventually to become the START (Strategic Arms Reduction Talks) treaties. However, before these could eventuate, the build-up of nuclear weapons, and the possibility of the end-game played by finely balanced nuclear brinkmanship on a plateau of mutual assured destruction, peaked during the mid-1980s. It was at this point in 1986 that the global stockpile of nuclear warheads reached 69,490. This was the equivalent of an explosive yield of 18 billion tons of TNT, or 3.6 tons for every human being.[53]

The first real break-through in nuclear arms controls in the period came with the 1987 Intermediate Range Nuclear Forces Treaty (INF)[54] which eliminated an entire class of nuclear offensive arms and established an intrusive on-site inspection regime. Soon after came START I,[55] which limited US and Soviet strategic offensive forces. In addition, START I built elaborate verification and on-site inspection regimes. As the Soviet Union began to disintegrate and the economic burden of the nuclear arms race came home to both superpowers in the early 1990s, unilateral reductions were announced by both the USA and the USSR. These unilateral actions were seized upon with the 1993 START II[56] agreement, which mandated even deeper cuts in strategic forces. This second treaty, which has *not* yet been ratified by Russia (but has by the

USA), has been supplemented by a framework START III which has detailed verification and dismantling regimes.[57] If all the START agreements come to fruition, the numbers of strategic warheads will be reduced to between 3000 and 3500 on each side. This is about a quarter of their peak during the Cold War. Although this is unquestionably an impressive reduction, the total still represents at least 3000 warheads on each side *above* what would actually be suitable for effective deterrence (500 warheads per superpower) as opposed to overkill.[58]

The focus on nuclear arms reductions between the superpowers has meant that the other confirmed nuclear powers (China, France, India, Pakistan and the UK) have not partaken in reduction talks.[59] Moreover, the nuclear weapons 'club' is certainly not static. In addition to the declared nuclear states, there are also the undeclared but highly suspected state of Israel and the four states believed to be trying to develop nuclear weapons (Libya, Iraq, Iran and North Korea). The specific case of Iraq and its pursuit of a wide range of advanced arms – including nuclear weaponry – despite being a member of the NPT and subject to IAEA inspections frightened many observers.[60] Similar concerns with the way North Korea avoided the IAEA, and then threatened to withdraw from the NPT entirely, have also led to questions of how successful the non-proliferation of nuclear weapons has actually been.[61] Additionally, proliferation concerns have been heightened with the break-up of the USSR and the 'leakage' of many forms of their weaponry.[62]

Such concerns as those noted above helped lead to the 1995 NPT Review and Extension Conference[63] and the Comprehensive Test Ban Treaty (CTBT).[64] The CTBT was eventually agreed to (in principle) by all five nuclear powers.[65] However, in 1999, the US Senate refused to ratify the CTBT. This effectively killed the Treaty, as to come into effect it had to be ratified by all 44 countries which possess nuclear power, including the USA.[66]

This failure was doubly important as the successful conclusion of the CTBT was seen as an essential step towards the extension of the NPT, which had a follow-up conference to the 1995 meeting in 2000. The objective of this was to fulfil the NPT goals of becoming 'universal', of being of an 'indefinite duration',[67] and of achieving the 'systematic and progressive efforts to reduce nuclear weapons globally, with the ultimate goal of reducing those weapons'.[68] However, the 2000 Conference failed to achieve a timetable or specific commitments, although the five central nuclear powers renewed 'unequivocal commitment to the ultimate goals of a complete elimination of nuclear weapons and a treaty of general and complete disarmament under strict and effective international controls'.[69]

These failures of both the CTBT and the NPT have led a number of states to refuse to join either treaty.[70] This is because without targets and meaningful commitments by the existing superpowers, nothing has changed in the status quo of global security (via a nuclear inequality) between nations.[71] Although this argument has *not* been conclusive for some countries which have either removed or abandoned their nuclear weapons programmes, for others it has not. Therefore, the essential linkage between an end to testing and reversing the already established inequity in weapons by full nuclear disarmament (the unspecified promise of the NPT) has not been achieved.[72] The situation was well summarized by the 1996 Canberra Commission:

> '*nuclear weapons are held by a handful of states which insist that these weapons provide unique security benefits, and yet reserve uniquely to themselves the right to own them. This situation is highly discriminatory and thus unstable; it cannot be sustained. The possession of nuclear weapons by any state is a constant stimulus to other states to acquire them.*'[73]

A world made safe from nuclear threats requires more than a freeze on production for the haves and have nots. It requires equality in a sense that *no* state should have the right to possess nuclear capability over others.[74]

Arms Control beyond Nuclear Weapons

Traditionally, arms control has adopted a myopic approach, focusing on specific classes of weapons (predominantly nuclear). This has engendered difficulties, as today arms control needs to be much more comprehensive than ever before as new varieties and types of weapons are developed. Recent attempts to control these new varieties include the 1993 Chemical Weapons Convention[75] and the 1972 Biological and Toxin Weapons Convention.[76] Both of these mandate the renunciation of these weapons, and the destruction of any stockpiles and production facilities that the signatories may possess.

Despite this progress, the effectiveness of these Conventions is under examination, as a number of countries outside the main signatories (the USA and Russia) explore the options that these new weapons offer. As it stands, Iraq, China, Egypt, Taiwan, Iran and North Korea are all believed to be involved in direct research efforts into biological warfare.[77] Likewise, a number of states believed to be pursuing chemical weapons have either refused to sign the Convention or have expressed reservations.[78] Moreover, even with the signatories to both of the Conventions, questions remain of how far they can be overseen due to the restricted natures (both economically and politically) of the Secretariats and the Conventions themselves.[79]

The control of conventional arms represents a different set of problems for the international community. The trade in small arms is worth between US$5 and 10 billion per year, and represents 10–20 per cent of the total worldwide trade in conventional arms. This figure helped to generate some 125 million automatic weapons, which are currently in circulation around the world. These weapons (along with other 'small arms') are responsible for some 80–90 per cent of all casualties in recent wars. Moreover, since 1990, light weapons were the only arms used in 46 of 49 conflicts.[80]

In some areas, such as in Europe, attempts to control the spread and build-up of conventional arms have also met with limited success with the 1990 and 1992 Conventional Forces in Europe (CFE) Treaties, which dramatically limited the size and structure of conventional forces.[81] However, apart from the European reductions, attempts to control the spread and build-up of conventional arms have been fraught with difficulty as there are no internationally (as opposed to unilateral or regional)[82] accepted norms or standards regarding small arms. Their production, trade and possession are essentially unmonitored and unregulated – subject to the ups and downs of demand rather than international policy.

At best, attempts are being made to come to grips with the *illegal* trade in small arms.[83] That is, only deals between sovereign nations are deemed legitimate, irrespective of its internal policies such as human rights violations. Aside from the failure to identify which countries obtain small arms, and the purposes to which they are put, is the problem that the focus on the legal trade does not cover weapons which are resold by the purchaser, stolen or copied. In addition, it fails to address the often legitimate needs of peoples within states, who may have to defend themselves against oppressive regimes with minimum force, especially where the international community fails to offer effective protection.

The failures of the international community to address this problem have been attributed to a number of reasons. The first problem is the difficulties of international, regional and domestic politics (as opposed to bi-polar negotiations) which was fully manifested with all the problems in such trouble areas as Bosnia and Rwanda.[84] Such situations make traditional approaches to questions of genocide, arms and peace-keeping notoriously difficult. Indeed, from deep-seated ethnic conflicts, through to the internal disintegration of nation states, the traditional approaches to security, let alone the actors in the debate, have fundamentally changed.[85]

Finally, powerful economic limitations are often imposed on those who should be pursuing security for other countries. These limitations arise through the export market for conventional weapons.[86] This consideration has made a number of countries unwilling to seriously commit themselves to reducing their trade in conventional weaponry, even if the recipients are utilizing their imported weapons for purposes in contravention of international law. This drive is not surprising given that the global arms transfer market was approximately US\$ 21 billion in 1998. The USA is the largest player in this trade, controlling over 45 per cent of the trade.[87]

The difficulties in reducing conventional weapons are evident in the attempt to obtain a worldwide ban on landmines. These weapons injure or kill 26,000 people annually, of which an estimated 80 per cent are civilians.[88] Members of the international community have been attempting to ban these weapons since 1980.[89] However, although 121 countries signed the 1997 Convention on the Prohibition of the Use, Stockpiling, Production and Transfer of Anti-Personnel Mines and on Their Destruction, major players (such as China, the USA and Russia) in the manufacture and sale of landmines refused to sign it on the grounds that they are necessary for self defence.[90]

REALISM IN A WORLD WITHOUT A SUPRA-SOVEREIGN

In overtly simplistic terms, disarmament is a strategy to secure peace. Conversely, arms control is a strategy to secure advantage. Proponents of arms control often do not think 'peace' is achievable because of deep conflicts that remain between opposing nations.[91] Nevertheless, arms controls are pursued because of the risks that are presented if such controls are not achieved. Such an approach is supported by 'realist' paradigms which suggest that disarmament in a world of antagonistic states, without any form of *suitable* international security guarantor, is extreme folly.[92] Quite simply, peace is not possible in a radically decentralized world full of power-hungry despots. Accordingly, it makes sense to remain fully armed to the highest point of security. Conversely, any weaponry reductions in a situation of antagonism between opponents is a high risk gamble.[93] This gamble nearly went terribly wrong with the disarmament talks prior to the Second World War, which both Japan and Germany ignored. Accordingly, in a world system without international security, *real* national security can only be counted by the size of a country's defence structure and capabilities, which sit on a nuclear hair trigger alert of between 15 and 30 minutes.[94]

Such a position raises two issues. The first deals with the idea of the nuclear deterrent, and the second with defence generally. Firstly, it is assumed that nuclear weapons are a suitable deterrent to other states, and do actually go towards maintaining peace.[95] However, this is highly arguable, from both traditional evidence and changing situations. The problem with the nuclear maintenance of peace argument is that nuclear weapons did *not* create more peace in the world, or necessarily act as a deterrent to war.

The failure of this proposition can be seen with the continuing conflict over Kashmir between India and Pakistan, or through the simple numbers and types of war during and since the Cold War. For example, between 1945 and 1989 there were 138 wars.[96] In recent years, a series of long-standing conflicts have been, or are in the process of being, settled and the number of major wars (in which over 1000 people have died) on the planet each year has consistently fallen since the end of the Cold War. For example, in 1989 there were 36 major wars, whereas in 1998 there were only 27 in 26 locations throughout the world.[97] Another important distinction to note with this statistic is that all but two of these conflicts were internal. In such situations, the viability of weapons of mass destruction must be re-examined, as the threat to the state is not necessarily a foreign power.

Even when the superpowers were involved in conflict which they lost against foreign enemies (Korea, Vietnam and Afghanistan), nuclear weapons could not be used against their victorious opponents for a variety of reasons.[98] This idea of when nuclear weapons may actually be suitable and the way that they act as a deterrent also ignores the fact that the way that wars originate often has little to do with 'profound causes' and tends to follow much more chaotic paths that rapidly escalate.[99] The First World War is the exemplar of this position, where the idea of deterrents did not stop the conflict once it unravelled in a way which few could have predicted.[100] The costs of a failure to deter in the modern age are much greater.

Despite these problems with the idea of deterrence, what of course is obvious is that a full-blown nuclear exchange did not take place. The failure of this to happen may have had more to do with good luck than two super-powers held in a form of check.[101] Indeed, there were over 100 accidents involving damaged nuclear weapons that 'could have caused unintended detonation' between 1945 and 1980.[102] The fact that any one of these incidents could have sparked nuclear exchanges should make people realize that the world has not experienced a nuclear weapons catastrophe more because of good fortune, rather than good management.[103]

Irrespective of whether the nuclear balance of terror maintained peace during the Cold War, the realization must now be accepted that the balance of terror between two finely balanced superpowers does not apply in a number of unstable situations around the world. That is, deterrence may not necessarily apply to despotic regimes which may acquire nuclear weapons and are prone to high risk-taking and have a willingness to absorb (and inflict) high levels of casualties. Such a situation does not lead to *mutual* deterrence. Accordingly, as the Canberra Commission suggested:

> *'The end of the bipolar confrontation has not removed the danger of nuclear catastrophe. In some respects the risk of use by accident or miscalculation has increased. Political upheaval or the weakening of state authority in a nuclear weapon state could cripple existing systems for ensuring the safe handling and control of nuclear weapons and weapons material, increasing the odds of a calamity.'*[104]

Such a situation led the Commission to conclude that: 'The proposition that nuclear weapons can be retained in perpetuity and never used – accidentally or by decision – defies credibility.'[105] The only solution to the problem that could bring about the extinction of humanity is 'The ... elimination of nuclear weapons and the assurance that they will never be produced again.'[106] A very similar conclusion was also reached in 1996 by the Generals for Peace and Disarmament, who recognized that 'the continuing existence of nuclear weapons ... constitutes a peril to the safety and survival of the people we are dedicated to protect.'[107]

Despite this growing recognition that nuclear deterrence and nuclear security is only a paper charade that creates much greater dangers than it prevents, the nuclear powers insist on retaining *their* nuclear forces. This is because, quite simply, no one and nothing else is believed to be strong enough to guarantee their security. Hence, they become engaged in a game of retaining their nuclear weapons, no matter how unstable the overall situation actually is, while denying the proliferation of them to other players. The political will to fully disarm their nuclear arsenals – which is essential for any successful negotiations – is not present.[108] This would only be present if their security could be guaranteed by other means. *Ultimately, the only way this may be achieved is by powerful supra-sovereign institutions that are capable of robust peace-keeping, non-violent dispute resolution and war prevention.* This recognition was first forcefully made in the nuclear age with the 1955 (Bertrand) Russell–(Albert) Einstein Declaration pertaining to the threat of nuclear weapons. The Declaration, after explaining the absolute threat to humanity that nuclear war represented, went on to suggest:

> *'Here then is the problem we present to you, stark and dreadful and inescapable: Shall we put an end to the human race; or shall mankind renounce war ... the abolition of war will demand distasteful limitations on national sovereignty.'*[109]

Both of the leaders of this Declaration recognized that a new and powerful supra-sovereign body must be created to control the possibility of an exchange of weapons of mass destruction.[110] Such a body would thus guarantee against the primary threat to global security – that of conflict between heavily armed states.[111] This body would also have to prevent the second major threat to security (which neither Russell nor Einstein predicted), which is the demilitarization of conflict, where warfare has become primarily internal within countries, as opposed to between them.

Despite the merit (and possible legality)[112] involved in this suggestion, the way that the global community is currently constructed suggests that any such powerful supra-sovereign body is highly unlikely.[113] This conflict between need and reality can already be seen in the arms context, with something as necessary as effective verification of the compliance of international nuclear regimes. Such verification is critical to the achievement and maintenance of a nuclear weapon-free world.[114] However, distinct questions are being raised over how far verification processes can be pursued.

Early arms control agreements such as the CTBT and the SALT agreements could be verified by technical equipment outside the superpower countries and through overhead surveillance. However, new agreements seeking to control further types of nuclear, conventional and chemical weapons all present problems that require additional verification measures which go beyond those which were adequate in the past.[115] That is, 'highly intrusive verification' is required which is often both expensive and a challenge to national sovereignty. Such challenges are unpalatable to many states.[116] This is not surprising, as many aspiring nuclear states (such as North Korea and Iraq) have already shown a willingness to actively deceive the international community in their pursuit of nuclear weaponry. Even the established superpowers have shown either active disregard[117] or manipulative intent to alter international arms control treaties that they have signed.[118]

CONCLUSION

War and the preparation for war is the antithesis of any meaningful form of sustainable development. This antithesis is found in the diversion of scarce financial resources from other needy areas to military budgets, right through to the actual threat or manifestation of war.

The threat of Armageddon has receded since the end of the Cold War. However, despite previously unknown opportunities to take the already impressive arms reductions even further and make the world even safer, these steps have not been taken. Moreover, the end of the 20th century saw two monumental failures with the refusal of the US Senate to ratify the CTBT, as well as the failure of the Non-proliferation Treaty to give either a timetable or specific commitments for reduction. These failures can only act as encouragement for states aspiring to possess weapons of mass destruction.

Additional efforts to control new types of weapons, from the biological to the chemical, right down to simple conventional armaments as deadly as the landmine, have proved to be limited. These limitations are a stark manifestation of one fact – that as the political world currently stands, nation states will continue to be very reluctant to relinquish any weaponry which could leave them at a disadvantage. This disadvantage is apparent because as yet there is no suitable supra-sovereign body that can offer and ensure a better type of security for both internal and external threats to the nation state. Accordingly, humanity is stuck, and sustainable development is hemmed in, by a system which is outdated, wasteful and directly threatens the very survival of the planet.

Chapter 8

Sovereignty

'*The Earth is one, but the world is not.*'[1]

THE BASIS OF INTERNATIONAL LAW

The absolute basis of international law is the 'deeply engrained' vision of 'larger than life' nations.[2] Nation states are seen as entities that are tangible, intelligent, independent and absolute. Implicit within this is the 'incubus' of sovereignty.[3] Although the idea of sovereignty has roots back to antiquity, it was only with the birth of modernity that it appeared with force. Around this point in 1583, Jean Bodin defined sovereignty as 'the absolute and perpetual power of a [monarchal] commonwealth'. He added: 'there is nothing greater on earth, after God, than sovereign princes'.[4] Likewise, Thomas Hobbes speculated, 'the State is unique only in having no superior'.[5] This idea of sovereignty remains the corner piece of international law.[6]

In practice this means that each state remains autonomous to the extent that it can make and execute policies for its own national interest. Essential to this is the necessity and centrality of the ideal of territorial sovereignty. For our purposes, territorial sovereignty includes the right to, and unrestricted use and control of, natural resources. This means that for all practical purposes nations may effectively 'own' or control certain resources that are situated in their territories.

Post-Second World War references to the concept of permanent sovereignty of a state over its natural resources occurred during the debates on human rights in the United Nations.[7] In 1952, the UNGA adopted a resolution recognizing that to achieve economic development and self-determination, states have the 'right to freely use and exploit their material wealth and resources'.[8] In 1962, the UNGA passed Resolution 1803, which stressed the importance of permanent sovereignty over natural resources.[9] Resolution 1803 was the first of a series of resolutions adopted on the topic of 'permanent sovereignty over natural resources'.[10] Prominent later examples included Article 2 of the United Nations 1974 Charter of the Economic Duties and Rights of States, which recorded, 'Every State has and shall freely exercise full and permanent sovereignty, including possession, and the use and disposal, over all its wealth, natural resources and economic activities.'[11]

Sovereignty over natural resources is particularly important to Southern countries. This is because of quests for independent control, a recognition of the leverage that sovereignty gives in an age of interdependent concerns, and fears of international regimes that could divest them of what they believe is 'theirs'.[12]

SOVEREIGNTY AND INTERNATIONAL ENVIRONMENTAL LAW ISSUES

Most modern international environmental documents and pronouncements reaffirm the sovereignty of states over their natural resources.[13] For example, Principle 2 of the 1992 Rio Declaration on Environment and Development recognizes that:

> *'States have in accordance with the Charter of the United Nations and the principles of international law, the sovereign right to exploit their own resources pursuant to their own environmental and developmental policies.'*[14]

This principle is recorded in a multitude of international environmental documents.[15]

SOCIAL ECOLOGY AND SOVEREIGNTY

Social ecology begins with the observation that sovereignty is a political creation. Such a concept is determined by social and not geographical considerations. Accordingly, when an issue is recognized as being important enough, sovereignty can be radically re-arranged – to make it fit what is needed.

In this regard, what is needed is a complete reorganization of the sovereign-based society; sovereignty is typically seen as inherently dangerous and as the antithesis of what ideologies seeking to 'liberate' are trying to achieve. With such views, social ecology mirrors anarchist theory on the question of nation states.[16] With special regard to the question of social and environmental sustainability, nation states are seen as either too small to handle both domestic and international environmental problems adequately, or too large to address the needs of a decentralized, democratic imperative.[17] Thus, as Anthony Giddens suggested, the nation state has become 'too small for the big problems of life, and too big for the small problems of life'.[18]

The solution to the above paradox is hinted at in the dictum, 'Think globally, act locally.' This ideal of global thinking is important as, although much Green theory argues for a decentralized, self-managing future, the powers of central government, or in this instance a powerful global government, may have to be strengthened to meet the demands of future international environmental needs. Such needs range from restructuring aspects of the international market economy through to creating and policing effective and equitable international environmental agreements. Such objectives will probably not be achieved in a world of self-interested actors who all seek differing goals.[19] Due to such a vast objective, many environmental theorists have suggested that a movement away from an international system, where the cornerstone of consent of every state always leads to the lowest common-denominator, needs to be contemplated.[20]

A POWERFUL INTERNATIONAL ENVIRONMENTAL BODY

The realization that there is an 'international institutions vacuum'[21] and that a new, or modified, international environmental body is needed to correct this imbalance has led to 'serious' calls for a powerful international legislative body.[22] However, the recognition of the need for a new and powerful international body to work in the international sphere for environmental considerations is not new. It was first mooted in 1910 at the Eighth International Zoological Congress in Graz.[23] However, it never eventuated and the idea did not appear again in substance until the 1972 Stockholm Conference on the Human Environment, where Maurice Strong argued that global environmental demands required new concepts of sovereignty, new codes of international law, and new international means of managing the oceans and the atmosphere for the benefit of all humanity.[24] He eventually went on to suggest, 'the international community may need to develop a new mission for the United Nations Trusteeship Council that includes guardianship of the global commons.'[25]

In 1980 the first Brandt report repeatedly talked of the increasing 'internationalization' of issues. It suggested that there was 'a need to review the state of international organisations; in some areas the existing ones may need to be supplemented to meet emerging concerns.'[26] The international environment was included in this context. The call for change in the international environmental arena was cautiously reiterated by the 1987 WCED.[27] However, it was not until 1989 at the UN that the former New Zealand Prime Minister Sir Geoffrey Palmer fully elaborated and advanced this line of thought. He argued that international law was too slow and too incremental to deal with the 'highly complex environmental problems of the future'. Consequently he suggested 'a conceptual leap forward in institutional terms' through the establishment of:

> *'a new organ in the United Nations system ... a body empowered to take binding decisions on global environmental issues. Nothing less than an institution with this status will command the necessary respect and authority to achieve what is required.'*[28]

In the same year, the G7 suggested that 'the establishment within the United Nations of a new [environmental] institution may be worth considering'.[29] More importantly in 1989, 17 Heads of State signed the Declaration of the

Hague that provided some indication of the magnitude of the necessary institutional innovations. These countries agreed to:

> 'The principle of developing, within the framework of the United Nations, new institutional authority, either by strengthening existing institutions or by creating a new institution ... which ... shall involve such decision making procedures as may be effective even if on occasion unanimous agreement has not been reached.'[30]

This body would be able to impose penalties for violations of its decisions. Disputes would be referred to the World Court for binding settlement. This Declaration did not advocate that the nation state would be superseded, but merely complemented by a more authoritative world political body. Nevertheless, this was still a radical document as it proposed a new institutional authority to combat global environmental problems, with decision-making and enforcement powers, and not requiring a unanimous vote for its decisions.[31]

Similar calls for 'strengthened international institutions',[32] 'a strengthened system of global governance'[33] and 'the need to further improve the existing international organisations and integrate the environmental dimension into the UN system'[34] were reiterated by international commissions prior to, and at (by individual countries),[35] the 1992 Earth Summit. Although nothing impressively innovative appeared from the Summit[36] after the event, it was suggested that 'A consciousness of One World [was] emerging above the din of individualistic and nationalistic self interest.'[37] However, this was not crystallizing into effective changes at the international level, and the final two international commissions of the mid-1990s reiterated the need for an 'apex body' that would provide leadership in economic, social and environmental fields,[38] as 'a political transition with new institutions and instruments of work is needed'.[39]

THE DECLINE OF THE NATION STATE SYSTEM

Implicit in many of the above views is what is commonly recognized as a *neo-liberal* view of the international system. This perspective emphasizes the changing nature of the international arena, its growing interdependence, a failure of individual states to solve international problems and an increasing pluralism through the infusion with new, non-state actors. These new actors from international organizations such as the Commission on Sustainable Development (CSD), through to the anathema of TNCs, or the 'promise' of NGOs, supposedly all alter the role and acting space of the nation state.[40] Therefore, far-reaching mechanisms for global management need to be considered[41] to meet the demands of a new age.[42]

The increasing globalization and interdependence which is believed to be radically changing the ground-rules by which sovereign states can operate is seen through economic, technological and ecological spheres. Such global interdependence radically alters the possibilities for sovereign national control.[43] The 1995 Commission on Global Governance expressed the position well: 'In an increasingly interdependent world, old notions of territoriality, independence, and non-intervention lose some of their meaning ... the principle of sovereignty must be adapted to recognise changing realities.'[44]

Although this trend has been evident since the beginning of the 20th century, it has been with ecological interdependence that this factor has perhaps been most 'dramatically emphasised'.[45] The nature of modern environmental problems is not compatible with concepts of national boundaries. This is because the ecological world has little to do with the territorial lines drawn on geographical maps.[46]

A second consideration in the justification for strengthened international environmental governance has been the recognition of the futility of unilateral actions to protect the environment from international concerns.[47] Such concerns typically require what the first Brandt report labelled as 'international solutions';[48] that is, no one nation can solve the problem alone. This reality may apply in both social and environmental contexts.[49]

This problem is increasingly complicated by the fact that unilateral action by some states to protect the environment may nowadays not only create domestic and international economic problems, but may also actually worsen the environmental problem they are trying to solve. Such results may occur due to delayed international impetus to meet the problem and through the associated creation of 'free riders', who make no effort to protect the environment themselves but benefit from the efforts of others.[50] This practice has a long historical record.[51] In a modern context this problem has developed a new twist through the imposition of economic costs on nations that attempt to protect the environment. For example, one of the main ways to deal with international environmental problems is through the correction of externalities through taxation, and some countries have acted unilaterally in this regard. However, as shown in Chapters 3 and 4, such options are becoming increasingly problematic. As such, the necessity for joint international actions becomes increasingly pertinent and forceful international bodies may be required to force international agreements.

The third reason why sovereign states are seen as declining in importance has to do with the traditional neo-liberal realization pertaining to the growth of non-state actors and their increasing recognition on the international stage. Allegedly, such bodies demonstrate that if the sovereign-driven system is not being eclipsed, then it is at least incapable of performing all the necessary functions for the international community at the beginning of the 21st century.[52] This realization is especially evident with NGOs. NGOs are growing at a rapid pace, with tens (if not hundreds) of thousands of international NGOs in existence.[53] Some of these NGOs command annual incomes in the tens of millions of dollars, and represent millions of people worldwide.[54]

These bodies, according to Agenda 21, 'play a vital role in the shaping and implementation of participatory democracy'.[55] Their importance is emphasized because of their ability to draw together and involve citizens from all levels of society to engage in forms of public participation, their ability to expose, challenge and change situations, and make sure that governments honour their agreements.[56] With such positive aspects behind them, it is not surprising that NGOs are receiving an increasing prominence in world politics. This prominence has ranged from direct participation (for some) in the creation of international environmental regimes, through to enhanced 'observer status' where previously there was none.[57]

Next to NGOs are the 'technical elites' or 'epistemic communities' of inter-state technical professionals. These bodies are at the core of a number of transnational networks of knowledge-based communities that are both politically empowered through their claims to exercise authoritative knowledge and motivated by shared casual and principled beliefs. Such bodies are commonly believed to foster epistemic solidarity across frontiers.[58]

INTERNATIONAL ENVIRONMENTAL LAW

The final justification for the call for a new and powerful institution has to do with the perceived failure of the sovereign-based world to manage the international environmental situation. This failure relates to a number of areas.

The first failure relates broadly to the inability of international environmental law to not only implement sustainable development, but also to broadly recognize the principle that development must be sustainable.[59] This alleged failure is despite the existence of hundreds of international, bilateral or multilateral treaties dealing with international environmental concerns,[60] and long-established precedents, such as that from the Trail Smelter arbitration which held that:

> 'No State has the right to use or permit the use of its territory in such a manner as to cause injury ... to the territory of another or the property or the persons therein.'[61]

This principle was duly recognized in international environmental law with Principle 21 from the 1972 Declaration on the Human Environment,[62] and has subsequently been repeated in a number of international environmental documents.[63] International environmental law also has precedents in respect of shared resources which incorporate the objectives of equity and conservation.[64] It further recognizes that states can take action against other states that are damaging the international commons.[65] Finally, there has also been a growth in international procedural requirements (ie information exchange) and conceptual schemas which reorganize the balance of power in environmental disputes (such as the precautionary principle and the polluter pays principle) and are believed to help lead to sustainable development.[66] Together, these principles are believed to make international environmental law suitable for the tasks ahead.

These developments in international environmental law have been primarily criticized, not because of what they proscribe (and associated problems of implementation, compliance and effectiveness), but because of the system that they are built upon. The problem is that *if* agreement cannot be reached with the *consent* of sovereign nations, then beyond moving to increasingly softer, lowest common-denominator types of consensus, little can be done to achieve progress.

The realists who support the sovereign-based system (and reject the above implications) retort with the following factors which suggest that moving to some form of world environmental governance is premature.[67]

The first point is that the process of some international environmental laws is already changing in some places, in that some international bodies *already* exercise certain powers and set international standards. In some cases these bodies, which were set up to implement treaties and which are composed of representatives of member states, can agree to set standards by a two-thirds majority, rather than a unanimous vote.[68] Unquestionably, such a proposal is an important departure from the former rules on unanimity, which frequently stalled the progress of treaties.

The problem of non-compliance with international environmental law is also believed to be slowly worked around by moving away from traditional mechanisms. That is, in the past the problem has been that there has been little compulsory jurisdiction for settling disputes within multilateral environmental regimes. However, this has begun to change with a number of international regimes which now prescribe compulsory settlement of disputes between antagonists *within* the multilateral forum in question.[69]

Finally, the defenders of the status quo like to point out the existence of new international institutions which have placed sustainable development permanently on the international stage. The exemplar of this is the CSD, which was created to act as a follow-up to the Earth Summit, as well as to 'enhance international co-operation and rationalise the inter-governmental decision making capacity'.[70] As it currently operates, the CSD has 'catalysed new action and commitments'[71] as well as monitoring progress on Agenda 21, including making governments and international institutions 'accountable to representatives of civil society'.[72] It also provides a forum for 'dialogue on priority issues of concern'[73] and makes recommendations to the UNGA.

Against the above position is the fundamental realization that international law, in a world of all-powerful sovereign states, is an oxymoron. This can be seen in a number of areas.

The central concern is that there is currently no international legislature which can force or oblige any nation state to become a party to a particular treaty or bring a matter to international adjudication. Such actions require the *consent* of the states concerned. Thus the overall utility (or willingness)[74] of bodies such as the International Court of Justice (ICJ) as a method to resolve international environmental disputes should not be overrated.[75] Despite the growth in ICJ activity in this area of international law,[76] the fundamental point remains that the ICJ does *not* possess compulsory jurisdiction over states that may choose to violate. This very problem led the WCED to call for a method of 'binding settlement' as a last resort to avoid prolonged disputes and possible serious environmental damage, and also to encourage and provide an incentive for all parties to reach agreement within a reasonable time.[77] This idea was also raised in Agenda 21, which called for an 'expanded role for the International Court of Justice'.[78] Finally, the Commission on Global Governance was adamant that the rule of international law must be respected and the authority of the ICJ compulsory.[79] However, as the international arena currently operates, these demands remain far from becoming a reality.

Even if the ICJ or similar bodies did have compulsory jurisdiction, there are still distinct difficulties in terms of which countries would be willing to initiate such actions as well as concerns pertaining to the adversarial process as a way to enforce international environmental law.[80] These concerns range from the difficulties of the adversarial method, problems of causation, defining 'unreasonable' behaviour,[81] and overt lacunae within international law which allow for incidents like Bhopal to occur without adequate redress.[82] The current situation on international environmental law was well summarized by the CSD in 1997:

> '*On the national level, implementation of international treaties in the field of sustainable development through national law remains piecemeal... Complete compliance with international treaties on sustainable development has not been attained. Factors contributing to this deficiency include lack of political will.*'[83]

The bottom line of this area is the possible refusal of states to contribute towards the growth of international environmental law. Due to such limitations, *nations are ultimately free to choose to violate, or simply withdraw from, international arrangements if they no longer consider them to be in accordance with their ultimate interests.*[84] This reality was starkly demonstrated when the standing of the ICJ was challenged by the actions of both France[85] and the USA.[86] In both instances, two of the most powerful nations on the planet refused to be bound by the ICJ when it became obvious that the Court would deliver decisions that could be detrimental to their interests. Moreover, the growth of the new international tribunals within international environmental law have to be seen in the same light. That is, at base, these organizations are ultimately nothing more than the creations of sovereign states. These institutions exist below sovereign states, not above them.

Aside from the possibility that states may change their mind about being bound by international law, there is the related problem that they may also decline to participate in the creation of it. A good example of this is tropical deforestation, where concern with this specific environmental problem led some Northern countries to suggest that inroads be made into the sovereignty of the countries where these tropical forests are found, so as to protect them. Such realizations have been continually and forcefully resisted by the heavily forested countries.[87] Accordingly, the international documents that have been created in this area contain minimal substantive duties or obligations. These soft obligations reflect what is acceptable to the most reticent signatory.[88]

The other area where international environmental law has had difficulties has been with the protection of the international commons. The commons are the areas of the planet which are owned by no single state. In such a situation, as the WCED noted, 'Traditional forms of national sovereignty raise particular problems in managing the "global commons" and their ecosystems.' Although the Commission noted that 'Some progress has been made' in this area, they noted that 'much remains to be done'.[89] Eight years later, the 1995 Commission on Global Governance noted that, 'What is becoming apparent is the lack of any consistent approach and oversight of the global commons ... one body should exercise overall responsibility.'[90] The same conclusion was reiterated in 1996 by the Independent Commission on Population and Quality of Life.[91]

The traditionally held solution to this problem was believed to be in classifying such areas as 'common heritage' where they will be governed for the good of all nations, with no one nation being able to claim ownership or exploit them.[92] Such a classification is a distinct negation of claims of national sovereignty. This idea, was suggested in a broad sense in the 1969 UN Declaration on Social Progress and Development, which suggested:

> *'Social progress and economic growth require recognition of the common interests of all nations in the exploration, conservation, use and exploitation, exclusively for peaceful purposes and in the interests of all mankind, of those areas of the environment such as outer space and sea-bed and ocean floor and the subsoil thereof, beyond the limits of national jurisdiction, in accordance with the purposes and principles of the Charter of the United Nations ... in order to supplement national resources available for the achievement of economic and social progress and development in every country, irrespective of its geographical location, special consideration being given to the interests and needs of the developing countries.'[93]*

The idealism of this paragraph materialized in the term 'common heritage', which appeared in a number of international documents, such as those pertaining to Outer Space,[94] Antarctica,[95] and the ocean floor. It is with the last area that the principle was most fully stated. The UN Convention on the Law of the Sea (UNCLOS) stated:

> *'The Area and its resources are the common heritage of mankind. No State shall claim or exercise sovereignty or sovereign rights over any part of the Area or its resources... All rights in the resources of the Area are vested in mankind as a whole ... the*

> *Authority shall provide for the equitable sharing of financial and other economic benefits derived from the area.*[96]

This idea of a common heritage does not invoke a legal phenomenon which is clearly understood in international law. It is a moral or political aspiration which has *no* independent legal content.[97] This has been demonstrated in a number of areas. The foremost example of this has been with the classification of the deep seabed as a common heritage for all.

The central difficulty in this area was one of ideology. This difficulty came to a climax with the devout ideological views of the Republican and Conservative administrations that came to power in Northern countries in the 1980s. For example, former President Reagan classified the International Seabed Authority (as set up by UNCLOS III, to manage the commons of the ocean floor) as an international socialist forum. Former presidential aides called the UNCLOS negotiations 'history's greatest rip-off' and warned of 'ideological surrender to a super-OPEC in minerals ... operated under the United Nations and dominated by the world's socialist nations.'[98] The mining aspect of the Convention was then 'Deemed to be against the economic, social, political and philosophical beliefs of the American system, and as such, against the national interests of the United States.'[99] Hence, the 'sound principles of capitalism, or good business' were given absolute priority over 'basic charity'.[100] With such principles in mind, the USA created an alternative international framework for the development of deep sea mining, guided by market forces.[101] Such alternative arrangements eventually came to succeed the offending parts of the Law of the Sea Convention. The eventual success in getting the Convention to recognize free market principles and move away from any powerful internationalist controls allowed the USA to view the 1994 revised document without the same level of antagonism as in the past (although they have still not signed).[102]

The difficulties that the common heritage principle caused for the Law of the Sea, was also replicated with the 1979 Agreement Concerning Activities of States on the Moon and Other Celestial Bodies (which the USA also refused to accept).[103] Due to such problems, the trend is now away from placing international concerns within the 'common heritage' ambit and more towards classification[104] of international environmental issues as 'common concern'[105] or 'common resources'.[106] Such moves are implicitly against any attempts to internationalize the ownership of the environment.[107] This conclusion has already been played out within the questions of Antarctica[108] and biological diversity.[109]

INTERDEPENDENCE, PLURALISM AND REALISM

The overt pursuit of national self-interest is known within the theories of international politics as realism or power politics. At its hardest edge, this position suggests that the only thing that matters to the nation state is the pursuit and protection of its own power. Accordingly, all ideas of interdependence, pluralism and a willingness on the part of nation states to cede sovereign power to international bodies are nothing more than charades. To make such a statement, it is essential to clarify some difficulties.

The community of nations is so-called because of the common occupancy of the Earth and increasing interdependencies, not because of shared assumptions or expectations. There are large and basic areas of human experience and value where no consensus exists and some in which open hostility is the norm. Patterns of transactions may indicate a growing togetherness, but political actions and economic systems are often at variance and reflect large schisms within international society. In this regard, it should be recognized that a large amount of the literature on the 'growing unity of the world' confuses interdependency with interconnectedness, suggesting by inference that interrelationships between nations imply beneficial interdependencies. This is a mistake and the idea of 'community of nations' is more an apparition than a reality.[110] For example, as the 1990 South Commission stated with regard to the North–South divide:

> 'Global interdependence is not symmetrical: the South is not an equal partner of the North, but is in a position of subordination. In international economic relations the South is not allowed a fair share but is exploited. So far from participating in decision-making at the world level, it is in fact excluded. It has little influence on its external environment; it is by and large at its mercy.'[111]

These aspects have been elaborated on in many of the previous chapters of this book. In such situations, certain traits that are seen as interdependence are better viewed as co-dependence. This is where policies that affect others are unilaterally determined, a relationship of inequality exists, and exchanges are mediated by powerful institutions and shaped by governments with quite exclusive bases of power.[112] In such a situation, these interconnections have *not* made the state less important. Rather, the state has reinforced its position of dominance.[113]

Just as there has been confusion with the idea of interdependence, so too has there been with the suggestion of the supposed pluralism of the international system in allowing new actors to emerge, such as NGOs. Here, it should be recognized that these communities often have only a marginal influence in the international area because of an overt unwillingness of nation states to yield too much control to anything other than themselves.[114] If states do decide to yield power, a close scrutiny of the institution to whom the power is yielded is necessary, as there is a diametrical opposition between yielding a little power to the WTO and yielding it to Friends of the Earth, or for that matter, the ICJ.[115]

In this regard, it must be recognized that state antagonism against NGOs is, despite their co-option into certain pockets of dialogue, often still overt.

This may range from international terrorism on the part of states (such as with the French government and Greenpeace's *Rainbow Warrior*)[116] through to the more common 'marginalization' of NGO positions at many international forums or within international institutions (such as those under the Bretton Woods rubric).[117] Thus, as the CSD noted in 1997:

> '*Both national and international non-governmental organisations ... feel that their growing role and contribution in environmental and other economic and social fields is not matched by equal growth in financial, political and technical support from Governments and international organisations.*'[118]

It is also important to recognize that the term 'NGO' has many uses and connotations. It is difficult to characterize the entire phenomenon, as there is often a failure to recognize the extreme diversity in the global NGO community. This diversity derives from differences in size, duration, range and scope of activities, ideology, philosophy, cultural background, power, organizational structure and legal status. With such diversity, it should not come as a surprise that not all NGOs are 'friendly' towards the methods that are ultimately needed to protect the environment. Indeed, distinct disputes, as well as a litany of failures on the part of many NGOs, lie beneath the simplistic facade that all NGOs are 'good', successful in their objectives, and are all seeking the same ends.[119]

Finally, the suggestion that new international environmental bodies may be just around the corner needs to be critically examined. As it stands, UNEP is distinctly hemmed in with a restricted operational mandate and small budget,[120] while simultaneously, the CSD has been deliberately excluded from direct policy dialogue. Moreover, the CSD lacks both the ability to make binding decisions and its own financial resources to fund programmes.[121] This drive to create a new powerful environmental body was again avoided at Earth Summit II, where the need for institutional rearrangement in this area was restricted to calls for greater coordination of environmental concerns within the UN ambit.[122]

Such proposals have been continually defeated because of the overt power these bodies could come to possess over nation states.[123] Such a body is perceived to be, according to Al Gore, 'both politically impossible and practically unworkable'.[124] This refusal to hand over real power to such bodies must be seen in light of the efforts made by a number of countries to move away from bodies that could detrimentally affect them. Although this is a problem with many Southern countries, it is also a distinct problem with many Northern countries who have, in places, moved away from international forums.[125] Many of these countries have attempted to keep the UN in check and reform it, so as not to allow it to continue its populist pressures and, through group action, demand structural changes to the world economy. To achieve these last two objectives, many Northern countries have attempted to shift the centre of gravity through economic control to the Bretton Woods institutions with which they hold much more power and control.[126]

CONCLUSION

The world is becoming increasingly interdependent. This is being manifested in a number of areas, but none more so than in the context of international environmental issues. Many people and organizations, when linking this interdependence with the growth of a number of non-state actors and the failure of international environmental law to meet the expectations of a new age, have called for a radical revision of the way the international world works. In essence, they have called for various forms of powerful international bodies to govern and control these issues. Moreover, in many areas, it appears that these concerns are being listened to, and progress has been made in expanding the way that the international community appears to be working.

However, when all of the supposed progress in this area is deconstructed, it becomes easy to be sceptical of how much has changed. That is because there is a *structure* within international environmental relations which goes much deeper than the rhetoric of sustainable development and framework treaties. It is this structure which has been instrumental in creating the gap between the burgeoning hundreds of international environmental laws and the actual condition of the international environment – perhaps one of the largest contradictions of our time.

The central problem in this context is that although attitudes towards sovereignty may have been softened in some instances, the fundamental reality that the international environmental system is without effective governance remains. The preference for soft law, the failure to accept binding jurisdictions of international courts, and the marginalization of all actors other than sovereign states, all point towards the fact that the status quo has not really changed. This situation was well concluded in UNEP's 1997 *Global Environmental Outlook* report which noted, when speaking of the general global failure to achieve sustainability, that 'Global governance structures and global environmental solidarity remain too weak to make progress a worldwide reality.'[127]

Conclusion

At the beginning of the 21st century, few people would argue that there is no environmental problem. Although argument would exist over the extent of the problem and how to deal with it, it is now largely taken as given that a problem of some proportion exists. The prima facie solution to this problem is sustainable development. However, it has been my contention that this ephemeral term has allowed the (green) wool to be pulled over the eyes of most people involved in the debate. The overall difficulty is that the epicentre of the entire development structure and the vast underpinnings of the debate are being sidestepped or manipulated. The critically important questions – ones which would call into question the legitimacy of the system itself – have not been asked, or have been answered in a way which suits and does not hinder the status quo. The critical questions that are at the centre of any meaningful form of sustainable development relate to economic growth, market structure, free trade, aid, debt, security and sovereignty.

Growth, as manifested in all of its diverse forms, is an essential part of most conventional ideologies. It is also now considered intrinsic to the quest for sustainable development. The idea of limits to how far humanity can grow, both in terms of numbers and their effect on the environment, has been traditionally dismissed. However, over the past 20 years the realization has grown that there may indeed be physical limits to growth which humanity may be facing; not necessarily those to do with static resources, but more to do with the absorption capacity of the environment. On the traditional Malthusian question of whether humanity will be able to feed the forthcoming doubling of world population, the commentators and international institutions remain divided.

The above realizations have begun to force the international community to consider ways of lowering human impact on the environment; firstly, through reducing consumption and, secondly, by reducing population growth. Unfortunately, both directions have, to date, proved largely fruitless.

The difficulty with current attempts to reduce consumption is twofold. Firstly, it is focusing on ideals of efficiency, and getting 'more for less'. The overall question of whether to consume or not is steadfastly avoided. Rather, the misplaced assumption remains that consumption itself is not the problem. However, even this very restricted approach to blunting the edges of consumption is restricted by the continuing failure to set international goals or targets about how to achieve the desired efficiencies. This failure to even consider if consumption itself is the central difficulty feeds into the second issue, which is that the considerations of reducing the impacts of consumption are only placed on Northern countries. This myopia will radically adjust itself as Southern countries soon eclipse Northern countries with their overall impact on the environment.

The second area, where the international community has been struggling for 25 years, has been in efforts to reduce population growth. Here, despite slow progress towards actually recognizing that population growth can directly contribute towards environmental problems, specific mandates or goals (beyond trying to achieve universal access to contraception) of what are sustainable levels of population remain off the international agenda.

The failure to confront growth is partly because of its intimate connection with economic liberalism, which has returned to the global community with a force that few would have predicted 30 years ago. Within this ethos, new types of instruments and emphases within the market economy have been brought to bear upon environmental issues. From this perspective, it is argued that once governmental subsidies and environmental externalities which have negative environmental results have been removed, then a perfectly functioning free market will secure positive environmental objectives.

Once these impediments have been removed, then the conscience of the consumer and the corporation can be relied on to direct the market towards environmentally protective choices through consumer directives, and/or through behaviour designed to maximize the economic self-interest of both. Self-interest is believed to be most fully maximized in a world where individuals own the environment, or have a direct interest in its preservation.

Many of these goals are laudable, and those who focus on the social side of sustainability agree that governmental subsidies which destroy the environment should be removed, and environmental externalities should be internalized and the importance of property as an incentive to conservation should be recognized. However, such an approach differs over the suggestion that all property must be private. Rather, it is suggested that common property regimes may be just as effective, if not more effective, than private property. Moreover, it may be necessary to actually redistribute private property to both suitable individuals and communities. This is the antithesis of the neo-liberal approach. Likewise, despite this recognition within much of the literature, it is barely recognized in international environmental law and policy.

Scepticism has also been introduced with questions of how far the market may be trusted to truly protect the environment. In this regard, it should be noted that the market does not necessarily promote nor even acknowledge equity, and without this, sustainable development can never be fully achieved. This failure to recognize goals of either social or environmental sustainability is because the market *ultimately* has only the objective to make profit. Because of this overriding goal, at times it is necessary that the market and the actors within are controlled and structured. The foremost example of this is with TNCs, which have only minimal constraints upon them in international law and policy.

The near complete freedom of TNCs and the fullest extent of the free market are manifested in free trade. Such a global market is not believed to be a danger to environmental concerns. If such effects do exist, then it is suggested that these must be dealt with within multilateral settings, away from the possibility of unilateral, trade discriminating measures.

Unfortunately, whether the international free trade system which the world is currently embracing will lead to environmental and social sustainability is far from given, and it appears highly possible that it is actually leading in the opposite direction. This is because the current regime of free trade is radically distanced from its theoretical roots, and revolves much more around power than equity and fairness. It is predicated upon actively excluding large parts of environmental externalities. It actively discourages unilateral acts to protect the international environment (despite the importance of these in the past) and seeks to foster multilateral scientific standards that are based on neither the precautionary principle nor democratic deliberation of these standards.

Moreover, free trade may also exacerbate the prerequisites of social and environmental sustainability in a number of ways. This may be done by encouraging the reckless use of domestic environmental resources, the allowance of environmental dumping in countries with low environmental standards, and the economic exploitation of the overall poverty of Southern countries – at the expense of Northern workers. That is, free trade as it currently works is based on commercial viability in an international market-place with few meaningful social or environmental markers.

With regard to the question of debt, the overall external debt situation of many Southern countries appears to be improving. However, this progress has been largely confined to middle-income Southern countries, while the more severely indebted countries continue to struggle with debts that are economically, socially and environmentally unsustainable. Despite the extreme costs that these forms of unsustainability cause, it currently appears unlikely that further bilateral debt reductions may be made. Additionally, although some progress has been made with commercial and multilateral debt, much remains to be achieved.

International financial assistance (aid) has a distinct role to play in moving towards a society which is both socially and environmentally sustainable. Moreover, it has a pivotal role to play in enticing a number of countries into international environmental agreements. However, as it currently operates, international financial assistance is commonly abused and misused by both donors and recipients alike. In this regard, movements towards goals where aid has to be spent on socially and environmentally deserving projects represented a good starting point. However, such attempts to delink financial assistance have failed, as have attempts to raise international aid flows to the requisite level of 0.7 per cent of GNP. Even where assistance has broadly kept up with its demands and promises, such as with the Global Environmental Facility, its ambit has been tightly curtailed to exclude addressing a number of 'structural' issues.

War and the preparation for war is the antithesis of any meaningful form of sustainable development. This antithesis is found in the diversion of scarce financial resources from other needy areas to military budgets, right through to the actual threat or manifestation of war.

Unquestionably, the threat of Armageddon has receded since the end of the Cold War. However, despite previously unknown opportunities before humanity to take the already impressive reductions even further and make the world even safer by complete nuclear disarmament of the existing nuclear powers, these steps have not been taken. The failure to achieve this has already left a number of nuclear and nuclear-aspiring states outside the realm of the new controls.

Moreover, additional efforts to control new types of weapons, from the biological to the chemical, right down to simple conventional armaments as deadly as the landmine, have proved to be limited. These limitations are a stark manifestation of one fact: that as the political world currently stands, nation states are very reluctant to relinquish any weaponry which could leave them at a disadvantage. This disadvantage is, above all other considerations, apparent because as yet there is no suitable supra-sovereign body that can offer and ensure a better type of security than that manifested by an outdated, wasteful and highly dangerous system.

The failure of the superpowers to disarm, and the overt risk that this continues to present, is only one manifestation of the contradiction between the sovereign state and the needs of an increasingly interdependent world. This interdependence is manifested in a number of areas, but none more so than in the context of international environmental issues. Many people and organizations, when linking this interdependence with the growth of a number of non-state actors and the failure of international environmental law to meet the expectations of a new age, have called for a radical revision of the way the international world works. In essence, they have called for various forms of powerful international bodies to govern and control these issues. Moreover, in many areas, it appears that these concerns are being listened to, and progress has been made in expanding the way that the international community appears to be working.

However, when all of the supposed progress in this area is deconstructed, it becomes very easy to be sceptical of how much has changed. That is because there is a *structure* within international relations which goes much deeper than the rhetoric of sustainable development and framework treaties. The central problem in this context is that although attitudes towards sovereignty may have been softened in some instances, the fundamental reality that the international environmental system is without effective governance (from leadership to compulsion) remains.

In a nutshell, the world is facing a potentially very large problem. However, beyond the rhetoric of sustainable development, it may well be that the community of nations is heading in the wrong direction. That is, if the objective is to solve the problem.

Notes and References

INTRODUCTION

1   Bookchin, M, *The Ecology of Freedom*. Cheshire Books, California, 1982.
2   Porritt, J, *Seeing Green*. Blackwell, London, 1986.

CHAPTER 1 DEVELOPMENT

1   For discussions of this, see Sachs, W, 'On the Archaeology of the Development Idea', *Ecologist* 20, 1990, 42; Sachs, W, 'Development: A Guide to the Ruins', *New Internationalist* 232, 1992, 4. Of course, it must be remembered that Truman was only one figure among many speaking of the fruits of modernization and technology from this period. For a fuller discussion of the paradigm of this epoch, see Rich, B, *Mortgaging the Earth: The World Bank, Environmental Impoverishment and the Crisis of Development*. Earthscan, London, 1994, 54–72.
2   Ekins, P, *A New World Order: Grassroots Movements for Global Change*. Routledge, London, 1992, 35. Sachs, 1990, supra n1, 42–43. Addo, H, 'Developmentalism: A Eurocentric Hoax, Delusion and Chicanery', in Chew, S C (ed), *The Underdevelopment of Development: Essays in Honour of Andre Gunder Frank*. Blackwell, Cambridge, 1996, 126–134.
3   For a full discussion of this idea and how it relates to environmental thinking, see Gillespie, A, *International Environmental Law, Policy and Ethics*. Oxford University Press, Oxford, 1997.
4   Shiva, V, 'Recovering the Real Meaning of Sustainability', in Cooper, E and Palmer, J A (eds), *The Environment in Question: Ethics and Global Issues*. Routledge, London, 1992, 187. Shiva, V, 'Development?', *Ecologist* 19, 1989, 3. Shiva, V, 'Development, Ecology and Women', in Plant, J, *Healing the Wounds: The Promise of Ecofeminism*. Green Print, London, 1989, 80, 82. Shiva, V 'Is Development Good for the Third World?', *Ecologist* 30(2), 2000, 22–26.
5   Winner, L, *Autonomous Technology: Technics Out-of-Control As a Theme in Political Thought*. Cambridge University Press, London, 1977, 100–01
6   Garcia-Amador, F V, *The Emerging International Law of Development*. Oceana, New York, 1990, 31–37, 66. Chowdhury, S R, *The Right To Development in International Law*. Nijhoff, Dordrecht, 1992, 35, 199–233.
7   Philadelphia Declaration, *American Journal of International Law* 38, 1944, 203.
8   Universal Declaration of Human Rights, proclaimed by UNGA Res 217(III), 10 December 1948. UNGA Official Records, 3rd Sess, Resolutions (A/810), 71, Article 25.
9   International Covenant on Economic, Social and Cultural Rights, UNGA Res 2200(XXI), 19 December 1966, Article II.

10   Charter of Economic Rights and Duties of States, UNGA Res 3281(XXIX), 12 December 1974.

11   'Right to Development', Annexed to UN Res 41/128, 4 December 1986, Article 1. Accordingly, 'The right to development is an inalienable human right...' Articles 2(3), 3 and 4 (ibid), emphasize that States have a duty to implement the right to development. An earlier UN Document which dealt with similar ideas, but did not invoke an actual right to development, was the 1968 Declaration on Social Progress and Development, UNGA Res 2542(XXIV), 24, UN GAOR Supp (No 30) at 49, UN Doc a/7630, 1969.

12   Paragraph 15 of the Preamble of the Declaration suggested 'efforts at the international level to promote and protect human rights should be accompanied by efforts to establish a new international economic order'. See also Article 3(3).

13   See Principle 10(1) and 10(3). Vienna Declaration and Program of Action, World Conference on Human Rights. Vienna, 14–25 June 1993. UN Doc A/CONF 157/24(Part I) at 20, 1993.

14   Report of the International Conference on Population and Development. A/CONF 171/13, 18 October 1994, Principle 3. See also paragraph 23 of the Habitat Agenda: Goals and Principles and Global Plan of Action. A/CONF 165/L, 6, Add 10, 14 June 1996. Note, however, that the United States retains its objection that development is not a right, but a goal. Nevertheless, it remains much easier to digest without the question of how development may be implemented being evident to the same degree as previously.

15   Rome Declaration on World Food Security. World Food Summit. 1996. This is reprinted in Report of the World Food Summit. FAO. WFS 96/REP. Paragraph 1. Note, this right was initially proclaimed at the 1974 World Food Conference, with 'the determination' of 'all governments' 'to eliminate within a decade hunger and malnutrition'. See Resolution V, Report of the World Food Conference, Rome, 5–16 November 1974, UN Doc E/CONF 65/20, 1975.

16   Istanbul Declaration on Human Settlements. A/CONF 165/L, 6, Add 10, Paragraph 1. Note, although the 'right to adequate housing' is reaffirmed in each part of the document, it is qualified by references such as 'progressive realization'.

17   International Bank for Reconstruction and Development, *The Basis of a Development Program for Colombia*. IBRD, Baltimore, 1950, xv.

18   Pearson Commission, *Partners in Development*. Pall Mall Press, London, 1969.

19   The first environmental difficulties caused by the conventional development process date back to at least the early 1970s. See Farvar, M T and Milton, J P, *The Careless Technology: Ecology and International Development*. Washington University Press, Washington, 1972. For an introduction of some critiques of the development crisis, see Trainer, T, *Developed to Death: Rethinking Third World Development*. Green Print, London, 1989, 3, 51–56. Trainer, T, *Towards A Sustainable Economy: The Need For Fundamental Change*. Carpenter, Sydney, 1996, 26–35, 60–65, 107. Trainer, F E, *Abandon Affluence*. Zed, London, 1989, 7, 115–134. Riddell, R, *Ecodevelopment*. Gower, Aldershot, 1981, 146–47. Sen, G and Grown, C, *Development Crisis and Alternative Visions*. Earthscan, London, 1988, 15–25. Adams, D M, *Green Development: Environment and Sustainability in the Third World*. Routledge, London, 1990, 172–179, 201. Norgaard, R, *Development Betrayed: The End of Progress and a Co-Evolutionary Revisioning of the Future*. Routledge, London, 1994, 1–10, 58–60, 120–121, 126. Friedman, J, *Empowerment: The Politics of Alternative Development*. Blackwell, Cambridge, 1994, 5–6. Engel, J R and J G (eds), *The Ethics of Environment and Development: Global Challenge, International Response*. Belhaven, London, 1990, 21–27, 29–31, 38, 145. Chatterjee, P and Finger, M, *The Earth Brokers: Power, Politics and World Development*. Routledge, London, 1994, 3–9. Schrijvers, J *The Violence of Development: A Choice for Intellectuals*. University of Amsterdam, Amsterdam, 1993, 11, 9–12, 20, 33. Goldsmith, E, 'Is Development the Solution or the

Problem?', *Ecologist* 15, 1985, 210, 214. Lohmann, L, 'Whose Common Future?', *Ecologist* 20, 1990, 82. Rees, W E, 'The Ecology of Sustainable Development', *Ecologist* 20, 1990, 19, 22. Sachs, W, 'Resisting Development Monoculture', *Ecologist* 21, 1991, 186.

20 WCED, *Our Common Future*. Oxford University Press, Oxford, 1987, 2. For similar comments to this in 1990, see the South Commission, *The Challenge to the South*. Oxford University Press, Oxford, 1990, 35.

21 The word 'crisis' is from the Istanbul Declaration, supra n16, Paragraph 4. The word 'civilization' is from UNICEF, *State of the World's Children: 1995*, Oxford University Press, Oxford, 1995, 3.

22 Copenhagen Declaration on Social Development. A/CONF 166/PC.L.22. Paragraph 15.

23 Rome Declaration, supra n15, Paragraph 3. The figure of 12 million children is from UNICEF. *The State of the World's Children: 1998*. UNICEF, New York, 1998, 2.

24 UNDP, *Human Development Report 1999*. Oxford University Press, Oxford, 1999, 2–3. Similar figures may also be ascertained from the UNDP reports for 1996, 1997 and 1998. See also Commission on Sustainable Development, 1997. Overall Progress Achieved Since UNCED. E/CN.17/1997/2, Paragraphs 9, 14, 20. Commission on Sustainable Development, 1997. Overall Progress Achieved Since UNCED: Combating Poverty. E/CN.17/1997/2/Add.2. Paragraphs 24–27. United Nations, *Critical Trends: Global Change and Sustainable Development*. UN, New York, 1997, 50–61. World Bank, *Poverty Reduction and the World Bank: Progress and Challenges in the 1990s*. World Bank, Washington, DC, 1996, 1–12. The Report of the Independent Commission on Population and Quality of Life, *Caring for the Future*. Oxford University Press, Oxford, 1996, 18–28. With regard to the increasing numbers of poor people at the end of the 20th century, see World Bank, 'World Bank Warns Global Poverty Fight Failing', Press Release 2000/059/S. World Bank, Washington, DC.

25 UNDP, *Human Development Report 1997*. Oxford University Press, Oxford, 1997, 1–5. UNDP, 1996, supra n23, 3–4. UNDP, 1999, supra n23, 4. Moreover, the 200 most wealthy people on the planet more than doubled their net worth in the four years leading to 1998, to US$1 trillion.

26 See WHO, *The World Health Report 1995: Bridging the Gaps*. WHO, Geneva, 1995, 1–2, 31–32, 38–39, 63. UNDP, *Human Development Report 1995*. Oxford University Press, Oxford, 1995, iii, 3. UNICEF, supra n21, 4–6.

27 Wolfensohn, J, *Rethinking Development: Challenges and Opportunities*. Remarks at the Tenth Ministerial Meeting of UNCTAD. 16 February 2000. (Available from the World Bank, Washington, DC.)

28 International Commission on Peace and Food, *Uncommon Opportunities: An Agenda For Peace and Equitable Development*. Zed, London, 1994, 163.

29 Dowdeswell, E, *Statement at the Oslo Conference on Consumption*, UNEP Speech 1995/1, 1995a, 2. Dowdeswell, E, *Speech to the World Summit for Social Development*, UNEP Speech 1995/3, 1995b. This view is not accepted by all people. For a defence of the traditional view, see Stiglitz, J E, 'International Development: Is It Possible', *Foreign Policy*, 1998, 138–151.

30 International Development Strategy for the First United Nations Development Decade, UNGA Res 1710(XVI), 1960. International Development Strategy for the Third United Nations Development Decade, UNGA Doc A /RES/35/56, Point 72, 1980. This echoed the earlier Lima Declaration and Plan of Action on Industrial Development and Co-operation which urged Southern governments to 'accelerate industrialization', Doc ID/B/155, Add 1, 14 April 1975.

31 Article 17, UNGA Declaration on Social Progress and Development in 1969, UNGA Res 2542(XXIV), 1969. The Declaration went on to call for 'economic growth rate targets ... high enough to lead to a substantial acceleration of their rates of growth'. re, Article 23(a).

32   Brandt Commission, *North–South: A Program for Survival*. Pan Books, London, 1980, 48. This was as the Pearson Commission on Development had done 11 years earlier. Pearson Commission, *Partners in Development*. Pall Mall Press, London, 1969, 7.

33   Brandt Commission; supra n32, 23, 24.

34   Ekins, P, *A New World Order: Grassroots Movements for Global Change*. Routledge, London, 1992, 23, 29. Hunt, G, 'Is There a Conflict Between Environment and Development in the Third World?', in Attfield, R (ed), *International Justice and the Third World*. Routledge, 1992, 117, 123. Matsui, Y, 'The Road to Sustainable Development: Evolution of the Concept of Development in the UN', in Ginther, K (ed), *Sustainable Development and Good Governance*. Kluwer, Netherlands, 1995, 53–71.

35   Brandt Commission, *Common Crisis*. Pan, London, 1983, 20. Marshall, B, *Willy Brandt*. Cardinal, 1990, 125, cf. 133–135.

36   O'Riordan, T, 'The Politics of Sustainability', in Turner, R K (ed), *Sustainable Environmental Economics: Principles and Practice*. Belhaven, London, 1993, 37, 50–52. Redclift, M, 'Redefining the Environmental Crisis in the South', in Weston, J (ed), *Development and the Environment: Red or Green Alternatives The New Politics of the Environment*. Pluto, London, 1984, 50. Adams, 1990, supra n19, 51.

37   See Chapter 2 of this book.

38   UNGA Res 1831 XVII. 1962 UNGA Official Records, 17th Session; Supplement No 17, p21.

39   Article XIV; African Convention on the Conservation of Nature and Natural Resources. 'In the formation of all development plans, full consideration should be given to ecological ... factors', UNTS Vol 1001, No 14689, pp3–33.

40   United Nations Second Development Decade. UNGA Res 2626, at 39. UN Doc A/8028, 1970. As the preamble of the UNGA Res 2849, at 26, 7 December 1970, on Development and the Environment noted, 'Development plans should be compatible with a sound ecology'.

41   McNamara, R, 'Address to Stockholm Conference', in World Bank, *World Bank Report*. World Bank, Washington, DC, 1972, 8–12.

42   Founex Report, *Development and Environment* Reprinted as Annex I to UN Doc A/CONF 48/10. 1971.

43   Principles 13. See also principles 11 and 14 of the 1972 Stockholm Declaration, UN Doc A/CONF 48/14/Rev. 1(E. 73.II.A.14).

44   Consider, for some examples, Preamble; Charter of Economic Rights and Duties of States. UNGA Res 2200 (XXI) December 19, 1966. See also points 2 and 4, OECD; Declaration of Environmental Policy, 1974, in Ruster, B and Simma, B (eds), *International Protection of the Environment*, Oceana, New York, 1980, Volume 1, 293. Resolution number 1, Second European Ministerial Conference on the Environment. Also in Ruster, Volume XVIII, 9172. Treaty for Amazonian Cooperation. 1978, in Kiss, A C (ed), *Selected Multilateral Treaties in the Field of the Environment*. UNEP, Kenya, 1982, Volume 1, 496.

45   World Conservation Strategy, 1980, Article XX. See also paragraph 3(b) of the title page, 'the main obstacle of achieving conservation ... [is] ... the consequent failure to integrate conservation with development'. Reprinted in *International Protection of the Environment*. Ibid, Volume XIII, 424.

46   Paragraph 3(b), ibid. See also Allen, R, *How to Save the World: Strategy For World Conservation*. Kogan Page, London, 1980, 7, 137–144.

47   Council on Environmental Quality, 'Global Future: Time to Act: Report to the President on Global Resources', reprinted in *Environmental Affairs* 9, 1980, 261–265, 281–282.

48   Brandt Commission, 1980, supra n32, 114.

49   This necessity was also recognized by point 41 of the International Development Strategy of the Third United Nations Development Decade. UNGA Doc A/RES/35/56.

50 Paragraph 6, World Charter for Nature. UNGA Res 37/7. UN. GAOR Supp No 51.
   UN Doc A/37/51, 1982. See also Wood, H W, 'The United Nations World Charter for
   Nature: The Developing Nations' Initiative to Establish Protections for the
   Environment', *Ecology Law Quarterly* 12, 1985, 977, 987–988.
51 Preamble, Regional Conventions for the Conservation of the Red Sea and the Gulf of
   Aden Environment. Jeddah, 14 February 1982. UN Doc UNEP/GG/INF II Rev. I, 1985,
   191–192. Preamble, Convention for the Protection, Management and Development of
   the Marine and Coastal Environment of the Eastern African Region. 1985. Nairobi, 21
   June 1985. (French) *Journal Officiel* 1989, 7728. Section 2, Arab League Declaration
   on Environment. *Environmental Policy and the Law* 16, 1986, 218. Articles 1 and 6 of
   the ASEAN Agreement on the Conservation of Nature and Natural Resources, 1985.
   Text in Burhenne No 985, 47. Also reprinted in Rummel-Bulska, I and Osafo, S (eds),
   Selected Multilateral Treaties in the Field of the Environment. Grotius, Cambridge,
   1991, 343–344.
52 WCED, 1987, supra n20, Principle 7.
53 Tickell, C, 'Diplomacy and Sustainable Development', in Angell, D J R, Commer, J D
   and Wilkinson, L N (eds), *Sustaining Earth: Response to Environmental Threats*.
   Macmillan, London, 1990, 172, 175. Caccia, C, 'OECD Nations and Sustainable
   Development', in Angell, 1990, 123–124. Perez de Cuellar, J, 'The United Nations
   System and Sustainable Development', in Angell, 1990, 164.
54 Perez de Cuellar, ibid, 164, 171.
55 G7 Economic Declaration. Toronto Summit. In *Environmental Policy and the Law* 18,
   1988, 106. G7 Economic Declaration. Summit of the Arch, Paris, 16 July 1989.
   Environmental Policy and the Law 19, 1989, 183. Paragraph 1, Kampala Declaration
   on Sustainable Development in Africa. *Environmental Law and Policy* 19, 1989, 222.
   'OECD Agreement to Link Environment and Economy', *Environmental Law and
   Policy* 21, 1991, 57. Note, however, that the OECD had been moving this way for a
   number of years. See the 'OECD Conference Summary', *Environmental Law and
   Policy* 13, 1984, 39.
56 Strong, M, 'ECO 92: Critical Challenges and Global Solutions', *Journal of
   International Affairs* 44, 1991, 287, 291.
57 Principle 3, *Rio Declaration on Environment and Development* UNCED Doc A/CONF
   151/5/Rev. 1. *International Legal Materials* 31, 1992, 877.
58 Article 3(4), 'The Parties have a right to, and should, promote sustainable
   development'. Framework Convention on Climate Change. A/AC. 237/18(Part II), Add
   1, 5 May 1992. See also paragraph C of the Preamble, and Article 1(b) of the
   Statement of Principles For A Global Consensus on the Management, Conservation and
   Sustainable Development of all Types of Forests. UNCED Doc A/CONF 151/6/Rev 1.
59 Rio Declaration, supra n57
60 Dowdeswell, E, 1995b, supra n29
61 Preamble, Paragraph 9 and Article 9. UNGA Declaration on Social Progress and
   Development in 1969. UNGA Res 2542(XXIV). This declaration not only placed the
   human person as the centre of development, it is also suggested that development was
   also about equity and social progress. For a useful discussion of the development of this
   approach, see Matsui, supra n34. 60–64. See also Sutcliffe, B, 'Development after
   Ecology', in Bhaskar, V (ed), *The North, The South and the Environment: Ecological
   Constraints and the Global Economy*. Earthscan, London, 1995, 232–244, 255.
62 United Nations Declaration on Development, supra n11.
63 Paragraphs 1 and 3, The Manila Declaration on People's Participation and Sustainable
   Development, Manila, 10 June 1989, recorded in Starke, L, *Signs of Hope: Working
   Towards Our Common Future*. Oxford University Press, Oxford, 1990, 80. With such
   a background, the first UNDP *Human Development Report 1990* (UNDP, New York,
   1990) opened with the lines: 'The real wealth of a nation is its people. And the purpose

of development is to create an enabling environment for people to enjoy long, healthy and creative lives. This simple but powerful truth is often forgotten in the pursuit of material and financial wealth'.

64   The idea of a socially aware alternative development can be traced back in international literature to the 1974 Cocoyoc seminar on environment and development, under the auspice of UNEP and UNCTAD. See the Cocoyoc Declaration: Patterns of Resource Use, Environment and Development Strategies, UN Doc A/C2/292, 1974.

65   See Ghai, D, *Development and Environment: Sustaining People and Nature.* Blackwell, Cambridge, 1994, 1, 5, 9–10.

66   'The ultimate goal of social development is to improve and enhance the quality of life of all people. It requires democratic institutions, respect for all human rights and fundamental freedoms ... empowerment and participation are essential for democracy, harmony and social development.' re: Program of Action of the World Summit For Social Development. Annex II of the Report of the World Summit For Social Development. A/CONF 166/9, Paragraph 1.7. The final Declaration stated: 'economic development, social development and environmental protection are interdependent and mutually reinforcing components of sustainable development'. Copenhagen Declaration, supra n22, Paragraph 6.

67   Overall Progress Achieved Since UNCED, supra n24, Paragraph 5.

68   See the Vienna Declaration and Program of Action, World Conference on Human Rights. Vienna, 14–25 June 1993. UN Doc A/CONF 157/24(Part I) at 20, 1993, Paragraphs 10 and 27.

69   See Article 21 of the Universal Declaration of Human Rights. UNGA Res 217 A(III), 10 December 1948. See also Article 25 of the International Covenant on Civil and Political Rights. UNGA Res 2200 A(XXI), 16 December, 1966. The importance of democracy has been reinforced by the United Nations following the end of the Cold War through its Support of the Efforts of Governments to Promote and Consolidate New or Restored Democracies. See documents, UNGA Doc A/49/713, 23 November 1994 and UNGA Doc A/52/334, 11 September 1997.

70   UNDP, *Human Development Report 1993.* Oxford University Press, Oxford, 1993, 21–28, 65–80.

71   WRI,UNEP,UNDP, *World Resources: A Guide to the Global Environment.* Oxford University Press, Oxford, 1996, xi, 103–104, 125–126. Dobson, A, *Green Political Thought.* Allen and Unwin, London, 1990, 93–97, 123. Bookchin, M, *The Ecology of Freedom.* Cheshire, California, 1982, 98–103. Bookchin, M, 'Ecology and the Left', in Chase, S (ed), *Murray Bookchin and Dave Foreman: Defending the Earth: A Dialogue.* South End, Boston, 1991, 54–57. Hempel, L C, *Environmental Governance: The Global Challenge.* Island Press, California, 1996, 219–223, 236–239. Paehkle, R C, 'Environmental Values and Democracy: The Challenge of the Next Century', in Vig, N J and Kraft, M E (eds), *Environmental Policy in the 1990s.* Congressional Quarterly Press, Washington, 1990, 349–363. Lauber, V, 'Ecology, Politics and Liberal Democracy', *Government and Opposition* 13, 1978, 199–217. Kane, M J, 'Promoting Political Rights to Protect the Environment', *Yale Journal of International Law* 18, 1993, 389, 396–99. Hartmann, J, 'Democracy, Development and Environmental Sustainability', in Fridtjof Nansen Institute (ed), *Green Globe Yearbook.* Oxford University Press, Oxford, 1992, 49–62. Sharp, R, 'Organising For Change: People Power and the Role of Institutions', in Holmberg, J (ed), *Policies for a Small Planet.* Earthscan, London, 1992, 39–48. Friedmann, 1994, supra n19, 30–36, 59, 72–80, 130–135. Doeleman, J, 'Democracy and Environment', *International Journal of Social Economics* 24, 1997, 105–127. McCloskey, H J, *Ecological Ethics and Politics.* Englewood Cliffs Publishers. New Jersey, 1983, 158–162. Johnston, R J, *Environmental Problems: Nature, Economy and State.* Belhaven, London, 1989, 120–121, 159–165. Commoner, B, 'Environmental Democracy is the Planet's Best Hope', in Plant, C and J (eds), *Green*

Business: Hope or Hoax? Green Books, Devon, 1991, 52–56. Redclift, M, 'Sustainable Development and Popular Participation', in Ghai, D and Vivian, J M (eds), *Grassroots Environmental Action: People's Participation in Sustainable Development*. Routledge, London, 1992, 23, 30–37. Note, however, that some Green theorists have no faith in democratic procedures. These theorists are often of the 'deep ecology' variety. This is an important dividing line from the more socially orientated views.

72 'Social ecology' is a body of theory which has sought to establish the political ground-rules for the establishment of a truly sustainable society. As a generalization, it has a strong link with anarchist precepts, and often seeks a synthesis with aspects of the philosophies of deep ecology.

73 Rousseau, J J, *The Social Contract*. Penguin, Harmondsworth, 1976, Book III, Chapters 1 and XV. See also the *Geneva Manuscript*. Penguin, Harmondsworth, 1976, Book II, Chapter III. *Emile*. Penguin, Harmondsworth, London, 1976, 34–36. Note that Rousseau was only one important theorist in this area. William Godwin, Charles Fourier, Pierre-Joseph Proudhon, Peter Kropotkin, William Morris and John Stuart Mill are also relevant.

74 Paehlke, R C, *Environmentalism and the Future of Progressive Politics*. MIT Press, Massachusetts, 1989, 145, 155–57, 346–251. Rahman, A, 'People's Self Development', in Ekins, P and Max-Neef, M (eds), *Real Life Economics: Understanding Wealth Creation*. Routledge, London, 1992, 165–170. Sale, K, *Human Scale*. Coward, New York, 1990, 490–501. Naess, A, *Ecology, Community and Lifestyle*. Cambridge University Press, Cambridge, 1989, 141–145. Kemp, P and Wall, D, *A Green Manifesto for the 1990s*. Penguin, Harmondsworth, 1990, 19–20, 171–186. Norgaard, 1994, supra n19, 136–157, 167–170. Ecologist, *A Blueprint For Survival*. Penguin, Harmondsworth, 1972, 50–53, 57, 62–63. Bahro, R, *Socialism and Survival*. Heretic, London, 1982, 62–74, 112–121. Goodin, R E, *Green Political Theory*. Polity, Cambridge, 1992, 124–131, 139–146. Kothari, R, 'Grassroots Development', in Woodhouse, T (ed), *People and Planet*. Green Books, Devon, 1987, 191–200. Esteva, G and Prakash, M S, 'Grassroots Resistance to Sustainable Development', *Ecologist* 22, 1992, 45, 50.

75 Carlie, M and Christie, I, *Managing Sustainable Development*. Earthscan, London, 1992, 81. See also Sale, supra n74, 352–391. Wall and Kemp, supra n74, 81.

76 UNDP, *Governance for Sustainable Human Development*. UN, New York, 1996. UNDP, *Reconceptualising Governance*. UN, New York, 1996. Bookchin, M, *Post Scarcity Anarchism*. Wildwood, London, 1974, 69, 68–75.

77 Baugh, G, 'The Politics of Social Ecology', in Clark, J (ed), *Renewing the Earth: The Promise of Social Ecology*. Green Print, London, 1990, 97–101. Max-Neef, M, 'Development and Human Needs', in Ekins, P and Max-Neef, M (eds), 1992, supra n74, 197–199. Bookchin, M, *Towards An Ecological Society*. Black Rose, Montreal, 1986, 42, 48, 80. Bookchin, supra n71, 336–341. Vivian, J M, 'Foundations for Sustainable Development: Participation, Empowerment and Local Resource Management', in Ghai, D and Vivian, J M, *Grassroots Environmental Action: People's Participation in Sustainable Development*. Routledge, London, 1992, 1–2, 14–17, 50, 53–54. Redclift, M, 'Sustainable Development and Popular Participation: A Framework For Analysis', Also in Ghai and Vivian, 23–27. Chambers, R, 'Sustainable Rural Livelihoods: A Key Strategy For People, Environment and Development', in Conroy, C and Litvinoff, M (eds), *The Greening of Aid: Sustainable Livelihoods in Practice*. Earthscan, London, 1989, 3–11. Redclift, M, *Sustainable Development: Exploring The Contradictions*. Routledge, London, 1987, 45, 154–162, 170, 250. Agarwal, A, 'Towards Green Villages', in Sachs, W (ed), *Global Ecology*. Zed, London, 1993, 242–249. Pearce, F, *Green Warriors; The People and Politics Behind the Green Revolution*. Bodley Head, London, 1991, 68–106. Schrijvers, 1993, supra n19, 39–50. Sale, 1990, supra n74, 38–39, 352–391, 505.

78   Chambers, R, 'Sustainable Rural Livelihoods', in Conroy and Litvinoff (eds), 1989, supra n77, 1–12. Brecher, J and Costello, T, *Global Pillage: Economic Reconstruction from the Bottom Up*. South End Press, Boston, 1994, 8–9, 28–29. Rich, supra n1, 274, 281, 284–285, 290–293, 306–307.
79   Brandt Commission, 1980, supra n32, 133.
80   See Chapter 18 of the *World Conservation Strategy*, supra n45. See also Allen, supra n46, 135.
81   WCED, 1987, supra n20, 8–9.
82   Ibid, 38, 62–63.
83   See for example, IUCN, *World Conservation Strategy for the 1990s*. IUCN, Gland, 1990, 137, 138, 156–157.
84   The Rio Declaration on Environment and Development, UNCED Doc A/CONF 151/5/Rev/1, 1992. See also Chapters 3, 11 and 14 of Agenda 21, UNCED Doc A/CONF 151/4, 1992.
85   Commission on Global Governance, *Our Global Neighbourhood*. Oxford University Press, Oxford, 1995, 35–37, 65–67.
86   Principle 4. Copenhagen Declaration, supra n22. See also paragraphs 1.8, 16 and 71 of the Program of Action of the World Summit for Social Development.
87   See paragraphs 115–118, 165 and 180–183 of the Habitat Agenda: Global Plan of Action: Strategies for Implementation, supra n14.
88   Independent Commission on Population and Quality of Life, 1996, supra n24, 312, 260–261.
89   See for example Kropotkin, P, *Fields, Factories and Workshops*. Swann, London, 1901, 213–218. A slightly later book was Lewis Mumford's *The Culture of Cities*. Secker, London, 1938.
90   See Schumacher, F, *Small is Beautiful*. Abacus, London, 1974, 47–50. Roszak, T, *Person/Planet: The Creative Disintegration of Industrial Society*. Gollancz, London, 1979, 36–38, 132–133, 241–270, 306. Bahro, R, *Avoiding Social and Ecological Disaster: The Politics of World Transformation*. Gateway, Bath, 1994, 1, 22, 87, 110, 233, 323, 326. Goldsmith, E, *The Way: An Ecological Worldview*. Rider, London, 1992, 288–291. Merchant, C, *Radical Ecology: The Search for a Livable World*. Routledge, London, 1992, 221–224. Sale, 1990, supra n74, 37, 394, 505. Albery, N and Peeters, Y (eds), *How To Save The World: A Fourth World Guide To The Politics of Scale*. Fourth World Research Trust, London, 1982, 18–21, 34, 329–333.
91   Mellor, M, *Breaking the Boundaries: Towards A Feminist Green Socialism*. Virago, London, 1992, 33–34. Goodin, 1992, supra n74, 151. Sale, 1990, supra n74, 192–208, 487. Ecologist, 1972, supra n74, 15. Goldsmith, supra n90, 288–291.
92   See paragraph 1.10. of the Program of Action from the Cairo Conference on Population, A/CONF 171/L1, 1994. See also the Habitat Action Plan, supra n14. Paragraph 55 and 109.
93   See WRI, UNEP, UNDP and the World Bank, *World Resources: A Guide to the Global Environment: The Urban Environment*. Oxford University Press, Oxford, 1996, 1–30, 57–80.
94   See for example, Ezcurra, E and Mazari-Hiriart, M, 'Are Megacities Viable? A Cautionary Tale From Mexico City', *Environment* 38, 1996, 7–15.
95   WHO, *Environmental Health in Urban Development*. Technical Report 807. WHO, Geneva, 1991, 2.
96   WRI,UNEP, UNDP and the World Bank, supra n93, x.
97   Bookchin, supra n77, 68, 104–06. Sale, supra n74, 38–39. Naess, supra n74, 143–145. Friedmann, 1994, supra n19, 11, 140–142, 158.
98   Ibid.
99   Lewis, M W, *Green Delusions: An Environmentalist's Critique of Radical Environmentalism*. Duke University Press, London, 1992, 91–95, 98–101. IUCN,

Caring For the Earth: A Strategy For Survival. Beazley, London, 1990, 79–85. McMichael, A J, *Planetary Overload: Global Environmental Change and the Health of the Human Species.* Canto, London, 1995, 259–290. Morris, D, 'Free Cities At Work', in Plant, 1991, supra n71, 133–136.

100 Cairo Conference, supra n92, Paragraphs 9.1–9.18.

101 Istanbul Declaration, supra n16, Paragraphs 5, 8, 12 and 15. Habitat Action Plan, supra n14, Paragraphs 102, 115–120, 128–136, 165, 180–182. WRI,UNEP, UNDP and the World Bank, supra n93, xi, 103–148.

102 See UNDP, *Human Development Report 1995.* Oxford University Press, Oxford, 1995, 2–4. Report of the Independent Commission on Population and Quality of Life, 1996, supra n24, 234–250, 311–312. WRI, UNEP and UNDP, *World Resources 1994–1995: A Guide to the Global Environment: People and the Environment.* Oxford University Press, Oxford, 1994, 43–61. Sontheimer, S, *Women and the Environment: A Reader.* Earthscan, London, 1988.

103 Principle 20 of the Rio Declaration recognizes 'Women have a vital role in environmental management and development. Their full participation is therefore essential to achieve sustainable development'. Rio Declaration, supra n57.

104 Cairo Conference, supra n92. Principle 4 and chapter IV.

105 Rome Declaration, supra n15. Paragraph 8. World Food Summit Plan of Action, supra n15. Objective 1, 1.3. See also the Habitat Conference, supra n14. Paragraph 82 and 119.

106 Fourth World Conference on Women, Beijing. Program of Action. A/CONF 177/20, Paragraph 36.

107 Paragraphs 248 and 251.

108 Bellamy, C, 'Women and the Environment', *Our Planet* 7, 1995, 6–8. See also OECD, *Gender Equality: Moving Towards Sustainable People-Centered Development.* OECD, Paris, 1995, 1–7.

109 Copenhagen Declaration, supra n22. Paragraphs 4, 7, 9, 16, 26. Commitments 2, 3 and 6. Action Plan, paragraphs 7, 8, 16, 18, 34, 35, 66–74. Report of the Fourth World Conference on Women. A/CONF 177/20, 17 October 1995, Paragraphs 3, 27 and 36. Habitat Agenda: Global Plan of Action, Paragraphs 55, 115–125, 165, 180. The Madrid Declaration and a Partnership For Growth and Development, UNCTAD IX, TD/377, 1996, Paragraphs 5–7. See the Rome Declaration on World Food Security, 1996, Paragraph 8. World Food Summit Plan of Action, supra n15, Objective 1 and 2.1. Cairo Conference, supra n92, Principles 2, 3, 4, 7, 10, Chapters 3.13, 3.15, 4.1, 11.1–11.2. It may be with this last issue, that of population, where the link between the empowerment of women, and the reduction in birth rates – as a perceived environmental 'good' – is most direct. See United Nations Population Fund. *Population Briefing Kit: 1995.* UNPF, New York, 1995, Section II.

110 See World Bank, *Annual Report 1999.* Oxford University Press, Oxford, 1999, 2.

111 Commission on Sustainable Development, 1997, 'Overall Progress Achieved Since UNCED: Financial Resources', E/CN.17/1992/2/Add 23, Paragraph 31. Steer, A, 'Overview: The Year in Perspective', *Environment Matters*, 1996, 5–6. For the difficulties in this area, see Chapter 6 of this book.

112 See Ranis, G, 'Defining the Mission of the World Bank Group', in Bretton Woods Commission (ed), *Bretton Woods: Looking to the Future.* World Bank. Washington, DC, 1994, 73–77. See also Brandon, K, 'Environment and Development at the Bretton Woods Institutions', in Bretton Woods Commission, 1994, 133–142.

113 McNamara, R, *The McNamara Years At the World Bank: Major Policy Addresses 1968–1981.* Johns Hopkins University Press, Baltimore, 1981, 193–206.

114 The importance and coordination of international organizations, such as the World Bank, with regard to environmental considerations was noted in Principle 25 of the

Stockholm Declaration, supra n43. At the Earth Summit, Agenda 21, Chapter 33, paragraph 1.3 acknowledged the importance of international organizations in achieving sustainable development. Agenda 21, supra n84. The Program for the Further Implementation of Agenda 21 in 1997 encouraged 'multilateral development banks ... to strengthen their commitments to supporting investment ... in a manner that jointly promotes economic growth, social development and environmental protection'. Program for the Further Implementation of Agenda 21, GA Res S–19/2, Annex, 28 June, *International Legal Materials* 36, 1997, 1639. Such perspectives were also recognized earlier by the banks themselves. For example, the 1980 *Declaration by International Banks on Environmental Policies and Procedures* which noted that 'International Development Assistance institutions have a responsibility to ensure the sustainability of the economic development activities financed by them', *International Legal Materials* 19, 1980, 524–525.

115 See World Bank, *Striking A Balance: The Environmental Challenge of Development.* Oxford University Press, Oxford, 1989, 9, 11. Goodland, R J A, 'The World Bank's Environmental Policy', *Hastings International and Comparative Law Review* 14, 1991, 811. Piddington, K, 'The Role of the World Bank', in Hurrel, A. and Kingsbury, B (eds), *The International Politics of the Environment.* Oxford University Press, Oxford, 1992, 212–218.

116 World Bank, *World Bank President Outlines A New Agenda*, News Release 97/1153, Washington, DC, 1996. See also World Bank Operations Policy Department, *The World Bank and Participation.* World Bank, Washington, DC, 1994. World Bank, *Learning from the Past: Embracing the Future.* World Bank, Washington, DC, 1994.

117 McNamara, R, *One Hundred Countries, Two Billion People: The Dimensions of Development.* Praeger, New York, 1973, 18–19.

118 McNamara, R, ibid, 8.

119 McNamara, R, ibid, 8. Indeed, on this count, McNamara suggested that 'current development programs are seriously inadequate'. *The McNamara Years*, supra n113, 194.

120 World Bank, *Annual Report 1999*, supra n110, 3–4. See also World Bank, *Poverty Reduction and the World Bank.* World Bank, Washington, DC, 1993, 4–8. Denny, C, 'World Bank in Surprise Policy U-Turn', *Guardian Weekly*, 6 July 1997, 19.

121 World Bank, 'Social Assessment', Environment Department, Dissemination Notes 36, World Bank, Washington, DC, 1995.

122 Rio Declaration, supra n57.

123 Nanda, V P, 'Human Rights and Environmental Considerations in the Lending Policies of International Development Agencies', *Denver Journal of International Law and Policy* 17, 1989, 29–39. Rich, B, 'The Cuckoo in the Nest: Fifty Years of Political Meddling By the World Bank', *Ecologist* 24, 1994, 8–14. Wilks, A, 'Evicted! The World Bank and Forced Resettlement', *Ecologist* 24(6), 1994, 225–229. Rich, supra n1, 84–106. Chatterjee, P, 'How to Waste $5 Billion A Year', *Guardian*, 6 November 1993, 143–148, 151–156. Werksman, J D, 'Greening Bretton Woods', in Sands, P (ed), *Greening International Law.* Earthscan, London, 1993, 65–84. Horta, K, 'The World Bank and the International Monetary Fund', in Werksman, J (ed), *Greening International Institutions.* Earthscan, London, 1996, 135–142. Watkins, K, *The Oxfam Poverty Report.* Oxfam, Oxford, 1995, 79–86, 103–104, 202–206.

124 This was a 150 per cent rise over the last ten years. Wapenhans, W, *Effective Implementation: Key to Development Impact.* World Bank, Washington, DC, 1992, 3. See also Wapenhans, W, *Report of the Portfolio Management Task Force, July 1, 1992.* World Bank, Washington, DC, 1992, 1, 4–8, 12, 14.

125 Rich, B, supra n1, 24–48, 113–140, 149–175. Friends of the Earth, *50 Years is Enough: 50 Years of World Bank Development Projects.* FOE, London, 1994. Friends of the Earth, *Financing Ecological Destruction: The World Bank and the International Monetary Fund.* FOE, London, 1988, 4–5.

126 Morse, B and Berger, T, *Sardar Sarovar: Report of the Independent Review. Morse Commission.* Resources Futures International, Ottawa, 1992, xxii–xxv, 233–34, 329, 336.

127 See United States Foreign Operations, Export Financing and Related Programs Appropriations Act 1993. Public Law 102–391, 6 October 1992.

128 See Report of the House/Senate Committee of Conference on HR2295, Report 103–267 of 28 September 1993. The document establishing the Inspection Panel can be found in International Bank for Reconstruction and Development 1993. 'Inspection Panel Operating Procedures, Including Executive Resolution', *International Legal Materials* 34, 1995, 503–510. See also Bradlow, D D, 'The World Bank's Independent Inspection Panel', *Indian Journal of International Law* 33, 1993, 59–71.

129 As created under World Bank Resolution No 93–10 and Resolution No IDA 93–6, 22 September 1993.

130 See Oxfam, *The World Bank Inspection Panel: Analysis and Recommendations.* Oxfam, Oxford, 1996, 3–7. Horta, supra n123, 131–135, 144–145. Watkins, supra n123, 202–205.

131 Dowdeswell, E, *The Role of The United Nations in the Twenty-first Century*, UNEP Speech 1995/25, 1995c, 6.

132 See World Bank, 'World Bank–United Nations Enhance Partnership.' Press Release. 2000/251/S, 1999. World Bank, *Annual Report 1999*, supra n110, 4–5. The increased transparency was provided by making country assessment reports available to the public – *at government request.*

133 Copenhagen Action Plan, supra n22, Paragraph 92. See also Chapter 7 of this book.

134 See Colclough, C, 'Structuralism versus Neo-liberalism', in Colclough (ed), 1995, 1, 6–7. Walton, J and Seddon, D, *Free Markets and Food Riots: The Politics of Global Adjustment.* Blackwell, Oxford, 1994, 6–7, 18–19. Rich, 1994, supra n1, 182–196. Adams, supra n19, 69–74. Martin, B, *In The Public Interest: Privatisation and Public Sector Reform.* Zed, London, 1993, 79–81, 128–129, 139. The detrimental role of the World Bank in the issue of the debt crisis suggests similar 'structural' concerns with their overall direction. See Reed, D, *Structural Adjustment, the Environment and Sustainable Development.* Earthscan, London, 1996, 8–21.

135 See Article 1(iii) *Articles of Agreement of the International Bank for Reconstruction and Development.* TIAS No 1507. 2 UNTS 134.

136 For example, although the Bank has dropped out of funding oil and gas exploration (from US$842 billion in 1990–94, down to US$17.5 billion in 1999) it has increased its portfolio on transportation (from US$2802 billion in 1990–94 up to US$3021 billion in 1999). See World Bank, 'Lending by Sector 1990–1999', in World Bank, *Annual Report 1999.* Oxford University Press, Oxford, 5. These investments will probably have a detrimental effect on attempts to slow climate change. See 'Banking on Climate Change: The World Bank', *Ecologist* 29(3), 1999, 3.

137 See Handl, G, 'The Legal Mandate of Multilateral Development Banks as Agents for Change Towards Sustainable Development', *American Journal of International Law* 92, 1998, 642–665.

138 See Dowdeswell, E, 'Building Sustainable Production and Consumption Patterns', in Dodds, F (ed), *The Way Forward: Beyond Agenda 21.* Earthscan, London, 1997, 206, 208.

CHAPTER 2 GROWTH

1   Godwin, W, (1793) *An Inquiry Concerning Political Justice.* Penguin, Harmondsworth, 1966, 276.

2   Condorcet, M, (1793) *Sketch for a Historical Picture of the Progress of the Human Mind*. Weidenfeld, London, 1955, 219.

3   OECD, *Technology in a Changing World*. OECD, Paris, 1991, 17.

4   WCED, *Our Common Future*. Oxford University Press, Oxford, 1987, 8, 16, 217.

5   Meadows, D H, Meadows, D L, Randers, J and Behrens, W M, *The Limits To Growth*. Earth Island, London, 1972, 17, 66–69.

6   Dzioubinski, O, *Trends in Consumption and Production: Selected Minerals*. United Nations, DESA Discussion Paper No 5, ST/ESA/1999/DP.5, 1999, 12–13. Commission on Sustainable Development, Background Paper: Assessing Long-term Trends in Resource Consumption: The Role of Models and Scenario Analysis, 1996, paragraphs 25–34. The debate pertaining to the availability of oil may be swinging back towards the possibility of scarcity. See Campbell, C, 'The End of Cheap Oil', *Scientific American* (March), 1998, 60–66.

7   World Bank, *Report on the Limits to Growth*. World Bank, Washington, 1972, 42. Beckerman, W, *In Defence of Economic Growth*. Cape, London, 1974, 227–235.

8   Indeed, as Julian Simon suggested, 'There is no limit to our capacity to keep growing forever.' Simon, J, *The Ultimate Resource*. Princeton University Press, New Jersey, 1981, 11, 348. Simon, J, *The State of Humanity*. Blackwell, London, 1995, 279–609. Simon, J, *The Ultimate Resource 2*. Princeton University, New Jersey, 1996, 578–589. For some more forthright no-limits advocates, see Bailey, R, *Eco-Scam: The False Prophets of Ecological Apocalypse*. St Martins Press, New York, 1994, 7, 22–23, 40–62. Moore, S, 'The Coming Age of Abundance', in Bailey, R, (ed), *The True State of the Planet*. Freedom Press, New York, 1995, 109–139. One of the earliest advocates of this position was Maddox, J, *The Doomsday Syndrome*. Macmillan, London, 1972, 1, 4, 16–17, 24, 27–28, 65–66, 78, 217–218, 231–233.

9   Bailey, R, 'Environmentalism for the Twenty-first Century', in Bailey, 1995, supra n8, 1, 5.

10 Summers, L, noted in 'The True price of Development', *Guardian Supplement* (26 May) 1992, 2. This should not be taken as the World Bank's position on this question. Indeed, their influential 1992 Report, *Development and the Environment* did recognize that 'many problems are exacerbated by the growth of economic activity... The earth's 'sources' are limited, and so is the absorptive capacity of its sinks ... with some ... natural resources ... demand exceeds supply', 8–9.

11 Kelley, D P, Stunkel, K R and Westcott, R R, *The Economic Superpowers and The Environment*. Freeman, San Francisco, 1976, 178–184. Ragsdale, J W, 'Ecology, Growth and the Law', *California Western Law Review* 16, 1980, 200, 267, 295–299. Mishan, E J, 'Growthmania', in Dorfman, R S and Dorfman N S (eds), *The Economics of the Environment*. Norton, New York, 1977, 324–327.

12 For a justification of this position, see Engels, F (1844), *The Condition of the Working Class in England*. Panther, London, 1969, 78–79, 82–84.

13 Richards, F, 'Can Capitalism Go Green?', *Living Marxism* 4, 1989, 18–22. Such a postulation mirrors Marx's position that, 'Man is distinct from all other animal species in that his needs have no limits and are completely elastic.' 'The Economics', in McLean, D (ed), *Karl Marx: Selected Writings*. Oxford University Press, Oxford, 1978, 521. Osborne, P, *Socialism and the Limits of Liberalism*. Verso, London, 1991, 260–267. Pepper, D, *Eco-Socialism: From Deep Ecology to Social Justice*. London, 1993, 60–62.

14 Thus, as Marx said of Mathus's postulation, 'This is a law of population peculiar to the capitalist mode of production'. Marx, K, *Capital*. Kerr, London, 1867, 692–693. Thus, when social considerations are taken into account, it becomes apparent for Marx that, 'an abstract law of population exists for plants and animals only.' Also in *Capital*, vol 1, 693.

15 ZumBrunnen, C, 'The Environmental Challenges in Eastern Europe', in Rowlands, I. (ed), *Global Environmental Change and International Relations*. Macmillan, London,

1992, 88–122. See also Spretnak, C and Capra, F, *Green Politics: The Global Promise*. Bear, New Mexico, 1986, 78. Kelley et al, supra n11, 180. Irvine, S and Ponton, A, *A Green Manifesto: Policies For A Green Future*. Optima, London, 1988, 142–144. Barnet, R J, *The Lean Years: Politics In The Age of Scarcity*. Abacus, London, 1981, 298, 301.

16 Locke argued that as people can only consume so many physical things, hence there must be a limit to physical consumption. Thus, a substitute (money) was needed so that humans do not reach physical limits. Locke, J (1690), *Two Treatise on Government*. Cambridge University Press, Cambridge, 1967, Treatise 2, paragraph 33.

17 Leeson, S M, 'Philosophical Implications of the Ecological Crisis: The Authoritarian Challenge to Liberalism', *Polity* 11, 1979, 303, 305, 306. Keekok-Lee, 1989, supra n13, 163–169, 180–181, 186.

18 Durning, A T, *How Much is Enough? The Consumer Society and the Future of the Earth*. Earthscan, London, 1992, 22–23, 36. Ophuls, W, *Ecology and the Politics of Scarcity*. Freeman, San Francisco, 1977, 184–189. Ekins, P, 'The Sustainable Consumer Society: A Contradiction in Terms?', *International Environmental Affairs* 3, 1991, 243, 245.

19 See Smith, A (1776), *An Inquiry into the Wealth and Causes of the Wealth of Nations*. Methuen, London, 1904, Book 1, Chapter 5, Vol 1, 70–84, cf 89. See also Barber, W J, *A History of Economic Thought*. Penguin, Harmondsworth, 1967, 41, 42, 47–48.

20 Thus, as Marx said, 'Accumulation for accumulation's sake, production for production's sake.' Marx, 1867, supra n14, 649, 652. Elsewhere, Marx observed, 'The circulation of capital therefore has no limits.' 'The Economics', in McLean, 1978, supra n13, 449.

21 Vogal, D, 'The Politics of the Environment: 1970–1990', *Western Quarterly* 1987, 51, 61. Vig, N J, 'Presidential Leadership: From the Reagan To The Bush Administration', in Vig, N J and Kraft, M E (eds), *Environmental Policies in the 1990s*. Washington, 1990, 33, 39. McCormick, J, *British Politics and the Environment*. Earthscan, London, 1991, 108–110. Ekins, 1991, supra n18, 243, 253.

22 WCED, 1987, supra n4, 1, 40. Council for Environmental Quality, 'Global Future: Time to Act. Report to the President on Global Resources', *Environmental Affairs* 9, 1981, 261, 263. Carlie, M and Christie, I, *Managing Sustainable Development*. Earthscan, London, 1992, 42. Schmidheiny, S/Business Council for Sustainable Development, *Changing Course*. MIT Press, Massachusetts, 1992, 12. Note, this is a strong assumption. Others, such as Paul Ekin, argue that 'prosperity does not automatically lead to a cleaner environment.' See 'Growing Up Cleaner', *New Scientist* 11 December 1999, 48–49.

23 Brandt Commission, *North-South: A Programme For Survival*. Pan, London, 1980, 33.

24 Pearce, D, 'The Global Commons', in Pearce, D (ed), *Blueprint 2: Greening The World Economy*. Earthscan, London, 1991, 11.

25 Preamble, Charter of Economic Rights and Duties of States, UNGA Res 3281 (XXIX), 12 December 1974.

26 The report then added 'but they need not follow the path taken by the rich and high-growth economies over the past half century.' UNDP, *Human Development Report: 1998*. UNDP, New York, 1998, 2.

27 O'Riordan, T, *Environmentalism*. Pion, London, 1981, 112. Adams, W M, *Green Development: Environment and Sustainability in the Third World*. Routledge, London, 1990, 68–69.

28 Gandhi, I, 'The Unfinished Revolution', *Bulletin Atomic Scientists* 28, 1974, 35. Szekely, G, 'Pollution for Export', *Mazingira* 3/4, 1977, 38. Centre for Science and Environment, *The State of India's Environment: A Citizens Report*. Centre for Science and Environment, New Delhi, 1983, 45.

29 Declaration of the Establishment of a New International Economic Order, UNGA Res 3201 (S-UI, 1 May 1974.

30 Commonwealth Group of Experts, *Climate Change: Meeting The Challenge*. London, 1989, 24. The 1989 International Conference on Global Warming and Developing Countries (The Tata Conference) went even further, suggesting that, 'In the immediate future, developing countries may have no choice but to pursue larger production, distribution and use of petroleum products', see point 6.2.2. (4). 'International Conference on Global Warming and Developing Countries', *American University Journal of International Law and Politics* 5, 1990, 547.

31 Principle 11, Stockholm Conference on the Environment, UN Doc A/CONF. 48/14/Rev 1, 1972, 4–5. Note that this principle was largely a reiteration of the 1970 United Nations General Assembly Resolution on 'Development and the Environment' which stated that, 'No environmental policy should adversely affect the present or future development possibilities of developing countries' and that it is necessary to 'respect fully the sovereign right of each country to ... determine its own environmental standards.' See principles 4 (b) and (d), UNGA Res 2849 (XXVI), 7 December 1970.

32 Principle 11 of the Rio Declaration, A/CONF. 151/5/Rev. 1, 13 June 1992.

33 Principle 9, Stockholm Declaration, 1972, supra n31.

34 Beijing Declaration on Environment and Development, General Overseas News Service, Item no 062135, Lexis Database, 20 June 1991. Also in *Environmental Policy and the Law* 21, 1991, 213.

35 Recommendation 659, Council of Europe 1972. In Ruster, B and Simma, B (eds), *International Protection of the Environment*. Oceana, New York, 1981, Vol 18, 9054.

36 McNamara, R, 'Speech to UN Conference on the Human Environment', in McNamara, R, *The McNamara Years At the World Bank: The Major Policy Addresses 1968–1981*. Johns Hopkins University Press, Baltimore, 1981, 196–197.

37 United Nations Declaration of Environmental Policies and Procedures Relating to Economic Development, reprinted in *Environmental Policy and the Law* 6, 1980, 78, 104–105.

38 Brandt Commission, 1980, supra n23, 33, 58, 115.

39 Principle II (b) of the 1982 Nairobi Declaration. Proclaimed as Annex to UNGA Res 37/7, 28 October 1982. Also in *Environmental Policy and the Law* 9, 1982, 47.

40 Inaugural Session of the Non-Aligned Countries. *Indian Journal of International Law* 23, 1983, 301, 304.

41 G7, '1984 London Declaration', *Environmental Policy and the Law* 15, 1985, 35.

42 G7, 'Bonn Declaration', *Environmental Policy and the Law* 14, 1984, 70.

43 WCED, 1987, supra n4, 44–45, 89. See also Brundtland, G H, 'Our Common Future: A Call For Action', in Polunin, N and Burnett, J H (eds), *Maintenance of the Biosphere: Proceedings of the Third International Conference on Environmental Future*. Edinburgh University Press, Edinburgh, 1990, 186, 188–189.

44 Point 37, G7 Paris Declaration, Paris 1989. *Environmental Policy and the Law* 19, 1989, 183. Paragraph 5, Lankawi Declaration on Environment, Commonwealth Heads of Government Meeting. Malaysia, Kuala Lumpur, 21 October 1989. Reprinted in Starke, L (ed), *Signs of Hope: Working Towards Our Common Future*. Oxford, Oxford University Press, 1990, 35–36. Paragraph 1, The Kampala Declaration on Sustainable Development in Africa. Kampala, Uganda, 12 June 1989. *Environmental Policy and Law* 19, 1989, 222.

45 'Report of the United Nations Conference on the Environment and Development'. UNCED A/CONF. 151/26/Rev 1, Vol 3, 77. 1992.

46 Rio Declaration, 1992, supra n32.

47 Report of the World Summit for Social Development. A/CONF. 166/9, point 26(a).

48 Goodin, R E, *Green Political Theory*. Polity, Cambridge, 1992, 65, 98–103, 193–196. Dobson, A, *Green Political Thought*. Unwin, London, 1990, 73–116. Porritt, J, *Seeing*

Green; The Politics of Ecology Explained. Blackwell, Cambridge, 1984, 26–29, 45–50, 134–139. Spretnak, C and Capra, F, *Green Politics: The Global Promise*. Bear, New Mexico, 1986, 82–106. Irvine and Ponton, 1988, supra n15, 13–15, 24–31. Sale, K, *Human Scale*. Coward, New York, 1980, 20–37, 59, 243–250. Naess, A, *Ecology, Community and Lifestyle*. Cambridge University Press, Cambridge, 1989, 30, 151–153, 162. Trainer, F E, *Abandon Affluence*. Zed, London, 1989, 2–3, 40–58, 68–82. Trainer, T, *Developed To Death: Rethinking Third World Development*. Green Print, London, 1989, 126–130. Trainer, T, *Towards A Sustainable Economy: The Need For Fundamental Change*. Carpenter, Oxford, 1996, 36–47. McMichael, A J, *Planetary Overload: Global Environmental Change and the Health of the Human Species*. Cambridge University Press, Cambridge, 1995, 82–87. Smil, V, *Global Ecology*. Routledge, London, 1994, 125–126, 131, 159, 173–177, 183–185, 202–208. Ecologist, *A Blueprint For Survival*. Penguin, Harmondsworth, 1972, 15–19. Hardin, G, *Living Within Limits*. Oxford University Press, Oxford, 1993, 204–214, 309.

49 Plato, 'The Laws', in *The Collected Dialogues*. New York, 1961, 615–620.

50 Aristotle, *Politics*. Penguin, Harmondsworth, 1979, 125.

51 Seneca, L K, *Epistola*. Penguin, Harmondsworth, 1973, x.

52 'We men have actually become a burden to the earth, the fruits of nature hardly suffice to sustain us, there is a general pressure of scarcity giving rise to complaints ... the earth can no longer support us.' Noted in Nisbet, R, *A History of the Idea of Progress*. Basic Books, New York, 1980, 52.

53 Mill, J S (1848), *Principles of Political Economy*. Longman, London, 1871, vol 2, 328–330. For an earlier example of this type of idea, see Fourier, F (1822), 'The Economics of Harmony', in *Selections From the Works of Fourier*. Gordon, New York, 1972, 196–198.

54 For the classic exposition of this position, see Boulding, K, 'The Economics of Coming Spaceship Earth', in Barr, J (ed), *The Environmental Handbook*. Ballantine, 1971, 77.

55 Rees, W E, 'The Ecology of Sustainable Development', *Ecologist* 20, 1990, 18, 21. Olson, M and Landsberg, H H (eds), *The No Growth Society*. Woburn, London, 1975, 15–63. Boulding, K E, 'The Shadow of the Stationary State', in Olson and Landsberg, *The No Growth Society*, 89, 92. Meadows, D H, Meadows, D L, Randers, J and Behrans, W H, *The Limits to Growth*. Earth Island, London, 1972, 177. Meadows, D H, Meadows, D L and Randers, J, *Beyond the Limits: Global Collapse or a Sustainable Future?* Earthscan, London, 1992, 214–215. Boulding, 1971, supra n54, 77–78. Sale, 1980, supra n48, 331.

56 Sale, 1980, supra n48, 332–333. Meadows et al, 1992, supra n55, xvi. Jacobs, M, *The Green Economy*. Pluto, London, 1991, 56–57. Spretnak and Capra, 1986, supra n15, 87. Ophuls, 1977, supra n18, 229–230, 241–242. Trainer, 1989, *Developed to Death*, supra n48, 135.

57 International Labour Office, *Meeting Basic Needs*. ILO, Geneva, 1977, 1–15.

58 Marcuse, H, *One Dimensional Man*. Routledge, London, 1964, 4–5. See also Bahro, R, *From Red to Green*. Heretic Books. London, 1984, 222. Pepper, D, *The Roots of Modern Environmentalism*. Routledge, London, 1984, 198. Meadows et al, 1992, supra n55, 216.

59 For some examples of where the lines have been drawn, see Goldsmith, E, *The Great U-Turn: Deindustrialising Society*. Green Books, Devon, 1988, 216. Hoogendijk, W, *The Economic Revolution: Freeing the Economy From Money Making*. Green Books, Devon, 1991, 57–61. Erhlich, P, *How To Be A Survivor*. Ballantine, New York, 1971, 82, 124–125. Trainer, T, 1996, supra n48, 16–20, 124–125. Lewis, M W, *Green Delusions: An Environmentalist's Critique of Radical Environmentalism*. Duke University Press, London, 1992, 120–121. Bahro, R, *Avoiding Social and Ecological Disaster: The Politics of World Transformation*. Gateway, Bath, 1994, 325–327.

60 Spretnak and Capra, 1986, supra n15, 91. Boulding, 1971, supra n54, 89, 97. Ecologist, 1972, supra n48, 17. Ophuls, 1977, supra n18, 227–229. Trainer, *Abandon Affluence*, 1989, supra n48, 267–270. Paehlke, R C, *Environmentalism and the Future of Progressive Politics*. MIT Press, Massachusetts, 1989, 54–60.

61 Stretton, H, *Capitalism, Socialism and the Environment*. Cambridge University Press, Cambridge, 1976, 20–26. Faramelli, N, 'Ecological Responsibility and Economic Justice', in Barbour, I (ed), *Western Man and Environmental Ethics*. Addison Wesley, Massachusetts, 1973, 188–203.

62 Meadows, 1972, supra n15, 158. Meadows, 1992, supra n15, 10, 215.

63 Meadows et al, 1972, supra n15, 191. Carley, M and Christie, I, *Managing Sustainable Development*. Earthscan, London, 1992, 46. Barnet, 1981, supra n15, 303, 310.

64 Meadows et al, 1972, supra n15, 178–180. Seabrook, J, *The Race For Riches: The Human Cost of Wealth*. Green Print, Basingstoke, 1988, 166–170. Dumont, R, 'Manifesto For An Alternative Culture', *Undercurrents* 10, 1975, 6. Johnson, W R, 'Should The Poor Buy No-Growth?' also in Olson and Landsberg, supra n55, 165, 186–187. Kemp, P and Wall, D, *A Green Manifesto For the 1990s*. Penguin, Harmondsworth, 1990, 64, 87–102.

65 Malthus, T (1798), *On the Principle of Population*. Penguin, Harmondsworth, 1970, 70–72.

66 Two important 1960s predecessors to the 1970s debate were Mishan, E J, *The Costs of Economic Growth*. Penguin, Harmondsworth, 1967, 219; and Packard, V, *The Waste Makers*. Penguin, Harmondsworth, 1960, 184–202, 255–263.

67 Ponting, C, *A Green History of the World*. Sinclair-Stevenson, 1991, 1–7, 70–87, 393–408. Wall, D, *Green History: A Reader in Environmental Literature, Philosophy and Politics*. Routledge, London, 1994, 31–43. McMichael, 1995, supra n48, 82–87. Sale, 1980, supra n48, 147–155.

68 Scharlemann, R P, 'A Theological Model of Nature', *Bucknell Review* 20, 1972, 101. For a discussion of such approaches, see Lewis, 1992, supra n59, 117–118, 121–125.

69 See Wall, 1994, supra n67, 140–145, 230–231.

70 Heidegger, M, 'The Question Concerning Technology', in Farrell, D (ed), *Basic Writings*. Routledge, London, 1947, 296. Zimmerman, M, 'Towards A Heideggerean Ethos For Radical Environmentalism', *Environmental Ethics* 5, 1983.

71 Mumford, L, *Technics and Civilisation*. Routledge, London, 1934. Mumford, L, *The Pentagon of Power*. Routledge, New York, 1964, 410–415.

72 Bahro, R, 1994, supra n59, 22–23, 39–43, 82–83, 86–87.

73 Orr, DW, 'Technological Fundamentalism', *Ecologist* 28(6), 1998, 329–323. See also Commoner, B, *Making Peace With the Planet*. Gollancz, London, 1990. Commoner, B, *The Closing Circle: Confronting the Environmental Crisis*. Cape, London, 1974. With regard to the issue of appropriate technology, see Bhalla, A S, *Towards Global Action for Appropriate Technology*. Pergamon, London, 1979, 1–61.

74 See Lovins, B, *Soft Energy Paths: Towards A Durable Peace*. Penguin, Harmondsworth, 1977, 54–59, 153–157. Dobson, 1990, supra n48, 101–103. Meadows, 1972, supra n15, 154. Lewis, 1992, supra n59, 127–132, 139–143. Trainer, 1996, supra n48, 160.

75 See Marx, K, 'The Economics', in McLean, 1978, supra n13, 380–381.

76 Clarke, R, *Science and Technology in World Development*. Oxford University Press, Oxford, 1985, 17–43. Menghistu, F T, *International Transfer of Technology to Developing Countries*. Boek, Amsterdam, 1988, 98–140.

77 Hobson, J A, *Imperialism: A Study*. Nisbet, London, 1902, 48.

78 Gandhi, M K, *Young India*. New Delhi, India, 1924, 38–39. For a good discussion of this see Sach, W, 'The Economist's Prejudice', in Ekins, P and Max-Neef, M, *Real Life Economics: Understanding Wealth Creation*. Routledge, London, 1992, 5. Brazier, S, 'The Economist's Blind Eye: The Vital Argument Between Gandhi and Nehru', *New Internationalist* 232, 1992, 15–18.

79 Schumacher, E F, *Small is Beautiful*. Abacus, London, 1974, 26–29, 34, 140–142, 166. Schumacher, E F, *Good Work*. Abacus, London, 1980, 57. Norgaard, R B, *Development Betrayed*. Routledge, London, 1994, 55–58, 170–171. McRobie, G, 'Intermediate Technology: Small Simple, Cheap and Non-Violent', in Albery, N and Peeters, Y (eds), *How to Save the World: A Fourth World Guide to the Politics of Scale*. Fourth World Research Trust, London, 1982, 219–221.

80 See Froggart, A, 'Brave New World Revisited', *Ecologist* 29(8), 1999, 464–468. Sale, K, 'The Triumph of Technology', *Ecologist* 29(3), 1999, 187–189.

81 For the classic example of this, see Carson, R, *Silent Spring*. Hamilton, London, 1962.

82 See UNEP, *Global Environmental Outlook: GEO 2000*. Earthscan, London, 2000, xxix. See also Ekins, P, 'The Sustainable Consumer Society: A Contradiction in Terms?', *International Environmental Affairs* 3(4), 1991, 251. For the specific problem of waste and recycling, see Connett, P and Connett, E, 'Municipal Waste Incineration: Wrong Question, Wrong Answer', *Ecologist* 24, 1994, 14–20.

83 Commission on Sustainable Development, *Overall Progress Achieved Since UNCED: Changing Consumption Patterns*. E/CN.17/1997/2/Add.3, paragraph 34, 1997. The same rule applies for increased energy efficiency in domestic housing, whereby national gains in industrialized countries are offset by the sheer growth of households in non-industrialized. See Dzioubinski, O, *Trends in Consumption and Production: Household Energy Consumption*. UN, DESA Discussion Paper No 6, ST/ESA/1999/DP.6, 1999.

84 Meadows et al, 1972, supra n15, 150–151. Carley and Christie, 1992, supra n63, 68–69. Hardin, G, 'The Tragedy of the Commons', *Science* 162, 1968, 1243, 1244, 1248. Hardin, G, *Exploring New Ethics for Survival*. Penguin, Baltimore, 1972, 120–121.

85 'Scientists Say Future Is In The Balance', reported in *Rachel's Environment and Health Weekly* 669, 23 September 1999.

86 Meadows, 1972, supra n15, 145, 181–182. Irvine and Ponton, 1988, supra n15, 41. Trainer, *Abandon Affluence*, 1989, supra n48, 211–212. McMichael, 1995, supra n48, 329–332. Hardin, 1993, supra n48, 7–8, 128–130.

87 Meadows et al, 1972, supra n15, 146–149.

88 Shiva, V, *The Violence of the Green Revolution*. Zed, London, 1989, 21–23, 135, 147, 151. Shiva, V, 'The Green Revolution in the Punjab', *Ecologist* 21, 1991, 57–58. Conway, G R and Barbier, E B, *After the Green Revolution: Sustainable Agriculture for Development*. Earthscan, London, 1990, 11–26. Scoones, I, *Beyond Farmer First*. Intermediate Technology, Exeter, 1994, 1–15. Redclift, M, *Sustainable Development: Exploring the Contradictions*. Routledge, London, 1987, 64.

89 United Nations Population Division, *World Population Prospects: 1950–2050: The 1998 Revision*. UN, New York, 1998, 13. Note, this figure is less than the 1997 figure of 9.4 billion (*The 1996 Revision*, 11–45) and even more than the 1994–1995 figure of 10 billion. See United Nations Population Fund, *The State of World Population*. UNFPA, New York, 1995, 1–2, 16–17. See also Report of the International Conference on Population and Development, A/CONF.171/13, paragraphs 1.3–1.4, chapter VI.

90 See Proceedings of the United Nations Expert Group Meeting On Population, Environment and Development, *Population, Environment and Development*. Department for Economic and Social Information and Policy Analysis, United Nations, New York, 1994, 5, 12. Engleman, R, *Population and the Environment: Impacts in the Developing World*. Population Action International, New York, 1992, 1–7. Leisinger, K and Schmitt, K, *All Our People: Population Policy with a Human Face*. Island Press, Washington, 1995, 46–98.

91 See Amalric, F, 'Beyond Growth and the Environmental Crisis: Beyond the Obvious', in Bhaskar, V (ed), *The North, The South and the Environment: Ecological Constraints and the Global Economy*. Earthscan, London, 1995, 85–101.

92 Report of the International Conference on Population and Development, A/CONF.171/13, paragraphs 3.25–3.26.

93   World Resources Institute, World Bank, UNDP and UNEP, *World Resources: 1994–1995*. Oxford University Press, Oxford, 1994, 4, 32–41.

94   Packard, 1960, supra n66, 15–162. McCracken, G, *Culture and Consumption*. Indiana University Press, Indianapolis, 1990, 28–29.

95   MacNeil, J, 'Sustainable Development: Meeting The Growth Imperative for the Twenty-first Century', in Angel, D J R, Comer, J D and Wilkinson, M L N (eds), *Sustaining Earth: Response to Environmental Threats*. Macmillan, London, 1990, 91–93.

96   Chayes, A, 'Post Stockholm', *American Society of International Law Proceedings 66*, 1972, 3, 8.

97   Ehrlich, P, 'Too Many Rich People – Weighing Relative Burdens upon the Planet'. UNEP Feature, 1994/1998. Rowley, J and Holmberg, J, 'Living in a Sustainable World', in Holmberg, J (ed), *Policies for a Small Planet*. Earthscan, London, 1992, 321, 333–335. Durning, 1992, supra n18, 23, 25, 49–55. Trainer, *Abandon Affluence*, 1989, supra n48, 1–9. Trainer, *Developed to Death*, 1989, supra n48, 137–143, 196–198. Gore, A, 'Keynote Address to Commission on Sustainable Development', *Environmental Policy and the Law* 23, 1993, 183, 184. WCED, 1987, supra n4, 14. Brandt Commission, 1980, supra n23, 162.

98   WCED, 1987, supra n4, 95.

99   UNDP, *Human Development Report: 1993*. Oxford University Press, Oxford, 1993, 13. See also UNICEF, *State of the World's Children: 1994*. Oxford University Press, Oxford, 1994, 23, 34–35. Adriaanse, A, *The Material Basis of Industrial Economies*. World Resource Institute, Washington, 1997, iv–v.

100 Office of the South Commission, *Environment and Development: Towards A Common Strategy for the South in the UNCED Negotiations*. Geneva, 1991, 8. UNDP, *Human Development Report: 1992*. Oxford University Press, Oxford, 1992, 13–18. In 1998, similar figures were produced by UNDP, which suggested that globally, 20% of the world's populations in the highest income countries account for 86% of private expenditures; the poorest 20% consume a minuscule 1.3%. Moreover, the richest 20% consume 45% of all meat and fish; the poorest fifth consume 5%; the richest consume 58% of total energy, the poorest less than 4%; the richest have 74% of all telephone lines, the poorest 1.5%; the top 20% use 84% of all paper, the poorest fifth use 1.1%; and finally the richest 20% own 87% of all the world's vehicle fleet, the poorest less than 1%. UNDP, 1998, supra n26, 2–3.

101 World Resources Institute, 1994, supra n93, 8–17. Ehrlich, P, 'Too Many Rich People', *Our Planet* 6(3), 1994, 12–13.

102 World Resources Institute, *World Resources: A Guide to the Global Environment 1996–1997*. Oxford University Press, Oxford, 1996, 315–320. This disproportionate contribution, and subsequent necessity for a differentiated responsibility from the countries which are less causally responsible is recognized in Articles 2 and 4. United Nations Convention on Climate Change. UNCED A/AC. 237/18 (Part II) Add 1, 15 May 1992.

103 World Resources Institute, 1994, supra n93, 201.

104 The 1998 *Human Development Report* suggested that a child born in the industrial world adds more to consumption and pollution over his or her lifetime than do 30–50 children born in the developing world. UNDP, 1998, supra n26. 2–3. See also Harrison, P, *The Third Revolution: Environment, Population and a Sustainable World*. Taurus, London, 1992, 255–258, 272–273, 275–277. Vittachi, A, 'Consuming Passions', *New Internationalist* 235, 1992, 6, 9.

105 Vittachi, A, 'Garbage Galore', *New Internationalist* 235, 1992, 9.

106 King, A and Schneider, B, *The First Global Revolution*. Simon and Schuster, London, 1991, 55–63. Tolba, M, 'Heeding Nature's Tug: An Environmental Agenda for International Relations', *Fletcher Forum* 14, 1990, 239, 244. Meadows et al, 1972,

supra n15, 146–149. MacNeil, 1990, supra n95, 191, 193. Ekins, P (ed), *The Living Economy*. Routledge, London, 1986, 128–129.

107 See Redclift, M, *Wasted: Counting the Costs of Global Combination*. Earthscan, London, 1995, 72–90. Harrison, P, 'Not Just a Numbers Game', *Our Planet* 6(3), 1994, 5–8. Gardner, G, 'Forging A Sustainable Materials Economy', in Brown, L et al (eds), *State of the World: 1999*. Worldwatch Institute, New York, 1999, 41, 44–48. Also, consumption is clearly rising faster in some Southern countries. Whereas the increase per capita for industrial countries was 2.3% per annum over the last few decades, in South Asia it was 2%, and in South East Asia it was 6.1%. See UNDP, 1998, supra n26, 1–2.

108 Dowdeswell, E, Speech to the International Conference on Population and Development. UNEP, Speech 1994/15, 1.

109 Dowdeswell, E, 1995), Speech at the Oslo Conference on Sustainable Production and Consumption. UNEP, Speech 1995/1, 5.

110 In terms of minerals, metals and wood products (alone), a sixfold increase would be required if the rest of the world was brought to the same per capita consumption levels as the United States. See Durning, 1992, supra n18, 36, 107. Trainer, 1989, *Abandon Affluence*, supra n48, 176–78. Ekins, P, 'Making Development Sustainable', in Sachs, W (ed), *Global Ecology*. Zed, London, 1993, 91, 97. Douthwaite, R, *The Growth Illusion*. Green Books, Devon, 1992, 150–169. Trainer, 1989, *Developed to Death*, supra n48, 121–124. Trainer, 1996, supra n48, 37, 42, 44–45.

111 Report of the Independent Commission on Population and Quality of Life, *Caring for the Future*. Oxford University Press, Oxford, 1996, 52.

112 Meadows, 1972, supra n55, 23, 126.

113 Ibid, 66.

114 World Resources Institute, 1996, supra n102, 225–228.

115 Postel, S, 'Carrying Capacity: The Earth's Bottom Line', in Mazur, L A (ed), *Beyond The Numbers: A Reader in Population, Consumption and the Environment*. Island Press, Washington, 1994, 48, 49.

116 See Dowdeswell, E, Environment and Food Security. UNEP Speech 1996/19, 4–7. For the declining per capita amounts, see World Resources Institute, *World Resources: 1998–1999, A Guide to the Global Environment*. WRI, Oxford University Press, 1999, 152–158.

117 See Alexandratos, N, *World Agriculture Towards 2010: An FAO Study*. Wiley, Chichester, 1995, 38–44, 184–185. For some of the supporters of this view, see Eberstadt, N, 'Population, Food and Income', in Bailey, R (ed), 1995, supra n8, 7–47. Bailey, 1994, supra n8, 40–62.

118 Rome Declaration on World Food Security. World Food Summit, 1996. This is reprinted in Report of the World Food Summit. FAO WFS 96/REP, Paragraph 5. Elsewhere, the FAO has stated 'Agricultural growth is expected to ... outpace population growth.' See FAO, 'Looking Forward', FAO, Fact Sheet, 1996, 1. For similar optimistic outlooks, see Sasson, A, *Feeding Tomorrow's World*. UNESCO, Paris, 1990, 703–708. For a similar view (but of opposing ideology) that suggests politics, not ecological scarcity, is the main problem in this debate, see Hildyard, N, 'Too Many For What: The Social Generation of Food 'Scarcity' and 'Overpopulation'', *Ecologist* 26(6), 1996, 248–249, 282–289.

119 Dowdeswell, E, Environment and Food Security. UNEP Speech 1996/19, 7.

120 Brown, L and Kane, H, *Full House: Reassessing the Earth's Population Carrying Capacity*. Earthscan, London, 1994. Brown, L R, 'Facing the Prospect of Food Scarcity', in Brown, L R (ed), *State of the World: 1997*. Norton, New York, 1997, 23–41.

121 World Resources Institute, 1996, supra n102, xiii. 'Food Scarcity', *Environmental Policy and the Law* 26(1), 1996, 14–16.

122 Commission on Sustainable Development, *Overall Progress Achieved Since UNCED: Report of the Secretary General.* E/CN.17/1997/2, Paragraph 29, 1997. This issue was earlier recognized by Chapter 14 of Agenda 21 which stated, 'the capacity of available resources and technologies to satisfy the demands of this growing population for food and other agricultural commodities remains uncertain.' *Agenda 21.* UNCED Doc A. CONF.151/4, Paragraph 14.1, 1992.

123 See Commission on Sustainable Development, 'Changing Consumption and Production Patterns'. E/CN.17/1996/5, 1996.

124 Council on Environmental Quality, *The Global 2000 Report to the President of the United States: Entering the 21st Century: the Summary Report.* Penguin, New York, 1980, 3. Very similar conclusions were reached in the same year by the World Conservation Strategy, which recognized that 'Human beings in their quest for economic development and enjoyment from the riches of nature, must come to terms with the resource limitation and the carrying capacity of ecosystems.' World Conservation Strategy, Switzerland, 1980, 1. Reprinted in Ruster, B and Simma, B (eds), *International Protection of the Environment.* Oceana, New York, 1983, Vol 13.

125 Independent Commission, 1996, supra n111, 96–113, 292–293.

126 Meadows, et al, 1992, supra n15, xv–xvi, 2, 47.

127 'projections ... clearly indicate that pursuit of business as usual development patterns is most unlikely to result in sustainable development patterns in the near future'. Commission on Sustainable Development, *Global Change and Sustainable Development: Critical Trends.* E/CN.17/1997/3, Paragraphs 14–15, 1997.

128 'the overall trends for sustainable development are worse today than they were in 1992'. Programme for the Further Implementation of Agenda 21. Reprinted in Osborn, D, *Earth Summit II: Outcomes and Analysis.* Earthscan, London, 1998, 128. See also UNGA, Special Session, 'Overall Review and Appraisal of the Implementation of Agenda 21'. A/S-19/15, 12 May 1997.

129 UNEP, 2000, supra n82, xii, xxiii, xxix. Earlier, the 1997 UNEP Global Environmental Outlook concluded 'The environment has continued to degrade in nations of all regions. Progress towards a sustainable future has simply been too slow.'

130 See World Meteorological Organisation, *Comprehensive Assessment of the Freshwater Resources of the World.* WMO, Geneva, 1997, 9, 20, 21. It expected that this could rise to two-thirds by 2025.

131 WRI, 1994, supra n93, 6–8. WRI, 1996, supra n102, 57–81, 201–225, 247–273, 295–315.

132 FAO, *The State of the World's Fisheries and Aquaculture.* FAO, Rome, 1997, 13. Thirty-five per cent of the world's commercially important stocks are showing patterns of decline, whereas another 25% are believed to be at their limit.

133 FAO, *Forest Resources Assessment 1990: Global Synthesis.* FAO, Rome, 1995, ix. Commission on Sustainable Development, 'Assessing Long-term Trends in Resource Consumption: Background Paper', Paragraphs 40–41, 1996.

134 UNEP, *Global Biodiversity Assessment.* Cambridge University Press, Cambridge, 1995, 6.

135 Ibid, 1, 118, 234.

136 WMO, *Scientific Assessment of Ozone Depletion: 1994: Executive Summary.* UNEP, Nairobi, 1995, 7–19.

137 See IPCC, *Climate Change 1995: The Science of Climate Change: Summary for Policy Makers.* WMO, Geneva, 1996, 44–51.

138 Paragraph 10, Cocoyoc Declaration. UN Doc A/C.2/292, 1 November 1974. Also in Ruster, B and Simma, B (eds), *International Protection of the Environment.* Oceana, New York, 1978, Vol 18, 9075–9082. The issue of overconsumption by Northern countries was also recognized at the 1974 World Food Conference, Resolution V, Paragraph 1. See Report of the World Food Conference, Rome, 5–16 November 1974.

UN Doc E/CONF.65/20, 1975. However, the overconsumption of this setting was only seen in terms of the consumption of food, not natural resources overall.

139 Brandt Commission, 1980, supra n23, 113, 163.

140 Paragraph 4, Nairobi Declaration. Doc UNEP/GC. 10/INF. 5, 19 May 1982.

141 Note, however, the Commission still called for 'rapid economic growth' in both Southern and industrialized countries. See WCED, 1987, supra n4, 44, 89.

142 See *Plan of Action for Implementing the World Declaration on the Survival, Protection and Development of Children in the 1990s*. UNICEF, Geneva, 1990, Paragraph 27.

143 The Bergen Ministerial Declaration on Sustainable Development, *Environmental Policy and the Law* 20, 1990104.

144 See Dr Castro's and Dr Mohammed's speeches in 'Report of the United Nations Conference on Environment and Development'. A/CONF. 151/26/REV 1, Vol 3, 38–39, 232–233. See also Maurice Strong, in Brown, P, 'Rio Opens With Plea for Proof of Global Brotherhood', *The Guardian* 4 June 1992, 22.

145 Sections 4.3, 4.4, 4.5 and 4.8, Agenda 21. UNCED DOC A/CONF 151/4 1992. Also in Johnson, S P (ed), *The Earth Summit*. Graham and Trotman, London, 1993, 152–153.

146 Principle 8, The Rio Declaration on Environment and Development. A/CONF. 151/5/Rev 1, 13 June 1992.

147 The Oslo Roundtable on Sustainable Production and Consumption, 'The Imperative of Sustainable Production and Consumption' Part 1.1, 1994. <http://www.iisd.ca/linkages/>.

148 Report of the International Conference on Population and Development. A/CONF.171/13. Chapter 3.1.

149 Report of the World Summit for Social Development. A/CONF. 166/9, point 16 (d).

150 'To keep global resource use within prudent limits while the poor raise their living standards, affluent societies need to consume less.' Commission on Global Governance, *Our Global Neighbourhood*. Oxford University Press, Oxford, 1995, 30.

151 'the continuing unsustainable trends in consumption and production patterns is undeniably contributing greatly to the continued deterioration of the environment.' Commission on Sustainable Development, 'Cross–Sectoral Issues, With Particular Reference To the Critical Elements of Sustainability'. E/CN.17/1996/27, 1996.

152 Istanbul Declaration on Human Settlements. A/CONF 165/L 6, Add 10, Principle 4.

153 Independent Commission on Population and Quality of Life, 1996, supra n111, 57.

154 'Unsustainable consumption patterns, common within today's developed nations, are also occurring among affluent income groups in developing countries experiencing rapid economic growth.' The Tokyo Declaration is reproduced in UNGA Special Session, Overall Review and Appraisal of the Implementation of Agenda 21. A/S-19/10, 18 April 1997. The quote is from paragraph 39.

155 Programme for the Further Implementation of Agenda 21. Adopted by the Special Session of the General Assembly 23–27 June 1997, Paragraph 28. This is reprinted in Osborn, 1998, supra n128, 140. For the failure to set targets at UNCED II, see pages 33–35, 118, 140–141.

156 See 'Summary of the Seventh Session of the Commission on Sustainable Development', *Earth Negotiations Bulletin* 5(132), 1999.

157 UNEP, 2000, supra n82, At 12. For the issue of newly industrialized countries, see pages 4–5.

158 IUCN, 'Draft International Covenant on Environment and Development', *Environmental Policy and the Law* 35, 1995, Article 28. A similar approach was reiterated in the *Overall Progress* report, Commission on Sustainable Development, 1997, supra n122, for the Earth Summit II in 1997. See paragraphs 52–54.

159 See for example the 1968 Human Rights Aspects of Family Planning Conference. Tehran, 22 April–13 May, Paragraph 1. 'The present rapid rate of population growth in some areas of the world hampers the struggle against hunger and poverty'.

160 Pearson Commission, *Partners in Development*. Pall Mall Press, London, 1969.
161 Declaration of the United Nations Conference on the Human Environment. UN Doc A/CONF.48/14, Principle 16.
162 For a discussion of this conference, see Johnson, S P, *World Population – Turning the Tide: Three Decades of Progress*. Graham and Trotman, London, 1995, 109–125.
163 Brandt Commission, 1980, supra n23, 105–108.
164 Council on Environmental Quality, 1980, supra n125, 40–41.
165 Mexico City Declaration on Population and Development, International Conference on Population. Mexico City, 6–14 August 1984. This is reprinted in Johnson, 1995, supra n162, 165–185, Paragraph 8.
166 Johnson, 1995, supra n162, 165–185.
167 WCED, 1987, supra n4, 95.
168 Amsterdam Declaration: A Better Life for Future Generations. Adopted by the International Forum on Population in the Twenty-first Century. Amsterdam, 6–9 November 1989, 1.13–1.16.
169 The Report of the South Commission, *The Challenge of the South*. Oxford University Press, Oxford, 1990, 281.
170 Johnson, 1995, supra n162, 218–220.
171 Report of the International Conference on Population and Development. A/CONF.171/13, Principle 6.
172 Report of the International Conference on Population and Development. A/CONF.171/13, Paragraph 3.14.
173 Report of the World Summit for Social Development. A/CONF. 166/9, Point 16 (e).
174 Report of the Independent Commission on Population and Quality of Life, 1996, supra n111, 29–31.
175 See Commission on Sustainable Development, *Overall Progress Achieved Since UNCED: Demographic Dynamics and Sustainability*. E/CN.17/1997/2/Add.4, Paragraphs 10–23, 1997. The United Nations General Assembly reiterated its support and concern over this issue in 1998; see vote 52/188. This was reprinted in *Environmental Policy and the Law* 28(1), 1998, 45. In 1999, UNEP and the United Nations Population Fund signed a memorandum of understanding, aimed at strengthening co-operation between the two bodies as 'population and environmental issues are interdependent'. See 'UNEP and UNFPA Sign Agreement on Strengthening Co-operation', *UNEP News Release* 1999/26.
176 See Johnson, 1995, supra n165, 14, 29, 37, 40–44, 56–57, 190, 194, 222.
177 See Potts, S, 'The Unmet Need for Family Planning', *Scientific American* January 2000, 70–75.
178 See *Report of the Ad-Hoc Committee of the Whole of the Twenty-first Special Session of the General Assembly*. A/S-21/5/Add.1. Key Actions for the Further Implementation of the Programme of Action of the International Conference on Population and Development, Paragraph 58.
179 That is, limitations of consumption in international policy clearly exist with regard to concerns such as ozone depleting chemicals, and the protection of certain endangered species. Moreover, a limit is appearing with regard to various atmospheric gases which have both localized and international effects. However, the broad question of consumption per se, remains unexamined.

CHAPTER 3 MARKETS

1   Hayek, F A, *The Road to Serfdom*. Routledge, London, 1944, 24–32, 42–54.
Friedman, M, *Capitalism and Freedom*. University of Chicago Press, Chicago, 1962,

7–21. Martin, B, *In the Public Interest: Privatisation and Public Sector Reform*. Zed, London, 1993, 5–15, 45–55.

2   South Commission, *The Challenge of the South*. Oxford University Press, Oxford, 1990, 71. For further discussions of this agenda, see Bello, W, *Dark Victory: The United States, Structural Adjustment and Global Poverty*. Pluto, London, 1994, 3, 5, 18–31, 86–104.

3   Reagan, R, 'Programme for Economic Recovery', *Weekly Compilation Press Documents* 17, 18 February 1981, 130, 135–136. Vig, N J, 'Presidential Leadership: From the Reagan to the Bush Administration', in Vig, N J and Kraft, M E (eds), *Environmental Policy in the 1990s*. Congressional Quarterly Press, Washington, 1990, 33, 35–36. King, D S, *The New Right, Politics, Markets and Citizenship*. Macmillan, London, 1987, 138.

4   See Landy, M K, Roberts, M and Thomas, S, *The Environmental Protection Agency: Asking the Wrong Questions from Nixon to Clinton*. Oxford University Press, Oxford, 1994, 245–279. King, 1987, supra n3, 155–158.

5   King, supra n3, 110. McCormick, J, *British Politics and the Environment*. Earthscan, London, 1991, 1, 51, 113, 133.

6   For economic sovereignty, see Article 1, Charter of Economic Rights and Duties of States. UNGA Res 3281 (XXIX), 12 December 1974. See also Swedberg, R, 'The Doctrine of Economic Neutrality of the IMF and World Bank', *Journal of Peace Research* 23(4), 1986, 377–390.

7   George, S, *A Fate Worse than Debt*. Penguin, Harmondsworth, 1990, 55, 56. Pirzio-Biroli, C, 'Making Sense of the IMF Conditionality Debate', in Snyder, F E and Sathirathai, S (ed), *Third World Attitudes Towards International Law*. Nijhoff, Dordrecht, 1987, 501–505. Reed, D, *Structural Adjustment, The Environment and Sustainable Development*. Earthscan, London, 1996, 8–12. Adams, P, *Odious Debts*. Earthscan, London, 1991, 75–81. Bello, supra n2, 5, 26–31, 70.

8   Due to such control, it is not surprising that the G7 continues to express its faith in the IMF process. For an early example of the recognition of 'the great importance of the role of the IMF' and the 'full support' offered by the G7, see the 1982 Versailles Summit. *International Legal Materials* 21, 1982, 562. Similar reiterations occurred thereafter.

9   See Articles I, VI, VIII and XIV of the Articles of Agreement of the International Monetary Fund. 60 Stat. 1401. TIAS No 1501 2 UNTS 39, 1947, amended 1969; 20 UST 2775, TIAS No 6748 726 UNTS 266, 1976 and 29 UST 2203, TIAS No 8939, 1978.

10   Ibid Article V (3).

11   1981 Group of 24 Communique 10(9), IMF Survey, 1981. See also the 1984 Communique 24, *International Legal Materials* 23, 1984, 1179, 1180, 1699–1710.

12   13 IMF Survey, 15 October 1984. See also the World Bank and IMF Statement, *International Legal Materials* 24, 1985, 886. Proposal of US Treasury Baker, *International Legal Materials* 25, 1986, 412, 416. IMF, 1981.

13   17 IMF Survey, 29 August 1988, 275.

14   For a discussion of these conditions, see Polak, J J, 'The Changing Nature of IMF Conditionality', in Polak, J J, *Essays in International Finance*. Princeton University Press, New Jersey, 1991, 1– 29. Chossudovsky, M, 'India Under IMF Rule', *Ecologist* 22, 1992, 271. Ghai, D, 'The Crisis of the 1980s', in Ghai, D (ed), *The IMF and the South: The Social Impact of Crisis and Adjustment*. Zed, London, 1991, 25. George, supra n7, 22–23, 51.

15   See Griffith-Jones, S, *Managing World Debt*. Wheatsheaf, Brighton, 1988, 3–7. Ghai, supra n14, 80, 91, 183–185. Brandt Commission, *Common Crisis. North-South: Co-operation for World Recovery*. Pan, London, 1983, 28. Pirzio-Biroli, supra n7, 501, 515. Zamora, S, 'The International Monetary Fund', in Zamora, S (ed), *Basic Documents of International Economic Law*. Commerce Clearing House, Illinois, 1990,

391–392. Gerster, R, 'The IMF and Basic Needs Conditionality', in Snyder and Sathirathai, supra n7, 535, 543. Martin, supra n1, 72–83.

16   Vogel, D, 'The Politics of the Environment: 1970–1987', *Wilson Quarterly* 11, 1987, 50, 57. Kraft, M E and Vig, J J, 'Environmental Policy from the Seventies to the Nineties: Continuity and Change', in Vig and Kraft, supra n3, 3, 16. Landy, supra n4, 245–279.

17   Baker, D C, 'The Environmental Focus of the Reagan Administration', *Law Notes* 18, 1982, 37–40. Vig and Kraft, supra n3, 18. Vig, supra n3, 33, 35–38, 41, 45. Koviacic, M E, 'The Reagan Judiciary and Environmental Policy', *Boston College of Environmental Affairs Law Review* 18, 1991, 668. Vogel, supra n16, 50, 65. Turner, T, 'Scuttling Environmental Progress', *Business and Society Review* Summer, 1982, 48, 50. Train, R E, 'The Destruction of the EPA', *Environmental Policy and the Law* 8, 1982, 128–130.

18   As George Bush stated at UNCED when speaking of the failure of state environmental control in the former USSR, 'Only the new breeze of [economic] freedom is allowing the clean-up.' In Report of the UNCED. A/CONF.151/26/Rev 1, Vol 3, 77. For further discussions on Bush's approach to environmental issues, see Landy, supra n4, 279–306.

19   Wirth, E and Heinz, J, *Project 88: Harnessing Market Forces to Protect our Environment*. Congress, Washington, DC, 1988, 54. The follow-up to this report was Stavins, D, *Project 88: Round Two: Incentives for Action: Designing Market Based Environmental Strategies*. Congress, Washington, DC, 1991, 36. See also EPA, *Economic Incentives: Options for Environmental Protection*. EPA, Washington, DC, 1991.

20   See Landy, supra n4, 306–310.

21   Gore, A, 'Interview', *Green Magazine* October, 1992, 30, 31. Gore, A, *Earth in the Balance: Forging A Common Purpose*. Earthscan, London, 1992, 333, 336, 349.

22   McCormick, supra n5, 3, 26–27, 58–67, 92–93.

23   Howard, noted in Brown, P, 'Market Forces Key To Greener Britain', *The Guardian* 2 October 1992, 4. See also *This Common Inheritance; The Second Year Report*. Cm 2068, HMSO, London, 1992, 34–35. See also 'DOE in Talks with Industry on S02 Permit Trading', *ENDS Reports* 230, 1994, 39–40.

24   See *This Common Inheritance*, supra n23, 33. For the history of this process in 1993, see the *ENDS Reports* 216, 26; 217, 18–21; 219, 21–22; 220, 15–16; 221, 3; 222, 19–21; 224, 32 and 226, 29–30, 31–32; 228, 36–37 and 230, 27, 34. Lean, G, 'War on Red Tape Hits Protection of Environment', *Observer* 18 July 1993, 9.

25   Point 4, Nairobi Declaration. UNEP Doc UNEP/GC. 10/INF. 5, 19 May 1982. Also in *Environmental Policy and the Law* 9, 1982, 46.

26   G7 1984 London Summit, *Environmental Policy and the Law* 15, 1985, 35.

27   International Chamber of Commerce, *Environmental Policy and the Law* 17, 1987, 262.

28   See the section on 'Economic Liberty and Responsibility', Charter of Paris: Section on the Environment, *Environmental Policy and the Law* 21, 1991, 36.

29   See paragraph L of the Dorbris Conference on the Environment in Europe. Reprinted in Prins, G (ed), *Threats Without Enemies: Facing Environmental Insecurity*. Earthscan, London, 1993, 109–112. See also Principle 5, The Bellagio Declaration on the Environment. Reprinted in *Environmental Affairs* 19, 1992, 499.

30   OECD, *Recent Developments in the Use of Economic Instruments: Environmental Monographs Number 41*. OECD, London, 1991, 65, 66. OECD, 'Agreement to Link Environment and Economy', *Environmental Policy and the Law* 21, 1991, 57, 60. OECD, 'Economic Instruments: Proposals By the Secretariat', *Environmental Policy and the Law* 23, 1993, 53.

31   Schmidheiny, S, and Business Council for Sustainable Development, *Changing Course*. MIT Press, Massachusetts, 1992, 172.

32 World Bank, *World Development Report 1992: Development and the Environment.* Oxford University Press, Oxford, 1992, 13.

33 Principle 12, Rio Declaration on Environment and Development. A/Conf. 151/5/Rev 1, 13 June 1992. See also Articles 3(5) of the United Nations Framework Convention on Climate Change. UNCED A/AC. 237/18 (PART II) Add 1, 5 May 1992.

34 Section 2 38 (e). Similar objectives attempting to establish 'open and free' economic markets and their link to sustainable development were repeated in Chapters 2.12, 2.27 and 33.6 of Agenda 21. UNCED Doc A/CONF 151 4. Also in Johnson, S P (ed), *The Earth Summit.* Graham and Trotman, London, 1993, 142.

35 'World Industry Council for the Environment', *Environmental Policy and the Law* 23, 1993, 54, 55. The IMF came to a very similar conclusion in their 1993 Report when they assessed UNCED as 'support[ing] the need for open markets as part of international efforts to achieve sustainable development.' See the IMF, *Annual Report.* IMF, Washington, DC, 1993, 12.

36 Commission on Sustainable Development, Sixth Session, 1998. Decision 6/2, Paragraph 14.

37 See World Bank, *Greening Industry: New Roles for Communities, Markets and Governments.* World Bank, Washington, DC, 2000.

38 For example Article 2 of the 1958 Geneva Convention on the High Seas provided, 'The high seas being open to all nations, no State may validly purport to subject any part of them to its sovereignty. Freedom of the high seas ... comprises ... inter alia ... 2. Freedom of fishing'. See Article 2 of the 1958 Convention on High Seas. UNTS Vol 559, 1966, 295–342. Despite these freedoms, limits on fishing were still theoretically recognized. See the end of Article 2 of the 1958 Convention, and articles 116 and 118 of the 1982 Convention. Such problems were more adequately addressed with the 1995 United Nations Agreement on Straddling Fish Stocks and Highly Migratory Fish Stocks. A/CONF.164/22, 23 August 1994.

39 It should be noted that these freedoms were initially curtailed by the 1982 United Nations Convention on the Law of the Sea. UN Doc A/CONF.62/122, Article 87 (2), 1982. This denial of the freedom of the international commons was furthered by the 1995 Agreement on the Implementation of the Law of the Sea Relating to the Conservation and Management of Straddling Fish Stocks and Highly Migratory Fish Stocks. A/CONF.164/22, Article 21.

40 Hardin, G, 'The Tragedy of the Commons', *Science* 162, 1968, 1244.

41 Hardin, G, 'Living in a Lifeboat', *Bioscience* 24, 1974561, 565–567.

42 Hardin, G, 'Carrying Capacity As An Ethical Concept', *Soundings* 59, 1976, 120. Smith, R J, 'Privatising the Environment', *Policy Review* 20, 1982, 11, 28. Stroup, R L and Baden, J A, 'Property Rights and Natural Resource Management', *Literature of Liberty* 2, 1979, 12. See also Barbier, E W, 'Economic Policy and Sustainable Natural Resource Management', in Holmberg, J (ed), *Policies For A Small Planet.* Earthscan, London, 1992, 65, 68.

43 See World Resources Institute, World Bank, UNEP and UNDP, *World Resources: A Guide to the Global Environment.* Oxford University Press, Oxford, 1996, 295–315.

44 Section 17.45 of Agenda 21, Commission on Sustainable Development, supra n36.

45 Hardin, supra n41, 1244–1245.

46 Hardin, supra n42, 264–265. Note, however, that Hardin came to argue that the free market, when it does invoke responsibility, and if necessary coercion, could lead to environmental devastation just as easily as either socialism or the commons. See Hardin, G, *Exploring New Ethics for Survival.* Penguin, Baltimore, 1972, 114–140. Hardin, G, *Living With Limits.* Oxford University Press, Oxford, 1993, 218–224, 294–297.

47 Anderson, T L and Leal, P R, *Free Market Environmentalism.* Westview, Boulder, 1991, 3, 22–23, 34, 58–59, 95–96, 118, 150, 170–172. Anderson, T L and Leal, P R, 'Free

Market Versus Political Environmentalism', *Harvard Journal of Law and Public Policy* 15, 1992, 297, 302. World Bank, supra n32, 12, 69. Pearce, D W and Warford, J J, *World Without End: Economics, Environment and Sustainable Development*. World Bank, Washington, DC, 1993, 253–256. Stewart, R B, 'Models for Environmental Regulation: Central Planning Versus Market-based Approaches', *Environmental Affairs* 19, 1992547, 555–559. Smith, supra n42, 11, 26, 33, 43. Stroup, R L and Goodman, S L, 'Property Rights, Environmental Resources and the Future', *Harvard Journal of Law and Public Policy* 15, 1992, 427, 433–435. Stroup, R L and Shaw, J S, 'The Free Market and the Environment', *Public Interest* 97, 1989, 30, 33.

48   Baden, J and Stroup, R (eds), *Bureaucracy vs Environment: The Environmental Costs of Bureacracy*. University of Michigan Press, Michigan, 1981. Libecap, G D, 'Bureaucratic Issues and Environmental Concerns', *Harvard Journal of Law and Public Policy* 15, 1992, 468. Ackerman, B A and Stewart, R B, 'Reforming Environmental Law', *Stanford Law Review* 37, 1985, 1333, 1335. Stewart, R B, 'Economics, Environment and the Limits of Legal Control', *Harvard Environmental Law Review* 9, 1985, 1, 11. Stewart, R B, 'Controlling Environmental Risks Through Economic Incentives', *Columbia Journal of Environmental Law* 13, 1988, 153–160. Stewart, 'Models for Environmental Regulation', supra n47, 547, 553–555. Stroup and Shaw, supra n47, 30–33. Smith, R J, 'Privatising the Environment', *Policy Review* 20, 1982, 11, 36. Helm, D and Pearce, D, 'Economic Policy Towards the Environment: An Overview', in Helm, D (ed), *Economic Policy Towards the Environment*. Blackwell, Oxford, 1991, 1, 20–21. Stavins, R N and Whitehead, B W, 'Dealing With Pollution: Market Based Incentives for Environmental Protection', *Environment* 34(7), 1992, 6–41.

49   See Gillespie, A. 'Common Property, Private Property and Equity: The Clash of Values and the Quest to Preserve Biodiversity', *Environmental and Planning Law Journal* 12, 1995, 388–399.

50   See Gillespie, A, *International Environmental Law, Policy and Ethics*. Oxford University Press, Oxford, 1997, Chapter 3.

51   Weizsacker, E U, 'Let Prices Tell the Ecological Truth', *Our Planet* 7(1), 1995.

52   Pigou, A C 1920), *The Economics of Welfare*. Macmillan, London, 1962. Mansfield, M, *Microeconomics: Theory and Applications*. Norton, New York, 1991, 372. Ruff, L E, 'The Economic Common Sense of Pollution', in Dorfman, R D and Dorfman, N S (eds), *The Economics of the Environment*. Norton, New York, 1977, 3, 16.

53   Dorfman and Dorfman, supra n52, xviii. Daly, H E and Cobb, J, *For the Common Good: Redirecting the Economy Towards the Community, the Environment and a Sustainable Future*. Beacon, Boston, 1989, 56. Cairncross, F, *Costing the Earth*. Economist, London, 1991, 46–47. Breslaw, J, 'Economics and Ecosystems', in Barr, J (ed), *The Environmental Handbook*. Ballantine, London, 1971, 83, 84–86. Note, I have discussed this idea in detail elsewhere. See Gillespie, supra n50.

54   Commission on Sustainable Development, *Changing Consumption and Production Patterns: Report of the Secretary General*. E/CN.17/1996/5, 30 January 1996, Paragraph 36. Commission on Sustainable Development, *Global Change and Sustainable Development: Critical Trends*. E/CN.17/1997/3, 20 January 1997, Paragraph 217. See also Roodman, D M, 'Harnessing the Market for the Environment', in Brown, L (ed), *State of the World: 1996*. Earthscan, London, 1996, 172–174. Brown, L (ed), *Vital Signs 1998*. Earthscan, London, 1998, 140–143.

55   Principle 16, Rio Declaration on Environment and Development. A/Conf. 151/5/Rev 1, 13 June 1992.

56   World Bank, *World Development Report*. Oxford University Press, Oxford, 1992, 11.

57   UNGA Special Session. *Programme for the Further Implementation of Agenda 21*. 1 July 1997, Paragraph 85. This is reprinted in Osborn, D, *Earth Summit II: Outcomes and Analysis*. Earthscan, London, 1988, Appendix D.

58 See Commission on Sustainable Development, *Financial Resources and Mechanisms: Report of the Secretary General*. E/CN.17/1996/4/Add.1, 22 February 1996, paragraphs 61–74. See also The Commission on Global Governance, *Our Global Neighbourhood*. Oxford University Press, Oxford, 1995, 211–212. World Bank, 'Reforming Subsidies: Now Is the Time to Act', *Environment Matters* Winter/Spring, 1997, 24–25. Gorelick, S, *Small is Beautiful, Big is Subsidised*. Ecologist Publications, Devon, 1998. UNDP, *Human Development Report: 1998*. United Nations, New York, 1998, Point 3, Agenda For Action, 6–7. Commission on Sustainable Development, *Outcomes of the Sixth Session*. Decision 6/2, paragraph 25, 1998.

59 See UNEP, *Global Environmental Outlook 2000*. Earthscan, London, 2000, 208. See also Roodman, supra n54, 174.

60 World Bank, supra n56, 68–69.

61 World Bank, supra n58, 2

62 Scott, A, 'CFC Recycling: Why Free Markets Won't Work', *Environmental Policy and the Law* 22, 1992, 150, 151. Fairlie, S, 'Long Distance, Short Life: Why Big Business Favours Recycling', *Ecologist* 22, 1992, 276–283. Boerner, C and Chilton, K, 'False Economy – The Folly of Demand-side Recycling', *Environment* 36(1), 1994, 7–15, 32.

63 See Report of the Independent Commission on Population and Quality of Life, *Caring for the Future*. Oxford University Press, Oxford, 1996. 'Official incentives should induce more sustainable practices... A centralised policy priority must be a reduction in the costs of renewable technologies', 55, 109.

64 See Reed, supra n7, 316–333, 350–354.

65 Dales, J H, *Pollution, Policy and Prices*. The Brookings Institute, New York, 1968, 17.

66 Section 33.18 (b), Agenda 21, supra n34.

67 Pearse, P H, *Building on Progress: Fisheries Policy Development in New Zealand*. Wellington, 1991. Hide, R P, *Depoliticising Fisherieies Management: Chatham Islands As A Case Study*. Lincoln University, Christchurch, 1990, 42–62. For the difficulties within this process, see Duncam, L, 'Closed Competition: Fish Quotas in New Zealand', *Ecologist* 25(2/3), 1995, 97–105.

68 Clean Air Amendments of 1990, Pub. L. No 101–154 d 401, 104 Stat. 2399, 2584–2631. 42 U SC dd 7651–7651 (0), Supp 1990.

69 See US Congress, *The Omnibus Reconciliation Act of 1989, Section 7506: Excise Tax on Chemicals Which Damage the Ozone Layer*. Congress, Washington, DC, 1989.

70 See Hahn, R W, *A Primer on Environmental Policy Design*. Harwood Academic Publishers, London, 1989, 33–49.

71 See The Commission on Global Governance, supra n58, 213–214. UNCTAD, *Combatting Global Warming: A Study on a Global System of Tradeable Carbon Emission Entitlements*. United Nations, New York, 1992. Pearce, D, Barratt, S, Markandya, A, Barbier, E, Turner, K and Swanson, T, 'Global Warming: The Economics of Tradable Permits', in Kirkby, J, O'Keefe, P and Timberlake, L (eds), *The Earthscan Reader in Sustainable Development*. Earthscan, London, 1996, 348–353.

72 Boulding, K E, 'Marketable Licences For Babies', in Hardin, G (ed), *Population, Evolution and Birth Control: A Collage of Controversial Ideas*. Freeman, San Francisco, 1969, 340. Cowles, R B, 'The Non Baby Bonus', also in *Population, Evolution and Birth Control* 339.

73 Kemball-Cook, D, *The Green Budget*. Green Print, London, 1991, 15–45. Goldsmith, E and *Ecologist*, *Blueprint For Survival*. Penguin, Harmondsworth, 1972, 37. Goodin, R E, *Green Political Theory*. Polity, Cambridge, 1992, 196–197. Lang, T and Hines, C, *The New Protectionism: Protecting the World Against Free Trade*. Earthscan, London, 1993, 143–145.

74 See Roodman, D M, 'Environmental Taxes Spread', in Starke, L (ed), *Vital Signs: The Trends That Are Shaping Our Future 1996–1997*. Earthscan, London, 1996, 114–115.

75 For example, see the Commission on Global Governance, supra n58, 212–213. See also section 18.3 of the Lucerne Declaration in *Environmental Policy and the Law* 23, 1993, 185, 186.

76 Pigou, supra n52.

77 Jacobs, M, *The Green Economy*. Pluto, London, 1991, 150, 153. Daly and Cobb, supra n53, 142–143. Dorfman and Dorfman, supra n52, I, xxxviii. Smets, H, 'The Polluter Pays Principle in the Early 1990s', in Campiglio, L and Pineschi, L (eds), *The Environment After Rio: International Law and Economics*. Graham and Trotman, London, 1994, 131–134, 139. Ruff, L E, 'The Economic Common Sense of Pollution', in Dorfman and Dorfman, supra n52, 1, 17. Tietenberg, T H, 'Economic Instruments for Environmental Regulation', in Helm, supra n48, 86, 105. Lewis, M W, *Green Delusions: An Environmentalist's Critique of Radical Environmentalism*. Duke University Press, London, 1992, 183–186. Kemball-Cook, supra n73, 6–7, 19–23.

78 Note that this is a matter of contention and the debate is still open. For as the Commission on Sustainable Development noted, 'there is far too little evidence available on the practical achievements of economic instruments ... so that no definitive answer can be given to the question of whether they really live up to the expectations'. Commission on Sustainable Development, *Financial Resources and Mechanisms: Report of the Secretary General*. E/CN.17/1996/4/Add.1, 22 February 1996.

79 WCED, *Our Common Future*. Oxford University Press, Oxford, 1987, 222, 329.

80 Nash, J and Ehrenfeld, J, 'Code Green: Business Adopts Voluntary Environmental Standards', *Environment* 38(1), 1996, 17–20, 36–45. United Nations, *World Investment Report: Transnational Corporations as Engines of Growth*. United Nations, New York, 1992, 90–95. Robins, N and Trisoglio, A, 'Restructuring Industry For Sustainable Development', in Holmberg (ed), supra n42, 157–167. Hampson, C, 'Industry and the Environment: A Question of Balance', in Angell, D J R, Comer, J D and Wilkinson, M L N (eds), *Sustaining Earth: Response to Environmental Threats*. Macmillan, London, 1990, 108, 111–123. Dionee, E, 'Consumers Make Them Just Do It', *Guardian Weekly* 31 May 1998. Maitland, A, 'Exporting Better Business Practices', *Financial Times* 26 January 1999, A12.

81 UNCTC, *Benchmark Corporate Environmental Survey*. UNCTC, New York, 1991, 4–6. Commission on Sustainable Development, *Towards Corporate Environmental Excellence*. E/CN.17/1996/30, 19 March 1996.

82 International Chamber of Commerce, *Environmental Guidelines for World Industry*. ICC, Paris, 1974. These were revised in 1981. See *Environmental Policy and the Law* 7, 1981, 45.

83 World Industry Council, *Environmental Policy and the Law*, 23, 1993, 17.

84 See Smith, J A, 'A Voluntary Code for Corporate Environmental Responsibility', *Yale Journal of International Law* 18, 1993, 307.

85 'The Rise of Japan', *New Internationalist* 231, 1992, 14.

86 Chemical Manufacturers Association, *Improving Responsible Care Implementation: Enhancing Performance and Credibility*. CMA, Washington, DC, 1993.

87 International Chamber of Commerce, *Business Charter for Sustainable Development*. ICC, Paris, 1991.

88 Schmidheiny, S and the Business Council for Sustainable Development, *Changing Course*. MIT Press, Massachusetts, 1992, 6–7. The Business Council for Sustainable Development changed into the World Business Council for Sustainable Development in 1995. See Stigson, B, 'The Business Charter for Sustainable Development', in Dodds, F (ed), *The Way Forward: Beyond Agenda 21*. Earthscan, London, 1997, 113–123.

89 See International Organisation for Standardisation, *Environmental Management Systems*. Committee Draft, ISO TC 207/SC1/WG1. ISO, Switzerland, 1995.

90 See UNEP, *Statement of Environmental Commitment by the Insurance Industry*. UNEP, Nairobi, 1995. UNEP, *A Statement by Banks on the Environment and Sustainable Development*. UNEP, Nairobi, 1993.

91 See Section 30.9, 30.10, 30.18 and 30.26 of Agenda 21, supra n. 36.
92 See Schmidheiney, S, *Financing Change: The Financial Community, Eco-Efficiency and Sustainable Development*. MIT Press, Massachusetts, 1996, 68.
93 Council of Environmental Quality: Twentieth Annual Report: 1990. Washington, DC, 1990, 12–13. See also Elkington, J and Burke, T, *The Green Capitalists*. London, 1987, 162.
94 Holdgate, M, 'Agenda for Action', in Commission on Sustainable Development, *Cross-Sectoral Issues*. E/CN.17/1996/30, 19 March 1996. See also Porter, M, 'Green and Competitive: Ending the Stalemate', in Welford, R (ed), *The Earthscan Reader in Business and the Environment*. Earthscan, London, 1996, 61–77.
95 *Tokyo Declaration from the Global Partnership on the Environment Summit*. Noted in UNGA, Special Session, Overall Review and Appraisal of the Implementation of Agenda 21. A/S-19/10, 18 April 1997, Paragraph 44.
96 Pirie, M, *Privatisation in Theory and Practice*. Adam Smith Institute, London, 1987, 6.
97 Elkington and Burke, supra n93, 14–23, 250. Elkington, J and Hails, J, *The Green Consumers Guide 1988*. Gollancz, London, 1988, 1–5. Faulkner, J H, 'Towards Simultaneously Achieving Economic Growth and Improving the Global Environment', *International Environmental Affairs* 2, 1990, 287, 294–296. McCormick, J, *British Politics and the Environment*. Earthscan, London, 1991, 107–120. Fazal, A, 'The Consumer Movement', in Woodhouse, T (ed), *People and Planet*. Green Books, Devon, 1987, 124–128. Cairncross, supra n53, 143, 154–155, 161. Ekins, P, 'Towards A Progressive Market', in Ekins, P and Max-Neef, M (eds), *Real-life Economics: Understanding Wealth Creation*. Routledge, London, 1992, 322.
98 See Oslo Roundtable on Sustainable Production and Consumption, *The Imperative of Sustainable Production and Consumption*. 1994, Paragraph 1. See also OECD-MIT Experts Seminar on Sustainable Consumption and Production Patterns, 1994. These are both available via the Linkages Server. <http://www.iisd.ca/linkages/>.
99 Irvine, S and Ponton, A, *A Green Manifesto: Policies For A Green Future*. Optima, London, 1988, 60.
100 It is useful to note that this position is not advocating the Marxist position of the abolition of the market, just the intervention within it and control of objectionable parts of it. This is normally identified as a 'Structuralist' position. For a useful discussion of this area, see Colclough, C, 'Structuralism versus Neo-Liberalism', in Colclough, C (ed), *States or Markets: Neo-Liberalism and the Development Policy Debate*. Clarendon, Oxford, 1995, 1–7.
101 It is important to realize that centralized planning is only an effective way to protect the environment when it is not subject to 'production biases' or 'dysfunctional motivational factors'. In such situations, as operated in the former Soviet Union, central planning may be worse than not having a central structure. See Pepper, D, *The Roots of Modern Environmentalism*. Croom Helm, London, 1995, 14–16. Ross, L and Silk, M A, 'Post Mao China and Environmental Protection', *Pacific Basin Law Journal* 4, 1985, 63–66, 85. Routley, V, 'Karl Marx as Environmental Hero', *Environmental Ethics* 3, 1981, 242. Maggs, P B, 'Marxism and Soviet Environmental Law', *Columbia Journal of Transnational Law* 23, 1984–85, 355, 357.
102 Letter from Marx to Engels, Manchester, 25 March 1868, in Progress Publishers (ed), *Marx and Engels: Selected Correspondence*. Progress Publishers, Moscow, 1965, 202.
103 See Steidlmeier, P, 'The Morality of Pollution Permits', *Environmental Ethics* 15, 1993.
104 See Gillespie, supra n50.
105 Chew, S C and Denemark, R A, *The Underdevelopment of Development*. Sage, California, 1996, 2–13, 18–19, 28, 50–51, 136–137. Sutcliffe, B, 'Development After Ecology', in Bhaskar, V (ed), *The North, The South and the Environment: Ecological Constraints and the Global Economy*. Earthscan, London, 1995, 232, 246–255. Friedmann, J, *Empowerment: The Politics of Alternative Development*. Blackwell,

Cambridge, 1994, 31–36, 64–65, 82–84, 160. Martin, supra n1, 149–200. Eckersley, R, 'Green Versus Ecosocialist Economic Programmes: The Market Rules OK?', *Political Studies* 40, 1992, 315, 322–323. Robins and Trisoglio, supra n80, 157, 179–82. Goodin, supra n73, 102–103.

106 See Smith, A (1776), *An Inquiry Into the Nature and Causes of the Wealth of Nations*. Random, New York, 1923 reprint, 650–651.

107 'It is ... necessary to recognise that the establishment of a market economy is not a turn-key operation... Nor can the market provide all the answers to the formidable social problems that inevitably arise in the process of rapid change. There is need for social safety-nets ... all reforms have to be related to the larger goal of enabling all people to live a life of dignity.' South Commission, supra n2, 275.

108 Here it iterated that it was necessary for governments to, 'intervene in markets, to the extent necessary, to prevent or counteract market failure, promote stability or long-term investment, ensure fair competition and ethical conduct, and harmonise economic and social development ... social progress will not be realised simply through the free interaction of market forces. Public policies are necessary to correct market failures'. *Copenhagen Declaration on Social Development, in World Summit for Social Development*. A/CONF.166/9, 19 April 1995, Commitment One, Paragraph (e). The second part of the quote comes from the Programme of Action of the World Summit, Chapter 1, paragraph 6.

109 World Bank, *Rethinking the Money and Ideas of Aid*. World Bank, Washington, DC, 1999, 2.

110 WCED, supra n79, 60, 219–220, 222.

111 Brundtland, G H, 'Our Common Future: A Call For Action', in Polunin, N and Burnett, J H (eds), *Maintenance of the Biosphere: Proceedings of the Third International Conference on Environmental Future*. Edinburgh University Press, Edinburgh, 1990, 186, 190.

112 Council of Europe, 'Conference on the Protection of the Environment', *Environmental Policy and the Law* 21, 1991, 37.

113 Section 20.13 (b) of *Agenda 21*, supra n36.

114 Bello, supra n2, 8, 111–115. Manser, R, 'Going West: Market Reform and the Environment in Eastern Europe', *Ecologist* 24, 1994, 27, 28–29.

115 Mintz, J A, 'Economic Reform of Environmental Protection: A Brief Comment on a Recent Debate', *Harvard Environmental Law Review* 15, 1991, 149, 158. Zambagni, S, 'Global Environmental Change: Rationality and Ethics', in Campiglio, L and Pineschi, L (eds), *The Environment After Rio: International Law and Economics*. Graham and Trotman, 1994, 235, 240–42.

116 Brunet, E, 'Debunking Wholesale Private Enforcement of Environmental Rights', *Harvard Journal of Law and Public Policy* 15, 1992, 312–318, 321–322. Menell, P S, 'Institutional Fantasylands: From Scientific Management to Free Market Environmentalism', *Harvard Journal of Law and Public Policy* 15, 1992, 489, 496, 503–505. Plantico, R C, 'A Property Rights Strategy For Protecting the Environment: A Comment on Stroup and Goodman', *Harvard Journal of Law and Public Policy* 15, 1992, 455, 463. Recently, enforcement has become more necessary as the illegal nature of many environmental problems is becoming paramount. See for example, Hooper, J, 'Mafia Turns to Eco-Gangsterism', *Guardian Weekly* 26 April 1998. UNEP, 'UNEP and Partners Step Up Efforts to Combat Illegal Trade and Other Related Environmental Crimes', *UNEP News Release* 1999/80. For the specific problem of ozone depleting chemicals, see Environmental Investigation Agency, *CFC Smuggling in the European Union*. EIA, London.

117 See Gray, A, 'Corporate Reporting for Sustainable Development: Accounting for Sustainability in AD2000', in Welford, supra n94, 173–196.

118 As the 1997 UNGASS Review of Agenda 21 suggested: 'access to information ... is fundamental to sustainable development', UNGA Special Session, 1997. *Programme for the Further Implementation of Agenda 21*, 1 July 1997, Paragraph 108. This is reprinted in Osborn, D, *Earth Summit II: Outcomes and Analysis*. Earthscan, London, 1988, Appendix D. For further discussion of this, see UNEP, *Companies' Organisation and Public Communication on Environmental Issues*. UNEP, Nairobi, 1991. World Bank, *Greening Industry: New Roles for Communities, Markets and Governments*. World Bank, Washington, DC, 2000, Chapter 3. Blumm, M C, 'The Fallacies of Free Market Environmentalism', *Harvard Journal of Law and Public Policy* 15, 1992, 371, 379. Pearce, D, Markandya, A and Barbier, E B, *Blueprint For A Green Economy*. Earthscan, London, 1989, 88, 92. For the recognition of this point in international environmental law and policy, see Section 4.21, *Agenda 21*, supra n36. See also Brady, K, 'New Convention on Access to Information and Public Participation in Environmental Matters', *Environmental Policy and the Law* 28, 1998, 69–74.

119 West, K, 'Ecolabels: The Industrialisation of Environmental Standards', *Ecologist* 25, 1995, 16–20. Welsh, D F, 'Environmental Marketing and Federal Pre-emption of State Law: Eliminating the Gray From Behind the Green', *California Law Review* 81, 1993, 991–993. Stauber, J C, 'Democracy for Hire: Public Relations and Environmental Movements', *Ecologist* 25, 1995, 173–180. Cairncross, supra n53, 12–16, 163, 171.

120 Commission on Sustainable Development, *Changing Consumption and Production Patterns: Report of the Secretary General*. E/CN.17/1995/13, 20 March 1995, Paragraph 48.

121 UNEP, supra n116, 12–13, 16, 30.

122 Streeton, H, 'Three Levels of State Action', in Ekins and Max-Neef (eds), supra n97, 328, 332. Holmberg, J, 'Financing Sustainable Development', in Holmberg, J (ed), supra n42, 298, 316.

123 See Chapter One of this book.

124 See Roodman, supra n54, 168–169, 179–182.

125 Jacobs, supra n77, 158–162. Kemball-Cook, D, *The Green Budget 1991*. Green Print, London, 1991, 6–7, 42–43. *Ecologist*, 'Whose Common Future?', *Ecologist* 22, 1992, 178. Stretton, H, *Capitalism, Socialism and the Environment*. Cambridge University Press, Cambridge, 1976, 214–215. Manser, supra n111, 27–29.

126 Commission on Sustainable Development, *Financial Resources and Mechanisms: Report of the Secretary General*. E/CN.17/1996/4/Add.1, 22 February 1996, Paragraphs 45 and 46.

127 For a useful analysis of all green consumer figures, see Commission on Sustainable Development, *Background Paper: Eco-Labeling*. 1996, paragraphs 17–25.

128 Jacobs, supra n77, 43. Cairncross, supra n53, 158.

129 McCully, P, 'Discord in the Greenhouse: How the WRI is Attempting to Shift the Blame for Global Warming', *Ecologist* 21, 1991, 154–160.

130 Smith, K R, 'The Basics of Greenhouse Gas Indices', in Hayes, P and Smith, K (eds), *The Global Greenhouse Regime: Who Pays?* Earthscan, London, 1993, 20–51. Subak, S, 'Assessing Emissions: Five Approaches Compared', also in Hayes and Smith, 51–70. Gillespie, A, *Burning Issues: The Failure of the New Zealand Response to Confront Climatic Change*. Dunmore Press, Palmerston, 1997, Chapter 3.

131 See Hempel, L C, *Environmental Governance: The Global Challenge*. Island Press, San Francisco, 1996, 196–202. Kverndokk, S, 'Tradable CO_2 Emission Permits: Initial Distribution as A Justice Problem', *Environmental Values* 4, 1995, 129–148. See also Commission on Sustainable Development, *Financial Resources and Mechanisms: Report of the Secretary General*. E/CN.17/1995/8, 24 March 1995, Paragraph 236.

132 Commission on Sustainable Development, *Financial Resources and Mechanisms for Sustainable Development*. E/CN.17/1996/4, 22 February 1996, Paragraph 20.

133 See Walley, N, 'Its Not Easy Being Green', in Welford, supra n94, 5–16.

134 World Bank, supra n32, 13. Commission on Sustainable Development, *Background Paper: Eco-labeling*. 1996, Paragraphs 34 and 39. Jacobs, supra n77, 43. Lang and Hines, supra n73, 113–114.

135 Pearce et al, supra n118, 154. Jacobs, supra n77, 43. Cairncross, supra n53, 166. Lang and Hines, supra n73, 111.

136 Jacobs, supra n77, 159. Clunies-Ross, T, 'Taxing Nitrogen Fertilizers', *Ecologist* 23, 1993, 13, 15.

137 Commission on Sustainable Development, *Changing Consumption and Production Patterns: Report of the Secretary General*. E/CN.17/1996/5, 30 January 1996, Paragraph 28. See also World Bank, supra n32, 13. Kemball-Cook, supra n 73, 29–30. Jacobs, supra n 77, 156–157. Helm and Pearce, supra n48, 1, 8. Turner, R K (ed), *Sustainable Environmental Economics: Principles and Practice*. Belhaven, London, 1993, 25–26. Roodman, supra n54, 174–175.

138 World Bank, *Greening Industry: New Roles for Communities, Markets and Governments*. World Bank, Washington, DC, 2000, 28. Or as Marx stated, 'No capitalist ever voluntarily introduces a new method of production, no matter how much more productive it may be, and how much it may increase the rate of surplus value, so long as it reduces the rate of profit.' In 'The Economics', in McLean, D (ed), *Karl Marx: Selected Writings*. Oxford University Press, Oxford, 1978, 490. Trainer, T, *Towards A Sustainable Economy: The Need For Fundamental Change*. Carpenter, Oxford, 1996, 10–15, 24–25, 31, 82–89. Bahro, R, *Avoiding Social and Ecological Disaster: The Politics of World Transformation*. Gateway, Bath, 1994, 99–111, 233. McBurney, S, *Ecology into Economics Won't Go*. Green Books, Devon, 1990, 87–95. England, R and Bluestone, B, 'Ecology and Class Conflict: Can Capitalism Go Green?' *Living Marxism* 4, 1989, 18, 19–27. Frolov, I, 'The Marxist Approach to Ecological Problems', in USSR Academy of Sciences (ed), *Environmental Protection and Society*. USSR Academy of Sciences, Moscow, 1983, 24, 28–35. Gorizontov, B, *Capitalism and the Ecological Crisis*. Progress Publishers, Moscow, 1985, 17–21, 39–40.

139 Friedman, M, Noted in Donaldson, J, *The Ethics of International Business*. Oxford University Press, Oxford, 1989, 45.

140 Office of Technology Assessment, US Congress, *Multinationals and the National Interest: Playing By Different Rules*. US Government Printing Office, Washington, DC, 1993, 1–4, 10.

141 See Rowell, A, *Green Backlash: Global Subversion of the Environmental Movement*. Routledge, London, 1996. Edward, D W, 'Greenwash: Co-opting Dissent', *Ecologist* 29, 1999, 172–175.

142 Greenpeace International, *The Oil Industry and Climate Change*. Greenpeace, Amsterdam, 1998. Kraft, M E, 'Environmental Gridlock: Searching for Consensus in Congress', in Vig, N J and Kraft, M E (eds), *Environmental Policy in the 1990s*. Washington, DC, 1990, 103, 113. Slawson, W D, 'The Right To Protection From Air Pollution', *Southern Californian Law Review* 59, 1986, 674–675, 678–679, 728–739.

143 Boehmer-Christiansen, S and Skea, J, *Acid Politics: Environmental and Energy Policies in Britain and Germany*. Belhaven, London, 1991, 94–195. McCormick, J, *Acid Earth: The Global Threat of Acid Pollution*. Earthscan, London, 1989, 68–69, 119, 149–153, 185. McCormick, J, *British Politics and the Environment*. Earthscan, London, 1991, 10, 20–23, 54–57, 93, 145, 170–171. Carroll, J E, 'The Acid Rain Issue in Canadian-American Relations', in Carroll, J E (ed), *International Environmental Diplomacy*. Cambridge University Press, Cambridge, 1988, 141–145, 146, 158–159, 173, 178–179, 184–185.

144 Maxwell, J H, 'Green Consciousness or Dollar Diplomacy?', *International Environmental Affairs* 5, 1993, 19, 36–37. Doyle, J, 'Hold the Applause: A Case Study of Corporate Environmentalism', *Ecologist* 22, 1992, 94–91. Roan, S L, *The Evolution of a Sudden Global Emergency: Ozone Crisis*. Wiley, New York, 1989, 42, 51, 99, 108–109, 229, 240–141.

145 Marshall, G, 'The Political Economy of Logging: Corruption of the Papua New Guinea Timber Industry', *Ecologist* 20, 1990, 174. Witte, J, 'Deforestation in Zaire', *Ecologist* 22, 1992, 58. Hurrell, A, 'The Politics of Amazonian Deforestation', *Journal of Latin American Studies* 23, 1991, 198–205. Pearce, F, *Green Warriors: The People and Politics Behind the Green Revolution*. Bodley Head, London, 1991, 168–170. Colchester, M, 'Asian Loggers Move in on Guyana's Forests', *Ecologist* 24, 1994, 45–47.

146 Marx, K, in Easton, D and Guddat, K H (eds), *Writings of the Young Marx on Philosophy and Society*. Anchor, New York, 1967, 245.

147 Castro, noted in Brown, P, 'Bush Lays Down Rio Gauntlet', *The Guardian* (13 June) 1992, 1.

148 Doyle, supra n144, 84. Roan, supra n144, 42, 99, 229, 240–141. Castro, F, *Tomorrow Is Too Late: Development and the Environmental Crisis in the Third World*. Ocean, Melbourne, 1993, 4, 22–23. Irvine, S, 'Consuming Fashions? The Limits of Green Consumerism', *Ecologist* 19, 1989, 88, 91. Cairncross, supra n53, 164. Pearce, supra n145, 168–170. Wallis, V, 'Socialism, Democracy and Ecology', *Monthly Review* 44, 1992, 1, 19.

149 Such as when there are only a small number of possible environmentally damaging companies, which all share the same possible fate via a public backlash, and there is a strong third party which provides independent verification of standards. See Gunningham, C, 'Environment, Self-Regulation and the Chemical Industry: Assessing Responsible Care', *Law and Policy* 17(1), 1995, 57–109. Very similar conclusions were recognized by the United Nations Centre on Transnational Corporations, which noted 'Some corporations still had not established the most basic procedures for managing their environmental impacts. One quarter of the respondents had no environmental policies and programs, International guidelines were rarely observed ... less than one third of the respondents utilised relatively inexpensive means of confidence building, such as disclosure of hazards and risks.' United Nations Centre on Transnational Corporations, *Environmental Mangement & Transnational Corporations: Report on the Benchmark Corporate Environmental Survey*. UN, New York, 1993, 91. See also World Resources Institute, *World Resources 1998–1999: A Guide to the Global Environment*. Oxford University Press, New York, 1998. The WRI study noted that 'the vast amount of smaller and medium sized enterprises' remain unconvinced of the benefits of 'going green', 168–169. For the best exemplar of this self-regulation actually working, see Rees, J, *Hostages of Each Other: The Transformation of Nuclear Safety Since Three Mile Island*. University of Chicago Press, Chicago, 1994. See also Welford, R, *Hijacking Environmentalism: Corporate Responses to Sustainable Development*. Earthscan, London, 1996, 54–56, 64–72, 76–77.

150 The first part of the quote is from the Commission on Sustainable Development, *Overall Progress Achieved Since UNCED: Role and Contribution on Major Groups*. E/CN.17/1997/Add 22, Paragraphs 80 and 81, 1997. The second part of the quote is from the Commission on Sustainable Development, *Financial Resources and Mechanisms: Addendum. Report of the Secretary General*. E/CN.17/1996/4/Add.1, 22 February 1996.

151 See World Bank, 'World Bank Debars Five Firms', *Press Release* no 2000/081/S. 2000. The movement to stop corruption in international society is one of the more promising areas in this arena. In 1997, the 'Combating Bribery of Foreign Public Officials in International Business Transactions' was agreed by the OECD.

152 See International Code of Marketing of Breast-Milk Substitutes, Annex to the Resolution WHA34.22 of 21 May 1981. For a useful discussion of this, see Prakash Sethi, S, *Multinational Corporations and the Impact of Public Advocacy on Corporate Strategy: Nestle and the Infant Formula Controversy*. Kluwer, Dordrecht, 1994. A good overall examination of overt direct anti-environmental approaches by TNCs is also to

be found in Rowell, supra n141. On the broader question of TNCs and human rights, see Meyer, W H, 'Human Rights and MNCs: Theory Versus Quantitive Analysis', *Human Rights Quarterly* 18, 1996, 369–397. Meyer concluded that TNCs have had a positive impact in this area.

153　Plant, C and Albert, D H, 'Green Business in a Grey World: Can It Be Done?', in Plant, C and Plant, J (eds), *Green Business: Hope or Hoax?* Green Books, Devon, 1991, 1, 3–4, 6–7. Watts, H, '"Green" Products Blamed For Rise in Animal Testing', *Independent* 9 November 1992, 3. Irvine, S, *Beyond Green Consumerism*. Friends of the Earth Discussion Paper no 1, 1989, 3, 9, and 17. Ekins, P, 'The Sustainable Consumer Society: A Contradiction in Terms?', *International Environmental Affairs* 3, 1991243, 251.

154　Plant and Albert, supra n153, 1, 7. See also Hawken, P, 'A Teasing Irony', in Welford R, supra n94, 5–16.

155　Porritt, J and Winner, D, *The Coming of the Greens*. Fontana, London, 1988, 150. Hoogendijk, W, *The Economic Revolution: Freeing the Economy From Money Making*. Green Books, London, 1990, 88.

156　See Friends of the Earth, *Position Paper for the UN Commission on Sustainable Development: 11–28 April, 1995. Sustainable Production and Consumption*. FOE, London, 1995. Dadd, D L and Carothers, A, 'Green Consuming In Perspective', in Plant, C and Plant, J, supra n153, 11, 18. Dodds, supra n88, 199–200.

157　Plant and Albert, supra n153, 1, 4. Dadd and Carothers, supra n156, 11–13, 19–20. Ellwood, W, 'Endorsing Green Capitalism: Should Environmental Groups Get into Bed With Business?', in Plant and Albert, supra n153, 39, 40–41. Tokar, B, 'Marketing the Environment', also in Plant and Albert, 42. Goodin, supra n73, 122. Cairncross, supra n53, 143.

158　Corry, S, 'The Rainforest Harvest: Who Reaps the Benefits?', *Ecologist* 23, 1993, 148, 153.

159　Meadows, D H, Meadows, D L and Randers, J, *Beyond the Limits: Global Collapse or a Sustainable Future?* Earthscan, London, 1992, 84, 181–182. Williams, H, *Autogeddon*. Cape, London, 1991. Hoogendijk, W, *The Economic Revolution*. Green Books, London, 1990, 129–133.

160　Dryzek, J, *Rational Ecology: Environment and Political Economy*. Blackwell, Oxford, 1987, 89–91, 91–95, 94–95, 96–107. Trainer, F E, *Abandon Affluence*. Zed, London, 1989, 267–270, 212–213, 367–270. Commoner, B, *The Closing Circle*. Cape, New York, 1974, 160–161, 195, 295. Commoner, B, *Making Peace With the Planet*. Gollancz, London, 1991, 160–161, 153–165. Commoner, B, *The Poverty of Power*. Bantam, New York, 1976, 257–258. Pepper, D, *Eco-Socialism; From Deep Ecology to Social Justice*. Routledge, London, 1993, 243. Bosselmann, K, *When Two Worlds Collide: Society and Ecology*. RSVP, Auckland, 1995, 112–119, 210, 222–223, 248–251, 268. Ophuls, W, *Ecology and the Politics of Scarcity*. Freeman, San Francisco, 1977, 184, 227–229. Johnston, R J, *Environmetnal Problems: Nature, Economy and State*. Belhaven, London, 1989, 82–87, 90–106, 111–143. Jacobs, supra n77, 154–156. Tietenberg, supra n77, 86, 106. Plantico, supra n116, 455, 458. Menell, supra n116, 489, 492, 502. Pearce and Warford, supra n44, 217–232. Bahro, supra n138, 338. Trainer, supra n138, 120–124, 147, 173–179. Manor, J, 'Politics and the Neo-Liberal', in Colclough, C, *States or Markets*, supra n100, 306–320. Toye, J, 'Is There a New Political Economy of Development?', also in Colclough, supra n100, 321–338.

161　See Welford, R, supra n149, 16–38, 49–50, 57–62, 64–70, 157–158, 172–173.

162　UNCTAD, 'Foreign Direct Investment Soars 40 Per Cent' TAD/INF/2680, 13 September 1996.

163　See Bailey, P, *Multinationals and Employment: The Global Economy of the 1990s*. International Labour Office, Geneva, 1991, 295.

164 See The Commission on Global Governance, supra n58, 25. See also Stopford, J, 'Multinational Corporations', *Foreign Policy* 1999, 15, 17.

165 See Korten, D, *When Corporations Rule the World*. Earthscan, London, 74–76, 166–167, 177–181, 214–226. Chatterjee, P and Finger, M, *The Earth Brokers: Power, Politics and World Development*. Routledge, London, 1994, 105–120. Watkins, K, *The Oxfam Poverty Report*. Oxfam, Oxford, 1995, 113, 145–147. Athanasiou, T, *Slow Reckoning: The Ecology of a Divided Planet*. Secker, London, 1997, 231–242. Martin, B, 'Privatisation and Globalistion', *Ecologist* 26, 1996, 145–155. Hildyard, N, 'Changing Landscapes of Corporate Control', *Ecologist* 26, 1996, 125–145. Welford, supra n149, 137–157. Doherty, A, 'Misshaping Europe: The European Roundtable of Industrialists', *Ecologist* 24, 1994, 135–140. Finger, M, 'Why Transnational Corporations Are Organising to "Save the Environment"', *Ecologist* 27, 1997, 138–142. For the 1970s and 1980s recognition and analysis of this problem, see Little, R and Smith, M (eds), *Perspectives on World Politics*. Routledge, London, 1994, 212–241, 291, 325–327, 336–338, 352–365. Spero, J, *The Politics of International Economic Relations*. Routledge, London, 1996, 136–140, 236–260.

166 WCED, supra n79, 229. Korten, supra n165, 66–68, 181, 208–214, 232–237, 276, 294–295, 308–324. Welford, supra n149, 5–15, 37, 82–89. Lang and Hines, supra n73, 34–38, 110–111. Brecher, supra n78, 3–4, 31, 51–52, 123–128. Chatterjee and Finger, supra n165, 126–127, 130–134. *Ecologist* 'Globalisation: Changing Landscapes of Corporate Control', *Ecologist, Special Issue* 26(4), 1996, 124, 142, 165. Trainer, supra n138, 153.

167 See United Nations, *Climate Change and Transnational Corporations: Analysis and Trends*. UN, New York, 1992, 2–3, 13–14.

168 *Benchmark Corporate Environmental Study*. United Nations Centre on Transnational Corportations, New York, 1991, 14. *Transnational Corporations in World Development: Third Survey*. United Nations Centre, New York, 1991, 224. See also Scovassi, T, 'Industrial Accidents and the Veil of Transational Corporations', in Francioni, F and Scovassi, S (eds), *International Responsibility for Environmental Harm*. Graham and Trotman, London, 1991, 381–397. Nanda, V P and Bailey, B, 'The Nature and Scope of the Problem', in Handl, G E and Lutz, R (eds), *Transferring Hazardous Technologies and Substances: The International Legal Challenge*. Graham and Trotman, London, 1989, 1–28. Note, in early 1997 there was some renewed movement in this area on the question of extra-territorial *voluntary* standards. See Blustein, P, 'Companies Agree Code of Conduct', *Guardian Weekly* 20 April 1997.

169 On the question of environmental protection within such a code, see Section B9, United Nations Commission on Transnationals, *Working Group Report Draft*. UN Doc E/C.10/1977/3, 4 May 1977. Articles 41–43, United Nations Commission on Transnationals, *Draft UN Code of Conduct*. UN Doc E/C.10/1982/6/1982, 5 June 1982. Section 8, United Nations Commission on Transnational Corporations, *Draft Code*. E/C.10/1984/5/5, 29 May 1984. Article 41 of the 'OECD Guidelines for Multilateral Enterprises on Environmental Concerns', *International Legal Materials* 25, 1986. 494.

170 United Nations, *World Investment Report: Transnational Corporations as Engines of Growth*. UN, New York, 1992, 240.

171 Brandt Commission, *North-South: A Programme For Survival*. Pan, London, 1980, 73, 200.

172 See point 9 of the *Nairobi Declaration*. UNEP Doc UNEP/GC.10/INF 5, 19 May 1982.

173 WCED, supra n79, 86, 219, 220, 329.

174 South Commission, supra n2, 233– 234.

175 The Commission on Global Governance, supra n58, 173.

176 Although the IUCN Covenant did not call for an international code, it did suggest that: 'Economic activities of foreign origin [comply with] the relevant environmental legal

requirements and standards applicable in the State of origin.' See IUCN, 'Draft International Covenant of Environmental Policy and Law', *Environmental Policy and the Law* 31, 1995, Article 31.

177 They suggested that: 'a multilateral code needs to be developed for multinational corporations ... multinationals are too important for their conduct to be left to voluntary and self-generated standards.' UNDP, *Human Development Report: 1999*. United Nations, New York, 1999, 6.

178 Commission on Sustainable Development, *Industry and Sustainable Development*. E/CN.17/1998/4, 1998, Paragraph 58.

179 The United Nations Centre on Transnational Corporations was set up in the early 1970s with the intention of creating some international guidelines for the practices of TNCs. Nineteen rounds of negotiations finally resulted in some draft regulations in 1992. However, these were not adopted, and the Centre itself was integrated into the UNCTAD. For some discussions on the loss of control over TNCs, see Hildyard, N, 'Foxes In Charge of the Chickens', in Sachs, W (ed), *Global Ecology*. Zed, London, 1993. 22, 28. Of late, the agenda may have changed somewhat, as TNCs have become more involved with the UN. See Karliner, J, 'Co-opting the UN', *Ecologist* 29, 1999, 318–321.

180 For the alleged positive environmental benefits of TNCs, and the preference for self regulation, see Sections 3, 9 and 26 of Chapter 30 of Agenda 21, supra n36.

181 Programme of Action for the World Summit for Social Development, A/CONF. 166/9, 19 April 1995, Paragraph 12 (e). See also the Commission on Global Governance which suggested that 'businesses must be encouraged to act responsibly', supra n58, 255.

182 *Report of the UN Conference on Human Settlements* (Habitat II). A/CONF.165/14. Global Plan of Action, Strategies for Implementation, Paragraph 204 (q).

183 See Gray, K, 'The Ambivalence of Property', in Prins, G (ed), *Threats Without Enemies: Facing Environmental Insecurity*. Earthscan, London, 1993, 150, 155. Buck, J S, 'Multi-Jurisdictional Resources: Testing a Typology for Problem-Structuring', in Berkes, F (ed), *Common Property Resources: Ecology and Community Based Sustainable Development*. Belhaven, London, 1989, 127, 128.

184 Grima, A P L, 'Natural Resources: Access, Rights to Use and Management', in Berkes, supra n183, 33, 39. Ruddle, K, 'Solving the Common-Property Dilemma', ibid, 5, 8–9, 168. Bromley, D W, 'Common Property Issues in International Development', *Developments* 5, 1985, 12.

185 *Ecologist*, 'The Commons: Where the Community Has Authority', in Kirkby, supra n71, 328–237. Miller, D L, 'The Evolution of Mexico's Caribbean Spiny Lobster Fishery', in Berkes, supra n183, 185. Gibbs, C and Bromley, D, 'Institutional Arrangements for Common Property Regimes', in Berkes, supra n183, 20, 22, 25–27. Berkes, F, 'Co-operation From the Perspective of Human Ecology', in Berkes, supra n183, 70, 84–85. Gadgil, M and Iyer, P, 'On the Diversification of Common-Property', also in Berkes, 240.

186 Metzger, M B, 'Private Property and Environmental Sanity', *Ecology Law Quarterly* 5, 1976, 793, 807.

187 Monbiot, G, 'The Real Tragedy of the Commons', *Guardian* 6 August 1993, 18, 19.

188 Helm, supra n48, 16. Vivian, J M, 'Local Resource Management', in Ghai, D and Vivian, J M (eds), *Grassroots Environmental Action*. Routledge, London, 1992, 50, 61.

189 Kurien, J, 'Ruining the Commons: Actions in South India', *Ecologist* 23, 1993, 5. Sale, K, *Human Scale*. Coward, New York, 1980, 334. Grima, supra n184, 33, 49. World Bank, supra n32, 20.

190 McNeely, J A, 'Common Property Resource Management', *International Relations* 10, 1991, 211, 213. Grima, supra n184, 33, 54. Moorehead, R, 'Changes Taking Place in Common Property Resource Management', in Berkes, supra n185, 256, 268.

191 Allaby, M and Bunyard, P, *The Politics of Self Sufficiency*. Oxford University Press, Oxford, 1980, 231. See also Pepper, supra n101, 198–199.

192 Paehlke, R C, *Environmentalism and the Future of Progressive Politics*. MIT Press, Massachusetts, 1989, 194. Goodin, supra n73, 105–109. Spretnak, C and Capra, F, *Green Politics: The Global Promise*. Bear, New Mexico, 1986, 93–94, 98. Bosselmann, supra n160, 247–253. Karp, J, 'A Private Property Duty of Stewardship: Changing Our Land Ethic', *Environmental Law* 23, 1993, 735–762.

193 For a full discussion of this important distinction, see Eckersley, R, *Markets, The State and The Environment*. Macmillan, Melbourne, 1995, 25–28, 294–309.

194 Winstanley, G (1649), 'A Declaration From the Poor Oppressed People of England', in Sabine, G (ed), *The Works of Gerrard Winstanley*. Russel, New York, 1965, 269–271.

195 Mill, J S, 'Principles of Political Economy', in Robinson, J M (ed), *The Collected Works of J.S. Mill*. University of Toronto Press, Toronto, 1965, 136.

196 Pinchot, G, *The Fight For Conservation*. Harcourt, New York, 1910, 46. See also McConnell, G, 'The Conservation Movement: Past and Present', in Burton, I and Kates, R W (eds), *Readings in Resource Management and Conservation*. University of Chicago Press, Chicago, 1965, 189, 192.

197 Pinchot, supra n196, 79–81. Pinchot, G, *Breaking New Ground*. Harcourt, New York, 1947, 506–507.

198 Ekins, P, *A New World Order: Grassroots Movements for Global Change*. Routledge, London, 1992, 142. McBurney, S, *Ecology into Economics Won't Go*. Green Books, Devon, 1990, 60–63. Trainer, T, *Developed to Death: Rethinking Third World Development*. Green Print, London, 1989, 17–18. Monbiot, G, 'The Lie of the Land', *New Internationalist* 235, 1992, 10–11. *Ecologist*, 'Whose Common Future?', supra n125, 141–144. Ponting, C, *A Green History of the World*. Sinclair-Stevenson, London, 1991, 251.

199 Buick, A, 'The Rich are Still There', *Socialist Standard* 89, 1992, 89. O'Toole, G, 'Brazil's Poor Pay Bloody Price in Battle for Land', *Guardian Weekly* 23 June 1996. Vidal, J, 'Landless on the Long March Home', *Guardian Weekly* 11 May 1997, 8–9.

200 Monbiot, supra n187, 18, 19.

201 Schumacher, E F, *Small is Beautiful*. Abacus, London, 1974, 223. Tawney, R H, *The Acquisitive Society*. Bell, London, 1962, 44, 53. Kemp, P and Wall, D, *A Green Manifesto For the 1990s*. Penguin, Harmondsworth, 1990, 68–69, 81.

202 See FAO, *Contemporary Thinking On Land Reform*. FAO, Rural Development Division, Rome, 2000. FAO, *Recent FAO Experiences in Land Reform and Land Tenure*. FAO, Rural Development Division, Rome, 1999. Dorner, P, *Land Reform and Economic Development*. Penguin, Harmondsworth, 1972.

203 See Walinsky, L J (ed), *The Selected Papers of Wolf Ladejinsky: Agrarian Reform as Unfinished Business*. World Bank, Oxford University Press, 1977, 10–12. Bello, W, *Brave New Third World: Strategies For Survival in the Global Economy*. Earthscan, London, 1990, 40–42. Cassen, R, *Does Aid Work?* Oxford University Press, Oxford, 1995, 48–50. Sasson, A, *Feeding Tomorrow's World*. UNESCO, Paris, 1990, 458–459. Watkins, supra n165, 34–37, 87, 90–91, 222.

204 Ghai, D (ed), *Development and Environment: Sustaining People and Nature*. Blackwell, Cambridge, 1994, 5–9. Holmberg, J, Bass, S and Timberlake, L (eds), *Defending the Future: A Guide to Sustainable Development*. Earthscan, London, 1991, 18–20. Hurst, P, *Rainforest Politics: Forest Destruction in South East Asia*. Zed, London, 1990, 269, 276. Middleton, N, O'Keefe, P and Moyo, S, *From Rio to Reality in the Developing World*. Pluto, London, 1993, 108–132.

205 Dowdeswell, E, *Speech at World Summit for Social Development*. UNEP, Speech 1995/3, 1995, 5.

206 See Dudley, N, Madeley, J and Stolton, S, *Land is Life: Land Reform and Sustainable Agriculture*. Intermediate Technology Publications, London, 1992, ix–xv. Sale, supra n189, 354–355, 366–367.

207 Chambers, R, *Sustainable Livelihoods, Environment and Development: Putting Poor Rural People First.* University of Sussex, Brighton, 1988, 13. Chambers, R, 'Sustainable Livelihoods: The Poor's Reconciliation of Environment and Development', in Ekins and Max-Neef (eds), supra n97, 214, 216. Toulman, C, 'The Future of Africa's Drylands', in Holmberg (ed), supra n42, 225, 243. Sargent, C and Bass, S, 'The Future Shape of Forests', also in Holmberg, 195, 220. Holmberg et al, supra n204, 10. Seitz, L, *The Politics of Development.* Blackwell, Oxford, 1988, 10.

208 Ibid, 12. Dorner, supra n202, 18, 29. Walinsky, supra n203, 11. Kemp and Wall, supra n201, 113. Hurst, supra n204, 270.

209 World Conference on Agrarian Reform and Rural Development. Rome 12–20 July 1979. UN Doc WCARRD/REP. Also contained in the Report to the Secretary General to the General Assembly A/34/485.

210 Brandt Commission, *North-South: A Programme For Survival.* Pan Books, London, 1980, 130.

211 South Commission, supra n2, 37.

212 WCED, supra n79, 13, 141.

213 Advisory Panel on Food Security, *Report to the World Commission on Environment and Development: Food 2000. Global Policies for Sustainable Agriculture.* Zed, London, 1987, 106.

214 Paragraph 6 and principle 2, *The Manila Declaration on People's Participation and Sustainable Development.* Manila, 10 June 1989. Reprinted in Starke, L (ed), *Signs of Hope: Working Towards Our Common Future.* Oxford University Press, Oxford, 1990, 80–81.

215 Principle 5, and 12 (d), *Statement of Principles for a Global Consensus on the Development of all Types of Forests.* UNCED Doc A/CONF. 151/6/Rev 1. 1992.

216 *Report of the World Food Summit.* WFS 96/REP. FAO, Rome. Rome Declaration on World Food Security and World Food Summit Plan of Action, Paragraph 19(d).

217 See 'Contemporary Thinking', FAO, supra n202.

218 Chapter 32, 32.6 (b) and 32.7 (d) *Agenda 21*, supra n36. This approach was reiterated with the 1997 UNGA Special Session Review of Agenda 21. See UNGA Special Session 1997, *Programme for the Further Implementation of Agenda 21,* 1 July 1997, Paragraph 62. In a similar sense, see World Bank, *World Bank and the Environment.* World Bank, Washington, DC, 1993, 88–91. For a discussion of this oversight, see Middleton, supra n204, 122–124, 51. Dorner, supra n202, 147.

219 Habitat II, supra n182, Paragraphs 63, 75, 76.

CHAPTER 4 TRADE

1 Smith, A, (1776) *An Inquiry Into the Nature and Causes of the Wealth of Nations.* Methuen, London, 1904.

2 Ibid, Book iv, Chapter 1.

3 Ricardo, D, *Principles of Political Economy and Taxation.* London, 1817, 133–134. Note, Adam Smith also realized that, 'both may find it more advantageous to buy off one another, than to make what does not belong to their particular trade'. Smith, supra n1, vol 1, 280.

4 Section 2.5, *Agenda 21.* UNCED Doc A/CONF. 151/4.

5 See Bolitho, A, 'The Return of Free Trade', *International Affairs* 72, 1996, 247–529. Kravis, I B, 'Trade as the Handmaiden of Growth', *Economic Journal* 80, 1970, 850–872. cf. Evans, D, 'Visible and Invisible Hands in Trade Policy Reform', in Colclough, C (ed), *States or Markets.* Clarendon Press, Oxford, 1995, 48–77.

6 Preamble, *General Agreement on Trade and Tariffs.* 55 UNTS 187. 1948.

7 International Monetary Fund, *Annual Report: 1993.* IMF, Washington, DC, 12.

8   See World Bank, *Trade and the Environment*. World Bank, Dissemination Notes no 13, 1995. cf. Lang, T and Hines, C, *The New Protectionism: Protecting the Future Against Free Trade*. Earthscan, London, 1993, 55–57.

9   *Weekly Presidential Documents*. Washington, DC, 22 July 1991, 969.

10 The Report is *Trade and the Environment*. World Trade Materials 4, 1992, 2. An earlier GATT Group was established in 1972 – the Group on Environmental Measures and International Trade – but has never been convened.

11 For the League of Nations example, see League of Nations Document CEI 22, article 21. For Article 20 of GATT, see GATT, TIAS no 1700; 55 UNTS 187, 262. Amended, TIAS no 3930; 278 UNTS 168, 200. For the European Example, see Article 12, Convention Establishing European Free Trade Agreement. UNTS 370, 5.

12 *The Rio Declaration on Environment and Development*. UNCED A/Conf. 151/5/Rev 1, 1992.

13 See Article 3 (5) of the *United Nations Convention on Climate Change*. UNCED A/AC. 237/18 (PART II) Add 1, 15 May 1992. See also Sections 2.3 (b), 11.23 (k), *Agenda 21*, supra note 4.

14 NAFTA actually goes so far as to call upon its signatories to 'promote sustainable development' and 'Strengthen the development and enforcement of environmental laws and regulations.' Preamble, 'North American Free Trade Agreement', *International Legal Materials* 32, 1993.

15 Preamble, *Agreement Establishing the World Trade Organisation*. MTN/FA II.

16 See *Report of the WTO Committee on Trade and the Environment*. WTO, Geneva, Press/TE 014, Paragraph 167. 1994.

17 Principle 10, *Stockholm Conference on the Human Environment*. UN Doc A/CONF. 48/14/Rev 1.

18 Pearson Commission, *Partners in Development*. Pall Mall Press, London, 1969, 14, 15, 97.

19 Brandt Commission, *North–South: A Programme For Survival*. Pan, London, 1980, 21, 32, 69–72, 100, 141–158, 186.

20 Brandt Commission, *North–South: Common Crisis*. Pan, London, 1983, 15.

21 WCED, *Our Common Future*. Oxford University Press, Oxford, 1987, 18.

22 South Commission, *The Challenge of the South*. Oxford University Press, Oxford, 1990, 224, 245, 247–53.

23 Strategy XX, WWF, *World Conservation Strategy*. Reprinted in Rusta, B and Simma, B (eds), *International Protection of the Environment*. Oceana, New York, 1981, vol 13, 424.

24 WCED, supra n21, 18, 36, 67, 79, 132.

25 'The Cartagena Commitment on Free Trade', *Environmental Policy and the Law* 22, 1992, 189, 190.

26 It should not be assumed that all countries that are heavily commodity dependent suffered because of the slumps in the 1980s. Indeed, several countries that are commodity dependent, such as Chile, Indonesia, Malaysia, Mexico, the Philippines and Thailand, have all grown strongly in their trade in commodities. Of course, these countries have also all had distinct environmental problems with the heavy nature of much of their commodity production.

27 Ponting, C, *A Green History of the World*. Sinclair-Stevenson, London, 1991, 116, 128, 195, 200, 214–220. See also Hudson, M, *Trade, Development and Foreign Debt*. Pluto, London, 1992, 24–26, 32–34.

28 Coote, B, *The Trade Trap: Poverty and the Global Commodity Markets*. Oxfam, Oxford, 1992, 3–13. Adams, W M, *Green Development: Environment and Sustainability in the Third World*. Routledge, London, 1992, 104–106. Bello, W, *Brave New Third World: Strategies For Survival in the Global Economy*. Earthscan, London, 1990, 18–23. Lang and Hines, supra n8, 16–19. Watkins, K, *The Oxfam Poverty Report*. Oxfam, Oxford, 1995, 115–117.

29 It is important to note that this is not a rule for developing countries generally. See Page, S, *How Developing Countries Trade: The Institutional Constraints*. Routledge, London, 1994, 92–98.

30 Brock, W E, 'Trade and Debt: The Vital Linkage', *Foreign Affairs* 62, 1984, 87. 'Cartagena Commitment on Foreign Debt', *International Legal Materials* 1985, 1699. George, S, *A Fate Worse Than Debt*. Penguin, Harmondsworth, 1990, 60. Hudson, supra n27, 280–281, 307. Brandt Commission, supra n19, 30.

31 These are non-tariff barriers, the Multi-Fibre Agreement and Anti-Dumping Measures. Indeed, in this regard, it must be recognized that Northern protectionism continues in a number of guises. Vaughan, S, *Trade and the Environment: Perspectives from Developing Countries*. UNEP, Nairobi, 1994, 2–3. Bello, W, *Dark Victory: The United States, Structural Adjustment and Global Poverty*. Pluto, London, 1994, 84–86. Watkins, K, *The Oxfam Poverty Report*. Oxfam, Oxford, 1995, 136–138.

32 South Commission, supra n22, 242–244. Brandt Commission, supra n19, 52. See also the World Bank, *The Challenge of Development*. Oxford University Press, Oxford, 1991, 113. Valley, P, *Bad Samaritans: First World Ethics and Third World Debt*. Hodder, London, 1990, 107–111.

33 GATT Secretariat, *Change For the Better*. Washington, DC, 1991, 7. See also Page, supra n29, 124–138, 284–290.

34 See Watkins, supra n28, 120–121.

35 South Commission, supra n22, 241–42. Jackson, B, *Poverty and the Planet: A Question of Survival*. Penguin, Harmondsworth, 1990, 75. Carlie, I and Christie, M, *Managing Sustainable Development*. Earthscan, London, 1992, 114–115. Coote, supra n28, 96, 102.

36 Pearson Commission, supra n18, 72. Note that the need for open Northern markets for a number of Southern goods, due to declining purchasing power predates the Pearson Commission. See for example points A and B of the 1967 *Charter of Algiers: Ministerial Meeting of 77 Developing Countries*. Reproduced from UN Doc MM 77/I/20, 20 October 1967. For two international discussions of this in the 1970s, see the 1975 *Conference of Developing Countries on Raw Materials*. UNCTAD Doc TD/B/C.1/L. 45, 17 February 1975. UNCTAD, *G:77 Manila Declaration*. UNCTAD Doc TD/195, 12 February 1976.

37 As one of the preparatory committees for the 1992 Earth Summit noted, between 1980 and 1988 the real prices of non-fuel commodities from Southern countries declined by 40%. Simultaneously, fuel prices declined by 50% in the same period. In sub-Saharan Africa alone, incomes fell by one-third between 1980 and 1988 as a result of the deterioration in the terms of trade. UNCED, *The International Economy and Environment and Development*. A/CONF. 151/PC/47, Geneva, 1991, 7. See also the South Commission, supra n22, 57–60. WCED, supra n21, 36. 15.

38 See UNCTAD, *Commodity Producers Call for International Action in the Short Term*. TAD/INF/2606, 1 November 1995. UNCTAD, *Modest Economic Growth in LDCs*. TAD/INF/2645, 28 March 1996.

39 World Bank, *Global Economic Outlook: 1994*. Oxford University Press, Oxford, 1994, 48–50. Coote, B, *The Hunger Crop: Poverty and the Sugar Industry*. Oxfam, Oxford, 1987, 28–32, 36. Bello, supra n28, 47–48, 74. Thomas, C, 'The Economic Crisis and the Commonwealth Caribbean', in Ghai, D (ed), *The IMF and the South: The Social Impact of Crisis Adjustment*. Zed, London, 1991, 43, 48–49.

40 Schmidheiny, S/Business Council for Sustainable Development, *Changing Course*. MIT Press, Massachusetts, 1992, 69. Report of the South Centre, *Environment and Development: Towards A Common Strategy for the South in the UNCED Negotiations and Beyond*. South Centre, Geneva, 1991, 8.

41 Principle 12, *The Rio Declaration*, supra n12, Sections 2.5, 2.7, 2.10 and 2.19 of *Agenda 21*, supra n4. See Section 13 (a) and (b) of the *Statement of Principles for a*

Global Consensus for the Conservation and Sustainable Development of All Types of Forests. UNCED Doc A/CONF. 151/6/Rev 1. 1992.

42 Mac Neil, J, Winsemius, P and Yakushiji, T, *Beyond Interdependence: The Meshing of the World's Economy and the Earth's Ecology.* Oxford University Press, Oxford, 1991, 61. Hurst, P, *Rainforest Politics: Forest Destruction in South-East Asia.* Zed, London, 1990, 267. Juniper, T, *Whose Hand on the Chainsaw.* Friends of the Earth, London, 1992, 34.

43 Pearce, F, 'A GATT To Our Heads', *BBC Wildlife* 10(5), 1992, 58. Housman, R and Zaelke, D, 'Trade, Environment, and Sustainable Development', *Hastings International and Comparative Law Review* 15, 1992, 535, 559. *Trade and the Environment*, supra n10, 28, 34.

44 Article 13 (b) of the *Statement of Principles on Forests*, supra n41. See also GATT, *International Trade 90–91.* GATT, Geneva, 1992, vol 1, Chapter 3. Pearce, D and Warford, J J, *World Without End: Economics, Environment and Sustainable Development.* World Bank, Washington, DC, 1993, 284–287, 298–299. Anderson, K and Blackhurst, R, 'Trade, The Environment and Public Purpose', in Anderson, K and Blackhurst, R (eds), *The Greening of World Trade Issues.* Harvester, London, 1992, 3, 14–15, 167.

45 See WTO, supra n16, Paragraph 197.

46 See Report of the Independent Commission on Population and Quality of Life, *Caring For the Future.* Oxford University Press, Oxford, 1996, 270–271.

47 UNGA Special Session. Overall Review and Appraisal of the Implementation of Agenda 21: Trade and Environmental Matters. A/S-19/4/E1997/13, 1997, Paragraph 25. Bergeikj, P A G, 'International Trade and the Environmental Challenge', *Journal of World Trade Law* 25, 1991, 105, 106. World Bank, *World Development Report 1992: Development and the Environment.* Oxford University Press, Oxford, 1992, 67. Schmidheiny, supra n40, xi–xii.

48 Sections 2.5, 2.19, *Agenda 21*, supra n4.

49 Jackson, J H, 'World Trade Rules and Environmental Policies: Congruence or Conflict', *Washington and Lee Law Review* 49, 1992, 1227, 1243–1244. Watkins, supra n28, 14.

50 *Trade and the Environment*, supra n10, 20.

51 See principle 6 of the OECD Guiding Principles on the Environment. U.S. Dept of State Release no 130, 1 June. *International Legal Materials* 11, 1972. 1172.

52 See Low, P (ed), *International Trade and the Environment.* World Bank Discussion Paper No 159, Washington, DC, 1992, iii. See also Jackson, supra n49, 1227, 1249. Schmidheiny, supra n40, 70.

53 Pearson, D, 'The Environment and International Economic Policy', in Joint Economic Committee, *The United States Role in a Changing World Economy.* Congressional Quarterly, Washington, DC, 1989, 114–115.

54 Anderson and Blackhurst, supra n44, 3, 16–17, 19–20, 167, 241–242.

55 Section 7, Cartagena Commitment, supra n25 189, 190. See also UNGA Special Session: Programme for the Further Implementation of Agenda 21, 1 July 1997, Paragraph 29.

56 *Agenda 21*, supra n4, Chapters 17.6 (e), 39.3 (d). *Trade and the Environment*, supra n10, 27–30. Anderson and Blackhurst, supra n44, 3, 16–17, 19–20, 167, 241–242. World Bank, supra n47, 67.

57 Ruggiero, R, 'Global Policy Coherence for Our Global Age', *Environmental Policy and the Law* 28, 1997, 79,80. For further discussions on this area, see *Trade and the Environment*, supra n10, 32–34. Pearce and Warford, supra n44, 58. Lang and Hines, supra n8, 64–65. World Bank, supra n47, 67. See also Chapter 3 of this book. Note, however, that this point is a matter of debate for some international guidelines such as point 5 of the *OECD's Guiding Principles on the Environment*, supra n51, which

emphasizes the Polluter Pays Principle (which should lead to correct environmental pricing). Note, however, the principle goes on to specify that the polluter pays principle 'Should be an objective of member countries ... provided that they do not lead to significant distortions of international trade and investment'.

58 Commission on Global Governance, *Our Global Neighbourhood*. Oxford University Press, Oxford, 1995, 169.

59 WTO, *United States–Import Prohibition of Certain Shrimp and Shrimp Products.* WT/DS58/AB/R, 12 October 1998, Paragraph 184. For a full discussion of this overall approach, see Hansen, P I, 'Transparency, Standards of Review, and Use of Trade Measures to Protect the Global Environment', *Virginia Journal of International Law* 39, 1999, 1017–1068.

60 Founex Report, *Environment and Development.* Reprinted as Annex 1 to UN Doc A/CONF. 48/10, 10 December 1971. Or *International Conciliation.* No 586, New York, 1972.

61 Recommendation 103. UN Doc A/Conf. 48/14, 1972. This ideal was earlier recognized in principle 4 (e) of the UNGA Res 2849(XXVI), 7 December 1970, on 'Development and the Environment' which suggested that the 1972 Stockholm Conference should 'avoid any adverse effects of environmental pricing on the economies of developing countries, including [through] international trade.'

62 Principle 12, Rio Declaration, supra n12.

63 Dunkel, noted in Pearce, supra n43, 58.

64 *Trade and the Environment,* supra n10, 4–6, 19–20. See also Charnovitz, S, 'Environmental Trade Measures: Multilateral or Unilateral', *Environmental Law and Policy* 23, 1993, 154, 157. Ruggiero, supra n57, 81.

65 Cartagena Commitment, supra n25, Paragraph 152.

66 Principle 12, supra n12. Sections 2.8, 2.22, 11.24, 17.6, 39.3 (d), Agenda 21, supra n4. Article 3 (5), *Convention on Climate Change,* supra n13. Article 13 (a), and 14, *Statement of Principles for a Global Consensus on the Management, Conservation and Sustainable Development of all Types of Forests.* UNCED Doc A/CONF. 151/6/Rev 1.

67 Caracas Declaration. LA/MM/77(VIII)/1, 30 January 1996, Paragraphs 34 and 35. See also the Addis Ababa Declaration on UNCTAD IX AF/MM/77(VIII)/1, 22 February 1996, Paragraphs 62 and 63.

68 *Tuna/Dolphin Panel Report.* GATT Doc DS 21/R, 3 September 1991, 46. US–Mexico Tuna Dolphin Panel. Also reprinted in *International Legal Materials* 30, 1991, 1594, 1622.

69 *Convention on International Trade in Endangered Species.* UNTS Vol 973 (No I. 14537), 243–438.

70 *Convention on the Control of Transboundary Movements of Hazardous Wastes and their Disposal.* UN Doc UNEP/WG.190/4. Also in *International Legal Materials* 28, 1989, 657. This trade was largely curtailed in 1994.

71 Montreal Protocol on Substances that Deplete the Ozone Layer. *International Legal Materials* 26, 1987, 1541, Article 1 (c), II (2), (3). For a very useful analysis of the overlap between trade and the Montreal Protocol see Brack, D, *International Trade and the Montreal Protocol.* Earthscan, London, 1996.

72 'Update: Summary of Panel's Decision', *Environmental Law and Policy* 21, 1991, 214. Hooley, M T, 'Resolving Conflict Between GATT and Domestic Environmental Laws', *William Mitchell Law Review* 18, 1992, 483, 489–98.

73 Some trade agreements, such as NAFTA, specifically mandate this. See article 104.

74 See World Trade Organisation, Report of the General Council to the 1996 Ministerial Conference, WT/MIN(96)/2, Vol 1, Paragraph 173 (IV), 1996. 'In practice, in cases where there is a consensus among Parties to an MEA to apply among themselves specifically mandated trade measures, disputes between them over the use of such measures are unlikely to occur in the WTO.' Ruggiero suggested although this area may 'be open

to question ... the reality is that – so far – the issue of legal compatibility is a theoretical, not a practical problem for the trading system.' Ruggiero, supra n57, 81. However, when a MEA involves action against non-signatories to the MEA, such as CITES or the Basel Convention, then it is highly possible that they could run foul of the GATT. See Makuck, Z, 'The World Trade Organisation and the General Agreement on Tariffs and Trade', in Werksman, J (ed), *Greening International Institutions*. Earthscan, London, 1996, 94, 100–106. Lang, W, 'Trade and the Environment: Progress in the WTO ?' *Environmental Policy and the Law* 27, 1997, 275, 278.

75   See UNCTAD, 'Report of the Workshop on Eco-Labeling and International Trade', TD/B/WG.6/Misc.2, 1994. See also OECD, 'Eco-Labelling and International Trade', 1994. This seminar was made available through the Linkages Network. <http://www.iisd.ca/linkages/>.

76   See *Report of the Topical Seminar on Environment, Competitiveness and Trade: A Development Perspective*. UNCTAD IX/Misc.2, 12 March 1996, Paragraphs 52 and 53.

77   See Chapter 40 of Agenda 21, supra n4.

78   See Hemenway, C G, *What is ISO 14,000: Questions and Answers*. Fairfax Station, Virginia, 1995.

79   *Treaty of Economic Association between El-Salvador, Honduras and Guatemala*. UNTS 383, 1960, Article 7. Note, this agreement is no longer in force.

80   Treaty Establishing A Free Trade Area and Instituting the Latin American Free Trade Association (1960), in Urquidi, V, *Free Trade and Economic Integration in Latin America*. University of California Press, Berkeley, 1962, Article 16.

81   Recommendations 103 and 104 of the Stockholm Action Plan. This is annexed to the Declaration, supra n17.

82   Brandt Commission, supra n19, 114.

83   Asia-Pacific Economic Co-operation Forum, *Achieving the APEC Vision*. Singapore, 1994, 20. Note, this was not accepted by APEC, although it may be in the future.

84   See chapters 1, 2 and 3 of the *Programme of Action of the European Communities on the Environment*. The Programme goes on to emphasize that 'the expenditure [ie the economic cost of anti-pollution measures] should be apportioned in such a way, that it does not jeopardise free trade and competition.' Annex, Part II, Chapter 9, *Official Journal of the European Communities* 16(C 112), 20 December 1973.

85   This idea was earlier noted by the OECD in 1972, which suggested 'Where products [that involve 'environmental questions'] are traded internationally and where there could be significant obstacles to trade, Governments should seek common starndards.' See point 10. OECD, supra note 51. See also Schmidheiny, supra n40, 30.

86   See Broman, M F, 'The United States and the European Community Hormone Treated Beef Conflict', *Harvard International Law Journal* 30, 1989, 549, 554. For earlier attempts to deal with harmonization, see the Preamble and Articles 2.2 and 2.3 of the *Agreement on Technical Barriers to Trade*. GATT Doc L/4907, BISD (26th Suppl) 8, 1980.

87   See the Preamble, and Articles 6, 9,10 and 17 of Annex 1.A: 4, *Agreement on the Application of Sanitary and Phytosanitary Measures*. GATT, Sanitary Measures, MTN/FA II-A/A-3. See also the Preamble and Article 2.2 and 2.5 of the *Agreement on Technical Barriers to Trade*. GATT, Technical Barriers, MTN/FA II-A/A-6. See also Article 6 and 17 of the Sanitary Measures. The difference between the SPS Agreement, and the TBT Agreement, is that the SPS refers specifically to laws and regulations that concern food and food safety, including pesticide regulation and biotechnology. The TBT takes a somewhat broader focus, and may encompass environmental standards from other sources. The above quote on 'sound scientific evidence' is from Ruggiero, supra n57, 81.

88   WCED, supra n21, 65.

89   Principle 6 (f), 'Bergen Conference: Ministerial Declaration on Sustainable Development', *Environmental Policy and the Law* 20, 1990, 105.

90   See UNEP, 'UNEP Calls for Integrated Approach to Trade and Environment Policy Making at WTO Seattle Conference', *UNEP News Release* 1999/132. UNEP, 'UNEP Highlights Five Key Environmental Considerations in the Trade-Environment Debate', *UNEP News Release* 1999/136.

91   Daly, H E and Cobb, J, *For the Common Good: Redirecting the Economy Towards the Community, the Environment and a Sustainable Future.* Beacon, Boston, 1989, 214. Lever, H and Huhne, C, *Debt and Danger: The World's Financial Crisis.* Penguin, Harmondsworth, 1985, 7.

92   Smith, A (1776), *An Enquiry into the Wealth of Nations.* Methuen, London, 1904, 423. For the critiques of this belief, see Keynes, J M, 'National Self Sufficiency', in Moggridge, D (ed), *The Collected Works of J.M. Keynes.* Macmillan, London, 1989, 230–236. Lang and Hines, supra n8, 22–23. Morris, D, 'Free Trade: The Great Destroyer', *Ecologist* 20, 1990, 190–194.

93   Hudson, supra n27, 141, 185–188. Ruigrok, W, 'Paradigm Crisis in International Trade Theory', *Journal of World Trade Law* 25, 1991, 61.

94   Goodman, D and Redclift, M, *Refashioning Nature: Food, Ecology and Culture.* Routledge, London, 1991, 188–191. Bello, supra n28, 16–18. Thomas, C, 'The Economic Crisis and the Commonwealth Caribbean', in Ghai (ed), supra n39, 43, 48–49. Lang and Hines, supra n8, 76–77.

95   Commission on Global Governance, supra n58, 178.

96   See Costanza, R, 'Sustainable Trade: A New Paradigm for World Welfare', *Environment* 17(5), 1995, 16–20. Hudson, supra n27, 120–141.

97   For the issue of debt, see Chapter 5 of this book. For some analysis of the effect of debt upon trade, see Claessens, S, *Analytical Aspects of the Debt Problem of Heavily Indebted Poor Countries.* World Bank, 1996.

98   Even Adam Smith was adamant upon this point, supra n92, 422–423, 431, 455–461.

99   Logan, B I, 'An Assessment of the Environmental and Economic Implications of Toxic Waste Disposal in Sub–Saharan Africa', *Journal of World Trade Law* 25, 1991, 61, 73–74. Handl, G F and Lutz, R, 'The Transboundary Trade in Hazardous Technologies and Substances from a Policy Perspective', in Handl, G E and Lutz, R (eds), *Transferring Hazardous Technologies and Substances: The International Legal Challenge.* Graham and Trotman, London, 1989, 41. Daly and Cobb, supra n91, 213. Tolba, M, 'The Global Agenda and the Hazardous Wastes Challenge', *Marine Policy* 1990, 208.

100   This is a past tense conversation because the international trade in toxic waste has now been largely curtailed, and is dealt with under the specific multilateral environmental agreement (the Basel Convention). See Krueger, J, *International Trade and the Basel Convention.* Earthscan, London, 1999.

101   Ramsay, R, 'UNCTAD's Failures: The Rich Get Richer', in Snyder, F E and Sathirathai, S (eds), *Third World Attitudes Towards International Law.* Nijhoff, Dordecht, 1987, 407. Raghaven, C, *Recolonisation; GATT; the Uruguay Round and the Third World.* Third World Network, Penang, 1990, 333, 41, 295. Ekins, P, 'Trade and Self Reliance', *Ecologist* 19, 1989, 186. Goldin, I, *Trade Liberalisation: Global Economic Implications.* OECD/World Bank, Paris, 1993.

102   See Gereffi, G, 'Power and Dependence in an Interdependent World', in Little, R and Smith, M, *Perspectives on World Politics.* Routledge, London, 1994, 318–324.

103   See Francois, J, *Economy-wide Effects of the Uruguay Round.* GATT Background Paper No 3, Geneva, 1993. Denny, C, 'New Big Five Are Set to Redraw Global Trade Map', *Guardian International* 21 September 1997. According to the World Bank, the big five are Brazil, China, India, Indonesia and Russia.

104   Midrand Declaration and A Partnership for Growth and Development. TD/377. UNCTAD IX, 1996, Paragraphs 2, 16, 21.

105   Commission on Sustainable Development, *Development Issues Facing Island Developing Countries: Basic Issues and Prospects in the Context of Trade*

Liberalisation and Globalisation. E/CN.17/1996/IDC/2. UNCTAD/LLDC/IDC/2, 1997, Paragraph 29, 64.

106 UNGA Special Session. Programme for the Further Implementation of Agenda 21, 1 July 1997, Paragraph 7. See also UNGA, *Overall Review of UNCED: Trade and Environmental Matters.* A/S-19/4/E/1997/13, 1997, Paragraph 18.

107 Page, S, *How Developing Countries Trade: The Institutional Constraints.* Routledge, London, 1994, 99–123. Martin, B, *In The Public Interest: Privatisation and Public Sector Reform.* Zed, London, 1994, 160–169. Sexton, S, 'Transnational Corporations and Trade', *Ecologist* 26(6), 1996, 256–258. Hudson, supra n27, 139–141, 280–281. Additionally, there are differences with who benefits from free trade *within* countries, as the benefits are not usually distributed equitably. See Chirchilnisky, G, 'North–South Trade, Property Rights and the Dynamics of the Environment', in Campiglio, L and Pineschi, L (eds), *The Environment After Rio: International Law and Economics.* Graham and Trotman, London, 1994, 131, 139–143. Watkins, supra n31, 110–111.

108 See Gibbon, P, *A Blighted Harvest: The World Bank and African Agriculture in the 1980s.* James Currie, London, 1993, Chapter 4. Kneen, B, 'The Invisible Giant: Cargill and its Transnational Strategies', *Ecologist* 25(5), 1995, 195–199. See also Watkins, supra n31, 130–132. Korten, D C, *When Corporations Rule the World.* Earthscan, London, 1995, 75–76, 179–182, 224–226.

109 See Barratt-Brown, M, *Fair Trade: Reform and Realities in the International Trade System.* Zed, London, 1993, 68.

110 See Dowdeswell, E, *Speech to the Oslo Roundtable on Sustainable Consumption.* UNEP Speech 1995/1, 1995, 6.

111 UNEP, *Global Environmental Outlook.* Oxford University Press, Oxford, 1997, 3.

112 See Chapter 3.

113 UNCTAD VIII *Report by the UNCTAD Secretariat to the Conference.* TD/358, 1992, 269–270.

114 See Andersson, T, Folke, C and Nystrom, S, *Trading with the Environment: Ecology, Economics, Institutions and Policy.* Earthscan, London, 1995, 22–23, 28–31, 53, 64–65, 112–113.

115 Dowdeswell, E, *Speech to the World Summit on Social Development.* UNEP Speech 1995/3, 1995, 5.

116 World Bank, supra n8.

117 UNEP, 'UNEP & UNCTAD Join Forces', *UNEP Press Release* 27 September 1996.

118 *Midrand Declaration and A Partnership for Growth and Development.* TD/377. UNCTAD IX, 1996, Paragraph 34.

119 Commission on Sustainable Development, *Trade, Environment and Sustainable Development: Report of the Secretary General.* E/CN.17/1996/8, 3 April 1996, Paragraphs 21, 23, 38(b). Commission on Sustainable Development, *General Discussion on Progress in the Implementation of Agenda 21: Trade, Environment and Sustainable Development: Report of the Secretary General.* E/CN.17/1995/12, 31 March 1995, Paragraphs 37–38, 43, 51–55, 90.

120 Gillespie, A, 'The Contradiction in International Environmental Law between the Free Market, Environmental Protection and Free Trade', *Waikato Law Review* 3, 1995, 127–137.

121 Principle 16, *Rio Declaration,* supra n12.

122 OECD, Guiding Principles Concerning International Economic Aspects of Environmental Policies. Paris, 1972, Annex A (a) (5). See also the 'World Industry Council for the Environment', Environmental Policy and Law 23, 1993, 55.

123 Schmidheiny, supra n40, 80. The BCSD revisited this question in 1994 and suggested that the best way that internalization could be achieved was, in essence, to allow the countries to develop economically and then, over a long time period seek to incorporate the costs. Most importantly, the BCSD stressed that trade restrictions upon

such non-internalizing sources should not be invoked. See BCSD, *Internalising Environmental Costs to Promote Eco-Efficiency*. BCSD, Geneva, 1994, 6–9, 56–71. This position seems broadly in congruence with the Intergovernmental Work Programme on the Environment and Sustainable Development within the UNCTAD, which suggested that price internalization was a means towards the ultimate goal of the efficient avoidance of environmental costs, not a goal in itself. See UNCTAD, *Sustainable Development: A Policy Review of UNCTAD's Activities*. TD/B/41(2)/10, 1995, Geneva. For a full discussion of this, see Arda, M, 'The United Nations Conference on Trade and Development', in Werksman, supra n74, 71–93. The obvious problem with this back-seating of price internalization is that it will not be able to achieve the objective which it seeks – namely, stopping unsustainable development.

124 See UNEP, *Informal Summary of UNCTAD-UNEP High Level Meeting on Trade, Environment and Development*. UNEP, Nairobi, 1994, Paragraph 4 (c).

125 See UNCTAD, *Standing Committee on Commodities*. TAD/INF/2603, 27 October 1995.

126 *Agreement on Technical Barriers to Trade*. GATT Doc L/4907, BISD (26th Suppl) 56, 1980. See also Doane, M, 'Green Light Subsidies: Technology Policy in International Trade', *Syracuse Journal of International Law* 21, 1995, 155–177.

127 Ritchie, M, 'Free Trade versus Sustainable Agriculture: The Implications of NAFTA', *Ecologist* 22, 1992, 221, 225. Ritchie, M, 'GATT, Agriculture and the Environment: The US Double Zero Plan', *Ecologist* 20, 1990, 214. Smets, H, 'The Polluter Pays Principle in the Early 1990s', in Campiglio (ed), supra n107, 131, 139–143. Housman, R and Zaelke, D, 'Trade, Environment, and Sustainable Development: A Primer', *Hastings International and Comparative Law Review* 15, 1992, 535, 541, 555. Shrybman, S, 'International Trade and the Environment, An Environmental Assessment of GATT', *Ecologist* 20, 1990, 30, 32. Jackson, J H, 'World Trade Rules and Environmental Policies: Congruence or Conflict', *Washington and Lee Law Review* 49, 1992, 1227, 1247. Warnock, J W, *Free Trade and the New Right Agenda*. New Star, Vancouver, 1987, 159–162.

128 For the European example of this, see the Danish Bottles Case. Judgement of the ECJ, 20 September 1988, Case 302/86. This is fully discussed in Kramer, L, *European Environmental Law*. Sweet and Maxwell, London, 1993, 90–105.

129 Ruggiero, supra n57, 81. For the specific rulings on this point, see US–Mexico Tuna Dolphin Panel, *International Legal Materials* 30, 1991, 1594, 1618. US–EEC Tuna Dolphin Panel, *International Legal Materials* 33, 1994, 842, 888–890.

130 See Andersson et al, supra n114, 87–90.

131 See articles 20 (a), 20 (e), 21. For a useful discussion of this entire area, see Charnovitz, S 'The Moral Exception in Trade Policy', *Virginia Journal of International Law* 38, 1998, 689–745. With specific regard to the issue of national security, see Perez, A, 'WTO and UN Law: Institutional Comity in National Security', *Yale Journal of International Law* 23, 1998, 301–381.

132 See Wise, M and Gibb, R, *Single Market to Social Europe*. Longman, New York, 1993, Chapter 6.

133 See International Confederation of Free Trade Unions, *International Workers: Rights and Trade*. ILO, Geneva, 1994. Mehmet O, *Towards A Fair Global Labour Market*. Routledge, London, 1995.

134 Pearce and Warford, supra n44, 299–300. Note, however, Pearce and Warford suggest that although this is a problem, it is better to create 'corrective policies' such as international financial assistance and technology transfers, rather than distort international trade in an attempt to incorporate environmental costs. See also Goldman, P A, 'Resolving the Trade and Environment Debate: In Search of A Neutral Forum and Neutral Principles', *Washington and Lee Law Review* 49, 1992, 1279, 1290–1291. Lang and Hines, supra n8, 51–53, 89–91. Buckley, R, 'International Trade, Investment and Environmental Regulation', *Journal of World Trade* 27, 1993, 101, 104, 121, 123.

135 See Articles 9, 10, 11 of the *Agreement on the Application of Sanitary and Phytosanitary Measures. GATT: Agreement on Trade in Goods.* MTN/FA II-A/A-1. See also Article 712 (3)–(5), 2014, 2015 and 2015 (1) (2) of the North American Free Trade Agreement. *International Legal Materials* 32, 1992, 297, 377.

136 Article XVI, paragraph 4. *Agreement Establishing the World Trade Organisation,* supra n15.

137 For the harmonization provisions, see the Preamble and Article 9, ibid. For discussions of this, see Walker, V, 'Keeping the WTO From Becoming the 'World Trans-science Organisation', *Cornell International Law Journal* 31, 1998, 251–320. Stevens, C, 'Harmonisation, Trade and the Environment', *International Environmental Affairs 5,* 1993, 42, 48–49. Warnock, supra n127, 159–162. Shrybman, supra n127, 30, 33. Schorenbaum, T J, 'NAFTA: Good For Jobs, The Environment and America', *Georgia Journal of International and Comparative Law* 23, 1993, 461, 486, 491–492.

138 For an example of their work in the international trade arena, see the Codex Commission, *Code of Ethics for International Trade in Food.* Codex Doc CAC/RPC 20, 1979.

139 For the recognition of this decision within the Uruguay Round, see the Preamble and Article 12 of the Sanitary Measures, supra n87. Note that the suggestion that Codex should play a leading role in the creation of international standards goes back to Recommendation 82 of the *Stockholm Action Plan for the Environment.* Attached to the Declaration, supra n17.

140 Clunies-Ross, T and Hildyard, N, *The Politics of Industrial Agriculture.* Earthscan, London, 1992, 108. Note, it is believed that the NAFTA agreement will not 'harmonise down' environmental standards. See Articles 713–714 of NAFTA, supra n14. See also Hustis, B S, 'The Environmental Implications of NAFTA', *Texas International Law Journal* 23, 1993, 589, 614–617. Stewart, R B, 'The NAFTA: Trade, Competition and Environmental Protection', *International Lawyer* 27, 1993, 751, 760, 762.

141 Freestone, D (ed), *The Precautionary Principle and International Law.* Kluwer, Netherlands, 1996. See also Principle 15 of the Rio Declaration, supra n12. Shrader-Frechette, K, 'Environmental Ethics, Uncertainty and Limited Data', in UNEP/Brown, N J (eds), *Ethics and Agenda 21: Moral Implications of a Global Consensus.* UNEP, Nairobi, 1994, 77–83. Walker, supra n137, 290–296.

142 Article 22, Sanitary Measures, supra n87.

143 European Communities – Measures Affecting Meat and Meat Products. WT/DS26/AB/R, Paragraph 123.

144 See Articles 104, 723 (b), 904, 907, 914 (4) and 915, which reverse the burden of scientific causation, to those proposing new standards, as opposed to those defending them. For discussions on the 'environmentally friendly trade agreement' see Ludwiszewski, R B, 'Green Language in the NAFTA : Reconciling Free Trade and Environmental Protection', *International Lawyer* 27, 1993, 691–706. Stewart, supra n140, 760, 762.

145 See Article 712.2, 715.4, 904, 907.3.

146 Article 712.3.

147 Bates, S, 'Beef Hormone Ban Upheld', *Guardian Weekly* March 1996, 24.

148 Isi Siddiqui, a senior trade official in the US Government, said that Japanese plans to identify and label genetically modified foods was unacceptable because: 'Obligatory GM Labelling suggests a health risk where there is none ... I fear major trade disruptions.' This is reported in Pearce, F, 'Free For All', *New Scientist* 27 November 1999. See also Bates, S, 'Trade Clash Looms Over Maize', *Guardian Weekly* 15 March 1996.

149 For the background to this debate, see Nollkaemper, A (ed), *Trapped By Furs: The Legality of the European Community's Fur Import Ban in EC and International Law.* Kluwer, Dordrecht, 1997. This debate was usurped by the *European Commission*

Regulations (No 35/97) Laying Down Provisions on the Certification of Pelts and Goods Covered by Council Regulation 3254/91. With this, specific agreements were reached with the 'offending' countries (Canada, Russia and the United States). These are reprinted in *International Legal Materials* 37, 1998, 532.

150 See Stonehouse, J M and Mumford, J D, *Science, Risk & Environmental Policy Decisions.* UNEP, Environment and Trade Series, No 5, Nairobi, 1994. Nollkaemper, A, 'What You Risk Reveals What you Value and Other Dilemmas Encountered in the Legal Assault on Risks', In Freestone, supra n141, 73–94. Welford, R, *Hijacking Environmentalism: Corporate Responses to Sustainable Development.* Earthscan, London, 1996, 40–62. Lawrence, G, 'Indicators for Sustainable Development', in Dodds, F (ed), *The Way Forward: Beyond Agenda 21.* Earthscan, London, 1997, 179, 182–183, 188–189.

151 Avery, N, 'Codex Alimentarius: Who Is Allowed In? Who Is Left Out?' *Ecologist* 23, 1993, 110, 113.

152 Goldman, supra n134, 1279, 1287–88. Clunies-Ross and Hildyard, supra n140, 108–109.

153 Goldman, supra n134, 1279, 1287. Lang and Hines, supra n8, 100–102. Avery, supra n151, 110, 111–112. Clunies-Ross and Hildyard, supra n140, 110.

154 Commission on Sustainable Development, *Chairman's Text on Trade, Environment and Sustainable Development,* 26 May 1994. Bill Clinton declared: 'We must modernise the WTO by opening its doors to the scrutiny and participation of the public ... I propose that all hearings by the WTO be open to the public.' Quoted in Dionne, E, 'Sidetracked on Road to Global Growth', *Guardian International* 7 June 1998. See also Watkins, supra n31, 146–147. Korten, supra n108, 176–177. Makuck, supra n74, 94, 97–98, 113–115.

155 See WTO, *WTO Committee on Trade and the Environment.* WTO, 1997, 33, 36.

156 See Marceau, G, 'Is the WTO Open and Transparent?' *Journal of World Trade* 33, 1999, 5–51. Nader, R, 'GATT, NAFTA and the Subversion of the Democratic Process', in Mander, J (ed), *The Case Against the Global Economy.* Sierra Club Books, San Francisco, 1996, 92–108.

157 World Bank, *Development and Environment.* Oxford University Press, Oxford, 1992, 21.

158 See, Charnovitz, S, 'Environmental Trade Measures: Multilateral or Unilateral', *Environmental Law and Policy* 23, 1993, 154, 155.

159 Piper, D C, 'Uniateral Acts of States With Regard to Environmental Protection', in Orr, D W (ed), *The Global Predicament 1979.* Duke University Press, North Carolina, 1979, 267.

160 See Trudeau, P, 'Notes for Address to Annual Meeting of the Press', *International Legal Materials* 9, 1970, 600. Beesley, J A, 'The Arctic Pollution Prevention Act; The Canadian Perspective', *Syracuse Journal of International Law and Commerce* 1, 1973, 226.

161 See Chapter 9.

162 Comment, 'Canadian Fish and Spanish Practices', *Guardian Weekly* 19 April 1995. Carvel, J, 'EU and Canada End Fishing War', *Guardian Weekly* 23 April 1995. Palmer, J, 'Canada Fishing Dispute Grows', *Guardian Weekly* 19 March 1995. Trevena, C, 'U.S. Governors Back Canada in Cod War', *Guardian* 18 June 1994. Hewson, J, 'Why Canada Has Sprung to the Turbot's Defence', *Guardian Weekly* 16 April 1995.

163 Cook, E, *Ozone Protection in the United States: Elements of Success.* World Resources Institute, 1996, 11–21. Benedick, R E, *Ozone Diplomacy: New Directions in Safeguarding the Planet.* Harvard University Press, Harvard, 1991, 6–7, 51–68. Haas, P M, 'Stratospheric Ozone: Regime Formation in Stages', in Young, O R (ed), *Polar Politics: Creating International Environmental Regimes.* Cornell University Press, New York, 1993, 152, 161, 165.

164 See Marine Mammal Protection Act of 1972. Public Law No 92–252, 86 Stat 1027, 16 USC ss 1371. However, it is important to note that the ability of the US to continue this trend is debatable. See McLaughlin, R, 'UNCLOS and the Demise of the United States: Use of Trade Sanctions to Protect Dolphins, Sea Turtles, Whales and Other International Marine Living Resources', *Ecology Law Quarterly* 21, 1994, 1–78.

165 Pelly Amendment. Public Law No 92–219, 85 Stat 786, 22 USC ss 1978.

166 Clinton, B and Gore, A, *Putting People First*. Times Books, New York, 1992, 157.

167 This is a contravention of Article XX (g), which requires that conservation measures must be 'in conjunction with restrictions on domestic ... consumption.' GATT, supra n6. For useful discussions of this action, see Patterson, E, 'GATT and the Environment: Rules To Minimise Adverse Trade and Environmental Effects', *Journal of World Trade Law* 26, 1992, 99, 106–107. Shrybman, supra n127, 30, 32.

168 See World Trade Organisation Appellate Body, *United States – Standards for Reformulated and Conventional Gasoline*. WT/DS2/AB/R, 20 May 1996, 25–28.

169 See Gillespie, A, 'The Malaysian Agenda And Influence On The International Tropical Deforestation Debate', *Asia & Pacific Journal of Environmental Law* 1, 1996, 25–45.

170 See Princen, T, 'The Ivory Trade Ban: NGOs and International Conservation', in Princen, T and Finger, M (ed), *Environmental NGOs in World Politics*. Routledge, London, 1994, 121–159.

171 As required by Article XX(b).

172 Arden-Clarke, C, *The General Agreement on Tariffs and Trade: Environmental Protection and Sustainable Development*. WWF, Gland, 1991, 15. Porter, G and Brown, J W, *Global Environmental Politics*. Westview, Colorado, 1992, 100–101. Lang and Hines, supra n8, 63–64, 66.

173 EEC–US Tuna Dolphin Panel, supra n129, 894, 896–898.

174 Paragraph 164, Shrimp-Turtle Case, supra n59. See *Report of the WTO Committee on Trade and the Environment*. WTO, Geneva. Press/TE 014, Paragraphs 24–31, 171–173. For a fuller discussion of this point, see Andersson et al, supra n114, 94–97.

175 Sustainable Development, *Background Paper on Research Linkages between Trade, Environment and Sustainable Development*. United Nations, New York, 1996, Paragraphs 29–37.

176 See Gillespie, supra n169.

177 *Report of the Topical Seminar on Environment, Competitiveness and Trade*, supra n76, paragraph 53. See also Commission on Sustainable Development, *Changing Consumption and Production Patterns*. E/CN.17/1995/13, 20 March 1995, Paragraphs 49, 94–105.

178 See for example, *Report of the WTO Committee on Trade and the Environment*, supra n16, Paragraphs 55–81, 183–185. UNCTAD, *Discussions in UNCTAD Shed Light on Impact of Environmental Policies on Competitiveness*. TAD/INF/2553, 14 June 1995. For a general discussion on ecolabels, see Chapter 3 of this book.

179 See UNGA, Special Session: Overall Review and Appraisal of the Implementation of Agenda 21: Trade and Environmental Matters. A/S-19/4/E/1997/13, 1997, Paragraph 42. The second part of the quote comes from WTO, 'Eco-labelling', *Environment* (available from their website, 1999).

180 See UNCTAD, *Summary of Joint UNCTAD-UNEP Seminar on Trade and Development*. UNCTAD, New York, 1996.

181 See Postel, S, 'Carrying Capacity: The Earth's Bottom Line', in Mazur, L A (ed), *Beyond the Numbers: A Reader on Population, Consumption and the Environment*. Island Press, San Francisco, 1994, 48. 64–67.

182 Summers, L, 'Why the Rich Should Pollute the Poor', *Guardian* 14 February 1992, 29.

183 Principle 14, Rio Declaration, supra n12.

184 Article 1114 of NAFTA states that the signatories should not encourage investment by relaxing or derogating from domestic health, safety or environmental measures. It is

important to note that the provision only uses the hortatory word 'should' rather than the normative word 'shall'. Additionally, if it is believed that a country is breaching this provision, the solution is believed to be found in consultation between parties, *not* formalized NAFTA dispute settlements. For a full discussion of the limitations of this section, see Housman, R, *Reconciling Trade and the Environment: Lessons from the North American Free Trade Agreement*. UNEP, Nairobi, 1994, 7–10. The figures on the Maquiladoras are from the references in note 214. See especially the Wallach article.

185 See Coote, B, *NAFTA: Poverty and Free Trade in Mexico*. Oxfam Insight Series, Oxford, 1995. Goldsmith, E, 'Increasing Trade, Increasing Pollution', *Ecologist* 29, 1999, 209–215. Lennon, P, 'Profits of Doom on the Border of Blight', *Guardian* 21 August 1992, 23. Ghazi, P, 'America's Deadly Border', *Observer Magazine* 12 December 1993, 16. Bhernandex, A, 'Dirty Growth', *New Internationalist* 246, 1993, 10.

186 This problem developed despite environmental protection agreements between the United States and Mexico which were meant to pre-empt this problem. See the 'Mexico–United States Agreement on Co-operation for the Protection and the Improvement of the Environment', *International Legal Materials* 26, 1987, 15–37, and the 'North American Agreement on Environmental Co-operation', *International Legal Materials* 32, 1993, 1480.

187 'North American Agreement on Environmental Co-operation', in *NAFTA Supplemental Agreements*. US Governmental Printing Office, Washington, DC, 1993. See also US Trade Representatives Office, *NAFTA: Report on Environmental Issues*. Congressional Quarterly, Washington, DC, 1993.

188 See Shields, J, 'Social Dumping in Mexico Under NAFTA', *Multinational Monitor* April 1995, 5–8. Housman, supra n184, Chapter 3.

189 See Castleman, B, 'Workplace Health Standards and Multinational Corporations in the Developing World', in Pearson, C (ed), *Multinational Corporations, Environment and the Third World*. Duke University Press, Durham, 1987, 149–172. Watkins, supra n31, 124–125.

190 See Economic Policy Institute, *Jobs and the Environment: The Myth of a National Trade Off*. EPI, Washington, DC, 1995. United Nations, *World Investment Report: Transnational Corporations as Engines of Growth*. UN, New York, 1992, 226, 230–235. Note also the UNCTAD study, which suggests that environmental policies in Northern countries have only a generally modest effect upon the competitiveness of firms. UNCTAD, The Policy Debate on Trade, Environment and Development. TD/B/WG/6/10, 1995. Commission on Sustainable Development, *Background Paper: Note by UNCTAD on the Relationship of Environmental Protection to International Competitiveness, Job Creation and Development*. United Nations, New York, 1996.

191 See *Report of the Topical Seminar on Environment, Competitiveness and Trade: A Development Perspective*. UNCTAD IX/Misc.2, 12 March 1996, Paragraphs 22, 26. Sustainable Development, *Background Paper on Research Linkages Between Trade, Environment and Sustainable Development*. United Nations. New York, 1996, Paragraphs 48–53. See also Pearson, C, 'Environmental Standards, Industrial Relocation and Pollution Havens', in Pearson, supra n189, 113–128. Korten, supra n108, 229–237.

192 WTO, *Trade and the Environment*. Special Studies 4, 1999, 34, 46.

193 World Bank, *Global Economic Prospects: 1994*. World Bank, Washington, DC, 1994, Chapter 2.

194 WCED, supra n21, 6, 68. See also Commission on Sustainable Development, *Background Paper on Research Linkages between Trade, Environment and Sustainable Development*. United Nations, New York, 1996, Paragraph 20.

195 WTO, *Trade and the Environment*. Special Studies 4, 1999, 26.

196 See Certain Phosphate Lands in Nauru (Nauru v. Australia). ICJ, 1993, 7. For a discussion of this case, see Anghie, A, 'The Heart of My Home: Colonialism, Environmental Damage, and the Nauru Case', *Harvard Journal of International Law* 34, 1993, 445–506.

197 See Gillespie, supra n169. This position is contentious. Indeed, the *Report of the Topical Seminar on Environment, Competitiveness and Trade: A Development Perspective*, UNCTAD IX/Misc.2, 12 March 1996, stated 'there is no direct correlation between trade in forest products and deforestation.'

198 Adams, W M, *Green Development: Environment and Sustainability in the Third World*. Routledge, London, 1992, 122–127. Carriere, J, 'The Crisis in Costa Rica: An Ecological Perspective', in Goodman, D and Redclift, M (eds), *Environment and Development in Latin America*. Manchester University Press, Manchester, 1991, 188–190. Bello, supra n31, 56–64. Fowler, C and Mooney, P, *The Threatened Gene. Food, Politics and the Loss of Genetic Diversity*. Lutterworth, Cambridge, 1990, 98. Lewis, S A, 'Banana Bonanza', *Ecologist* 22, 1992, 289. Goldsmith, E, 'Is Development the Solution or the Problem?' *Ecologist* 15, 1985, 210, 213.

199 See Watkins, supra n31, 118–120.

200 Reed, D, *Structural Adjustment, the Environment, and Sustainable Development*. Earthscan, London, 1996, 17–18, 307–317. Johnston, R J, *Environmental Problems: Nature, Economy and State*. Belhaven, London, 1989, 93–101. Timberlake, L, *Africa in Crisis: The Causes and the Cures of Environmental Bankruptcy*. Earthscan, London, 1985, 144–150. Blaikie, P, *The Political Economy of Soil Erosion in Developing Countries*. Longman, London, 1985. Adams, supra n28, 44–48.

201 Thrupp, L, *Challenges in Latin America's Recent Agro-Export Boom*. World Resources Institute, Washington, 1994. Coote, supra n28, 148–153. Bello, supra n28, 58–59. Watkins, supra n31, 88, 124–127.

202 See the sections on property in Chapter 3.

203 Shamugaratnam, N, 'Development and Environment: A View from the South', *Race and Class* 30, 1989, 13, 26–29.

204 GATT. Article XVIII(11).

205 Or as Caroline LeQuesne stated, 'while the finance generated by increasing trade could be spent on environmental protection, it would require an extraordinary leap of faith to assume it necessarily would.' LeQuesne, C, 'Trade and Sustainable Development', in Dodds, supra n150, 167, 169.

206 See Gillespie, supra n169.

207 World Bank, *Forestry Subsector Study*. Oxford University Press, Oxford, 1992, 3.

208 Commission on Sustainable Development, *Background Paper on Research Linkages between Trade, Environment and Sustainable Development*. United Nations, New York, 1996, Paragraph 17. Of course, the converse may also hold true, with countries being forced to exploit more if import barriers are erected to generate the same amount of income.

209 Pearce and Warford, supra n44, 299.

210 See Chapter 1.

211 See ILO, *World Employment Record 1995*. ILO, Geneva, 1995. See also Bailey, P, *Multinationals and Employment*. ILO, Geneva, 1992, 295–299. Commission on Sustainable Development, supra n105, Paragraphs 33–44. UNCTAD/LLDC/IDC/Misc.2. paragraph 63.

212 Hume, D (1752), 'Of Money', in Rotwein, E (ed), *Writings On Economics*. Madison, Wisconsin, 1970, 34–35.

213 See Brecher, supra n78, 3–5, 8–9, 15–28, 68–72, 131–140. Hildyard, N, 'Who Competes? Changing Landscapes of Corporate Control', *Ecologist* 26(4), 1996,

125–144. Stewart, F, 'The New International Division of Labour', *World of Work* 8, 1994, 28–29.

214 For example, the NAFTA agreement is believed to have led to the exodus of at least 400,000 jobs from North America to Mexico. See Wallach, L, 'NAFTA: Four and a Half Years Later', *Ecologist* 28, 1998, 171–173. Warnock, supra n127, 78–79, 181–83, 279–282. Lang and Hines, supra n8, 73–82.

215 Daly and Cobb, supra n91, 227. Lennon, supra n185, 23.

216 NAFTA, supra n14, Article 1114(1)(2).

217 See Remarks and a Question and Answer Session on NAFTA. *Weekly Compilation of Presidential Documents* 38, 1993, 1766.

218 For the WTO outcome, see Ruggiero, supra n57, 82. The European Union has already got its Social Chapter, and the European Commission has endorsed NAFTA-like 'clauses to avoid social and environmental dumping which would inevitably create protectionist tendencies.' European Commission, 'An Industrial Competitiveness Policy for the European Union', *Bulletin of the European Union* (suppl 3), 1994, 32–33.

219 Sale, K, *Human Scale*. Coward, New York, 1980, 394–399. Naess, A, *Ecology, Community and Lifestyle*. Cambridge University Press, Cambridge, 1989, 143–145. Ekins, P, *A New World Order: Grassroots Movements For Global Change*. Routledge, London, 1992, 35, 186–187. Lang and Hines, supra n8, 27–29, 107–114, 125–154. Schumacher, F, *Small is Beautiful*. Abacus, London, 1974, 47–50, 55. Porritt, J, *Seeing Green*. Blackwell, Oxford, 1984, 166–170. Trainer, F, *Abandon Affluence*. Zed, London, 1989, 251–266. Mellos, K, *Perspectives on Ecology*. Macmillan, London, 1988, 69, 77–89, 112, 116–118, 140. Korten, supra n108, 307–333. For an early example, see Morris, W (1890), *News From Nowhere*. Longman, London, 1907, 94–95.

220 Point 3, *The Cocoyoc Declaration: Patterns of Resource Use, Environment and Development Strategies*. UN Doc A/C.2/292, 13 November 1974. Also in Ruster, B and Simma, B (eds), *International Protection of the Environment*. Oceana, New York, 1979, vol 18, 9075.

221 See Lappe, F M and Collins, J, *Food First: The Myth of Scarcity*. Condor, Bristol, 1980, 153–171, 297–327.

222 Economic Commission for Africa, *African Alternative Framework*. Addis Ababa, 1989, 11.

223 See *World Conference on Agrarian Reform and Rural Development*. UN Doc WCARRD/REP, 1979 Objective 1 a (iii). *Food and Agricultural Problems. General Assembly Resolution* 39/166, 17 December 1984, Paragraph 8. Article 46 of the Treaty Establishing the African Economic Community. *International Legal Materials* 30, 1991, 1241. For the recognition of self-sufficiency generally, see also the 1994 *Programme of Action for the Sustainable Development of Small Island Developing States*. A/CONF.167/9, Paragraph 55(a)(i).

224 *United Nations Conference on the Least Developed Countries*. Paris, 14 September 1981, Paragraphs 11 and 12.

225 See *Universal Declaration on the Eradication of Hunger and Malnutrition*. 16th Plenary Meeting, 16 November 1974, Paragraph 11. *World Food Conference, 1974. Report of the World Food Conference*. UN Doc E/CONF.65/20, 1975, Resolution V, Paragraph 2. *Programme of Action on the Establishment of a New International Economic Order*. General Assembly Resolution 3203 (S-VI) 1 May 1974, Principle 2, e-h. The 1978 *Mexico Declaration of the World Food Council*, 14 June 1978. Passed as General Assembly Resolution 33/90 of 15 December 1978, Paragraph 11.

226 See *World Food Summit Plan of Action*, Report of the World Food Summit. WFS 96/REP. FAO, Rome, 1996, Paragraph 5, 37–41. FAO, *International Trade and Food Security*. FAO, Rome, 1996.

227 World Resources Institute, World Bank, UNEP and UNDP, *World Resources: A Guide to the Global Environment.* Oxford University Press, Oxford, 1996, 235–236.

228 Goodman and Redclift, supra n94, 144. Trainer, supra n219, 160–162. Watkins, supra n31, 87–89.

229 Coote, supra n28, 144–148. Madeley, J, 'Does Economic Development Feed People?', *Ecologist* 15, 1985, 36. Shiva, V, *The Violence of the Green Revolution.* Zed, London, 1989, 154. cf Pearce and Warford, supra n44, 294–295.

230 Hildyard, N, 'Foxes In Charge of the Chickens', in Sachs, W (ed), *Global Ecology.* Zed, London, 1993, 22, 27. Madeley, supra n229, 36.

231 See the Preamble of the *Uruguay Agreement on Agriculture*, which states that the long-term objective 'is to establish a fair and market orientated agricultural trading system ... [and] ... to provide for substantial progressive reductions in agricultural supports and protection.' *Agreement on Agriculture.* GATT, Agriculture. MTN/FA II-A/A-3. For the movement towards this, see McMahon, J A, *Agricultural Trade, Protectionism and the Problems of Development.* University of Leicester Press, Leicester, 1992, 229–248. The importance of trade and agriculture was also noted at the Earth Summit in Chapters 2.7 and 14 of Agenda 21. Section 2.7, Agenda 21. UNCED Doc A/CONF. 151/4.

232 Raghaven, supra n101, 161. Lang and Hines, supra n8, 50.

233 Lehman, K, 'Control of the World's Food Supply', in Mander, supra n156, 122–131. Watkins, K, 'Free Trade and Farm Fallacies', *Ecologist* 26(6), 1996, 244–255. Body, R, *Our Food, Our Land.* Rider, London, 1991, 96–98, 112–115. Clunies-Ross and Hildyard, supra n140, 11, 40, 67, 75, 107. Ritchie, supra n127, 214–223. Simms, A, 'Big Corporations Tighten Grip on World Food Supply', *Guardian Weekly* 16 March 1999.

234 For the problem of coffee, see World Resources Institute, World Bank, UNEP and UNDP, *World Resources 1998–1999: A Guide to the Global Environment.* Oxford University Press, Oxford, 1998, 165–167.

235 See Commission on Sustainable Development, *Trade Issues and Development Prospects of Island Developing Countries of the Caribbean.* E/CN.17/1996/IDC/Misc.1. UNCTAD/LLDC/IDC/Misc.1, 1996, Paragraphs 19–29. Watkins, K, 'Fast Route to Poverty', *Guardian Weekly* 16 February 1997, 29.

236 See 'GATT Dispute Settlement Panel Report on the EEC–Import Regime for Bananas', *International Legal Materials* 34, 1995, 177. See also LeQuesne, supra n205, 167, 176–177.

237 See European Court of Justice, 'Judgement of the Court in Federal Republic of Germany v. Council of European Union', *International Legal Materials* 34, 1995, 154–229.

238 See WTO, *Report of the Appellate Body on the European Communities Regime for the Importation, Sale and Distribution of Bananas.* AB-1997-3. This is reprinted in *International Legal Materials* 37, 1998, 243.

239 Ritchie, supra n127, 221, 223. Raghaven, supra n101, 163. Watkins, supra n31, 140–141.

240 World Bank, *Trade and the Environment*, supra n8. For the specific problem that this presents for the Small Island States of the South Pacific, see Commission on Sustainable Development, *Trade Issues and Development Prospects of Island Developing Countries of the Pacific.* E/CN.17/1996/IDC/Misc.2. UNCTAD/LLDC/IDC/Misc.2, 1996, Paragraph 56.

241 Commission on Global Governance, supra n58, 167. Goldin, I and Knudsen, O, *Agricultural Trade Liberalisation: Implications For Developing Countries.* OECD/World Bank, Washington, DC, 1990, 275–477, 479–480. Watkins, supra n31, 88–89.

242 See World Resources Institute, supra n227, 228–229.

243 See Ritchie, supra n127, 214. Goodman and Redclift, supra n94, 146, 210. Clunies-Ross and Hildyard, supra n140, 11, 70, 107, 112–115, 140, 146.

244 Ritchie, supra n127, 214, 215. Patterson, supra n167, 99. Middleton, N, O'Keefe, P and Moyo, S, *Tears of the Crocodile: From Rio to Reality in the Developing World*. Pluto, London, 1993, 96–102. Raghaven, supra n101, 41. Shrybman, supra n127, 30, 31. Goodman, supra n94, 135, 139–156.

245 See point 8, GATT L/2314/Rev 1, 30 November 1964. See also UNCTAD, *Generalised System of Preferences*. UN Doc TD/B/330. Annex I, 14 October 1970. Note however that it was not the intention to remove this protection in the Uruguay Round. See *GATT Focus* 18, December 1982. For the current retention of this exemption within GATT, see GATT, *Final Act Embodying the Results of the Uruguay Round. Multilateral Trade Negotiations*. Doc MTN/FA, 15 December 1993, Section III.

246 See the Preamble of the Uruguay Agreement, ibid. See also the section on agriculture of the 'Decisions at the Mid-Term Review of the Uruguay Round', *GATT Focus* 61, May 1989. McMahon, supra n231, 9–11, 229–248.

247 Khor Kok Peng, M, 'The Uruguay Round and the Third World', *Ecologist* 20, 1990, 213. Raghaven, C, 'Recolonisation and GATT in its Historical Context', *Ecologist* 20, 1990, 207. Raghaven, supra n101, 16, 70, 76. Coote, supra n28, 114–117.

248 WCED, supra n21, 131.

249 FAO, *Agenda for Action on Sustainable Agriculture and Rural Development*. Netherlands, 1991, 14. cf Report of the Advisory Panel on Food Security to the World Commission on Environment and Development, *Food 2000: Global Policies for Sustainable Agriculture*. Zed, London, 1987, 82–84.

250 Preamble, Agreement on Agriculture, supra n231. See also Points 2 and 3 of *Ministerial Decisions and Declarations: Decisions in Favour of Least Developed Countries*, Declaration 6. *Decisions Concerning the Possible Negative Effects of the Reform Programme on Least Developed Net Food Importing Countries*. MTN/FA III. 6.

251 See *World Food Summit Plan of Action*, supra n226, Paragraph 38. See also World Food Summit, *Technical Background Document: Food and International Trade*. FAO, Rome, 1996, 2–4.

252 *Addis Ababa Declaration on UNCTAD IX*. AF/MM/77(VIII)/1, 22 February 1996, Paragraph 31.

253 *Programme for the Further Implementation of Agenda 21*. This is reprinted in Osborn, D, *Earth Summit II: Outcomes and Analysis*. Earthscan, London, 1998, Paragraph 29(b), 63. See also Commission on Sustainable Development, *Overall Progress Achieved Since UNCED*. E/CN.17/1997/2, 1997, Paragraphs 48–49.

254 Rome Declaration on World Food Security, supra n226. See paragraphs 22, 37–40.

CHAPTER 5 DEBT

1   For some of the 19th century problems of international financial debt, including some where 'submission to international financial controls' was necessary (including Tunisia in 1869, Egypt in 1876 and Turkey in 1880), as well as the ill-fated invasion of Mexico in 1861 on the pretext of debt repayment, see Nussbaum, A, *A Concise History of the Law of Nations*. Macmillan, London, 1947, 210–213. It is interesting to note also the inter-war situation in which the League of Nations had to become involved in the financial arrangements of Austria in 1922 and Hungary in 1924. Moreover, in the 1930s Washington 'forgave' the defaulted debts of Britain, France and Italy. For the arrival of the post-WWII debt crisis, see Pearson Commission, *Partners in Development*. Pall Mall Press, London, 1969, 72.

2   Brandt Commission, *Common Crisis: Cooperation for World Recovery*. Pan, London, 1983, 47. Lever, H and Huhne, C, *Debt and Danger: The World's Financial Crisis*.

Penguin, Harmondsworth, 1985, 11–13. Payer, C, *Lent and Lost: Foreign Credit and Third World Development*. Zed Books, London, 1991, 74. Valley, P, *Bad Samaritans: First World Ethics and Third World Debt*. Hodder, London, 1990, 143–149. Adams, P, *Odious Debts; Loose Lending, Corruption and The Third World's Environmental Legacy*. Earthscan, London, 1991, 60–65, 95–102.

3   George, S, *A Fate Worse Than Debt*. Penguin, Harmondsworth, 1990, 18, 23. Payer, supra n2, 109. Adams, supra n2, 119–143. Lever and Huhne, supra n2, 129–130. Valley, supra n2, 32–40, 150–151. Ekins, P, *A New World Order: Grassroots Movements for Global Change*. Routledge, London, 1992, 27. Adams, supra n2, 49–57. Pearce, D and Warford, J J, *World Without End: Economics, Environment and Sustainable Development*. World Bank, Washington, 1993, 313–324.

4   Pearson Commission, supra n1, 153.

5   Brandt Commission, *North–South: A Programme For Survival*. Pan, London, 1980, 47, 67, 223.

6   As the IMF stated in 1981, the economic problems of non-oil producing Southern countries 'has stemmed mainly from external developments unfavourable to them, including ... recessionary conditions in the industrialised world, the adverse movement of the terms of trade, including higher oil prices and the steep rise of interest rates in major financial markets.' See 'Interim Communique' 10 (9) *IMF Survey* 1981. Also in *International Legal Materials* 20, 1981, 1490–1492. See also South Commission, *The Challenge to the South*. Oxford University Press, Oxford, 1990, 55–60.

7   See World Bank, *The External Debt of Developing Countries and HIPCs*. World Bank, Washington, DC, Fact Sheet, 1998. Note, the 1.9 figure is actually reported for 1996. It is possible that it may be over 2 trillion by the end of 1999.

8   The 1984 *Consensus of Cartagena on Foreign Debt and Economic Development* noted that (regarding Latin America) the region was undergoing 'an unprecedented crisis characterised by severe decline in per-capita income ... Latin America [has seen] itself forced to reduce and in some areas halt its development process.' See points 4 and 6. Reprinted in *International Legal Materials* 23, 1984, 1169. For the position in the 1990s, see UNICEF, *State of the World's Children*. Oxford University Press, Oxford, 1992, 43. George, S, *The Debt Boomerang: How Third World Debt Harms Us All*. Pluto, London, 1992, XIV–XV. Castro, F, *Tomorrow Is Too Late: Development and the Environmental Crisis in the Third World*. Ocean, Melbourne, 1993, 15, 38. Jackson, B, *Poverty and the Planet: A Question of Survival*. Penguin, Harmondsworth, 1990, 94.

9   See World Bank, *World Debt Tables: 1996*. World Bank, Washington, DC, 1996, Vol 1. Ghai, D, *The IMF and the South: The Social Impact of Crisis and Adjustment*. Zed, London, 1991, 13–15, 17–18, 21, 23–24. For a discussion of the African positions, see Mkandawire, T, 'Crisis and Adjustment in sub-Saharan Africa', in Ghai, 80–90. Bello, W, *Dark Victory: The United States, Structural Adjustment and Global Poverty*. Pluto, London, 1994, 52–60. Valley, supra n2, 164–178. Adams, supra n2, 158–161. South Commission, supra n6, 61. Bello, W, *Brave New Third World; Strategies For Survival in the Global Economy*. Earthscan, London, 1990, 4–6, 8. Jackson, supra n8, 85–95.

10   For example, in 1986, Peru's Ambassador Antonio Belaunde-Moreyra suggested that Peru should not pay all of its foreign debt. He commented: 'This [position] ... rests on deep rational foundations... It is above all a call for equity ... Peru does not repudiate its debt; on the contrary, my country acknowledges and affirms its will to pay, but on conditions that should not be equivalent to a submission of a type of serfdom. The debt has to be restructured so that it may cease to be the insane and exorbitant load that it is now.' This quote is noted in Detlev, C D, *Foreign Debts in the Present and a New International Economic Order*. Fribourg, Switzerland, 1986, at 19–20.

11   See IMF, supra n6. It is worth noting that this directive must be carried out 'without resorting to measures destructive of national or international prosperity.'

12 See Chapter 3 of this book.

13 Brandt Commission, supra n2, 28, 66–69. Jackson, supra n8, 105, 108–111.

14 *Agenda 21.* UNCED Doc A/CONF./151 4, 1992. Also reprinted in Johnson, S P (ed), *The Earth Summit.* Graham and Trotman, London, 1993, 142.

15 UNDP, *Debt and Sustainable Human Development.* United Nations, New York, Technical Advisory Paper No 4. South Commission, supra n6, 68. Starr, P, *Feminist Critiques of Structural Adjustment.* Zed, London, 1994. Watkins, K, *The OXFAM Poverty Report.* Oxfam, Oxford, 1996, 78–107. Hansen, K, 'Sapping the Economy: Structural Adjustment Policies', *Ecologist* 23, 1993, 179–183. Middleton, N, O'Keefe, P and Moyo, S, *Tears of the Crocodile: From Rio to Reality in the Developing World.* Pluto, London, 1993, 193–197. Bello, supra n9, 32–50, 67. Valley, supra n2, 182–190. Jackson, supra n8, 89–85.

16 UNICEF, *State of the World's Children: 1994.* Oxford University Press, Oxford, 1994, 51.

17 Camdessus, M, 'World Debt', *Financial Times* 24 September 1990, 18. This view echoed the official position, which was recognized in the midst of the debt crisis, that structural adjustment would require 'painful and courageous efforts'. See 'Summit Communique Text Stresses Debtors Need Greater Assistance.' *13 IMF Survey* 18 June 1984, 188–90.

18 See Walton, J, *Free Markets and Food Riots: The Politics of Global Adjustment.* Blackwell, London, 1994, 4–8, 17–19, 333–338. Brecher, J, *Global Pillage: Economic Reconstruction from the Bottom Up.* South End Press, Cambridge, 1994, 28–32.

19 See South Commission, supra n6, 50, 68, 240. Hudson, M, *Trade, Development and Foreign Debt.* Pluto, London, 1992, 420–426. Watkins, supra n15, 73, 78–79. Cassen, R, *Does Aid Work?* Oxford University Press, Oxford, 1994, 65–68, 82–83, 125.

20 Elbadawi, I, *World Bank Adjustment Lending and Economic Performance in Sub-Saharan Africa.* World Bank Policy Research Paper, Washington, DC, 1992, 4. See also Sepehri, A, 'Back to the Future?' *Review of African Political Economy* 62, 1994, 559–568. Watkins, supra n15, 98–100. cf World Bank, *Adjustment in Africa: Reform, Results and the Road Ahead.* World Bank Policy Research Paper, Washington, DC, 1994.

21 See Watkins, supra n15, 101–102.

22 See Editors, 'Who Broke Mexico?' *Ecologist* 25(1), 1995, 2–5.

23 Commission on Global Governance, *Our Global Neighbourhood.* Oxford University Press, Oxford, 1995, 181–182.

24 See Collins, J, 'Free Market Miracle or Myth? Chile's Neo-Liberal Experiment', *Ecologist* 26(4), 1996, 156–165. Brecher, supra n18, 56–60. O'Connor, J, 'The Meaning of Economic Imperialism', in Little, R and Smith, M (eds), *Perspectives on World Politics.* Routledge, London, 1994, 277–291. Martin, B, *In the Public Interest? Privitisation and Public Sector Reform.* Zed, London, 1993, 95–125, 149–159. Reed, D, *Structural Adjustment, the Environment, and Sustainable Development.* Earthscan, London, 1996, 4–5, 312–314.

25 Hurrel, A, 'The Politics of Amazonian Deforestation', *Journal of Latin American Studies* 23, 1991, 199, 205, 213. Indeed, because of this, some commentators have gone so far as to assert that there is no direct link between destruction of the environment and structural adjustment. See for example, Munasinghe, M, *Environment, Economics and Sustainable Development.* World Bank, Washington, DC, 1993, 17–19. See also World Bank, *World Bank and the Environment.* World Bank, Washington, DC, 1993, 'a programme of economic liberalisation will generally be beneficial both economically and environmentally.' At 97, cf, page 96. Pearce and Warford, supra n3, 313–324; cf pages 316 (necessity for environmental programmes) and 324 (protection for the poor).

26 George, supra n3, 16. See also Myers, N, 'Tropical Forests', in Leggett, J (ed), *Global Warming: The Greenpeace Report*. Oxford University Press, Oxford, 1990, 372.

27 See Camdessus, M, 'Africa and the World', IMF Speech 28 November 1995, 3–4.

28 Hudson, M, *Trade, Development and Foreign Debt*. Pluto, London, 1992, 283. Middleton et al, supra n15, 192–193. Adams, supra n2.

29 George, supra n3, 1, 9. This claim is supported by the fact that the Southern countries that deforested the fastest in the 1980s were, on the whole, the largest debtors. In a number of smaller countries with less significant forest reserves, the fastest deforesters were also the most heavily indebted. Finally, countries with the highest debt service ratios or subject to the highest levels of structural adjustment conditionality, also tend to be the largest deforesters. See also Bello, supra n9, 56–66. See also Hayter, T, *Exploited Earth*. Earthscan, London, 1989, 7–10.

30 UNEP, *Global Environment Outlook 2000*. Earthscan, London, 2000, 11.

31 WCED, *Our Common Future*. Oxford University Press, Oxford, 1987, 68.

32 Reed, D, *Structural Adjustment and the Environment*. Westview Colorado, 1992, 7. Reed's initial conclusion was confirmed by his expanded investigation in Reed, supra n24, 299–354. WCED, supra n31, 68. Hayter, supra n29, 71–75. George, supra n3, 4, 8. Coote, B, *The Trade Trap; Poverty and the Global Commodity Markets*. Oxfam, Oxford, 1992, 32–36.

33 WCED, supra n31, 6, 36, 67–68.

34 Declaration of Brazilia. *International Legal Materials* 28, 1989, 1311. Similar sentiments can be located in the Amazonian Declaration. *International Legal Materials* 28, 1989, 1303 and the *Manila Declaration on People's Participation and Sustainable Development*. Reprinted in Starke, L (ed), *Signs of Hope: Working Towards Our Common Future*. Oxford University Press, Oxford, 1990, 80–81.

35 South Commission, supra n6, 226–227.

36 See *World Summit for Children*. UNICEF, Geneva, 1990. *World Declaration on the Survival, Protection and Development of Children*, Paragraphs 5, 16, 20 (10). See also paragraphs 30 and 31 of the Action Plan.

37 Principle 9(a), *Statement of Principles For a Global Consensus on the Management, Conservation and Sustainable Development of all Types of Forests*. UNCED Doc A/CONF. 151/6/Rev 1. 31, *International Legal Materials* 1992, 881. See also sections 2.3, 2.3.4, 2.23 and 33.16. of *Agenda 21*, supra n14. For further notable statements on the issue of foreign debt at UNCED see the *Report of the United Nations Conference on Environment and Development*. A/CONF. 151/26/Rev 1 (Volume 3), 29 and 44. See also the G77 *Statement*, in Robinson, N A (ed), *Agenda 21 and the UNCED Proceedings*. Oceana, 4, New York, 1993, 858.

38 Paragraphs 103–104. *Overall Progress Achieved Since UNCED*. E/CN.17/1997/Z, 31 January 1997. This is reprinted in Osborn, D, *Earth Summit II: Outcomes and Analysis*. Earthscan, London, 1998. The second part of the paragraph is from Paragraph 20 of the Special Session of the General Assembly. *Programme for the Further Implementation of Agenda 21*. United Nations, New York, 1997, Paragraph 20. This is also reprinted in Osborn, at 134.

39 UNEP, 'UNEP and Habitat Welcome G8 Cologne Debt Relief', *UNEP Press Release* 1999/73.

40 South Commission, supra n6, 228. Brandt Commission, supra n2. Oxfam, *Africa: Make or Break*. Oxfam, Oxford, 1993, 1. Hayter, supra n29. Watkins, supra n15, 11, 220. Bello, supra n9. George, supra n8, 241.

41 Other facilities such as the Debt Reduction Facility, which is run by the International Development Association, also deal with commercial debt.

42 The 1989 G7 Economic Summit talked of the necessity of rescheduling, flexibility, 'debt service reduction and new money' all done on a case by case basis. See points 30 and 31. Reprinted in *International Legal Materials* 28, 1989, 1293. For further discussions,

see Jackson, B, *Poverty and the Planet: A Question of Survival*. Penguin, Harmondsworth, 1990, 90. Lichtenstein, C, 'International Debt: How Can Developing Countries Regain Creditworthiness?' *Proceedings of the American Society of International Law* 83, 1989, 87, 88.

43   See 'U.S. Banks Over-reserved Against Potential Losses', *Independent* 28 July 1992, 6. Meacher, M, 'The Debt Crisis is Over, But Only For the Banks', *Guardian* 19 February 1993, 18.

44   Jones, S, 'Brazil Wins Accord To Reduce Debt With Commercial Banks', *Guardian* 10 July 1992, 11. Bradbury, A, 'Debt Deal of Little Benefit To Most Brazilians', *SPUR*, August 1992, 3.

45   See Watkins, supra n15, 176–179.

46   Randel, J and German, T (eds), *The Reality of Aid 1996: An Independent Review of International Aid*. Earthscan, London, 1996, 30–31.

47   See Overseas Development Institute, *Poor Country Debt: A Never Ending Story?* ODI, London, 1995, 4, 7. Oxfam International, *Position Paper: Multilateral Debt – The Human Cost*. Oxfam, Oxford, 1996, 5.

48   See Watkins, supra n15, 187–188, 220–223. Overseas Development Institute, supra n47, 4–5. Rich, B, *Mortgaging The Earth: The World Bank, Environmental Impoverishment and the Crisis of Development*. Earthscan, London, 1994, 310. Oxfam International, supra n47, 6–8, 10–13.

49   See Rich, supra n48, 108–111, 184–191, 244, 279–280, 310–312. Martin, supra n24, 72–83, 127–137. Cassen, supra n19, 82–83.

50   IMF, *Annual Report: 1993*. IMF, Washington, DC, 22.

51   See Randel and German, supra n46, 29–31.

52   See Martin, M, *Official Bilateral Debt: New Directions*. Eurodad, Brussels, 1993.

53   The main bilateral creditor is Japan, which is owed a total of 12 per cent of all bilateral debt. France, Germany and the USA are all owed 11 per cent. The UK is owed 6 per cent and Italy 5 per cent.

54   See UNCTAD, 'UNCTAD Analyses The Debt of Sub-Saharan African Countries to Non-OECD Countries', Correspondent Note 31, 7 November 1996.

55   Payer, supra n2, at 14.

56   George, supra n3, 163, 190–191, 213.

57   See the 'Proposal of U.S. Treasury Baker', *International Legal Materials* 25, 1986, 412. The notion that debtor countries should economically grow out of the debt crisis was at the centre of the idea. For as the World Bank stated, 'Sustained growth is at the heart of any satisfactory lasting resolution of debt problems.' World Bank, *World Debt Tables: 1985–1986*. Oxford University Press, Oxford, 1995, 1. For further discussions of the Baker plan, see Lichtenstein, C, 'International Debt: How Can Developing Countries Regain Creditworthiness?' *Proceedings of the American Society of International Law* 83, 1989, 87, 88. Lever, H and Huhne, C, *Debt and Danger: The World's Financial Crisis*. Penguin, 1985, XV–XVIII. Bello, W, *Dark Victory: The United States, Structural Adjustment and Global Poverty*. Pluto, London, 1994, 28–30.

58   George, supra n3, 163. Valley, supra n2, 294. Bello, supra n46, 37. Lever and Huhne, supra n57, XV–XVI. Toye, J, *Dilemmas of Development*. Blackwell, Oxford, 1993, 220–223. Valley, supra n2, 294–296.

59   See Toye, supra n58, 224–225.

60   Griffith-Jones, S (ed), *Managing World Debt*. Penguin, Harmondsworth, 1988, 37. 'Aid, Debt Relief and Reforms', *Middle East Executive Reports* 13, 1991, 9. Brittain, V, 'Deadly Rates of Self Interest', *Guardian* 15 May 1992, 25. 'Egypt Claims West Will Forgive 3m Debt After Reform Agreement', *Guardian* 7 July 1993, 4.

61   Wilkins, B, 'Debt and Underdevelopment: The Case For Cancelling Third World Debts', in Attfield, A and Wilkins, B (eds), *International Justice and the Third World*. Routledge, London, 1992, 169, 182.

62 For the development of this plan, see Valley, supra n2, 297–298. Toye, supra n58, 224–226.
63 Cole, D H, 'Debt–Equity Conversions, Debt for Nature Swaps and the Continuing World Debt Crisis', *Colombia Journal of Transnational Law* 30, 1992, 7, 30.
64 World Bank, supra n20, 5. Adams, supra n2, 92–94. Toye, supra n58, 228.
65 World Bank, *World Debt Tables: 1992*. Oxford University Press, Oxford, 3.
66 George, supra n3, 242.
67 See 'Special Session on Economic Co-operation and Development', *Environmental Policy and the Law* 20, 1990, 74. Barras, D, 'Promoting International Environmental Protection Through Foreign Debt Exchange Transactions', *Cornell International Law Journal* 24, 1991, 24, 36. Valley, supra n2, 296–99.
68 See footnotes 37 and 38 of this chapter.
69 Vidal, J, 'Good Intentions Doomed By Gulf Between Rich and Poor', *Guardian* 19 June 1992, 9. Brittain, V, 'Deadly Rates of Self Interest', *Guardian* 15 May 1992, 25. Middleton et al, supra n15, 194.
70 Brummer, A, 'US Offers to Write Off Half Debt of Poorest Countries', *Guardian* 14 May 1993.
71 Watkins, K, 'Summit For Nowt', *Guardian* 16 July 1993, 13. Watkins, supra n15, 11.
72 See Watkins, supra n15, 185–187. See also the *Addis Ababa Declaration from UNCTAD IX*. AF/MM/77(VIII)/1, 22 February 1996, Paragraphs 11–13. Overseas Development Institute, supra n47, 3.
73 World Bank, *World Debt Tables: 1996*. World Bank, Washington, DC, 1996, 33.
74 Commission on Sustainable Development, *Financial Resources and Mechanisms. Report of the Secretary General*. E/CN.17/1996/4/Add.1, 22 February 1996, Paragraph 19.
75 World Summit for Social Development. Declaration A/CONF.166/9, 19 April 1995, Commitment 1, Paragraph k.
76 Programme of Action of the World Summit. Annexed to the Declaration. Chapter 1. Paragraph 10 (e).
77 Declaration. Ibid, Commitment 7, Paragraph c.
78 Declaration. Ibid, Commitment 8. See also Paragraph 74 (f) and 91 of the Programme of Action.
79 Programme of Action. Ibid, Chapter II, Paragraph 38 (i).
80 The Heavily Indebted Poor Countries (HIPC) Debt Initiative Trust. Reprinted in *International Legal Materials* 39, 1997, 990. For discussions of this, see World Bank, *The Initiative for Heavily Indebted Poor Countries: Review and Outlook*. World Bank, Washington, DC, 1988. World Bank, *HIPC Initiative: A Progress Report*. World Bank, Washington, DC, 1998, 2–3.World Bank, *The Heavily Indebted Poor Countries Debt Initiative*. World Bank Backgrounder, Washington, DC, 1999, 1. World Bank, *Overview of the HIPC Initiative*. World Bank Backgrounder, Washington, DC, 1999, 1.
81 See Andrews, D, *Debt Relief for Low-Income Countries: The Enhanced HIPC Initiative*. International Monetary Fund, Washington, DC, Pamphlet Series No 51, 1999. World Bank, *Modifications to the HIPC Initiative*. World Bank, Washington, DC, 1999, Information Sheet.
82 Elliot, L, 'Britain to Cancel Debts Owed by Most Impoverished Countries.' *Guardian Weekly* 29 December 1999, 1. Burgess, J, 'Clinton Pledges to Cancel Debt Poor Nations Owe US', *Guardian Weekly* 7 October 1999, 36.
83 See UNDP, *Human Development Report: 1999*. UNDP, New York, 1999, 11. Oxfam, *Oxfam International Assessment of the IMF-World Bank Debt Reduction Initiative*. Oxfam, Oxford, 1996, 1–5. The other useful collection of critiques of the Initiative is in Annex II of the Review and Outlook. Supra n80. The figure for Mauritania comes from IMF, *Mauritania Qualifies for US1.1 Billion Debt Relief*. IMF Press Release No 00/9.
84 For an early example of this see World Bank, 'Memo on Debt Conversion in Chile', 24 September 1986, *International Legal Materials* 26, 1987, 819.

85   Alagiri, P, 'Give Us Sovereignty or Give Us Debt: Debtor Countries' Perspectives on Debt-For-Nature Swaps', *American University Law Review* 41, 1992, 485. Hrynik, T J, 'Debt For Nature Swaps: Effective But Not Enforceable', *Case Western Reserve Journal of International Law* 22, 1990, 141, 153.

86   Sadler, R M, 'Debt For Nature Swaps: Assessing the Future', *Journal of Contemporary Health and Policy* 61, 990, 337. Alagiri, supra n85, 485, 491. Middleton et al, supra n15, 68.

87   Lichtenstein, supra n42, 87, 97.

88   See Tucker, M, 'A Proposed Debt For Nature Swap in Madagascar and the Larger Problem of LDC Debt', *International Environmental Affairs*, 6, 1994, 59, 63–66. See also Cole, supra n63, 7, 18, 22, 25, 27.

89   The idea that debt for nature swaps 'could play a useful role in environmental protection' was mentioned approvingly in an international setting in the 1989 *G7 Economic Summit*. See point 38. Reprinted in *International Legal Materials* 28, 1989, 1293.

90   See *G7 Economic Summit*. Ibid. See also Moltkie, K, 'Debt-For-Nature: The Second Generation', *Hastings International and Comparative Law Review* 14, 1991, 973, 982. Hrynik, supra n85, 141, 155. Moline, M J, 'Debt for Nature Exchanges: Attempting to Deal Simultaneously With Two Global Problems', *Law and Policy in International Business* 22, 1991, 133, 138, 150–155. Cole, supra n63, 7, 33.

91   See World Bank, *Environment Bulletin* 7(4), 1996, 8–9.

92   Mahony, R, 'Debt for Nature Swaps: Who Really Benefits?', *Ecologist* 22, 1992, 97. Patterson, A, 'Debt For Nature Swaps and the Need for Alternatives', *Environment* 32(10), 1990, 5, 9–13. Sadler, R M, 'Debt for Nature Swaps: Assessing the Future', *Journal of Contemporary Health and Policy* 6, 1990, 319. Hrynik, supra n85, 141. Alagiri, supra n85, 285. Cole, supra n63, 7, 32. 301, 320. Tucker, supra n88, 59, 67–68. Note, although debt for nature swaps have not worked well so far, there is no reason to disregard the idea completely. Such swaps could, if more carefully thought out, be very beneficial. See George, supra n8, 30.

93   Adams, supra n2, 162–170. Ramphal, S, *Our Country, the Planet*. Lime Tree, London, 1992, 185. George, supra n2, 67.

94   See Schulze, D, 'Lifting the Loads Off Their Backs: Legal Solutions to the Third World Debt Crisis', *Indian Journal of International Law* 36, 1996, 54–75.

95   See Foorman, J L, 'Effects of State and Government Succession on Commercial Bank Loans to Foreign Sovereign Borrowers', *University of Illinois Law Review* 1982, 9–11, 21–23. Chomsky, N, 'The Poor Always Pay Debts of the Rich', *Guardian Weekly* 24 May 1998. Payer, supra n2, 78.

96   See note 10. See also Ferguson, T, *The Third World and Decision Making in the International Monetary Fund*. Pinter, London, 1992, 232–234.

97   Dowden, R, 'Nairobi Halts IMF and World Bank Reforms', *Independent* 24 March 1993, 12. Griffith-Jones, supra n60, 7, 338–342.

98   In 1983, the US Deputy Secretary of the Treasury, Robert McNamara suggested if a country decided to unilaterally repudiate their debt: 'the foreign assets of [the] country ... would be attached by creditors throughout the world; its exports seized ... its national airlines unable to operate ... its sources of desperately needed capital goods and spare parts virtually eliminated. In many countries, even food imports would be curtailed'. US Chamber of Commerce, 12 October 1983. This is discussed in Hudson, M, *Trade, Development and Foreign Debt*. Pluto, London, 1992, 307. George, supra n3, 67. George, supra n8, XVI. Bello, supra n9, 12–13.

99   George, supra n3, 239. George, supra n8, XVIII. Hayter, supra n29, 12. Payer, supra n2, 109. Gerster, R, 'The IMF and Basic Needs Conditionality', in Snyder, F E and Sathirathai, S (eds), *Third World Attitudes to International Law*. Nijhoff, Dordrecht, 1987, 535, 543.

100 See Commission on Sustainable Development, *Overall Progress Achieved Since UNCED*. E/CN.17/1997/2, 1997, Paragraphs 103–104. Commission on Sustainable Development, *Overall Progress Since UNCED; Addendum on Financial Resources and Mechanisms*. E/CN.17/1997/2/Add 23, 1997, Paragraphs 15–19. See also Addis Ababa Declaration from UNCTAD IX. AF/MM/77(VIII)/1, 22 February 1996, Paragraph 11. Midrand Declaration and A Partnership for Growth and Development. UNCTAD IX. TD/377, Paragraphs 16, 55, 56.
101 See Oxfam International, supra n47, 2.
102 See Randel and German, supra n46, 28–31.
103 See Watkins, supra n15, 10, 73, 75.
104 *Report of the United Nations Conference on Human Settlements* (Habitat II). A/CONF.165/14, Paragraph 204 (d).
105 See World Bank, *Social Security Reforms and Social Safety Nets in Reforming and Transforming Economies*. World Bank, Washington, DC, 1993.
106 In 1996, the IMF Executive Board adopted a policy on external evaluations for an experimental period of two years. This was reviewed in 2000.
107 See Camdessus, M, Speech to UN World Summit for Social Development. IMF Speech, Copenhagen, 7 March 1995. See also Camdessus, M, 1995 'Income Distribution and Sustainable Growth: The Perspective From the IMF at Fifty'. IMF Speech, 1 June 1995. Camdessus, M, 'An Agenda for the IMF at the Start of the 21st Century'. IMF Speech, New York, 1 February 2000. <http://www.imf.org/external/news.htm>.
108 See Horta, K, 'The World Bank and the International Monetary Fund', in Werksman, J (ed), *Greening International Institutions*. Earthscan, London, 1996, 131, 142–143.
109 See Watkins, supra n15, 82–86, 105–108.
110 See Gupta, S, *Social Issues in IMF-Supported Programmes*. IMF, Washington, DC, 2000, 2.
111 Reed, supra n24, 5–6, 326–328, 351–354.

CHAPTER 6 AID

1 For an early examination of this see, Hayter, T, *Aid as Imperialism*. Pelican, London, 1971. For some of the critiques on aid and environmental damage from the late 1980s onward, see Hayter, T, *Exploited Earth: Britain's Aid and the Environment*. Earthscan, London, 1989, 39–51, 91–103. Pearce, F, *Green Warriors: The People and Politics Behind the Environmental Revolution*. Bodley Head, London, 1991, 101–103, 223–225. Cassen, R, *Does Aid Work?* Oxford University Press, Oxford, 1994, 42–48. Keohane, R O and Levy, M (eds), *Institutions for Environmental Aid*. MIT Press, Cambridge, 1996. Adams, P, *Odious Debts: Loose Lending, Corruption and the Third World's Environmental Legacy*. Earthscan, London, 1991, 182–184. Turner, R K, 'Environmentally Sensitive Aid', in Pearce, D (ed), *Blueprint 2*. Earthscan, London, 1991, 167, 176–179. Forrest, R A, 'Japanese Aid and the Environment', *Ecologist* 21, 1991, 24–31. Colchester, M, 'Aid Money is Helping the Rape of Guyana', *Guardian International* 17 August 1997, 13.
2 *Programme of the German Green Party*. Heretic, London, 1983, 28. Irvine, S and Ponton, A, *A Green Manifesto*. Optima, London, 1988, 130–131. Ghai, D and Vivian, G M (eds), *Grassroots Environmental Action: People's Participation in Sustainable Development*. Routledge, London, 1992, 17. Watkins, K, *The Oxfam Poverty Report*. Oxfam, Oxford, 1995, 171–172.
3 Oxfam, *The Case For Aid*. Oxfam, Oxford, 1996, 2–4. Randel, J and German, T (eds), *The Reality of Aid 1996: An Independent Review of International Aid*. Earthscan, London, 1996, ix. Watkins, supra n2, 171–174, 190–192. Cassen, supra n1, 7, 9,

29–31, 35–36, 54–55, 94–96, 107–109, 121, 130. WCED, *Our Common Future*. Oxford University Press, Oxford, 1987, 313. Pearson Commission, *Partners in Development*. Pall Mall Press, London, 1969, 1. South Commission, *The Challenge to the South*. Oxford University Press, Oxford, 1990, 222–223. Patten, C, 'Common Future – Common Challenge: Aid Policy and the Environment', in Angell, D J R, Comer, J D and Wilkinson, M L N (eds), *Sustaining Earth: Response to Environmental Threat*. Macmillan, London, 1990, 135, 146–149.

4   Crosbie, L, 'Developing the New Economic Orthodoxy', in Dodds, F (ed), *Into the Twenty-first Century: An Agenda For Political Realignment*. Green Print, Basingstoke, 1988, 79, 84, 90–91. Lambert, J, 'Moves Towards a Green Future', also in Dodds, 137, 138. Devall, B, *Simple in Means, Rich in Ends: Practising Deep Ecology*. Green Print, London, 1990, 184. Goodin, R E, *Green Political Theory*. Polity, Cambridge, 1992, 200. Holmberg, J, 'Financing Sustainable Development', in Holmberg, J (ed), *Policies For a Small Planet*. Earthscan, London, 1992, 289, 304. Hayter, T, *Exploited Earth: Britain's Aid and the Environment*. Earthscan, London, 1989, 224–225, 248–250.

5   Section 33.15 of *Agenda 21*. UNCED Doc A/CONF. 151/4. Also in Johnson, S P (ed), *The Earth Summit*. Graham and Trotman, London, 1993, 452. See also Commission on Sustainable Development, *Financial Resources and Mechanisms*. E/CN.17/1995/8, 24 March 1995, Paragraphs 34, 42.

6   Commission on Global Governance, *Our Global Neighbourhood*. Oxford University Press, Oxford, 1995, 191. See also WCED, *Our Common Future*. Oxford University Press, Oxford, 1987, 76–77. World Bank, *World Development Report 1992: Development and the Environment*. Oxford University Press, Oxford, 1992, 176. Carlie, M and Christie, I, *Managing Sustainable Development*. Earthscan, London, 1992, 119. Johnson, supra n5, 450. Holmberg, supra n4, 289–291. Cassen, supra n1, 13–14. Watkins, supra n2, 189.

7   Brandt Commission, *North–South; A Programme for Survival*. Pan, London, 1980, 176.

8   The foremost example of this is when then US Secretary of State George C. Marshall launched in 1947 the idea of a US supported European recovery programme which combined massive amounts of aid for European countries with the strategy of reconciliation and reconstruction. For useful discussions of this plan, see 'The Marshall Plan and its Legacy', *Foreign Affairs* 76(3), 1997, 159–221.

9   In 1961, as the UNGA designated the United Nations Development Decade, they suggested that international assistance to developing countries should 'reach as soon as possible approximately 1% of the combined national incomes of the economically advanced countries.' The 0.7% target appeared in Article C of the *Charter of Algiers: Ministerial Declaration of 77 Developing Countries*. Reproduced from UN Doc MM. 77/7/20, 30 October 1967. Article 23 of the 1969 *UN Declaration on Social Progress and Development* called for: 'the implementation of the aid volume target of a minimum of 1% of the gross national product ... of economically advanced countries.' GA Res 2542(XXIV), 11 December 1969.

10   UNGA Res 2626(XXV). Independent Commission on Population and Quality of Life, *Caring for the Future*. Oxford University Press, Oxford, 1996, 272–273.

11   Pearson Commission, supra n3, 18. Brandt Commission, supra n7, 22, 43, 89, 214–15. Brandt Commisson, *North–South: Common Crisis*. Pan, London, 1983, 90–96, 111. WCED, supra n6, 313. Commission on Global Governance, supra n6, 191. Report of the International Conference on Population and Development, A/CONF.171/13, 1994, Paragraphs 14.8–14.18. World Summit for Social Development, A/CONF.166/9, 1995, Commitments 7(e) and 9(l). International Conference on Human Settlements, The Habitat Agenda: Goals and Principles and Global Plan of Action. A/CONF.165/L.6, Add 10, 14 June 1996. Habitat Agenda, Chapter II, Principle IX, Chapter IV, Paragraph 204(b). UNCTAD IX, The Caracas Declaration. LA/MM/77 (VIII)/1, 1996,

Paragraph 19. Rome Declaration on World Food Security. World Food Summit, 1996. This is reprinted in Report of the World Food Summit. FAO, WFS 96/REP, Objective 6.2, Paragraph e.

12   See points 7 and 8 of *Development and Environment*. UNGA Res 2849(XXVI), 7 December, 1970.

13   Brandt Commission, supra n7, 88–89.

14   WCED, supra n6.

15   The term Planetary Protection Fund is Rajiv Gandhi's. See Planet Protection Fund, Reprinted in Starke, L (ed), *Signs of Hope: Working Towards Our Common Future*. Oxford University Press, Oxford, 1990, 148, 149. The actual genesis of the GEF – as a Northern idea as opposed to the Southern demands for additional environmental finance – is French. For the development of the GEF, see Sjoberg, S, *From Idea to Reality: The Creation of the Global Environmental Facility*. World Bank, GEF, Working Paper No 10, 1993.

16   See International Bank for Reconstruction and Development Resolution on the Global Environmental Facility, World Bank, Washington, DC, 14 March 1991. UNEP, The Global Environmental Facility. *UNEP Press Release* 26 February 1991. These are both reprinted in Churchill, R (ed), *International Law and Climate Change*. Graham and Trotman, London, 1991, 302–312.

17   See UNEP, supra n16, Paragraph 4. Note that the question of whether this funding has been additional or not, and has not just been transferred from other areas, is a matter of debate. See Independent Evaluation of the Pilot Phase, *The Global Environmental Facility*. World Bank, Washington, DC, 1995, xv.

18   Udall, S L, 'Some Second Thoughts On Stockholm', *American University Law Review* 22, 1973, 724. Sullivan, E T, 'The Stockholm Conference: A Step Towards Environmental Co-operation and Involvement', *Indiana Law Review* 6, 1972, 267, 273.

19   See Articles 9 and 12 of the *Stockholm Declaration*. UN Doc A/CONF. 48/14/Rev I, *International Legal Materials* 11, 1972, 1416, 1418.

20   Principle 12 of the *Stockholm Declaration*, ibid.

21   Strategy XV and XX of the *World Conservation Strategy*. IUCN, Gland, 1980. Reprinted in Ruska, B and Simma, B (eds), *International Protection of the Environment*. Oceana, New York, 1981, Vol 13, 424. The IUCN's 1995 *Draft International Covenant on Environment and Development* reiterated this basic call. Specifically, Article 26 again emphasized 'new and additional financial resources' as well as the nations endeavouring 'to reach the United Nations General Assembly target of 0.7%'. IUCN, *Environmental Policy and Law* 31.

22   Brandt Commission, supra n7, 22.

23   Brandt Commission, supra n11, 14, 74.

24   WCED, supra n6, 313, 340.

25   *Declaration of Brasilia*. Adopted at the *Sixth Ministerial Meeting on the Environment in Latin America and the Caribbean*. Brasilia, March 1989. *International Legal Materials* 28, 1989, 450–453. Amazonian Declaration. *International Legal Materials* 28, 1989, 1303. See also *Summit of the Non-Aligned*. 7 September 1989 NAC 9/EC/Doc/8/Rev 4.

26   South Commission, supra n3, 281.

27   'Developing Countries and International Law', *Environmental Policy and Law* 21, 1991, 213. See also Ramphal, S, *Our Country, The Planet*. Lime Tree, London, 1992, 256–257.

28   Principle 7 of the *Rio Declaration* UNCED UN Doc A/CONF./151/5, 1992. Principles 1 (b), 7(b), 8(c) *Statement of Principles for a Global Consensus on the Management, Conservation and Sustainable Development of all Types of Forests*. UNCED Doc A/CONF. 151/6/Rev 1, 1992. *International Legal Materials* 31, 1992, 881, 883. Article

20 (2) UNEP/Bio. Div./CONF/L. 2, 1992. Preamble, Articles 3 (4), 4 (2), 4 (3–10), 11 (5), 12 (3). *United Nations Framework Convention on Climate Change*. A/AC. 237/18 (part II) Add 1, 15 May 1992.

29   United Nations Convention to Combat Desertification. A/AC.241/27, 1994. Articles 4(2) and 20. Report of the International Conference on Population and Development. A/CONF.171/13, 1994, Paragraphs 14.8–14.18.

30   Pearson Commission, supra n3, 8, 10. For an example of how these ethical ideals influenced earlier decades, see Black, M, *A Cause For Our Times: Oxfam – The First Fifty Years*. Oxford University Press, Oxford, 1992, 68–69.

31   See Development Assistance Committee, *Shaping the 21st Century: The Contribution of Development Co-operation*. OECD, Paris, 1996, 3–4.

32   See for example, Opeskin, B R, 'The Moral Foundation of Foreign Aid', *World Development* 24, 1996, 21–24. Collier, A, 'Marxism and Universalism: Group Interests or a Shared World', in Attfield, R and Wilkins, B (eds), *International Justice and the Third World*. Routledge, London, 1992, 77, 84–89. Jamieson, D, 'Global Environmental Justice', in Attfield, R (ed), *Philosophy and the Natural Environment*. Cambridge University Press, Cambridge, 1994, Chapter 7. Singer, P, *Practical Ethics*. Cambridge University Press, Cambridge, 1993, 218–246. Singer, P, 'Famine, Affluence and Morality', *Philosophy and Public Affairs* 1, 1972, 229, 231. Rawls, J, *A Theory of Justice*. Clarendon, Oxford, 1972.

33   Paragraph 13 *Toronto Conference on the Changing Atmosphere*. Reprinted in *American University Journal of International Law and Policy* 5, 1990, 539, 542. Article 4. 10 of the *International Conference of Global Warming and Climate Change*. In the same volume, at 555 Second World Climate Conference. Also in *American University Journal of International Law and Politics*. 540, 542. Principle (d) of the Hague Declaration on the Environment. *International Legal Materials* 28, 1989, 1308.

34   See the preamble and Article 4 (9) of the *Framework Convention*, supra n28.

35   See GATT Working Party, *Trade and the Environment*. World Trade Materials 4, 1992, 2, 27–30. See also Gillis, M, 'Mending the Broken Circle for Tropical Forests', in Borman, F H and Kellert, S R (eds), *Ecology, Economics and Ethics: The Broken Circle*. Yale University Press, New York, 1991, 155, 175.

36   See UNGA Res 2849(XXVI), 1971. For a recent example of this type of argument, see Castro, F, *Tomorrow Is Too Late: Development and the Environmental Crisis in the Third World*. Ocean, Melbourne, 1993, 19–20, 36–37. Strong, M, 'ECO' 92: Critical Challenges and Global Solutions', *Journal of International Affairs* 44, 1991, 287, 290.

37   For an example of this argument in the debates about the protection of biodiversity, see Gillespie, A, 'Common Property, Private Property & Equity: The Clash of Values and the Quest to Protect Biodiversity', *Environmental and Planning Law Journal* 12, 1995, 388–399.

38   See 'Australia v. The Republic of Nauru: Settlement of the Case in the ICJ Concerning Certain Phosphate Lands', *International Legal Materials* 32, 1993, 1471. Note also Dr Mohammed's speech at UNCED, in *Report of the United Nations Conference on Environment and Development*. A/CONF. 151/26/Rev 1, Vol 3, 232, 233.

39   Castro, supra n36, 22–24.

40   Brandt Commission, supra n7, 17–18.

41   Handl, G, 'Environmental Protection and Development in Third World Countries: Common Destiny – Common Responsibility', *New York University Journal of International Law and Politics* 20, 1988, 603. Holst, G, 'A New International Politics: Diplomacy in Complex Interdependence', *International Organs* 32, 1978, 513. Dorfman, R, 'Protecting the Global Environment: An Immodest Proposal', *World Development* 19, 1991, 105.

42   Pearson Commission, supra n3, 8–9.

43   Brandt Commission, supra n7, 9.

44 Shue, H, 'The Unavoidability of Justice', in Hurrell, A and Kingsbury, B (eds), *The International Politics of the Environment*. Oxford University Press, Oxford, 1992, 373, 374–75. Handl, supra n41, 608. Ramphal, supra n27, 187. Brandt Commission, supra n7, 16. Susskind, L E, *Environmental Diplomacy: Negotiating More Effective Global Agreements*. Oxford University Press, Oxford, 1994, 94–95.

45 Hyder, T, 1992 'Climate Negotiations: The North/South Perspective', in Mintzer, I (ed), *Confronting Climate Change*. Cambridge University Press, Cambridge, 1992, 336.

46 Williams, M, 'Re-Articulating the Third World Coalition: The Role of the Environmental Agenda', *Third World Quarterly* 14, 1993, 7–29. Shue, H, 'The Unavoidability of Justice', in Hurrell and Kingsbury (eds), supra n44, 273, 294, 373, 376. Susskind, supra n44, 92–93, 98, 133–34. Sachs, W, 'Global Ecology and the Shadow of Development', in Sachs, W (ed), *Global Ecology*. Zed, London, 1993, 1, 7. Poole, T, 'South's Spokesman Talks Tough', *Independent* 5 June 1992, 12.

47 See 'India Wants $2 Billion to Sign Montreal Protocol', *International Environmental Law Reporter* 12, 1989, 389.

48 *Treaty for the Preservation and Protection of Fur Seals*. 37 Stat 1542, Treaty Series, No 564. For discussions of this, see Paterson, D G and Wilen, J, 'Depletion and Diplomacy: The North Pacific Seal Hunt 1886–1910', *Research In Economic History* 2, 1977, 81, 111.

49 Article 19, Montreal Protocol. *International Legal Materials* 26, 1987, 1557.

50 Wood, A, 'The Multilateral Fund for the Implementation of the Montreal Protocol', *International Environmental Affairs* 5, 1993, 335, 338–340. Rosencranz, A, 'Montreal Protocol: "Bringing The Developing World On Board"', *Environmental Policy and The Law* 20, 1990, 202. Friends of the Earth, *Funding Change*. Friends of the Earth, London, 1990, 2, 3–6.

51 See the *Helsinki Declaration on the Protection of the Ozone Layer*. *International Legal Materials* 28, 1989, 1335–1336. *International Environmental Report (BNA)* 12, 1989, 225, 268. For a further discussion of this, see Wood, supra n50, 335, 338–340.

52 *London Amendment to the Montreal Protocol on Substances that Deplete the Ozone Layer*. *International Legal Materials* 30, 1991, 537. Also in Rummel-Bulska, B (ed), *Multilateral Treaties in the Field of the Environment*. Grotius, Cambridge, 1991, Vol 2, 311.

53 See Article 1 of Annex II, ibid.

54 Milne, K, 'CFC Clampdown Eases Pressure on Ozone Layer', *New Scientist* 7 July 1990, 21.

55 Susskind, supra n44, 83, 87, 90. French, H, 'Learning From the Ozone Experience', in Brown, L R (ed), *State of the World: 1997*. Earthscan, London, 1997, 151, 162–166. DeSombre, E, 'The Montreal Protocol Multilateral Fund: Partial Success Story', in Keohane, supra n1, 89–126. Haas, P M, 'Stratospheric Ozone: Regime Formation in Stages', in Young, O R (ed), *Polar Politics: Creating International Environmental Regimes*. Cornell University Press, New York, 1993, 152, 164, 169–170. Note that there were other significant factors leading to this agreement. See Haas, 161, 165, 176–180.

56 Pearson Commission, supra n3, 5, 17.

57 See Toye, J, *Dilemmas of Development*. Blackwell, Oxford, 1993, 231. Porter, G and Brown, J W, *Global Environmental Politics*. Westview, Colorado, 1991, 46. Susskind, supra n44, 24.

58 Hancock, G, *Lords of Poverty*. Macmillan, London, 1989, 189. For a similar conclusion, see Bauer, P and Yarney, B, 'Foreign Aid: What Is At Stake?', *The Public Interest* 1982, 54, 57, 60.

59 Hancock, supra n58, 5. Valley, P, *Bad Samaritans: First World Ethics and Third World Debt*. Hodder, London, 1990, 32–45. Pearson Commission, supra n3, 168–169. South Commission, supra n3, 51–52. Commission on Global Governance, supra n6, 63–65. Cassen, supra n1, 11–14. Watkins, supra n2, 40–41.

60   See for example, Turner, R, 'Minister's Dismissal Raises Green Doubts About Collor', *Independent* 24 March, 1992, 13. Tickell, O, 'Death By Design', *BBC Wildlife* 10(5), 1992, 28, 32. Shankland, A, 'Felling Mr Clean', *New Internationalist* 232, 1992, 30. Vidal, J, 'History Goes On Hold', *Guardian* 3 April 1992, 29.

61   Brummer, A, 'Lamont Pledges Foreign Aid To Assist Third World Clean Up', *Guardian* 29 April 1992, 13. Brown, P, 'Major Ties Signature to Veto on Spending', *Guardian* 13 June 1992, 3. Patten, C, 'Common Future – Common Challenge: Aid Policy and the Environment', in Angell et al, supra n3, 135, 145. McCarthy, M, 'Misuses of Wildlife Cash Feared: British Doubts Threaten Rio Treaty Signing', *Times* 9 June, 1992, 1.

62   'Tied aid limits competition, and therefore choice; it may encourage external dependence rather than self-reliance, and it creates opportunities for corruption on both sides of the tied transaction.' Cassen, supra n1, 219.

63   South Commission, supra n3, 29. It should also be recognized that it is affected by the public perception of various crises which make some more attractive to give to than others. Thus, the former Yugoslavia received most of its required aid, whereas Eritrea received less than one tenth of their amount, even though their need was equally compelling. See Randel and German, supra n3.

64   House of Commons Foreign Affairs Committee, *Bilateral Aid: Country Programmes*. London, 1987, Paragraph 16. Editors, 'Lies, Dam Lies and Ballistics', *Ecologist* 24, 1994, 44. Bello, W, *Dark Victory: The United States, Structural Adjustment and Global Poverty*. Pluto, London, 1994, 10, 25–26. Trainer, T, *Developed to Death; Rethinking Third World Development*. Green Print, London, 1989, 97–101. Hayter, supra n4, 75–76, 174–75. Hancock, supra n58, 156. Valley, supra n59, 74–85. Adams, supra n1, 82–90.

65   UNICEF, *The State of the World's Children: 1994*. Oxford University Press, Oxford, 1994, 21. See also Finger, M, 'Politics of the UNCED Process', in Sachs, supra n46, 36, 37.

66   Cassen, supra n1, 3. Randel and German, supra n3, x. UNDP, *Human Development Report: 1993*. UN, New York, 1993, 7, 22–23. Watkins, supra n2, 191–192. United Nations, *The Least Developed Countries Report: 1996*. UN, New York, 1996, 2–4. Development Assistance Committee, *Aid to Least Developed Countries*. OECD, Paris, 1999, Fact Sheet. Whereas in 1996 aid to the LDCs made up 28 per cent of the total aid given, by 1997 this was down to 23 per cent. Development Assistance Committee, *Total DAC Countries: Aid at a Glance*. OECD, Paris, 1999, Fact Sheet. In 1999, Israel and Indonesia received the highest amounts of foreign aid. No African or Latin American country was among the top 10 recipients.

67   The Report of the Independent Commission on Population and Quality of Life, *Caring for the Future*. Oxford University Press, Oxford, 1996, 274.

68   World Bank, *Rethinking the Money and Ideas of Aid*. World Bank, Washington, DC, 1999, 1–2. For the possible detrimental environmental effects of foreign aid, see note 1.

69   World Bank, ibid, 1–9, 14–25. Almost identical conclusions apply to the effectiveness of environmental aid. See Keohane, R, 'Analysing the Effectiveness of International Environmental Insitutions', in Keohane, supra n1, 1–27.

70   *The Reality of Aid* put this figure at one-third, supra n3, x, 18. Watkins, supra n2, 194–197. Holmberg, supra n4, 289, 307. The 25 per cent figure is from the World Bank, supra n68, 6.

71   OECD/DAC, *Co-operation for Sustainable Development*. OECD, Paris, 1997, 2. OECD/DAC, *Guidelines on Aid and Environment*. OECD, Paris, 1992, 2.

72   See Ross, M, 'Conditionality and Logging Reforms in the Tropics', in Keohane, supra n1, 166–197.

73   See the Recommendations of the 1962 Development Assistance Committee of the OECD. 'Joint efforts should be made to reverse the trend towards more tying of aid.' See also the Pearson Commission, supra n3, 191. Direct efforts to achieve the goal of

untying aid failed in 1970. It was only in 1992 that the use of tied aid in upper middle income countries, and the use of tied aid for any projects that may be commercially viable, was 'banned' by the DAC of the OECD. All of these documents are reprinted in OECD, *The Story of Official Development Assistance*. OECD, Paris, 1996, 14, 22, 57–58.

74 World Summit for Social Development. A/CONF.166/9, 1995, Programme of Action, Paragraph 88 (c). For an earlier example of this in the 1990s, see the Plan of Action for Implementing the World Declaration on the Survival, Protection and Development of Children in the 1990s. UNICEF, Geneva, 1990, Paragraph 31.

75 Independent Commission on Population and Quality of Life, supra n10, 269.

76 Habitat Agenda, 1996, supra n11, paragraph 204 dd.

77 OECD/DAC, *Shaping the 21st Century: The Contribution of Development Co-operation*. Paris, OECD, 1996. This document contains laudable and explicit targets on economic, social and sustainable development, 2–3. See also OECD/DAC, *Development Partnerships in the New Global Context*. OECD, Paris, 1995.

78 Independent Commission on Population and Quality of Life, supra n10, 269, 273–276. Randel and German, 1996, supra n3, ix, 35–37. Special Session of the General Assembly. Programme of Implementation of Agenda 21, 1 July 1997, Paragraph 27.

79 Randel and German, 1996, supra n3, ix. Watkins, supra n2, 192–195. Interpretation of this figure may be a source of debate. This is because in 1999 it was suggested that just over 30 per cent of OECD aid was spent on 'education, health, population and other social infrastructure'. See Development Assistance Committee, *Total DAC Countries: Aid at a Glance*. OECD, Paris, 1999, Fact Sheet.

80 GEF, *The Restructured GEF: Questions and Answers*. World Bank, Washington, DC, 1995, 1. GEF, *The Pilot Phase and Beyond*. World Bank, GEF Working Paper No 1, 1992, Principle 1.

81 See Sjoberg, S, 'The Global Environmental Facility', in Werksman, J (ed), *Greening International Institutions*. Earthscan, London, 1996, 148, 153–157. Reed, D, *The Global Environmental Facility: Sharing Responsibility for the Biosphere*. WWF, Washington, DC, 1993, 11–19. Rich, B, *Mortgaging the Earth: The World Bank, Environmental Impoverishment and the Crisis of Development*. Earthscan, London, 1994, 175–181, 260–261, 269–270, 279–280. Wells, M P, 'The Global Environmental Facility and the Prospects For Biodiversity', *International Environmental Affairs* 6, 1994, 69, 74, 80–81, 83–84. Jordan, A, 'The Evolving Role of the GEF', *Environment* 36(6), 1994, 31–34.

82 See Watkins, K, 'Trade Route of Evils', *Guardian* 6 March 1992, 29.

83 Shue, supra n44, 373, 376. Vidal, J, 'Earth Soundings', *Guardian* 3 April 1992, 29.

84 Forrest, supra n1, 26.

85 International Bank for Reconstruction, supra n16, Paragraph 1. For a discussion of this phase, see Jordan, supra n81, 13–16, 18–19.

86 See Chapter 1 of this book.

87 These calls were first heard in the World Bank in 1991, where it was suggested that 'developing country representation [in the GEF] is essential.' See World Bank Document Concerning the Establishment of the GEF. *International Legal Materials* 30, 1991, 1735. The calls for the expansion and democratization of the GEF are in Paragraph 33. 16 (iii), Agenda 21. UNCED Doc A/Conf. 151, 4. See also Articles 11 (2) and 21 (3) of the *United Nations Framework Convention on Climate Change*. UNCED A/AC. 237/18 (Part II), Add 1, 5 May 1992.

88 World Bank, 'Replenished and Restructured GEF', *Environment Bulletin* 6(2), 1995, 10. World Bank, *World Bank and the Environment: 1993*. Washington, 1993, 126–127. El-Ashry, M, 'Mechanisms For Funding', *Environmental Policy and the Law* 23, 1993, 48–50. GEF, 1992, supra n80, Principle 1. Sjoberg, supra n81, 156–158.

89 El-Ashry, supra n88, 48, 50.

90   Wells, supra n81, 79, 89–90.

91   Independent Evaluation of the Pilot Phase, supra n17, 12.

92   See Porter, G, Clemencon R, Waafas O and Philips, M, *Study of GEF's Overall Performance*. GEF, World Bank, Washington, DC, 1999, 1–4, 38–64.

93   Markandya, A, 'Economics and the Ozone Layer', in Pearce, supra n1, 53.

94   Tolba, M, 'Heeding Nature's Tug: An Environmental Agenda For International Relations', *Fletcher Forum* 14, 1990, 239, 247.

95   'Biological Diversity: Slow Progress', *Environmental Law and Policy* 15, 1991, 134. 'Financial Resources for Biodiversity Conservation', *Environmental Policy and the Law* 27, 1997, 9–13. Lake, R, 'Financing Biodiversity Conservation', *Environmental Policy and the Law* 27, 1997, 172–175.

96   Agarwal, A and Narain, S, *Global Warming in an Unequal World: A Case of Environmental Colonialism*. Third World Network, New Delhi, 1991, 20. Greenpeace, 'Prevent Climate Holocaust', *Newsletter* 21 June 1991, 3.

97   Strong, M, 'Costing The Earth', in World Development Movement, *Costing The Earth: Striking The Global Bargain at the Earth Summit in 1992*. Chameleon, London, 1991, 69. This was reiterated in paragraph 2.17 of Agenda 21. UNCED Doc/CONF. 151/4. See also Ramphal, supra n27, 253.

98   See Markandya, A, *Financing Sustainable Development: Agenda 21*. Harvard Institute for International Development, Harvard, 1994.

99   Breen C, 'Deal Emerging on Aid to Poor', *Independent* 9 June 1992, 14. Brown, P, 'Eleventh Hour Cash Deal is Near', *Guardian* 11 June 1992, 10. Schoon, N, 'Bush Defiant on Rio Signing', *Independent* 13 June 1992, 1. Tisdal, S, 'Defiant Bush Insists on US Development', *Guardian* 13 June 1992, 8. Tisdal, S, 'Money The Root Cause', *Guardian* 4 June 1992, 8.

100 See K Miyazawa's speech at UNCED, in *Report of the United Nations Conference on Environment and Development*. A/CONF. 151/26/Rev 1, Vol 3, 163–164. H Kohl's speech, in the *UNCED Report*, ibid, 29. John Major's speech is also in the *UNCED Report*, 25, 27. George Bush's speech, 73–78. See also Turner, R, 'Germans Pledge More Money', *Independent* 13 June 1992, 8. Vidal, J, 'Deadlock in Talks About Cash', *Guardian* 10 June 1992, 8.

101 Schoon, N, 'Bush Aims To Divert His Critics', *Independent* 12 June 1992, 9.

102 Resolution of the Common Aid Effort. Adopted by the Development Assistance Group (of the OECD) 1961. This is reprinted in OECD, supra n73, At 14.

103 Whereas some believed the year 2010 is a good aim, others suggested no firm timetables were possible and could only give a vague intention of 'as soon as possible'. Hurtado, M E, 'A Pledge for the World's Poor', *Guardian* 28 April 1992, 18. Vidal, J, 'Discord on Rise Before Rio Summit', *Guardian* 26 May 1992, 7. Brown, P, 'Bush Lays Down Rio Gauntlet', *Guardian* 13 June 1992, 1.

104 See Osborn, D, *Earth Summit II: Outcomes and Analysis*. Earthscan, London, 1998, 12, 26–27.

105 Paragraphs 18 and 77. Programme for the Further Implementation of Agenda 21. This is reprinted in Osborn, ibid, 127, 134.

106 See Bramble, B, 'Financial Resources for the Transition to Sustainable Development', in Dodds, F (ed), *The Way Forward: Beyond Agenda 21*. Earthscan, London, 1997, 191, 192–194.

107 'GEF In Trouble', Ecologist Campaigns, *Ecologist* 24, 1994, 2. Sjoberg, 1996, supra n81, 154–157.

108 *Special Session of the General Assembly*. Implementation of Agenda 21, 1 July 1997, Paragraph 13. See also UNEP, *Executive Committee of the Multilateral Fund: Report of the Twentieth Meeting*. UNEP, Nairobi, 1996, 2.

109 This fact is commonly juxtaposed against the situation that although aid has fallen, private investment in the developing world has increased. While this is correct, it must

be remembered that private investment is concentrated in a very small, select group of countries. See OECD, 'Financial Flows to Developing Countries in 1998: Rise in Aid', OECD, DAC, News Release, 10 June 1999. Moreover, private enterprise cannot be expected to fund social or environmental objectives.

110 UNICEF, supra n65, 23. UNDP, supra n66, 2. Randel and German, supra n3, ix, xii, 17. Commission on Sustainable Development, *Overall Progress Achieved Since UNCED: Report of the Secretary General.* E/CN.17/1997/2, Paragraphs 13, 1997, 98–102, 133.

111 OECD, 'Partnership is no Longer Just an Option', OECD, DAC, News Release, February 2000.

112 Commission on Sustainable Development, *Financial Resources and Mechanisms for Sustainable Development: Overview of Current Issues and Developments: Report of the Secretary General.* E/CN.17/1996/4, 22 February 1996, Paragraph 19. Commission on Sustainable Development, *Financial Resources and Mechanisms: Addendum.* E/CN.17/1996/4/Add.1, 1996, Paragraphs 79–91.

113 Commission on Global Governance, supra n6, 217–221.

114 Independent Commission, supra n10, 278–284, 318–319. See also Bramble, supra n106, 196–200.

115 Commission on Sustainable Development, *Overall Progress Achieved Since UNCED: Report of the Secretary General: Financial Resources and Mechanisms.* E/CN.17/1997/2/Add.23, 1997, Paragraph 38. For the background reasons to this failure, see Chapters 3 and 8 of this book.

116 See Osborn, supra n104, 47, 55–56.

CHAPTER 7 PEACE

1 Kemp, P, and Wall, D, *A Green Manifesto for the 1990s* Penguin, Harmondsworth, 1990, 129–146. Spretnak, C and Capra, F, *Green Politics: The Global Promise.* Bear, New Mexico, 1986, 43–49. Porritt, J, *Seeing Green: The Politics of Ecology Explained.* Blackwell, Oxford, 1984, 54–64.

2 See OECD, *Review of Environment, Security and Development Co-operation.* OECD, Paris, 2000. For some further background material, see Renner, M, *Fighting For Survival: Environmental Decline, Social Conflict and the New Age of Insecurity.* Norton, New York, 1996. Prins, G and Stamp, R, *Top Guns and Toxic Whales: The Environment and Global Security.* Earthscan, London, 1991. Renner, M, 'Ending Violent Conflict', in Brown, L R et al (eds), *State of the World: 1999.* Earthscan, London, 1999, 151–168. Swain, A, 'Environmental Migration and Conflict Dynamics', *Third World Quarterly* 17, 1996, 959–973. Homer-Dixon, T, 'Environmental Scarcities and Violent Conflict', *International Security* 9, 1994, 1–38.

3 WCED, *Our Common Future.* Oxford University Press, Oxford, 1987, 290.

4 International Commission on Peace and Food, *Uncommon Opportunities.* Zed, London, 1994, 43, 193, 197. The second part of the quote actually comes from the Commission on Global Governance, *Our Global Neighbourhood.* Oxford University Press, Oxford, 1995, 79.

5 See McNamara, R, *Development and the Arms Race.* University of Chicago Press, Chicago, 1979.

6 Brandt Commission, *North–South: A Programme For Survival.* Pan, London, 1980, 14, 123. Brandt Commission, *North–South: Common Crisis.* Pan, London, 1983, 38, 80. WCED, *Our Common Future.* Oxford University Press, Oxford, 1987, 7, 297–298. South Commission, *The Challenge of the South.* Oxford University Press, Oxford, 1990, 52–53. Independent Commission on Disarmament and Security Issues, *Common*

Security. Pan, London, 1982, 71–100. International Commission on Peace and Food, *Uncommon Opportunities.* Zed, London, 1994, 52–54. For some recent conferences that discussed this, see World Food Summit Actions Plan. In *Report of the World Food Summit.* WFS 96/REP. FAO, Rome, Objective 6.2. Paragraph G. The Habitat Agenda Global Plan of Action, in *Report of the UN Conference on Human Settlements.* (Habitat II). A/CONF.165/14, 1996, Paragraph 204 (l). World Summit for Social Development A/CONF.166/9, 1995, Paragraph 21.

7   Ul Haq, M, 'What Ever Happend to the Peace Dividend?', *Our Planet* 7(1), 1995, 8–10. UNICEF, *State of the World's Children: 1996.* Oxford University Press. Oxford, 1996. 4–5.

8   Independent Commission on Population and the Quality of Life, *Caring For the Future.* Oxford University Press, Oxford, 1996. 68.

9   See 'Military Expenditure', in *SIPRI Yearbook 1999: Armaments, Disarmament and International Security.* Oxford University Press, Oxford, 1999, 10–12 and Chapter 6. International Institute for Strategic Studies, *The Military Balance 1998–1999.* Oxford University Press, Oxford, 1996, 295–300. Klare, M T, 'The Arms Trade in the 1990s: Changing Patterns, Rising Dangers', *Third World Quarterly* 17, 1996, 857–874.

10   Independent Commission on Population and Quality of Life, *Caring for the Future.* Oxford University Press, Oxford, 1996, 69. Ul Haq, supra n7, 8–10.

11   International Institute for Strategic Studies, supra n9, 13–15, 295–300.

12   UNDP, *World Development Report: 1992.* Oxford University Press, Oxford, 1992, Tables 20 and 41, 166–167, 200. King, A and Schneider, B, *The First Global Revolution.* Simon and Schuster, London, 1991, 56, 67. Barnaby, F (ed), *The Gaia Peace Atlas: Survival In The Third Millennium.* Pan, London, 1988, 96–97. Ramphal, S, *Our Country, the Planet.* Lime Tree, London, 1992, 34.

13   International Commission on Peace and Food, supra n6, 42. Commission on Global Governance, supra n4, 122–129.

14   Watkins, K, *The OXFAM Poverty Report.* Oxfam, Oxford, 1996, 8. UNICEF, *The State of the World's Children: 1996.* Oxford University Press, Oxford, 1996, 4. International Institute for Strategic Studies, supra n9, 10–11, 14–15.

15   Report of the Independent Commission on Population and Quality of Life, *Caring For the Future.* Oxford University Press, Oxford, 1996, 68.

16   Declaration on the Rights of Peoples to Peace. Approved by the General Assembly Resolution 39/11 of 12 November 1984. In a similar vein, the 1994 Commission on Peace and Food also stated: 'The main prerequisite and condition for the fulfilment of the world's many different potentials is peace ... peace has become the fundamental imperative of development.' Report of the International Commission on Peace and Food, supra n6, 29–30.

17   Principle 24, *Rio Declaration on Environment and Development.* UNCED Doc A/CONF. 151/5/Rev 1, *International Legal Materials* 31, 1992, 877. Likewise, the 1968 Tehran Human Rights Conference stated: 'Peace is the underlying condition for the full observance of human rights and war is their negation.'

18   See Bates, D, 'The Medical and Ecological Effects of Nuclear War', *McGill Law Journal* 28, 1983, 717–719.

19   Director, 'Nine Minutes to Midnight', *Bulletin of Atomic Scientists* October 1998, 4–5.

20   Daneilsson, B and Daneilsson, M, *Poisoned Reign: French Nuclear Colonialism in the South Pacific.* Penguin, Australia, 1996. Walker, M, 'The Long View', *New Scientist* 16 October 1999.

21   These costs have become apparent for each nuclear power. For a small selection of these, see Zorpette, G, 'Hanford's Nuclear Wasteland', *Scientific American* May 1996, 72–81. Lluma, D, 'What the Russians Left Behind', *Bulletin of Atomic Scientists* June 2000, 14–17.

22   UNGA Res 36/100, 9 December 1981.

23 Independent Commission on Disarmament and Security Issues, *Common Security: A Blueprint for Survival*. Simon and Schuster, New York, 1982, 49–70.

24 Schell, J, *The Fate of the Earth*. Picador, London, 1982, 111.

25 WCED, supra n6. 295.

26 See Pittock, A B, *The Environmental Consequences of a Nuclear War: Volume 1: The Physical and Atmospheric Effects*. Wiley, New York, 1989. Harwell, M A, *The Environmental Consequences of a Nuclear War: Volume 2: The Ecological and Agricultural Effects*. Wiley, New York, 1989.

27 Turco, A, 'Nuclear Winter: The Global Consequences of Multiple Nuclear Explosions', *Science* 222, 1983, 1283. Ehrlich, P and Sagan, C, *The Nuclear Winter: The World After Nuclear War*. Sidgwick & Jackson, London, 1984.

28 Schell, supra n24, 69–70.

29 For the effects of radiation upon future generations, see World Health Organisation, *The Effects of Nuclear War Upon Health and Health Services*. WHO, Geneva, 1987. See also Abrams, H, 'Chernobyl and the Short Term Effects of Nuclear War', in Sixth World Conference of International Physicians Against Nuclear War (ed), *Maintain Life on Earth!* IPANW, Cologne, 1986, 122.

30 See ICJ, *Legality of the Threat or Use of Nuclear Weapons*. 8 July 1996, General List No 95, Paragraph 105. See also Matheson, M, 'The Opinion of the ICJ on the Threat or Use of Nuclear Weapons', *American Journal of International Law* 91, 1997 417–435. Kristjansdottir, E, 'The Legality of the Threat or Use of Nuclear Weapons Under Current International Law: The Arguments Behind the World Court's Advisory Opinion', *New York University Journal of International Law and Politics* 30, 1998, 291–369.

31 Noted in Lamb, J, *How To Think About Arms Control, Disarmament and Defence*. Prentice Hall, New Jersey, 1988, 11. See also Croft, S, *Strategies of Arms Control: A History and Typology*. Manchester University Press, Manchester, 1996. Chapter 1.

32 See Creveld, M, *Technology and War: From 2,000 BC to the Present*. Free Press, New York, 1989, 10–16.

33 Convention With Respect To The Laws And Customs Of War On Land (Hague, Ii) (29 July 1899. Entry into Force: 4 September 1900.

34 See Northedge, F S, *The League of Nations: Its Life and Times. 1920–1946*. Manchester University Press, Manchester, 1990, 113–136. Walters, F P, *A History of the League of Nations*. Simon and Schuster, London, 1949, 217–230, 361–376, 501–516, 541–555, 606–614.

35 See Bull, H, 'The Classical Approach to Arms Control Theory After Twenty Years', in Nerlich, U (ed), *Soviet Power and Western Negotiating Strategies*. Ballinger, Cambridge, 1983, Vol II, 21–30.

36 See Lieberman, J, *The Scorpion and the Tarantula: The Struggle to Control Atomic Weapons 1945–1949*. Houghton, Boston, 1970. Hewlett, R, *A History of the United States Atomic Energy Commission*. Pennsylvania State University, 1962, 540–549.

37 See Hewlett, R G, *Atoms For Peace and War, 1953–1961: Eisenhower and the Atomic Energy Commission*. University of California Press, Berkeley, 1989.

38 Statute of the International Atomic Energy Agency. IAEA, Vienna, 1957, 89–05761.

39 See The IAEA Safeguards System of 1965–68. INFCIRC/66/Rev 2. For a useful discussion of the IAEA in this context, see Harry, R, 'IAEA Safeguards and Non-Proliferation', in Leeuwen, M (ed), *The Future of the International Nuclear Non-proliferation Regime*. Kluwer, Dordrecht, 1995, 167–203. For a discussion on the future of the IAEA, see the special issue of the *IAEA Bulletin*, 'Safeguards and non-Proliferation', *IAEA Bulletin* 41(4), 1999. For earlier comments in the same journal, see 37(3), 2–10 and 39(3), 4–12. The new safeguards were assisted by the IAEA's 'Draft Protocol to Strengthen and Improve the Effectiveness and Efficiency of the IAEA Safeguards System', *International Legal Materials* 36, 1997, 1232. The idea of further

strengthening was recognized in the NPT extension treaty. See Final Document on the Extension of the Non-proliferation Treaty. *International Legal Materials* 34, 1995, 959–973, Decision 2, Paragraphs 9–13.

40 See Muller, H, *Nuclear Non-proliferation and Global Order*. SIPRI, Oxford University Press, 1994, 22–26. Goldenberg, S, 'Russia in Nuclear Deal with India', *Guardian Weekly* 28 June 1998, At 4.

41 See Muller, supra n40, 4–5.

42 For an examination of how 'close' things became in the Cuban Missile Crisis, see Gottfried, K and Blair, B, *Crisis Stability and Nuclear War*. Oxford University Press, Oxford, 1988, 169–198.

43 See Arkin, W, 'History of the Nuclear Stockpile', *Bulletin of Atomic Scientists* August 1985, 107.

44 See Schelling, T, 'On the Objectives of Arms Control', in Art, R J (ed), *The Use of Force*. Lanham, New York, 1988, 618.

45 Treaty Banning Nuclear Tests in the Atmosphere, In Outer Space and Under Water. United Nations Treaty Series, Vol 480.

46 Treaty on the Non-proliferation of Nuclear Weapons. United Nations Treaty Series, Vol 729. See also Shaker, M, *The Nuclear Non-proliferation Treaty: Origin and Implementation, 1959–1979*. Oceana, New York, 1980.

47 These assurances were originally made in 1968. See UN Security Council Resolution on Security Assurances to Non-nuclear States. UN Doc S/RES/255, 1968.

48 Agreement between the USA and the USSR on Certain Measures With Respect to the Limitation of Strategic Offensive Arms (SALT I), *Treaties and Other International Act Series*. 7653, US Dept of State, Washington, DC, 1972.

49 Treaty Between The United States of America And The Union of Soviet Socialist Republics On The Limitation Of Anti-Ballistic Missile Systems. 944 UNTS 13, 26 May 1972.

50 For a discussion of this system, see McNamara, R, *Blundering into Disaster*. Pantheon, New York, 1986, 157–173. Of late, there has been another American attempt to develop a new 'Star wars' system. This was a source of contention in the mid-1990s. See Kewusm, G, 'Portrait of a Bad Idea', *Bulletin of Atomic Scientists* August 1997, 18–25. However, in 1997 the two sides agreed on demarcation between strategic and non-strategic missile defence systems. Although this was useful, debate about it continues.

51 See Cowen, R, *The ABM Treaty: To Defend or Not to Defend*. Oxford University Press, Oxford, 1987. Some good discussions of the MAD policy are contained in Caldicott, H, *Nuclear Madness*. Autumn Press, Massachusetts, 1978, 72–85. Jervis, R, *The Meaning of Nuclear Revolution: Statecraft and the Prospect of Armageddon*. Cornell Press, Ithaca, 1989, 74–107.

52 Treaty between the USA and the USSR on the Limitation of Strategic Offensive Arms (SALT II), *Committee on Disarmament Documents*. CD/28, 27 June 1979 and CD/29, 2 July 1979.

53 See Renner, supra n2, 153–156. For one example among many of how sensitive the early 1980s were, see Knelman, F, *Reagan, God and the Bomb*. McClelland, Ontario, 1984.

54 Treaty between the USA and the USSR on the Elimination of Their Intermediate Range and Shorter Range Missiles. *International Legal Materials* 27, 1988, 84–254.

55 For a useful description of START I, see Karp, C, 'The START Treaty and Nuclear Arms Control', in *SIPRI Yearbook 1992: World Armaments and Disarmament*. Oxford University Press, Oxford, 1992, 13–26.

56 For a useful description and analysis of START II, see Lockwood, D, 'Nuclear Arms Control', in *SIPRI Yearbook 1993: World Armaments and Disarmament*. Oxford University Press, Oxford, 1993, 554–559.

57 See Simpson, J, 'The Nuclear Non-Proliferation Regime After the NPT Review and Extension Conference', in *SIPRI Yearbook 1998: Armaments, Disarmament and International Security*. Oxford University Press, Oxford, 1998, 404–432, 626–639.

58 See Muller, supra n40, 6.

59 Nevertheless, France and the UK have announced that they will be reducing aspects of their nuclear deterrents. See Black, I, 'Trident Nuclear Warheads To Be Cut By Half', *Guardian Weekly* 28 June 1998.

60 Albright, D, 'Iraq And the Bomb: Were They Even Close?', *Bulletin of Atomic Scientists* March 1991, 18. Albright, D, 'Iraq's Shop-Till-You-Drop Nuclear Programme', *Bulletin of Atomic Scientists* April 1992, 27–37.

61 Albright, D, 'How Much Plutonium Does North Korea Have?', *Bulletin of Atomic Scientists* October 1994, 46–53. Mack, A, 'Nuclear End-Game on the Korean Peninsula', in Leeuwen (ed), supra n39, 15–57.

62 See Potter, W, 'The Nuclear Proliferation Challenge from the Soviet Successor States: Myths and Realities', in Leeuwen (ed), supra n39, 155–166. 'Anti-Nuclear Trafficking', *IAEA Bulletin* 39(3), 1997, 10–11. Reuters, 'Russia Has Lost 100 Nuclear Bombs', *New Zealand Herald* 7 September 1997.

63 Extension of the Treaty on the Non-Proliferation of Nuclear Weapons. NPT/CONF.1995/32/DEC.3, 11 May 1995.

64 Comprehensive Test Ban Treaty. UN Doc A/50/1027 Annex, 26 August 1996. Also in *International Legal Materials* 35, 1996, 1439–1450.

65 Brown, P, 'Treaty Success', *Guardian Weekly* 29 September 1996. This was after some 'last minute' nuclear testing by China and France.

66 See 'Under a Cloud', *New Scientist* 6 November 1999, 18–19. The senate feared that 'rogue' States could manufacture 'first generation' nuclear weapons (robust fission weapons) without having to test them. Moreover, without having the ability to test their own arsenal, it could lose some of its potential.

67 Decision 3, Paragraph 2.

68 Comprehensive Nuclear Test Ban Treaty Principles and Objectives for Nuclear Non-Proliferation and Disarmament. A/50/1027, 26 August 1996, Paragraph 4(c).

69 Reuters, 'Nuclear Powers Reaffirm Pledge to Scrap Weapons', *NZ Herald* 3 May 2000.

70 See Simpson, supra n57, 563–589. Comment, 'The Nuclear Test of Time', *Guardian Weekly* 7 July 1996. Bedi, R, 'India Wrestles With Nuclear Status', *NZ Herald* 13 May 1998, B4. Editor, 'On the Nuclear Precipice', *Guardian Weekly* 7 June 1998. Black, I, 'Nuclear Club Tells South Asian Rivals to Cool Off', *Guardian Weekly* 14 June 1998.

71 See Muller, supra n40, 5–8, 12–14. Black, I, 'India Seeks Nuclear Convention', *Guardian Weekly* 7 June 1998. It is not only the emerging nuclear powers which have expressed unwillingness to accept the CTBT. See Lippman, T, 'Support for Test Ban Treaty May Be Lacking', *Washington Post* 3 September 1998.

72 See Perkovich, G, 'Nuclear Proliferation', *Foreign Policy* Fall, 1998, 12–23. The countries which have opted out of the nuclear arms race are South Africa, South Korea, Ukraine, Argentina, Kazakhstan and Brazil. For further discussion, see Hoekema, J, 'CTBT and NPT: An Essential Linkage?' in Leeuwen, supra n39, 231–241. Arnett, E, 'Implications of the Comprehensive Test Ban For Nuclear Weapons Programmes and Decision Making', in Arnett, E, *Nuclear Weapons After the Comprehensive Test Ban: Implications for Modernisation and Proliferation.* SIPRI, Oxford University Press, 1996, 2–23, 129–139. Simpson, supra n57, 563–564, 572–575.

73 *Canberra Commission on the Elimination of Nuclear Weapons.* Government Printer, Canberra, 1996, 9.

74 See Commission on Global Governance, supra n4, 114–117.

75 Convention on the Prohibition of the Development, Production, Stockpiling and Use of Chemical Weapons and On Their Destruction. (Corrected version in accordance with Depositary Notification C.N.246.1994.TREATIES-5 and the corresponding Procès-Verbal of Rectification of the Original of the Convention, issued on 8 August 1994.)

76 Convention on the Prohibition of the Development, Production and Stockpiling of Bacteriological (Biological) And Toxin Weapons and On Their Destruction. TIAS 8062,

1972. For a brief introduction to this area, see Rogers, P, 'Biological Warfare', *Scientific American* June, 1999, 62–67. For a more detailed analysis, see Dando, M, *Biotechnology, Weapons and Humanity*. Harwood, London, 1984.

77   See Harris, E, 'Chemical Weapon Proliferation', in Lanham, M (ed), *New Threats: Responding to the Proliferation of Nuclear, Chemical and Delivery Systems in the Third World*. University Press of America, Aspen, 1990, 211–218. Robinson, J P P, 'Implementing the Chemical Weapons Convention', *International Affairs* 72, 1996, 73–89. Hogendoorn, E, 'A Chemical Weapons Atlas', *Bulletin of Atomic Scientists* October 1997, 35–39. Kettle, M, 'UN Team in Iraq Discover Deadly Nerve Gas', *Guardian Weekly* 5 July 1998.

78   See Harris, ibid, 215-216.

79   Renner, supra n2, 161. Antony, I, 'Multilateral Military-Related Export Control Measures', in *SIPRI Yearbook: 1998* supra n9, 456–499. International Institute for Strategic Studies, supra n9, 291–294.

80   See 'Special Issue: Small Arms, Big Problem', *Bulletin of Atomic Scientists* February 1999. See also Renner, M, *Small Arms, Big Impact*. Worldwatch Institute, Washington, DC, 1997.

81   Treaty on the Conventional Forces in Europe, 1990. Reprinted in *SIPRI Yearbook 1991: Armaments, Disarmament and International Security*. Oxford University Press, Oxford, 1991, 407–409. The Concluding Act on the Negotiations on Personnel Strength of Conventional Armed Forces in Europe, 1992. Reprinted in *SIPRI Yearbook 1993: Armaments, Disarmament and International Security*. Oxford University Press, Oxford, 1993, 591–618. In 1996, the CFE was added to by the Flank Document Agreement to the Conventional Armed Forces in Europe, which added increased transparency, a reduction of the flank zone (map realignment) and additional constraints within the flank areas. *International Legal Materials* 36, 1997, 866. Despite these achievements, Europe continues to hold the largest conglomeration of advanced conventional arms in the world. See Pearson, F, *The Global Spread of Arms: The Political Economy of International Security*. Westview, Boulder, 1994, 96.

82   Such unilateral or regional bodies may attempt to stop the trade in small arms on the grounds of security, instability of recipient regimes, or human rights abuses. In 1998, the European Union adopted a Code of Conduct on arms exports which is 'politically, not legally, binding'. For discussions of the limitations of many such approaches, see Pearson, supra n81, 71–74, 86–88. *SIPRI Yearbook*, supra n9, 374–397. Black, I, 'Cook's Ethical Arms Policy in Disarray', *Guardian Weekly* 5 July 1998. MacAskill, E, 'Blair Shoots Down Ethical Policy on Arms Sales', *Guardian Weekly* 27 January 2000.

83   See for example, the 1995 Wassenaar Agreement, which seeks to establish export controls on conventional weapons. For a discussion of this, see Antony, supra n79, 537–550. See also International Institute for Strategic Studies, supra n9, 286–289. Renner, M, 'Arms Control Orphans', *Bulletin of Atomic Scientists* January 1999, 22–25.

84   Pearson, supra n81, 102–105.

85   McCausland, J D, 'Conventional Arms Control', in Larsen, J (ed), *Arms Control: Towards the 21st Century*. Lynne Rienner, Boulder, 1996, 138–152.

86   Husbands, J, 'Preventing the Spread of Conventional Arms', in Larsen, ibid, 228–245. Pearson, supra n81, 26–27, 70, 86–90, 101, 106–107. International Institute for Strategic Studies, supra n9, 281–283.

87   See SIPRI, supra n9, 9–10. International Institute for Strategic Studies, supra n9, 17–19.

88   See Commission on Global Governance, supra n4, 130–131. Randel, J and German, T (eds), *The Reality of Aid 1996: An Independent Review of International Aid*. Earthscan, London, 1996, 32–34. Comment, 'Setting A Lead for the World', *Guardian Weekly* 6 July 1997.

89 Arguably, landmines may have fallen foul of the Convention on the Prohibition or Restrictions on the Use of Certain Conventional Weapons, Which May Be Deemed Excessively Injurious or Have Indiscriminate Effects. BH790.txt. See also Araujo, S J, 'Anti-Personnel Mines and Preemptory Norms of International Law: Argument and Catalyst', *Vanderbilt Journal of Transnational Law* 30, 1997, 1–30.

90 Convention on the Prohibition of the Use, Stockpiling, Production and Transfer of Anti-personnel Mines and on Their Destruction. *International Legal Materials* 36, 1997, 1507. Lachowski, Z, 'The Ban on Anti-Personnel Mines', in *SIPRI Yearbook 1998*, supra n9, 545–560. 'Landmine Treaty: First Conference of the Parties', *Environmental Policy and Law* 29, 1999, 155–156.

91 See Noel-Baker, P, *Disarmament*. Garland, New York, 1972.

92 See Codevilla, A, *The Arms Control Delusion*. Institute for Contemporary Studies, San Francisco, 1987. Goldblat, J, *Nuclear Non-Proliferation: A Guide to the Debate*. SIPRI, Taylor & Francis, London, 1995, 17–28. cf Sagan, S, 'Why Do States Build Nuclear Weapons? Three Models in Search of A Bomb', *International Security* 21, 1996, 54–86.

93 See Kartchener, K, 'The Objectives of Arms Control', in Larsen, supra n85, 19, 20.

94 Pearson, supra n81, 3–4. *SIPRI Yearbook,* supra n9, 419. Blair, B, 'Taking Nuclear Weapons Off Their Hair Trigger Alert', *Scientific American* November, 1997, 42–49.

95 See Waltz, K N, 'Nuclear Myths and Political Realities', *American Political Science Review* 84, 1990, 731–744.

96 Commission on Global Governance, supra n4, 14.

97 See *SIPRI Yearbook*, supra n9, 8–9, 17–23.

98 Canberra Commission, supra n73, 23.

99 See Taylor, A, *How Wars Begin*. Futura, London, 1979, 14–15.

100 See Gottfried and Blair, supra n42, 28–33.

101 For a useful history of how close the super-powers came to war, see Moore, M, *Midnight Never Came: Five Decades of the Doomsday Clock*. Bulletin of Atomic Scientists/Educational Foundation for Nuclear Science, 1995.

102 This figure comes from the Canberra Commission, supra n73, 21. For some examinations of these accidents, see Sagan, S, *The Limits of Safety: Organisations, Accidents and Nuclear Weapons*. Princeton University Press, New Jersey, 1993. May, J, *The Greenpeace Book of the Nuclear Age: The Hidden History*. Gollancz, London, 1989.

103 See Buttler, R, *The Elimination of Nuclear Weapons: Reversing History's Greatest Mistake*. University of New England: The 1996 Lecture Series, Cambridge, 1996, 10–12.

104 Canberra Commission, supra n73, 10.

105 Canberra Commission, supra n73, 9.

106 Canberra Commission, supra n73, 9.

107 See Fairhall, B, 'Generals Call For End to Nuclear Weapons', *Guardian Weekly* 15 December 1996.

108 Domke, W, 1995, 'Proliferation, Threat and Learning', in Leeuwen, supra n39, 205–229. Taylor, T, 'The Arms Control Process: The International Context', in Larsen, supra n85, 42–43, 51–52.

109 The Declaration is reproduced in Nathan, O, *Einstein on Peace*. Methuen, London, 1963, 633–636.

110 See Russell, B, *Has Man A Future?* Penguin, Harmondsworth, 1962, Chapter 6. For Einstein's position, see Nathan, supra n109, 400–458.

111 Not only would it have to be able to defend all nations of the Earth from despotic regimes, it would also need to be able to enter, forcefully if necessary, all countries and verify that any suspect nations are not pursuing weapons programmes that could cause mass destruction.

112 See Smith, R K, 'The Legality of Coercive Arms Control', *Yale Journal of International Law* 19, 1994, 455–508.

113 See Chapter 9 of this book.

114 Canberra Commission, supra n73, 4–5.

115 Chevrier, M, 'Preventing the Spread of Arms: Chemical and Biological Weapons', in Larsen, supra n85, 201, 208.

116 Pilat, J, 'Arms Control, Verification and Transparency', In Larsen, supra n85, 89, 92–94. Larsen, J A, 'The Evolving Nature of Arms Control', in Larsen, supra n85, 285, 289–290. Pearson, supra n81, 80–84.

117 See for example, the former USSR and its build-up of biological weapons. Ailbek, K, *Biohazard*. Harwood, London, 1999. See also Chevrier, supra n115, 212–213. Consider also, Kurtz, K, 'Nerve Gas Allegations Spark Row', *Guardian Weekly* 28 June 1998.

118 See for example the debate about the ABM treaty, supra n51.

CHAPTER 8 SOVEREIGNTY

1   WCED, *Our Common Future*. Oxford University Press, Oxford, 1987, 27.

2   MacKenzie, M J M, *Politics and Social Science*. Penguin, Harmondsworth, 1967, 277–287. Beitz, C R, *Political Theory and International Relations*. Princeton University Press, Princeton, 1979, 144–145. Russell, B, *A History of Western Philosophy*. Unwin, London, 1946, 531–541.

3   Brierly, J L, *The Law of Nations*. Clarendon, Oxford, 1963, 47. cf Lauterpacht, E, 'Sovereignty: Myth or Reality', *International Affairs* 73, 1997, 137–150. Lauterpacht concludes: 'with regard to sovereignty on the international plane, that must be seen largely as myth – except when it is used as a word to describe a state's title to territory.' At 149.

4   Bodin, J, *On Sovereignty*. Cambridge University Press, Cambridge, 1992, 1, 46.

5   Hobbes, T, *Leviathan*. Penguin, Harmondsworth, 1974, 187–88. Sabine, G H and Thorson, T L, *A History of Political Theory*. Dryden, Illinois, 1987, 435, 437. Russell, supra n2, 531–41.

6   *Island of Palmas Case* (Netherlands v United States). 2 UN RIAA, 829, at 839. Additionally, as Article 8 of the 1933 *Montevideo Convention on the Rights and Duties of States* emphasized, 'No State has the right to intervene in the internal or external affairs of another.' 49 Stat 3097. 165 LNTS 19, 1934.

7   Banerjee, S K, 'The Concept of Permanent Sovereignty Over Natural Resources: An Analysis', *Indian Journal of International Law* 8, 1968, 515.

8   UNGA Res 626(VII), 1952.

9   See articles 1 and 7 of UNGA Res 1803(XVII), 19 December 1962.

10 See UNGA Res 2158(XXI), 1966. UNCTAD: *Trade and Development Board; Resolution on Permanent Sovereignty over Natural Resources.* 19 October 1972. UN Doc/D/B/421, 15 November 1972. Social Welfare, Progress and Development. UNGA Res 2542(XXIV), 11 December 1969. For some discussions of these, see Brandt Commission, *North–South: A Programme For Survival*. Pan, London, 1980, 200. See also Zakariya, H S, 'Sovereignty Over Natural Resources and the Search for a New International Economic Order', in Snyder, F E and Sathirathai, S (eds), *Third World Attitudes Towards International Law*. Nijhoff, Dordrecht, 1987, 637, 638.

11 UN Doc A/Res/3281, 1974. See also UNGA Doc A/Res/3016(XXVII), 15 January 1973.

12 Bryant, R L and Bailey, R, *Third World Political Ecology*. Routledge, London, 1997, 48–75. Goldemberg, J and Durham, E R, 'Amazonia and National Sovereignty', *International Environmental Affairs* 2, 1990, 22. McGhee, H W, 'The Deforestation of the Brazilian Amazon: Law, Politics and International Co-operation', *University of Miami Inter American Law Review* 21, 1990, 513. Banerjee, supra n7, 515, 541.

13   Birnie, P W and Boyle, A E, *International Law and the Environment.* Clarendon, Oxford, 1992, 112–114.

14   Principle 2, the *Rio Declaration on Environment and Development.* A/CONF.151/5/Rev 1, 13 June 1992.

15   Article 2 (3), *Convention on Wetlands of International Importance.* UNTS Vol 996, 1971, 244. Article 4, *World Heritage Convention.* UNTS Vol 1037 (No I 15511), 1972, 151–211. Article 49 and 55–58, *United Nations Convention on the Law of the Sea.* UN Doc A/CONF. 62/122 with corrections, 1982. Article XIV, *Convention on International Trade in Endangered Species of Wild Flora and Fauna.* UNTS Vol 973 (No I 14537), 1973, 243–438. Article 1, *International Tropical Timber Agreement,* 1983. In Rummel-Bulska, I (ed), *Multilateral Treaties in the Field of the Environment.* Grotius, Cambridge, 1991, Vol 2, 271. Article III (22), *World Charter for Nature.* Proclaimed as Annex to UNGA Res 37/7, 28 October 1982. The sovereignty of countries within environmental concerns has also been taken to include the rejection of plans of action if they are not within the 'ethical values and cultural background' of its people. See *Report of the International Conference on Population and Development.* A/CONF.171/13, 18 October 1994, Chapter II, Paragraph 1.

16   Pepper, D, *Eco-Socialism: From Deep Ecology to Social Justice.* Routledge, London, 1993, 43, 133, 155, 184–185, 227.

17   Spretnak, C and Capra, F, *Green Politics.* Bear, New Mexico, 1986, 60, 188, 206–208. Goldsmith, E, *The Way: An Ecological World-View.* Rider, London, 1992, 341. Bahro, R, *Avoiding Social and Ecological Disaster: The Politics of World Transformation.* Gateway, Bath, 1994, 154–156, 169, 175, 342–344. Bosselmann, K, *When Two Worlds Collide: Society and Ecology.* RSVP, Auckland, 1995, 74–77, 254–255, 264–265, 272–281, 285. Mellos, K, *Perspectives on Ecology.* Macmillan, London, 1988, 37–42. *Programme of the German Green Party.* Heretic, London, 1983, 25. Kohr, L, *The Breakdown of Nations.* Routledge, London, 1957, 97–98. Friedman, J, *Empowerment: The Politics of Alternative Development.* Blackwell, Cambridge, 1994, 7, 84, 158–162. Sale, K, *Human Scale.* Coward, New York, 1980, 107–142, 456–460, 480–481. Dryzek, J, *Rational Ecology: Environment and Political Economy.* Blackwell, Oxford, 1987, 162–179, 216–227, 231–238. Hempel, L C, *Environmental Governance: The Global Challenge.* Island Press, New York, 1996, 156–165.

18   Giddens, A, *The Consequences of Modernity.* Stanford University Press, California, 1990, 65. See also O'Riordan, T, *Environmentalism.* Pion, London, 1980, Section 9.1.1. Spretnak and Capra, supra n19, 170.

19   See Gillespie, A, *International Environmental Law, Policy and Ethics.* Oxford University Press, Oxford, 1997, Chapter 2. See also, Johnston, R J, *Environmental Problems: Nature, Economy and State.* Belhaven, London, 1989, 112–143.

20   Paehlke, R C, *Environmentalism and the Future of Progressive Politics.* MIT Press, Massachusetts, 1989, 155–157. Carlie, M and Christie, I, *Managing Sustainable Development.* Earthscan, London, 1992, 59, 130–135, 141–142. Ophuls, W, *Ecology and the Politics of Scarcity.* Freeman, San Francisco, 1977, 210, 219. Eckersley, R, *Environmentalism and Political Theory.* UCL Press, London, 1992, 172–176. Dobson, A, *Green Political Thought.* Unwin, London, 1990, 127–128. Frankel, B, *The Post Industrial Utopians.* Polity, Cambridge, 1987, 202–203, 270. Bodansky, D, 'The Legitimacy of International Governance: A Coming Challenge for International Environmental Law?' *American Journal of International Law* 93, 1999, 596–623.

21   Vavrousek, J, 'Institutions for Environmental Security', in Prins, G (ed), *Threats Without Enemies: Facing Environmental Insecurity.* Earthscan, London, 1993, 87, 90.

22   French, H, 'Making Environmental Treaties Work', *Scientific American* December 1994, 62–65. Sand, P H, 'Lessons Learnt In Global Environmental Governance', *Boston College of Environmental Affairs* 18, 1991, 213, 250–266. Caldwell, L K, 'Beyond Environmental Diplomacy', in Carrol, J E (ed), *International Environmental*

Diplomacy. Cambridge University Press, Cambridge, 1988, 13, 43. Caldwell, L K, *International Environmental Policy*. Duke University Press, London, 1994, 109.

23 For a discussion of this conference, see Nicholson, M, *The Environmental Revolution: A Guide For the New Masters of the World*. Penguin, Harmondsworth, 1970, 223–225. The first truly international body which looked (indirectly) at environmental issues was the International Meteorological Organization, which was founded in 1872. The first international arbitration on environmental matters was in the 1880s, with the Pacific Fur Seal Arbitration Tribunal, which made its award in 1893. In 1909 the International Joint Commission between Canada and the United States was established, which dealt with, among other things, transboundary environmental disputes between the two countries.

24 See Sullivan, E T, 'The Stockholm Conference: A Step Toward Global Environmental Cooperation and Involvement', *Indiana Law Review* 6, 1972, 267, 269.

25 Strong, M (1988), 'Proposal For An Extended UN Mandate', noted in Anderson, F R, 'Of Herdsmen and Nation States: The Global Environmental Commons', *American University Journal of International Law and Policy* 5, 1990, 217, 222. Strong, M, 'Eco 92: Critical Challenges and Global Solutions', *Journal of International Affairs* 44, 1991, 287, 297–298.

26 Brandt Commission, supra n10, 19, 26.

27 WCED, *Our Common Future*. Oxford University Press, Oxford, 1987, 18, 38–40, 261–286, 319–323, 326–328, 334.

28 Palmer, G, 'Verbatim Record of the 15th Meeting', GA, 44th Sessions at 61. UN Doc A/44/PV. 15, 1989. See also Palmer, G, 'An International Regime For Environmental Protection', *Journal of Urban and Contemporary Law* 42, 1992, 1–12. These ideas were advanced further in Palmer, G, *Environment: The International Challenge*. Victoria University Press, Wellington, 1995, 45–84.

29 Paragraph 8, *G7: Summit of the Arch*. Paris, 1989. Reprinted in Starke, L (ed), *Signs of Hope: Working Towards Our Common Future*. Oxford University Press, Oxford, 1990, 16.

30 Principle (a), The Hague Declaration. *International Legal Materials* 28, 1989, 1308.

31 French, H F, 'Strengthening Global Environmental Governance', in Brown, L R (ed), *State of the World: 1992*. Earthscan, London, 1992, 155, 169. It is important to note that the United States, China and the Soviet Union were absent from the signatories to the Declaration.

32 The South Commission, *The Challenge to the South*. Oxford University Press, Oxford, 1990, 264–265, 283–286.

33 The *Stockholm Initiative on Global Security and Governance; Common Responsibility in the 1990s*. Stockholm, 1991, 19. For a discussion of this initiative, see Susskind, L E, *Environmental Diplomacy: Negotiating More Effective Global Agreements*. Oxford University Press, Oxford, 1994, 147–149.

34 The *Dobris Conference Conclusions*. Reprinted in Prins, supra n21, 109, 112.

35 See the *Norwegian Policy Regarding Global Sustainable Development*. Reprinted in Starke, supra n29, 42, 43. See G Bruntland's speech in *Report of the United Nations Conference on Environment and Development*. A/CONF. 151/26/Rev 1, Vol 3, 1992, 192. See *Earth Charter Report*. A/CONF. 151/PC/WG. III/L.8/Rev 1, 1992.

36 The Earth Summit did not produce any radical suggestions. The emphasis of international institutional arrangements and the Commission on Sustainable Development are both set entirely within existing UN institutions (chapter 38. 13 of *Agenda 21*. UNCED Doc A/CONF. 151/4) and do not intend to create 'executive functions in itself'. See Imber, M, 'Too Many Cooks? The Post Rio Reform of the United Nations', *International Affairs* 69, 1993, 55, 56, 58. See also the tentative paragraphs 39.3 (h) and 39.9 in Agenda 21 which only hint at widening the ambit of the International Court of Justice. This was unlike the IUCN's *Draft International Covenant on Environment and Development* (IUCN, *Environmental Policy and Law*

31, Geneva, 1995) which suggested that all disputes between parties shall be settled either by the Permanent Court of Arbitration, judicial settlement, including the ICJ, or by the International Tribunal for the Law of the Sea. See Article 62.

37 International Commission on Peace and Food, *Uncommon Opportunities*. Zed, London, 1994, 14.

38 The Commission was adamant that it was not advocating 'world government or world federalism'. Commission on Global Governance, *Our Global Neighbourhood*. Oxford University Press, Oxford, 1995, 2–6, 326.

39 Report of the Independent Commission on Population and Quality of Life, *Caring For the Future*. Oxford University Press, Oxford, 1996, 257, 314.

40 See Malik, M, 'Do We Need A New Theory of International Relations?' in Bartlett, R (ed), *International Organisations and Environmental Policy*. Greenwood, New York, 1995 223–237.

41 See Hurrel, A, 'International Political Theory and the Global Environment', in Booth, K and Smith, S (eds), *International Relations Theory Today*. Polity, London, 1995, 129, 133.

42 Gosovic, B, *The Quest For World Environmental Co-operation: The Case of the UN Global Environmental Monitoring System*. Routledge, London, 1992, 246. Ward, P and Dubos, R, *Only One Earth: The Care and Maintenance of a Small Planet*. Penguin, Harmondswoth, 1972, 30, 291. French, supra n31, 155, 173. Brandt Commission, supra n10, 19, 258. WCED, supra n27, 27, 37–38, 312–13. Tarlock, D, 'Stewardship Sovereignty', *Journal of Urban and Contemporary Law* 42, 1992, 21, 27. Caldwell, L K, 'The Geopolitics of Environmental Policy: Transnational Modification of National Sovereignty', *Revista Juridica* 59, 1990, 693. Bragdon, S H, 'National Sovereignty and Global Environmental Responsibility: Can The Tension Be Reconciled', *Harvard International Law Journal* 33, 1992, 381, 384, 391–392.

43 Commission on Global Governance, supra n38, 10–11. Handrieder, W, 'Dissolving International Politics: Reflections on the Nation State', in Little, R and Smith, M (ed), *Perspectives on World Politics*. Routledge, London, 1994, 143–156.

44 Commission on Global Governance, supra n38, 70–71, 135–138.

45 Paragraph 4, *Summit of the Non-Aligned*. NAC 9/EC/DOC/8. Rev 1, 7 September 1989.

46 WCED, supra n27, 38–40. MacNeil, J, Winsemius, P and Yakushiji, T, *Beyond Interdependence: The Meshing of the World's Economy and the Earth's Ecology*. Oxford University Press, Oxford, 1991, 58–59.

47 Young, O R, 'Global Environmental Change and International Governance', in Rowlands, I H and Greene, M (eds), *Global Environmental Change and International Relations*. Macmillan, London, 1992, 6. Vavrousek, supra n21, 87, 88, 92.

48 Brandt Commission, supra n10, 33.

49 'Social development ... cannot be successfully achieved without the collective commitment and efforts of the international community.' See *Report of the World Summit for Social Development*. A/CONF.166/9, 19 April 1995, Paragraph 26 (e).

50 Hoel, M, 'Global Environmental Problems: The Effects of Unilateral Actions Taken By One Country', *Journal of Environmental Economics and Management* 20, 1991, 55, 70. Barrett, S, 'Global Warming: The Economics of a Carbon Tax', in Pearce, D (ed), *Blueprint 2: Greening The World Economy*. Earthscan, London, 1991, 31, 47–48.

51 Paterson, D G and Wilen, J, 'Depletion and Diplomacy: The North Pacific Seal Hunt 1886–1910', *Research In Economic History* 2, 1977, 81, 111. Swanson, T, 'The Regulation of Oceanic Resources: An Examination of the International Community's Record in the Regulation of One Global Resource', in Helm, D (ed), *Economic Policy Towards the Environment*. Blackwell, Oxford, 1991, 221–228.

52 Princen, T and Finger, M, *Environmental NGOs in World Politics: Linking the Local and the Global*. Routledge, London, 1994, 31.

53 Commission on Global Governance, supra n38, 32–35, 198–200, 254–255. It is suggested that 275,000 exist in the UK. See Salamon, L, 'The Rise of the Non-Profit Sector', *Foreign Affairs* 73, 1994, 109–115. And up to 2 million in the USA. See Editor, 'NGOs More Powerful Than Ever', *Ecologist* 30(2), 2000, 5.

54 See Princen and Finger, supra n52, 2–4.

55 Chapter 27 of Agenda 21 is titled: 'Strengthening the role of Non Governmental Organisations: Partners for Sustainable Development'. Agenda 21, supra n36. See also WCED, supra n27, 326–328.

56 Bothe, M, 'Compliance Control Beyond Diplomacy: The Role of Non-Governmental Actors', *Environmental Policy and the Law* 27, 1997, 293–297. Giorgetti, C, 'The Role of Nongovernmental Organisations in the Climate Change Negotiations', *Colorado Journal of International Environmental Law and Policy* 9, 1998, 115–132. Princen and Finger, supra n52, 10–11, 106–108, 161–163, 167, 179–182. Susskind, supra n33, 49–55, 114–117, 130–131. Commission on Global Governance, supra n38, 32–35.

57 Thus, with Treaties such as the World Heritage Convention, and the Convention on the International Trade in Endangered Species, specific NGOs have been assigned important roles in implementing the agreements. For a further example of NGO involvement, see Brady, K, 'Aarhus Convention Signed' and 'New Convention on Access to Information and Public Participation in Environmental Matters', *Environmental Policy and the Law* 28, 1998, 69–74, 171–189. See also Princen and Finger, supra n52, 3–6.

58 Haas, P M, 'Do Regimes Matter? Epistemic Communities and Mediterranean Pollution Control', *International Organisation* 42, 1989, 3777. Haas, P M, 'Obtaining International Environmental Protection Through Epistemic Communities', in Rowlands and Greene, supra n47, 52. Haas, P M, 'Stratospheric Ozone: Regime Formation in Stages', in Young, O R (ed), *Polar Politics: Creating International Environmental Regimes.* Cornell University Press, New York, 1993, 152, 176–180.

59 See Boyle, A and Freestone, D, *International Law and Sustainable Development.* Oxford University Press, Oxford, 1999, 16–17, 21, 25–26, 36–37. WCED, supra n1, 330–333.

60 Susskind, supra n33, 143.

61 *United States v Canada (Trail Smelter),* 3 International Arbitration Awards, 1941, at 1905. For confirmation of this principle, see *United Kingdom v. Albania.* 1949. ICJ 4, 22. *Spain v France. American Journal of International Law* 53, 1959, 156.

62 Principle 21. UN Doc A/CONF. 48/14/Rev 1.

63 *Charter of Economic Rights and Duties of States.* 31 GAOR Suppl (A/9631) at 50. UN Doc A/RES/3281, 1974. The Nairobi Conference in 1982. 37 UN GAOR, Annex 2, Suppl (25) at 49; or UN Doc A/37/25, 1982. *Report of the International Law Commission.* New York, 1989, 222–223. UN Doc A/44/10. American Law Institute, *Restatement of the Foreign Relations Law of the United States.* 1987, §601–604.

64 *Charter of Economic Rights and Duties,* supra n63, Article 3. See also the *Report of the Intergovernmental Working Group of Experts on Natural Resources Shared by Two or More States.* Re UNEPGC. 6/CRP 2, 19 May 1978. Also reprinted in *International Legal Materials* 17, 1978, 1094.

65 Vienna Convention on the Law of Treaties. *International Legal Materials* 1969, 679. *South West Africa Case.* ICJ 1966, 6, 32. *Barcelona Traction Case (Belgium v Spain)* ICJ 1970, 1, 32.

66 See principles 17, 18 and 19 of the *Rio Declaration.* UNCED A/CONF. 151/5/Rev 1. 13, 1992. Section 39.3 and 39.9, *Agenda 21,* supra n36. Such drives have also become increasingly regional. See for example, the exemplar of Europe and the 1998 Aarhus Convention on Access to Information, Public Participation in Decision Making and Access to Justice in Environmental Matters. For an examination of this Convention, see Brady, supra n57, 69–74, 171–189. See also 'OECD Greater Availability of Pertinent

Environmental Data', *Environmental Policy and the Law* 28, 1998, 191. The OECD
Council Recommendation on Environmental Information is C(98)67, 3 April 1998.

67 Young, O, *International Governance: Protecting the Environment in a Stateless Society*.
Cornell University Press, New York, 1994, 12–28. Gelfand, G, 'International
Environmental Legislation: Is the Cure Worse than the Disease', *Journal of Urban and
Contemporary Law* 42, 1992, 35, 45, 52–53. Susskind, L and Ozawa, S, 'Negotiating
More Effective International Environmental Agreements', in Hurrell, A and Kingsbury,
B (eds), *The International Politics of the Environment*. Oxford University Press,
Oxford, 1992, 85, 86–87, 109, 142–165. Gore, A, *Earth in Balance: Forging A New
Common Purpose*. Earthscan, London, 1992, 302. For further discussions about the
idea of compliance, see UNEP, *Enforcement and Compliance with MEAs*. UNEP,
Nairobi, 2000. Jacobson, H, 'Strengthening Compliance with International
Environmental Accords', in Diehl, P (ed), *The Politics of Global Governance*. Island
Press, Washington, DC, 1995, 305–330. Yoshida, O, 'Soft Enforcement of Treaties',
Colorado Journal of International Environmental Law and Policy 10, 1999, 95–141.
Faure, M, 'Compliance with International Environmental Agreements', in Vig, N (ed),
The Global Environment: Institutions, Law and Policy. Earthscan, London, 1999,
138–156. Susskind, supra n33, 122–149. Hempel, supra n17, 172–177. This debate is
currently unresolved, for as the UNEP *Global Environmental Outlook 2000* report
(Earthscan, London, 2000) suggested: 'it is still difficult to assess accurately the
effectiveness of MEAs and non-binding instruments because of the lack of accepted
indicators', at xiii.

68 Article 9(c)(2), Montreal Protocol. *International Legal Materials* 21, 1987, 951. See
also the 1990 London Amendments to the Montreal Protocol. *Environmental Policy
and the Law* 20, 1990, 75, 76, 134–135. Note that this type of arrangement is the
exception to international environmental agreements.

69 The 1982 United Nations Convention on the Law of the Sea, and the 1995 Agreement
relating to the Conservation and Management of Straddling Fish Stocks and Highly
Migratory Fish Stocks, contain provisions whereby disputes to the Agreement or the
Convention between signatories are submitted to an International Tribunal for resolu-
tion. Similar obligations exist with the 1973 Convention on the International Trade in
Endangered Species, the 1991 Protocol on Environmental Protection within Antarctica,
the 1987 Montreal Protocol and the 1994 Oslo Protocol on Further Reduction of
Sulphur Emissions; and the 1997 Kyoto Protocol to the UNFCCC. The International
Tribunal which evolved out of the 1982 UNCLOS, which has 'compulsory procedures
entailing binding decisions' is a very good example of movements in this field. This
Tribunal was successful in protecting the marine environment, via the precautionary
principle, in 1999, with the Southern Bluefin Tuna Cases (NZ and Australia v. Japan).
ITLOS/PV.99/19.

70 See Agenda 21, supra n36, Section 38.11.

71 Special Session of the General Assembly. *Programme for the Further Implementation of
Agenda 21*. 1 July 1997, Paragraph 16, 130–137.

72 See Biggs, T, 'The United Nations Commission on Sustainable Development', in Dodds,
F (ed), *The Way Forward: Beyond Agenda 21*. Earthscan, London, 1997, 15–33.
Mensah, C, 'The United Nations Commission on Sustainable Development', in
Werksman, J (ed), *Greening International Institutions*. Earthscan, London, 1996,
21–37.

73 Commission on Sustainable Development, *Institutional Arrangements to Follow Up
UNCED: Report of the Secretary General*. E/CN.17/1996/16, 1996, Paragraph 8.

74 Or as Judge Weeremantary stated in this case, 'The court has not availed itself of the
opportunity to enquire more fully into this matter and of making a contribution to
some of the seminal principles of the evolving corpus of international environmental
law. The Court has for too long been silent on these issues'. Nuclear Tests (New

Zealand v. France) Case. ICJ Reports 1995, 288, at 362. For a discussion of this, see Gillespie, A, 'The 1995 Nuclear Tests Case And The Failure Of The International Court Of Justice To Address The Merits Of An International Environmental Concern', *New Zealand Law Journal* May 1996, 195–200.

75 Palmer, 'An International Regime', supra n28, 1, 11. Postiglione, A, 'An International Court For The Environment?' *Environmental Policy and Law* 23, 1993, 73–78. Lutz, R E, 'The World Court in a Changing World: An Agenda For Expanding the World Court's Role', *Stanford Journal of International Law* 27, 1991, 265–2771. Birnie and Boyle, supra n13, 159, 179.

76 See 'Secretary General's Report', *Environmental Policy and the Law* 24, 1994, 2. 'Chamber For Environmental Matters', *Environmental Policy and the Law* 23, 1993, 243. Sands, P, 'The International Court of Justice', in Werksman (ed), supra n72, 221–227, 234–235.

77 WCED, supra n72, 334. A classic example of this was the 1992 Statement of Principles for a Global Consensus on the Management, Conservation and Sustainable Development of all Types of Forests, which is emphatic that it is a 'non-legally binding authoritative statement'. UNCED Doc A/CONF. 151/6/Rev 1.

78 See the Chapters 'Strengthening Institutions for Sustainable Development' and 'A Survey of International Agreements and Instruments', *Agenda 21*, supra n36.

79 Commission on Global Governance, supra n38, 303–313.

80 Schwabach, A, 'The Sandox Spill: The Failure of International Law to Protect the Rhine River', *Ecology Law Quarterly* 16, 1989, 443. Sands, P J, 'The Environmental Community and International Law', *Harvard Journal of International Law* 30, 1989, 393, 397. Howland, T, 'Chernobyl and Acid Deposition: An Analysis of the Failure of European Co-operation to Protect the Shared Environment', *Temple International and Comparative Law Journal* 2, 1988, 1, 31. Birnie and Boyle, supra n13, 159 and chapter 9. Schachter, O, 'The Emergence of International Environmental Law', *Journal of International Affairs* 44, 1991, 457, 464. 457.

81 Birnie, P, 'The Role of International Law In Solving Certain Environmental Conflicts', in Carroll, supra n22, 101. Lang, W, 'Environmental Protection: The Challenge of International Law', *Journal of World Trade Law* 1987, 490. Francioni, F and Scovazzi, T, *International Responsibility for Environmental Harm*. Graham and Trotman, 1991, 3, 10, 15, 31, 179–180, 429, 433, 443. Birnie and Boyle, supra n13, 92–94, 144, 159. Schachter, supra n80, 457, 463, 480, 484. Bosselmann, supra n17, 88–94. Note, however, that in certain areas of international environmental law, strict liability for international environmental damage is imposed. See for example the Vienna Convention on Civil Liability in the Field of Nuclear Energy. UNTS Vol 1063(No I 16197), 1963, 265–219. See also the IMO Convention on Civil Liability For Oil Pollution Damage. UNTS Vol 973, 1975, 3–55. For a useful discussion of this area and nuclear issues, see Rijswijk, J, 'The International Community and the Closure of Chernobyl', *Environmental Policy and the Law* 25(4/5), 1995, 207–216.

82 Hazarika, S, *Bhopal: The Lessons of a Tragedy*. Penguin, Harmondsworth, 1987, 101–137. Morehouse, W, 'Unfinished Business: Bhopal Ten Years After', *Ecologist* 24, 1994, 164–168.

83 Commission on Sustainable Development, *Overall Progress Achieved Since UNCED: International Legal Instruments*. E/CN.17/1997/2/Add.29, 1997, Paragraph 16. A similar conclusion was reached by the UNEP Governing Council at the end of 1995 when they noted '3 years after the adoption of Agenda 21 only limited progress has been made in the realisation of its goals and objectives and that existing and proposed legal and institutional instruments and arrangements have so far been ineffective in halting the deterioration of the environment.' Noted in 'Statement on International Environmental Law', *Environmental Policy and the Law* 25, 1995, 415.

84 Birnie, P, 'The Role of International Law', supra n81, 116. Taulbee, J L, 'Law Organisation and Environmental Concerns', in Orr, D W (ed), *The Global Predicament*. Duke University Press, North Carolina, 1979, 257. Piper, D C, 'Unilateral Acts of States With Regard to Environmental Protection', also in Orr, 277. Bjorkbom, L, 'Resolution of Environmental Problems: Use of Diplomacy', in Carroll, supra n22, 123. Slouka, Z K, 'International Environmental Controls In A Scientific Age', in Hargrove, J L (ed), *Law, Institutions and the Global Environment*. Ocean, New York, 1972, 208, 229–230. See for example the *Nuclear Test Cases*. Interim Protection, ICJ Rep 99 and 135, 1973. ICJ Rep 253 and 257, 1974.

85 See New Zealand v. France. ICJ Reports 476, 1973. For a discussion of this, see Gillespie, supra n74.

86 Nicaragua v. The United States. ICJ Reports 1, 1984.

87 Brock, L, 'The Colonisation of Amazonia', in Bolle, M (ed), *Amazonia and Siberia: Legal Aspects of the Preservation of the Environment and Development in the Last Open Spaces*. Graham and Trotman, London, 1993, 57, 69–70. For some specific legal reflections of this, see Treaty for Amazonian Co-operation. *International Legal Materials* 17, 1978, 1045. See Mendez, L B, 'Environmental Law and the Regional Approach: The Amazon Pact', also in Bolle, 199, 201, 205. The foremost recognition of sovereignty in this area is found with Principles 1(a) and 2(a) of the *Statement of Principles for a Global Consensus on the Management, Conservation and Sustainable Development of all Types of Forests*. UNCED Doc A/CONF. 151/6/Rev 1. The principles recognize that, 'States have, in accordance with the Charter of the United Nations and the principles of international law, the sovereign right to exploit their own resources pursuant to their own environmental policies ... [and] States have the sovereign and inalienable right to utilise, manage and develop their forests in accordance with their development needs and socio-economic development.'

88 Tinker, C, 'International Environmental Planet Management: An Idea Whose Time Has Not Yet Come', *International Law and Politics* 22, 1990, 793, 802–803. Springer, A L, *The International Law of Pollution: Protecting the Global Environment in a World of Sovereign States*. Quorum, Westport, 1983, 99–103. Pallemaerts, M, 'International Environmental Law From Stockholm to Rio: Back to the Future?' in Sands, supra n76, 1, 2–5. Birnie, P, 'International Environmental Law: Its Adequacies For Present and Future Needs', in Hurrell and Kingsbury, supra n67, 51, 53–54. Schachter, O, 'The Emergence of International Environmental Law', *Journal of International Affairs* 44, 1991, 457, 475–479, 487–488. Susskind, supra n33, 14, 32, 142–147. French, supra n31, 155, 161.

89 WCED, supra n27, 18, 261–286.

90 Commission on Global Governance, supra n38, 214–216.

91 Independent Commission on Population and Quality of Life, supra n39, 105, 294.

92 For a useful discussion of the idea of common heritage, and how it has changed over time, see Buck, S J, *The Global Commons*. Island Press, Washington, DC, 1998, 28–30. The idea of common heritage as an environmental protection mechanism appeared in the first Brandt report, which suggested, 'The biosphere is our common heritage ... all nations have to co-operate more urgently in international management of the atmosphere and other global commons, and in the prevention of irresistible ecological damage.' Brandt Commission, supra n10, 73, 115.

93 Social Welfare, Progress and Development. UNGA Res 2542(XXIV), 11 December 1969, Article 9.

94 1979 Agreement Concerning Activities of States on the Moon and Other Celestial Bodies. *International Legal Materials* 18, 1979, 1434. For a discussion of this, see Buck, supra n92, 148–153.

95 Antarctica Treaty. UNTS 402, 1959. See the ambiguous Article IV. For an introduction to this area, see Buck, supra n92, 64–68.

96 Article 136, *United Nations Convention on the Law of the Sea*. UN Doc A/CONF. 62/122, 1982, with corrections. See also Birnie and Boyle, supra n13, 415–418.

97 Richardson, E, 'The Politics of the Law of the Sea', *Ocean Development and the Law* 11, 1982, 16, 23. Birnie and Boyle, supra n13, 118.

98 For the American reasons for this decision, see *Department of State Bulletin* 84, February 1984, 41–42. Reagan, R, *Weekly Comp Press Document* 18, 1982, 94. Larson, R L, 'The Reagan Rejection of the United Nations Convention', *Ocean Development And International Law* 14, 1984, 342. Soto, A D, 'Reflections On UNCLOS III: Critical Junctures', *Law And Contemporary Problems* 46, 1983, 66–72. Boczek, B A, 'Ideology and the Law of the Sea: The Challenge of the New International Economic Order', *Boston College of International and Comparative Law Review* 7, 1984, 2. Richardson, supra n97, 16–28. Ratiner, L S, 'The Law of the Sea: A Crossroads for American Foreign Policy', *Foreign Affairs* 1982, 1008.

99 Bandow, D, 'The United States Versus the Law of the Sea', *Journal of Social, Political and Economic Studies* 7, 1982, 196, 197, 204. Larson, supra n98, 348. Ratiner, supra n98.

100 Smith, G P, 'The United Nations and the Environment: Sometimes a Great Notion?', *Texas International Law Journal* 19, 1984, 354. Malone, J L, 'The United States and the Law of the Sea', *Virginia Journal of International Law* 24, 1984, 786.

101 Malone, J L, 'The United States and the Law of the Sea After UNCLOS III', *Law and Contemporary Problems* 46, 1983, 32. 'Rejection of UNCLOS III', *Environmental Policy and the Law* 8, 1982, 127. Brewer, W C, 'Deep Seabed Mining: Can An Acceptable Regime Be Found?', *Ocean Development and International Law* 11, 1982, 42–45. For the continuing opposition to this, see 'Law of Sea: Soon In Force?' *Environmental Policy and the Law* 23, 1993, 62. Birnie and Boyle, supra n13, 415–418.

102 See United States President's Transmittal of the United Nations Convention on the Law of the Sea and the Agreement Relating to the Implementation of Part XI to the US Senate. *International Legal Materials* 34, 1995, 1393–1438.

103 See Christol, C Q, 'The International Law of Space Environment Resources', *Air and Outer Space Law* 1981, 581. Tennan, F, 'Outer Space: A Preserve for all Humankind', *Houston Journal of International Law* 2, 1979, 154. Griffin, N L, 'Americans and the Moon Treaty', *Journal of Air Law and Commerce* 46, 1981, 729, 751, 754. Birnie and Boyle, supra n13, 415–418.

104 See Kiss, A, 'The Common Concern of Mankind', *Environmental Policy and the Law* 27, 1997, 244–247. Kiss suggests that 'common concern' reflects 'a fundamental value of mankind'. This is considerably different from reflecting a distinctive ideological content. See also Churchill, R and Freestone, D (eds), *International Law and Global Climatic Change*. Graham and Trotman, London, 1991, Chapter 1.

105 See paragraphs 1–3 of the Preamble of the *United Nations Convention on Climate Change*. A. AC. 237/18 (Part II) Add 1, 15 May 1992. See also the Preamble of the *United Nations Convention on the Conservation of Biological Diversity*. UNCED BioDiv/CONF/L.2, 1992.

106 Principle 3, *Protection of the Atmosphere, Statement of Legal and Policy Experts*. Ottawa, 1989. Recorded in *American University Journal of International Law and Policy* 5, 1990, 531.

107 Birnie and Boyle, supra n13, 120–122. Anand, R P, 'Common Heritage of Mankind: The Mutilation of An Ideal', *Indian Journal of International Law* 37, 1997, 1–18.

108 See Gillespie, A M, *Antarctica 1991; Conservationist Victory or Hidden Agendas?* Nottingham University, Occasional Research Paper, 1993. Buck, supra n92, 64–66.

109 See Gillespie, A, 'Common Property, Private Property and Equity: The Clash of Values and the Quest to Preserve Biodiversity', *Environmental and Planning Law Journal* 12, 1995, 388–399.

110 South Commission, supra n32, 216–222. Banuri, T, 'The Landscape of Diplomatic Conflicts', in Sachs, W (ed), *Global Ecology*. Zed, London, 1993, 49, 65. Brock, supra n87, 73.

111 South Commission, supra n32, 284.

112 Doran, C F, 'Oil Politics and the Rise of Co-dependence', in Orr, D W (ed), *The Global Predicament*. Duke University Press, North Carolina, 1979, 199.

113 List, M and Rittberger, B, 'Regime Theory and International Environmental Management', in Hurrell and Kingsbury, supra n67, 85, 86–87.

114 See Rooy, A, 'The Frontiers of Influence: NGO Lobbying at the 1974 World Food Conference, the 1992 Earth Summit and Beyond', *World Development* 25, 1997, 93–114. Huntington, S, 'Transnational Organisations in World Power', in Little and Smith, supra n43, 212–217. Keohane, R, 'Transgovernamental Relations and International Organisations', also in Little and Smith, 229–241.

115 There is also a distinct question of how much power can actually be given to non-State bodies. The Vienna Convention on the Law of Treaties Between States and International Organisations, UN Doc A/Conf. 129/15, 1986, implicitly points out that international organisations do not enjoy the same status as States.

116 See Robie, D, *Eyes of Fire: The Last Voyage of the Rainbow Warrior*. Lindon, Auckland, 1986. For an excellent study of the growing antagonism against NGOs, see Rowell, A, *Green Blacklash: Global Subversion of the Environment Movement*. Routledge, London, 1996. Vidal, J, 'Government Gunning for Green Alliance', *Guardian International* 28 May 1995, 11.

117 See French, H, 'The Role of Non-State Actors', in Werksman, supra n72, 251, 255–258.

118 Commission on Sustainable Development, *Overall Progress Since UNCED: Role and Contribution of Major Groups*. E/CN.17/1997/2/Add 22, 1997, Paragraph 51.

119 See Commission on Sustainable Development, *Role of Major Groups in the Implementation of Agenda 21*. E/CN.17/1996/12, 1996, Paragraphs 8–11. Princen and Finger, supra n52, 5–8, 6–9, 144–153, 190–191, 198–211. Johnston, supra n19, 171–181. Commission on Global Governance, supra n38, 33. Susskind, supra n33, 46–47, 75–76. Watkins, K, *The Oxfam Poverty Report*. Oxfam, Oxford, 1995, 206–215. Weiss, T and Gordenker, L, *NGOs, The UN & Global Governance*. Reinner, London, 1996, 116–117, 209–213, 217–221. Chatterjee, P and Finger, M, *The Earth Brokers: Power, Politics and World Development*. Routledge, London, 1994, 65–104, 110. Bryant and Bailey, supra n12, 130–157. Gallarotti, G, 'The Limits of International Organisation: Systematic Failure in the Management of International Relations' in Diehl, supra n67, 375–414.

120 Imber, M, *Environment, Security and UN Reform*. St Martins Press, New York, 1994, 109–114. Timoshenko, A, 'The United Nations Environment Programme', in Werksman (ed), supra n72, 38–48. 'Progress in Restoring UNEP's Image', *Environmental Policy and the Law* 28, 1998, 141–143. Soroos, M, 'Global Institutions and the Environment: An Evolutionary Perspective', in Vig, supra n67, 27, 36–41. WCED, supra n27, 319–323. Imber, supra n36, 55, 58–677, 69–70. For UNEP's expanded role since 1995, see the Nairobi Declaration on the Role and Mandate of UNEP. Reprinted in *Special Session of the General Assembly on the Implementation of Agenda 21*. A/S-19/6, 4 March 1997. This mandate makes it clear that UNEP (in complete accordance with its original mandate) is to advance, co-ordinate and analyse international environmental issues. This renewed mandate followed division between UN members over the role and future of UNEP. See Osborn, D and Bigg, T, *Earth Summit II: Outcomes and Analysis*. Earthscan, London, 1998, 58–63.

121 Chatterjee and Finger, supra n119, 157–160. Werksman, supra n72, xxiii. Imber, supra n120, 104–109. Soroos, supra n120, 39–42.

122 Special Session of the General Assembly, supra n71, Paragraph 116. See also Commission on Sustainable Development, *Overall Progress Achieved Since UNCED*.

E/CN.17/1997/2, 1997, Paragraphs 139, 140. Commission on Sustainable Development, *Overall Progress Since UNCED: Institutional Arrangements.* E/CN.17/1997/2/Add 28, 1997.

123 Bailey, R, *Eco-Scam: The False Prophets of Ecological Apocalypse.* St Martins Press, New York, 1993, 16–18, 26–31, 76–78. Hardin, G, *Living Within Limits: Ecology, Economics and Population Taboos.* Oxford University Press, Oxford, 1993, 275, 294–296, 310–312. Richardson, E, 'Prospects For the 1992 Conference on the Environment and Development: A New World Order', *John Marshall Law Review* 25, 1991, 1, 7. Tinker, supra n88, 819.

124 Gore, supra n67, 301–302.

125 South Commission, supra n32, 71–72. Brandt Commission, *Common Crisis. North–South: Co-operation For World Recovery.* Pan, London, 1983, 34.

126 This contention may be asserted because organizations like the WTO not only have the ability to direct huge economic power, they also have the ability to set standards, and require compulsory adjudication of disputes. For a discussion of these, with regard to the question of sovereignty, see Shrybman, S, 'The WTO: The New World Constitution Laid Bare', *Ecologist* 29(4), 1999, 270–276. See also South Commission, supra n32, 72. Bello, W, *Dark Victory.* Pluto, London, 1994, 10–31. Gosovic, supra n42, 249–263.

127 UNEP, *Global Environmental Outlook.* Oxford University Press, Oxford, 1997, 3.

Index

www.ingramcontent.com/pod-product-compliance
Ingram Content Group UK Ltd.
Pitfield, Milton Keynes, MK11 3LW, UK
UKHW020356010325
455677UK00021B/484